Creative Belonging

China Understandings Today

Series Editors: Mary Gallagher and Emily Wilcox

China Understandings Today is dedicated to the study of contemporary China and seeks to present the latest and most innovative scholarship in social sciences and the humanities to the academic community as well as the general public. The series is sponsored by the Lieberthal-Rogel Center for Chinese Studies at the University of Michigan.

Creative Belonging: The Qiang and Multiethnic Imagination in Modern China
Yanshuo Zhang

Reportage in the Chinese-Speaking World
Edited by Charles A. Laughlin and Li Guo

Ethnic Minority Cinema in China's Nation-State Building
Kwai-Cheung Lo

Gendered Memories: An Imaginary Museum for Ding Ling and Chinese Female Revolutionary Martyrs
Xian Wang

Engineering Stability: Rebuilding the State in Twenty-First Century Chinese Universities
Yan Xiaojun

In Search of Admiration and Respect: Chinese Cultural Diplomacy in the United States, 1875–1974
Yanqiu Zheng

Seeking a Future for the Past: Space, Power, and Heritage in a Chinese City
Philipp Demgenski

China as Number One? The Emerging Values of a Rising Power
Yang Zhong and Ronald F. Inglehart

Paris and the Art of Transposition: Early Twentieth Century Sino-French Encounters
Angie Chau

A complete list of titles in the series can be found at www.press.umich.edu

Creative Belonging

The Qiang and Multiethnic Imagination in Modern China

Yanshuo Zhang

University of Michigan Press
Ann Arbor

Published in the United States of America by the
University of Michigan Press
First published January 2026

A CIP catalog record for this book is available from the British Library.

Library of Congress Control Number: 2025029043
LC record available at https://lccn.loc.gov/2025029043

ISBN: 978-0-472-07777-9 (hardcover : alk. paper)
ISBN: 978-0-472-05777-1 (paper : alk. paper)
ISBN: 978-0-472-90536-2 (OA ebook)

DOI: https://doi.org/10.3998/mpub.12136311

The University of Michigan Press's open-access publishing program is made possible thanks to additional funding from the University of Michigan Office of the Provost and the generous support of contributing libraries.

Cover image by Jingui Zhang, "Ancient Qiang Castle," oil on canvas (detail). This is an artistic depiction of Taoping Qiang Village, a historical Qiang village in China with a recorded history of about 2,000 years. Jingui Zhang is an artist devoted to the artistic portrayals of ethnic minority architectural and cultural heritage in China, particularly the cultural heritage that belongs to the Tibetan and Qiang groups in western China.

The authorized representative in the EU for product safety and compliance is Easy Access System Europe, Mustamäe tee 50, 10621 Tallinn, Estonia, gpsr.requests@easproject.com

To all the Qiang friends, scholars, and villagers whom I have had a chance to meet, who make me feel a strong sense of belonging whenever I set foot in the steep mountains and beautiful villages of the East Himalayas. I have learned so much from you.

To my father, Zhang Jingui, who has dedicated his life to the Qiang and other minority groups of China through his painting brushes and tireless advocacy for minority cultural preservations. It was my father who first planted in me the seeds of curiosity for scholarly inquiries and for studying the diverse and colorful shaoshu minzu of China.

谨以此书献给所有关心、帮助过我的羌族朋友和用热忱与创造力保护自己文化的

四川羌族人

谨以此书献给我的父亲张金贵，启发我致力于民族研究，多年来陪我走过青藏高原的高山深谷，一生用画笔致敬、爱护民族文化

CONTENTS

List of Illustrations ix
Acknowledgments xi

Introduction: Conceptualizing "Creative Belonging": Toward an Interdisciplinary and Multicultural Paradigm of China Studies 1

Part I: Imagining the "Qiang" in Chinese National Narratives and Minority Scholarly Debates

Chapter 1. From "Barbarians" to "Brothers" and Cultural Guardians: Race, Ethnicity, and the Invention of the "Qiang" in Chinese Textual Traditions and National Discourses 43

Chapter 2. "King Yu Rose from West Qiang": Minority Scholarly Production and the Cultural Politics of Imaginary Ancestry in the Qiang Regions of China 85

Part II: Visualizing the "Qiang" in Cinema, the Built Environment, and Tourism

Chapter 3. A Village's Affair with the World: Visual Culture and Representing the Qiang Native Village in Transnational Cinema and Tourism 125

Chapter 4. The Run-away Minority Bride: Fluid Indigeneity and Ethnographic Poetics in Qiang Indigenous Cinema 157

Part III: Reconstituting the "Qiang" in Literary Voices and Cultural Activism in the Himalayas

Chapter 5. Between the Languishing Ethnic Mother and the Bewitching "Poisonous Cat": Gender and Commercialization in Contemporary Chinese Minority Literature 187

Chapter 6. Paradise Recrafted: The Problems of Secular Modernity in Chinese Multiethnic Literature and Village-Level Cultural Activism 213

Conclusion: The "Qiang" as Concept, History, and People 242

Glossary 247
Notes 259
Bibliography 279
Index 297

Digital materials related to this title can be found on the Fulcrum platform via the following citable URL: https://doi.org/10.3998/mpub.12136311

ILLUSTRATIONS

Figure 1. A sight-seeing spot in Luobo Qiang Village, built in the form of an indigenous shrine or temple 2
Figure 2. Map of the geographical distribution of the modern Qiang ethnic group in Sichuan 21
Figure 3. Yanshuo Zhang interviewing Qiang embroidery master Li Xingxiu 23
Figure 4. Film poster of *Forbidden Kiss* 24
Figure 5. Overview of Taoping Qiang Village 38
Figure 6. Touristic promotion board of the cinematic representations of Taoping Qiang Village in domestic Chinese and international films 38
Figure 7. Book cover of *Qiangrong kaochaji*, original edition 53
Figure 8. Book cover of *Qiangrong kaochaji*, 2007 edition 66
Figure 9. The Jade Gate Pass (Yumenguan) as a tourist spot in Gansu Province 78
Figure 10. Qiang flute maker in Taoping Qiang Village 83
Figure 11. Mr. Wang in front of his Qiang culture museum in Taoping Qiang Village 86
Figure 12. Cover image of the journal *Xiqiang Wenhua* (*The Culture of West Qiang*) 91
Figure 13. Cover image of *Fengzhou Qiangge Sanbaishou* (*Three Hundred Qiang Songs from Feng County*) 93
Figure 14. Cover image of *Taoping Shihua* (*Historical Accounts of Taoping*) 113
Figure 15. Overview of Taoping Qiang Village 126
Figure 16. Movie poster of *Design of Death* 127
Figure 17. Tourism board at the entrance of Taoping Qiang Village 131
Figure 18. Fill still from *Design of Death* 134
Figure 19. Fill still from *Design of Death* 135
Figure 20. Film still from *Forbidden Kiss* 144

Figure 21. The inside of a Qiang house open for tourism 148
Figure 22. Tourists sitting inside a Qiang house open for tourism 150
Figure 23. Poster of *Ten Years in Search of the Qiang* 162
Figure 24. Film still from *Ten Years in Search of the Qiang* 164
Figure 25. Film still from *Ten Years in Search of the Qiang* 164
Figure 26. Film poster of *Erma's Wedding* 171
Figure 27. Film still from *Erma's Wedding* 177
Figure 28. Film still from *Erma's Wedding* 179
Figure 29. A traditional Qiang wedding 180
Figure 30. Film still from *Erma's Wedding* 180
Figure 31. Photograph of the Sacred Grove in Niuwei Qiang Village 217
Figure 32. Front and back covers of *A'er Archive* 233
Figure 33. Inner pages of *A'er Archive* 235
Figure 34. The author interviewing an old Qiang *shibi* and his apprentice 245

ACKNOWLEDGMENTS

This book grew out of my doctoral dissertation completed in the Department of East Asian Languages and Cultures at Stanford University in 2018. From the dissertation to the book, I have journeyed through various jobs in different states, several major moves, and survived the global COVID pandemic. From my years as a PhD student to a postdoctoral scholar to now an assistant professor, this book project has accompanied me throughout my extraordinary journey of finding my voice as a scholar and maturing in my interdisciplinary methodologies. As I acknowledge the people and events that have made this book possible, I also acknowledge the exciting, challenging, and transformative nature of scholarly discoveries as moments of intellectual growth and personal enlightenments.

The conception and completion of this book involved many people who have supported and sustained me and to whom I owe intellectual debt. First and foremost, I would like to thank my dissertation committee members at Stanford for their continuous mentorship throughout my graduate career. I was fortunate to work with Ban Wang, my main advisor. For eight years, his intellectual breadth, generous spirit, and unwavering patience were instrumental for my growth. Ban had provided invaluable insights, inspiring feedback, and personal attention to my scholarly and professional development. His unfailing support also cheered me up to overcome the challenges one inevitably runs into during the journey of an academic life.

I thank Thomas Mullaney for the rigorous training, incisive comments, and historical perspectives he shared with me. Taking his seminar "Race and Ethnicity in East Asia" at Stanford ignited my interest in pursuing research on the ethnic minority cultures of China. Working with Tom also helped cultivate a precious historian's perspective in my scholarly thinking, as I have learned the importance of tracing the historical origins of contemporary phenomena and maintaining a keen awareness of how ideas, institutions, and social systems emerge in the first place. Tom's meticulous and sharp comments on the drafts of my dissertation pushed me to think harder on my arguments and clarify my logic.

It was a truly rewarding experience to work with Ronald Egan. Ron carefully read my working drafts at various stages and proved to be a wonderful mentor for both my scholarly and professional pursuits. In addition to his always thoughtful feedback on my chapters, Ron encouraged me to think about the broader significance of my research and to articulate the political and cultural importance of studying the long-overlooked ethnic minority communities in modern Chinese literature and culture.

Since my scholarly endeavors have been interdisciplinary, the guidance I received from my committee members in anthropology and comparative literature was invaluable. My conversations with Matthew Kohrman were always illuminating. Ever so willing to help his students, Matthew tirelessly guided me in deepening my arguments and elucidating the conceptual complexity of my project. His anthropological perspectives have propelled me to make the human beings, or the minority people of China, stand out in my writing. David Palumbo-Liu and his scholarship on race, otherness, and literature in a global era have been influential for me. The literary criticism seminar I took with him during my first year at Stanford set the foundation for my literary inquiry. Mark Lewis, though not my official dissertation committee member, carefully read the entire dissertation and gave me insightful comments from the angle of a China historian. I am grateful for his interest and support.

My sincere gratitude goes to the Stanford East Asia Library and its wonderful staff. Zhaohui Xue never hesitated to listen to my needs and helped purchase a large collection of books and journals about the Qiang that facilitated my research. Grace Yang always greeted me with a bright smile upon my entry into the library, helping me access my research materials.

Immediately after obtaining my PhD at Stanford, my two years of serving as a lecturer at Stanford's undergraduate Program in Writing and Rhetoric (PWR) surrounded me with new friends and colleagues passionate about writing. PWR's collegial environment and emphasis on "stylish academic writing" helped me craft my prose and reflect on the persuasive power of ethos and pathos in making scholarly writing memorable and personal. Readers will likely find moments of emotional power and personal relevance throughout the book, as I worked to inject life and energy from my fieldwork into the human narratives of this scholarly volume.

The COVID pandemic posed both challenges and new opportunities as I left the bosom of Stanford to embrace the wider scholarly community. In the fall of 2020, I became a postdoctoral fellow at the University of Michigan's Lieberthal-Rogel Center for Chinese Studies (LRCCS). Despite being at the height of COVID, LRCCS and the warm, welcoming environment at Michigan provided me with a new home. I worked extensively with Emily Wilcox, who expanded my horizon into the study of Asia in a global context. Emily's illuminating scholarship on the early P.R.C's minority art politics was an inspiration for me. I will always cherish the contemplative walks I took with Emily along the Huron River on the colorful autumn days in Ann Arbor. Emily's smiling face, words of encouragement, and deep trust in my work fueled me during the difficult time of the pandemic.

My other colleagues and friends at the University of Michigan provided both emotional support and intellectual alliance. Fangfei Miao gave me detailed feedback on the earlier drafts of this book. I thank her for her comprehensive, nuanced reading of my work and the refreshing insights she shared from her perspective of a dance scholar immersed in the arts of China. Lang Chen organized many workshops in which I shared parts of my research with graduate students at the University. I appreciate the excitement and enthusiastic feedback I received from graduate students and junior scholars at Michigan, such as Yucong Hao and Yihui Sheng. Erik Mueggler and Hua-tse Gyal reaffirmed my passion for studying about China's ethnic minority cultures. As the past and current directors of LRCCS, Mary Gallagher, Twila Tardif, and Ann Lin have all shown tremendous support toward my work. Carol Stepanchuk, Ena Scholrff, and Do-Hee Morsman warmly welcomed me to the Michigan community and made my time in Ann Arbor home-like.

After departing from the University of Michigan, my brief time at Kalamazoo College allowed me to connect with new colleagues and revise and refine my chapters. I thank Cyndy Margarita Garcia-Weyandt for organizing our weekly writing workshops. I benefited from the friendship and support from my lovely former colleagues Kathryn Sederberg, Tris Faulkner, Carlos Vazquez-Cruz, Juan Carlos Guerrero-Hernadez, Brian White, Manfa Sanogo, and Eunice Uhm.

At Pomona College, my colleagues in the Department of Asian Languages and Literatures and beyond have been supportive of my book project. Conversations with Jun Lang, Feng Xiao, Eileen Cheng, Kyoko Kurita, and Angelina Chin are always joyful and encouraging.

Outside of my formal institutional affiliations, I am much indebted to many scholars who have generously shared their wisdom, advice, and time to instrument this project's maturation. Louisa Schein has been a faithful mentor and reader of my work. I enjoyed our morning coffees in Palo Alto, where she checked on my progress and we exchanged ideas on ethnic minority groups, culture, and contemporary China in general. Louisa also provided immensely helpful feedback and encouraged me to draw out the theoretical contributions of my work through a manuscript workshop organized by the University of Michigan. Carols Rojas was always happy to read my work and played a major role in the manuscript workshop in helping me elucidate the literary and cultural translations of important terms in my book, as this book traverses many conceptual, historical, and literary domains.

Sixiang Wang and Tristan Brown listened to multiple presentations I gave on various parts of my book in progress. They offered fruit for thought that helped me articulate the discursive contours of the idea of "Qiang." Ralph Litzinger, whose early work on the Yao ethnic group of China was already influential on me, showed keen interest in my progress. E.K. Tan was a kind mentor who never failed to encourage me even at moments of challenges and uncertainties. Participating in a special panel titled Chinese Literature Across Borderlands organized by David Der-wei Wang and contributing to a special issue edited by him for *Prism: Theory and Modern Chinese Literature* allowed me to connect my work with other stellar scholars working on borderlands in China and Asia. The two anonymous reviewers for the manuscript of this book provided informative feedback and important insights for me to consider my own positionality as a U.S.-trained Han Chinese scholar straddling different linguistic and cultural worlds. Such reflections were worked into the final version of the book that is in front of the reader.

The special group of people without whom my entire project would be inconceivable and whom I would like to particularly thank is the ethnic Qiang people of my home province, Sichuan. Whether it is ordinary villagers or renowned writers, intellectuals, and entrepreneurs, the Qiang people have always provided me with selfless help and unreserved enthusiasm during my many years of field research. I am touched by the resilient spirit that guided them in surviving the devastating 2008 Sichuan earthquake, and I am moved by their tremendous efforts to rebuild their culture and homeland. While it is impossible to name all of the Qiang people who have generously helped me, I would like to specially thank Long Xiaoqiong and Wang Jiajun from

Taoping Qiang Village. They have shared the treasures of Taoping's rich history and allowed me to conduct numerous oral history interviews with them. Mr. Wang's small bookstore and folk museum in Taoping also exposed me to exciting primary sources and original materials that later made their way into my dissertation and now book. Tang Jicheng of the Longxi Qiang People's Valley and Yu Zhengguo and his father of A'er Village educated me about the shamanism and oral traditions of the Qiang. They told me enchanting stories about the Qiang religious practices and spiritual pursuits. Furthermore, Zhang Shanyun introduced me to the Sichuan Qiang Studies Association and shared his knowledge of advocating for institutionally preserving Qiang cultural traditions in China and abroad. Liu Kui of the Southwest Minzu University in China showed great enthusiasm and encouragement for my project.

During the research and writing stage of my dissertation and book manuscript, the funding I have received has been vital. I am grateful for the Stanford Center for Comparative Studies in Race and Ethnicity (CCSRE) for the dissertation award I received in 2015–16. CCSRE's welcoming community and joyful weekly lunch seminars allowed me to get to know other scholars and students working on the topic of race and ethnicity in various parts of the world. During 2017–18, I received the dissertation award from the Chiang Ching-kuo Foundation for International Scholarly Exchange (CCKF). This award was important for me to bring my dissertation to completion. In addition, the generous summer grants I received from the Center for East Asian Studies (CEAS) at Stanford and the Stanford Graduate Research Opportunity Funds allowed me to conduct research in Taiwan and Mainland China. In summer 2017, my trip to the Institute of History and Philology at Academia Sinica resulted in many fruitful conversations with scholars in Taiwan. I am particularly grateful to Wang Ming-ke for hosting me at the Institute. I also benefited from my conversations with various scholars at Academia Sinica, such as Wang Peng-hui, Tsia Wei-chieh, and Hu Chi-jui, and the resources that they generously shared with me.

The many editors and editorial team members at the University of Michigan Press have been instrumental in ushering in the final publication of the book. They include: Marcella Landri, Delilah McCrea, Sara Cohen, Sarah Berg, Mary Hashman, and many others at the Press that I have not yet had a chance to meet. A subvention from the Center for Chinese Studies at the University of Michigan has made the open-access version of this book possible. I am grateful for these wonderful people and resources.

Last but certainly not the least, I owe great intellectual and personal debts to my wonderful parents, Zhang Jingui and Li Xiaoshuang. It was them who first planted in me the curiosity to explore the cultural diversity of China when they took the teenager me on numerous trips to the high mountains and rivers of southwest China, where the nation's many minority peoples reside. My parents encouraged me to step outside of my comfort zone and embrace the cultures that I came into contact with. This spirit of embracing difference has sustained me throughout the years and has been critical for my intellectual pursuits. Particularly, my father Zhang Jingui, a devoted artist and educator, has been helping me with my field research in the minority regions of Sichuan and has been instrumental for the development of this project. He introduced me to many local minority communities. We have conducted numerous research trips together in the steep mountains and remote villages of West China. My father is my guard and my guide all at once. He tirelessly drives for me, supports me, and guides me into the many remote and forgotten Qiang villages that he has discovered throughout the years. Many times, he has driven me and my mother on the treacherous mountain roads of Aba Tibetan and Qiang Autonomous Prefecture. Not once but a few times have we encountered weather-induced road problems and even fallen into scary car accidents. Yet none of these difficulties and disasters have deterred us. My father's great passion for the minority cultures of China and his artistic depictions of the natural and cultural landscape and architectural heritage of the Tibetans and the Qiang have been the soul of our connections as father and daughter. We both feel a calling and I am tremendously lucky to be his daughter. My father's public service efforts for the marginalized populations have taught me by example how as intellectuals, we can and should make our knowledge speak to public interest and the common good.

My two deceased grandfathers, Li Zhichun (1928–2017) and Zhang Hengdao (1930–2014), and my beloved departed paternal grandmother Zhou Suying, who taught me to recognize my first words in Chinese, would have certainly been most delighted to see me bring this extensive project to completion. They always trusted that my endeavors were worthwhile and held high expectations for me. It is to my loving and special family and to all my resilient Qiang friends that I dedicate this book.

INTRODUCTION

Conceptualizing "Creative Belonging"

Toward an Interdisciplinary and Multicultural Paradigm of China Studies

In the summer of 2014, in the heat of my field research in China's multiethnic southwestern Sichuan Province, I had an encounter with an ethnic Qiang villager that left an indelible impact on this book.

I was lodging in a guesthouse in a tourist village called the New Luobo Village. The New Luobo Village, with its distinctive Qiang-style architecture, had been newly opened up for tourism after the catastrophic 2008 Wenchuan earthquake. The Wenchuan earthquake ravaged many Qiang villages in northwestern Sichuan and forced large numbers of Qiang villagers to abandon their home villages, including the Old Luobo Village, in search for new livelihoods. Many of these villagers turned to tourism with the help of local governments, as the monumental Qiang fortressed villages lent themselves well to ethnic tourism and sightseeing even before the earthquake (Figure 1). Despite making its way into global breaking news, the Wenchuan earthquake was rarely associated with a Chinese ethnic minority community, the Qiang (羌) or Qiangzu (羌族), in international mass media. Yet, this catastrophe not only transformed a minority people's agricultural lifestyle forever, but also posed important scholarly questions about the entanglements between ethnic and national identities in multiethnic countries like China.

At the guesthouse, my hosts were a middle-aged Qiang couple. One morning, as I finished the breakfast prepared by the Qiang woman, I started a conversation with the couple. What I thought was a casual exchange turned out to be a transformative moment for me as an ethnic Han scholar. Lighting his cigarette, the Qiang man slowly but confidently stated to me: "The Qiang

Figure 1. A sightseeing spot in Luobo Qiang Village, built in the form of an indigenous shrine or temple. Photograph by author.

were the ancestors of the Han and the Tibetans. We Qiang people are the real ancestors of China. There wouldn't be *Zhonghua minzu* (the Chinese people or Chinese race) were it not for the Qiang people." The Qiang man said this matter-of-factly, as if repeating an adage. As our conversation drew to a close, he continued with his daily routine of going to the Old Luobo Village to pick up tourists looking for accommodations. Meanwhile, I was left in deep thoughts as I stayed in the house, facing the giant portrait of Mao hanging quietly in the living room.

As someone who grew up in China and had received the first twelve years of her education in China, I was caught in both surprise and awe by the words of the Qiang man. Nowhere else had I encountered any statements that prioritized the Qiang as the "real ancestors" of Chinese people and Chinese culture—not in news media, and certainly not in textbooks. Where did the Qiang man's claim that "the Qiang are the real ancestors of China" stem from? What propelled an ordinary minority villager to proudly call his ethnic group the "ancestors of the Han," the majority and dominant ethnic group of China?

What historical and social conditions gave rise to such epistemological declarations, which imply an irrevocable connection between ethnic and national identities in multiethnic China? Most importantly, what did the Qiang man's understanding of the relationship between the Han, the Qiang, and the Tibetans tell us about how ethnic identities are constructed in China and how such identity constructions have profoundly influenced both China's overall national consciousness and the ethnic awareness of minority communities? Finally, how have China's ethnic minority people (少数民族 *shaoshu minzu*) participated in the production of knowledge about ethnicity and the nation in their daily lives and in formal discourses, articulating a central place for themselves in China's national narratives and presenting their indigenous identities in a world of multicultural encounters?

This book seeks to answer these questions by investigating how the ethnic and the national are mutually constitutive as minority groups engage in discursive self-fashioning within the parameters of multiculturalism in reform-era China (roughly 1980 to the present). One core framework that runs throughout the book is the study of the formation of minority discourses by minority members themselves, or what I call minority "discursive self-fashioning." Discursive self-fashioning refers to the multilayered processes through which ethnic minority groups create discourses about their self-identities in the realm of both formal literature, such as poetry, fiction, and scholarly publications, as well as everyday encounters and interactions embedded in the architectural environments of minority villages. Ethnic minority members form discursive spaces as they traverse different genres of literature and different types of everyday encounters (such as touristic negotiations) and fashion the ethnic "self" vis-à-vis national narratives, transnational influences, and historical imaginaries. In this sense, minority groups like the Qiang engage in processes of cultural recognition as a relational practice: cultural recognition is not a "predetermined target" or a finite product, but a "work in progress," or what Canadian indigenous film scholars call "*relationships in the process of being formed*."[1]

The book integrates a decade of textual-archival research into ethnographic fieldwork in the Qiang ethnic regions of southwest China. As an interdisciplinary project combining historical contextualization and anthropological inquiries and grounded in literary, discursive, and textual analysis, this book probes how China's smaller ethnic minority groups interact strategically with mainstream Chinese society, challenging the historically entrenched hierarchies between the socio-political "centers" of China and the nation's non-Han "peripheries." The book further reveals how minority groups critique the secular, developmentalist agendas of the nation by asserting the spiritual values and alternative worldviews rooted in indigenous traditions. In doing so, minority groups like the Qiang question the basic tenets of modernity defined by a teleological, pragmatical outlook of the world, contending for a place for spiritually-driven and indigenously-rooted worldviews.

The Qiang minority writers, filmmakers, scholars, village activists, and entrepreneurs studied in this book engage in a collective enterprise of creative expression to articulate "minor thought as a theoretical mode of engagement that propels the minor author to evolve into an agent of transformative experimentation and collective awareness."[2] As the book will bear out, strands of "minor thought" as cultural movements that question state-defined frameworks of modernity are common among many of China's—as well as the world's—ethnic minority groups. These movements not only shape minority identities but also transform minority groups' relationships to nation-states and foster transnational connections between indigenous and ethnic groups from China and elsewhere around the globe.

In this introduction, I theorize about the strategies of "creative belonging" employed by the Qiang ethnic group of China. I argue that minority groups like the Qiang resist a simplifying, reductionist definition of their ethnic identities by creatively drawing from diverse ethnic, cultural, historical, and textual sources to imagine their place in China's past and present. Rather than seeing the "Qiang" as a stable concept, I probe into the very processes of the invention and re-invention of the linguistic and cultural conceptualizations of "Qiang" throughout Chinese history, dislodging an ethnic concept from immediate and specific circumstances to examine its signifying powers at different historical conjunctures in order to understand the dynamic and ever-evolving relationship between the ethnic and the national. As such, this book defines the "Qiang" not simply as one of the fifty-five officially recognized ethnic minorities of today's China, but as an ethnic, cultural, and historical signifier open to immense creative re-making and central to modern China's very concept of "Chinese-ness" rooted in its long history of interethnic exchanges.

I situate the identity-creation of Chinese minority groups within a global multicultural imaginary characterized by multi-lateral movements of transcultural influences among ethnic groups around the world—minority writers from southwest China invoke their shared destiny with their "Native American brothers" and Latin American literary counterparts, formulating a transnational solidarity in their literary innovations. I will also briefly trace the evolution of the concept of "Qiang" in Chinese cultural history to understand how the modern Qiangzu re-invents itself by re-creating and re-imagining the historical image of "Qiang" as a signifier for racial otherness and cultural strangeness in Chinese textual traditions. I will further examine how ethnic and national identities are intertwined in modern China, an intertwinement that has generated a productive space for minority groups like the Qiang to carve out a creative place for their cultural, political, and ethnic belonging. Furthermore, I will place my understanding of the contemporary Qiangzu's experience within China's globalizing neoliberal economy, where the political necessity of managing the nation's multicultural heritage is paired with the Chinese state's desire to develop the social economy in minority regions, packaging ethnic cultures into global spectacles and media sensations. Challenging mainstream media's tendency of reducing minority cultures to ready-made symbols and easy-to-consume stereotypes, Qiang grassroots and elite writers, filmmakers, and cultural activists create an innovative aesthetic style that I theorize as "ethnographic poetics." Similar to the socially-embedded poetics of indigenous media produced in Latin America that aim to reveal local struggles for cultural and linguistic autonomy, Chinese ethnic groups like the Qiang enact the rich, complex, and sometimes contradictory experience of being minority in a large multicultural nation, employing ethnographically-detailed and aesthetically-inspiring portrayals of their land and culture to "shape counter discourses and engender alternative public spheres."[3]

This will lead us to broader theoretical considerations of multiculturalism both as a domestic governmental strategy within China and as a global phenomenon defining the lives of indigenous and minority groups the world over. As Pamela Wilson and Michelle Stewart have noted, emerging from diverse locations of the world, indigenous media and multicultural expressions made by racial and ethnic minority groups "now occupy a significant place not only in local cultures and communities but also in national and global media discourses, policies, industries, and funding structures."[4] This book will examine how Chinese minority groups' creative endeavors and aesthetic impulses are part and parcel of this global tide of re-claiming indigenous identities but with ideological and cultural characteristics that are unique to China. Such examinations aim to foster fruitful future conversations between scholars of China and those who study race and ethnicity in other contexts.

Toward an Interdisciplinary Approach to China Studies: Ethnic Diversity in China and the Global Multicultural Imaginary

Home to fifty-five officially recognized ethnic minority groups spanning every corner of its enormous landmass, China is a multicultural country with diverse linguistic and ethnic traditions. Multiethnic literatures constitute an important part of Chinese literary production. In southwest China, one of the nation's most ethnically diverse regions, minority writers and poets have been energetically writing and forming regional literary centers since as early as the mid-1980s.[5] In Sichuan, Yunnan and Guizhou, three neighboring provinces with a galaxy of minority groups, writers, poets, and scholars from Qiang, Yi, Tibetan and Wa ethnic backgrounds regularly gather, write, publish and present their literary and scholarly writings in public venues and academic conventions.[6] Elsewhere in China, ethnic Mongolian (*Menggu zu*), Korean (*Chaoxian zu*), Uighur (*Weiwu'er zu*) and Zhuang writers, among writers from many other ethnic backgrounds, are prolifically documenting minority life and interpersonal relationships in their literary works, reflecting the changing social and moral landscapes of contemporary China.[7]

Such vibrant minority literary and cultural communities have produced some of the nation's highest-achieving literary figures. A prominent example is Alai (阿来 b. 1959), an ethnic Tibetan author from Sichuan, who won the Fifth Mao Dun Literary Prize, the most prestigious literary prize in China, as the youngest laureate in the history of this prize at the time of winning.[8] Not only are Alai's novels and stories about Tibet translated into over twenty languages and widely published in the West, the author himself cites global multicultural literature's influence on his career. In an interview that Alai conducted during his visit to UC Davis for a panel discussion on indigenous poetics with Native American scholars in 2016, he evoked Trinidadian Nobel laureate, V. S. Naipaul, for the latter's examination of the impact of cultural globalization on minority writers: like the Anglophone writer Naipaul, who made a name for himself in Britain, Alai leaves behind his native place of the Tibetan regions to write in his acquired language of Mandarin Chinese, expanding the conceptual and literary possibilities of the Chinese language with his Tibetan linguistic and cultural sensibilities.[9]

Like Alai, many of China's ethnic minority writers and artists engage in a process of "translating" their ethnic traditions and linguistic heritage into literature, cinema, and other cultural productions that aim to reach a larger audience both in China and abroad. In this process, minority writers and intellectuals negotiate with the dominant Han cultural influence and experiment with thematically and stylistically new ways of expressing their experience as cultural "hybrids" in a multiethnic nation.

Most significantly, many Chinese ethnic minority poets are actively seeking out transnational literary and cultural connections in an effort to probe into the shared spiritual origins, human quandaries, and cultural dilemmas across geographical and national boundaries. One prominent example of this is the ethnic Yi poet Aku Wuwu (阿库乌雾) from southwest China's Sichuan province. Aku traveled extensively in Native American regions in the United States and visited many Native American historical and sacred sites spanning Minnesota and Ohio.[10] Evoking the serpent-like Ohio River and other stunning landscapes of the American Midwest, Aku traces Native American cultural history as he credits Native Americans as the creators of an ancient civilization that has benefitted the entire world.[11] Aku also makes thematic and stylistic parallels between Native American cultural symbols and his native Yi tribes to locate the spiritual connections between Chinese ethnic groups and indigenous groups of North America. He reads tribal histories and spiritual miracles into the crescent moon, the corn crops, and the grandeur of the rock that he chances upon during his sojourn to Native America. Aku is but one of an abundance of Chinese minority poets who find global resonance in their literary and cultural endeavors. This, and many other transnational journeys made by China's ethnic minority writers, is indicative of a new trend of global ethnic literature that seeks to dissolve national boundaries in search of a common home for the human soul. These efforts are precious in helping to dislocate the centrality of Western epistemologies as indigenous communities search for alternative ways of accounting for human history and strive for a shared human destiny.

Currently, ethnic diversity has largely escaped major U.S. scholarly discussions about Chinese literature and art: not only are most Chinese literary and cinematic/artistic productions taught in American college classrooms produced by ethnic Han authors, to date, only very sporadic studies have been published about China's minority creative productions, including literature, cinema, and art.[12] This glaring lack of critical attention to ethnic diversity in Chinese literature and art has resulted in a Han majority-centric paradigm of Chinese literary and cultural studies, alienating Chinese minority experience from global multicultural studies. Furthermore, this lack of understanding of Asia's ethnic diversity contributes to creating a homogenous and flat image of Asian American and Pacific Islander experience in the U.S., suppressing the richness and diversity of "Asian-ness" in the U.S. or even other Western countries. This book responds to this urgent need to understand ethnic diversity in China and Asia both in the academy and in the global society by illuminating the often marginalized and even forgotten creative expressions made by China's ethnic minority groups through an interdisciplinary methodology crisscrossing literary studies, visual culture (including cinema and architecture), anthropology, and history.

Existing U.S. scholarship on ethnicity in China tends to fall into the fields of history, anthropology, and the social sciences. Scholarly works produced in these fields analyze the historical and socio-political aspects of Chinese minorities. Ample historical studies have been produced to examine China's formation as a polyethnic modern polity. For example, Thomas Mullaney's milestone study, *Coming to Terms with the Nation: Ethnic Classification in Modern China* and James Leibold's *Reconfiguring Chinese Nationalism: How the Qing and Its Indigenes Became Chinese* argue for the centrality of the non-Han peoples in the formation of the modern Chinese polity during multiple political regimes, from the late imperial Qing era (nineteenth century) to the Republican era (1911 or 1912–1949) and then the Communist period (1949–present).

Ethnic minority groups have further been extensively studied by American anthropologists. From the early 2000s to the present, a rich body of anthropological scholarship has been produced to examine the social aspects of minority life. Notable examples include Louisa Schein's 2000 study of the Miao titled *Minority Rules: The Miao and The Feminine in China's Cultural Politics*. In it, the author discusses issues of modernity, cultural production and gender in China, including the production of the Miao's cultural images in the intersections of local life, mass cultural imagination, and national discourses.[13] More recently, Jenny Chio's *A Landscape of Travel: The Work of Tourism in Rural Ethnic China* (2014) investigates how tourism activities reconfigure minority life in Guangxi and Guizhou, as migration and mobility are redefining what it means to be both rural and ethnic in contemporary China.[14]

In the field of literary studies, in recent years, there have been some important studies on China's minority literatures published in the U.S. Examples include Robin Visser's 2023 book, *Questioning Borders: Ecoliteratures of China and Taiwan*. Visser's book is a timely and critical study of indigenous ecoliteratures produced by the Han and various non-Han minority groups, such as the Mongol, Tibetan, Yi, Bai, and Kazakh and Uighur.[15] With a focus on indigenous ecoliteratures, Visser's study directly engages with ecocriticism and global postcolonial discourses. Similarly, Mark Bender's seminal 2017 book, *The Borderlands of Asia: Culture, Place, Poetry*, is an encyclopedic study of the poetry produced by writers from many ethnic groups in China, India, and other Himalayan countries, offering a panoramic view of the cosmological perspectives, cultural customs, and environmental concerns expressed by multiethnic poets.

Despite the individually luminous achievements the above-mentioned studies make to the study of China's *shaoshu minzu* in their respective fields, to date, there has been very little conversation among these fields. Most existing studies on the *shaoshu minzu* focus heavily or exclusively on their targeted field and audience, citing materials strictly from their primary field of concern (such as historical archives, anthropological theories, literary texts, and literary theories). While such disciplinary attention is invaluable in elucidating a certain area of minority life, the lack of conversation among these fields precludes a fuller, more dynamic understanding of the minority experience. The disciplinarily-defined methodology of studying minority cultures (or perhaps any community at all) also undermines the many surprising overlaps and shared motifs among different scholarly fields. For example, as the next section of this introduction will argue, the invention of the very idea of the *Zhonghua minzu* (Chinese people) in twentieth-century China's national and historical narratives necessitated a creative process not unlike that of literary imagination. In fact, the state historians who conceived of the multicultural *Zhonghua minzu* in various national discourses produced in the post-1949 era relied on pre-modern Chinese literary images, such as the Qiang flute that recurred in Tang-dynasty poetry, to imagine the Qiang into a multiethnic Chinese history. If we look only to either conventional "historical" sources or "literary" sources, we would miss the fascinating cross-fertilization that can be forged between the fields of history and literature.

Therefore, *Creative Belonging* strives to bridge the humanistic disciplines of literature, history, anthropology, and visual culture by offering perhaps the first in-depth English-language study of the "invention" of one ethnic group through many modes of creative expression and many methods of identity-making. Challenging the disciplinary boundaries among the above-mentioned fields, this book cuts across the creative realms of historical imagination, literary creativity, visual representation, as well as the everyday life as it seeks to understand the inventiveness of those categorized as the "Qiang" in constructing a place of belonging for themselves in multiethnic China and in the world.

The book investigates the changing ethno-national connotations of the very concept of "Qiang" during pivotal moments of Chinese history and examines the multifaceted creative activities carried out by the contemporary Qiangzu in diverse fields, from fictional literature and cinema to minority scholarly productions and historical writing; from tourism and the built environment to minority grassroots cultural activism. This book adopts an interdisciplinary/cross-disciplinary methodology that attends to both the socio-historical realities of the Qiang and the aesthetic motifs and creative agencies exercised by a minority group that has come to be known as the Qiang in today's China. In this sense, this book takes inspiration from both the well-developed fields of history and anthropology in the study of Chinese minority communities and contributes to the rising field of Chinese minority literary and cultural studies.

An interdisciplinary/cross-disciplinary approach is not only necessary, but also essential to studying China's *shaoshu minzu*. Many ethnic minority groups in China, especially the smaller ethnic groups from southwest China, such as the Qiang and the Naxi from Yunnan, historically lacked a standardized written script and did not have a tradition of secular written literature. Oral traditions, legends, and pictographic representations abounded. Writing—mostly in pictographic traditions embedded in religious contexts—was reserved for the religious elites. Literature in the sense of the written documentation of secular experience in fiction, poetry, drama and essays did not fully emerge among these ethnic groups until the 1980s, when the vibrant reform era allowed for the blossom of minority writers and various *minzu* (minority nationality) universities started training bilingual minority writers and writing elites.

Due to the relatively short time span of "minority literature," many *shaoshu minzu* are still in the process of forming their literary and cultural "canons." Furthermore, minority literatures and cultures are in perpetual flux vis-à-vis the changing national policies and social conditions in China. As such, it is not adequate to simply read a collection of published minority literature and write about minority experience solely from published work. As scholars, we need to attend to the historically non-logo-centric traditions of the smaller minority groups and pay attention to the living conditions of the *shaoshu minzu* that cannot or have not been fully captured by the written word.

As such, I root my research in an ethnographic methodology that investigates the lived experience of minority communities in addition to examining minority written discourses. This book is based on more than a decade of ethnographic research in the ethnic Qiang regions of southwest China, which includes interacting with and interviewing minority scholars, entrepreneurs, villagers, and writers, as well as attending minority cultural activities and events ranging from scholarly conventions, tourism festivals, to community rituals and ceremonies. I combine this ethnographic research with a textual-archival methodology that entails discovering and analyzing locally produced cultural texts.

Theoretically, this book is influenced by scholarly output both within and well beyond the bounds of Chinese and Sinophone studies. It takes inspiration from Sinophone studies' attention to the ethnic and linguistic diversity of Sinophone communities. Particularly, I seek to de-center the linguistic and cultural dominance of the Han/Hua ethnic group as the main producer of "Chinese" culture by acknowledging Shu-mei Shih's idea that "Sinophone culture [is] produced by people of various ethnicities," and that "Sinophone culture is place-based and belongs to the place where it is produced."[16] As many chapters of this book will illuminate, contemporary Qiang minority writers and historians produce Chinese-language literary and scholarly discourses that are deeply attached to the place-bound identity of the Qiang in the Eastern Himalayas. Many of these literary and historical discourses enrich and complicate a Han-centered understanding of Chinese culture.

Beyond China studies and Sinophone studies, this book draws from theories in indigenous studies. Particularly, the book builds upon indigenous studies scholars' theorization of the "rhetorical legitimacy" of indigenous groups to understand the creative agencies of the contemporary Qiangzu. Canadian indigenous studies scholars Dudemaine, Marcoux and St-Amand define rhetorical legitimacy as the following:

> Rhetorical legitimacy [. . .] cuts across the expressive forms—literature, theatre, cinema, media and the visual and performing arts—and (re)connects with unique territories, histories, and political contexts . . . [Indigenous artists] refuse to subscribe to any dynamic of victimization and folkorization, to which Indigenous artistic and media representations are often reduced.[17]

The idea of rhetorical legitimacy is intimately connected to my conception of creative belonging. Rhetorical legitimacy acknowledges the agency and autonomy of indigenous creative acts, viewing them not as derivatives of dominant discourses or inferior imitations of some external standards, but as fully self-assured, legitimate expressions of indigenous groups' experiences and worldviews. Similarly, the conception of creative belonging takes the minority subject as the main producer of legitimate discourses, rather than holding minority discourses against the light of dominant social ideologies. Many chapters of this book give the reader a deep dive into the rhetorical spaces and discursive productions of the Qiang people, exploring the interplay between different expressive forms in shaping the Qiang identity.

Just as indigenous studies scholars have observed, for the Qiang intellectuals and villagers that I have come into contact with, a conscious resistance against victimization and folkorization prevails. One older Qiang man has self-funded a private museum in his backyard, not willing to let any university or official organization buy out his museum because he wants to maintain the autonomy of his private museum about Qiang culture. Another young Qiang village leader from the A'er Village has mobilized his fellow villagers to write and publish a Qiang cultural manual because, as he expressed to me, he was deeply unsatisfied with the distortions of Qiang culture done by a certain famous Han scholar. These and many other acts of indigenous creativity are motivated by a strong desire to foster a sense of belonging between the indigenous actor and his/her/their land, people, and history. In these acts of creative belonging, the indigenous actor fosters new relations to his/her/their place and history.

Ultimately, my ethnographic-textual research methodology is rooted in a deep historical contextualization that places ethnic minority experience not simply in contemporary China, but in the long history of ethnic minority groups' influence on Chinese culture as a whole. As Chapter 1 will demonstrate, this method of excavating the historical conditions and textual presence of minority groups in Chinese culture is important for tracing the intellectual genealogy and understanding the dynamic evolution of ethnoracial concepts in China across different historical periods. It is also my hope that this historical excavation will help break down established boundaries between modern Chinese studies and pre-modern Chinese studies by connecting a seemingly contemporary phenomena—the Qiang's place in China's present multicultural politics—with pre-modern motifs of imagining "ethnic others" on China's borders. Such a trans-historical perspective will help us avoid making unwarranted assumptions about China's ethnic minority groups, assumptions that are often solely based on a presentist understanding of minority-related policies in the twenty-first century.

In terms of its content, the book discovers, translates, and presents a wide variety of previously unexamined literary, cinematic, cultural, and scholarly discourses produced by or about the "Qiang" as an evolving entity in Chinese culture and history. The genres studied in this book range from national history-making projects to local ethnic scholarly journals; from "native-language" cinema produce by minority artists to grassroots cultural revival publishing projects initiated by village leaders. These different genres stitch together the colorful tapestry of minority creativity and multicultural confluences in contemporary China.

This book advances two major arguments. First, it argues that indigenous and ethnic identities can be produced within the generative spaces of national discourses and ideologies. Instead of challenging the official discourse of a unitary, multiethnic Chinese nationhood, smaller minority groups like the Qiangzu engage in processes of creative belonging in the Chinese nation: they leverage and mobilize "orthodox" Sinitic-Chinese cultural symbols, historical memories, and textual traditions to invent their identities in contemporary China. Such efforts are two-fold: on the one hand, minority groups assert their centrality in Chinese cultural history by combatting the negative images of the non-Han others in Sinitic-Chinese textual traditions; on the other hand, minority groups embed their claims of their central place in Chinese culture within the alluring Chinese market economy to benefit from their articulations of ethnic differences within the frameworks of the Chinese state's version of multiculturalism. In doing so, minority groups create an "entrepreneurial identity" that allows them to thrive both culturally and economically, fostering a strong sense of belonging within Chinese society.

The book's second major argument is that, outside of national discourses, Chinese ethnic minorities resort to a powerful indigenous source of spirituality and mysticism to imagine their identity. By presenting and reviving shamanistic rituals, mystic beliefs, and community memories in literary and cinematic works, Qiang intellectuals and grassroots activists maintain their distinctive ethnic identities and establish transnational imaginary with indigenous peoples from other nations, such as Native Americans in the U.S. The indigenous legends, myths, spiritual practices, and alternative worldviews serve as a treasure trove of cultural sources for Qiang artists and cultural workers to critically imagine the Qiang identity without falling prey to the potentially assimilationist prowess of national policies and developmental agendas.

By combining these two main sources of identity—national narratives and indigenous traditions—Chinese ethnic minority groups join a global multicultural imaginary in our contemporary world. As Paula M.L. Moya, a scholar of Chicano/a American literature, reminds us, "identity involves a commitment to the idea that identities refer outward . . . to the social world within which they emerge."[18] Chinese ethnic minority writers and intellectuals are often bilingual in their native languages and in Mandarin Chinese. They have further been exposed to ethnic literatures and traditions from outside of China. Their construction of ethnic imaginary is by default multicultural and multi-perspectival, referring outwardly to China's encounter with globalization and inwardly to the status of indigenous traditions amidst rapid social transformations in China.

In terms of its source materials, this book focuses on two kinds of minority cultural productions: those produced in Mandarin Chinese and those produced in minority languages. Instead of pitting these two against each other, I demonstrate the thematic and cultural interplay between the two. For example, as Chapter 4 unveils, Qiang indigenous cinema is rarely about simply revitalizing the ethnic traditions of minority peoples, but usually unmasks the current struggles and negotiations minority communities undergo. A common theme in indigenous cinema is a scenario where minority villagers are lured by the material profitability of a modern lifestyle presented to them by the industrializing nation, yet they long to preserve collective memories in their native villages. Minority filmmakers and writers enact the complex "third space" suggested by Hombi Bhabha through their acts of negotiation: straddling the culturally hybrid space between the national "self" and the ethnic "other," minority communities produce an interstitial agency that enables them to creatively integrate different cultural sources and assert their subjectivities within the nation.[19]

Therefore, I propose that we should understand minority identities not as finished products or static aesthetic objects, but as *movements* between different genres, *interactions* between minority groups and the state and transnational cultural influences, and *processes* of negotiation and the *mobilization* of cultural and historical sources from multiple sites. In other words, given the dynamic reality of minority life in contemporary China, we need to study minority cultural and literary phenomena not in the traditional canon-centered way of reading a collection of established authors, but as a perpetual *flux of multicultural exchanges* between different ethnic groups and the world—minority peoples from different social classes are actively crafting their ethnic consciousness in today's China, such as the Qiang host who claimed that the Qiang are the ancestors of the Han and the Tibetans at the beginning of this introduction.

Beyond national narratives, transnational cultural influences have profoundly shaped the Qiangzu's self-perceptions. Many international researchers and tourists routinely visit the Qiang regions of Sichuan. During my field research, I met Qiang intellectuals and villagers who proudly shared about how Japanese and Italian researchers found possible linguistic and architectural connections between the Qiang language and architecture and the Japanese language and Italian architecture. The frequent presence of international researchers and visitors fosters a transnational imaginary that profoundly chisels the Qiang's self-awareness as a global ethnic group, even though sometimes the cross-cultural links established by international visitors are still rudimentary and even speculative. This global multicultural imaginary is important in shaping the ethnic consciousness of minority groups, having a profound effect in constructing a sense of ethnic belonging "equal to that of phenotypical or historical fact."[20]

What is most telling of southwestern Chinese indigenous ethnic groups' global connections is the fact that many Chinese minority authors and poets, such as the Qiang poet Yang Zi and Yi poet Jidi Majia, repetitively invoke the shared destiny between their ethnic groups and indigenous communities in the Americas, such as Native American tribes. In lyrical, nostalgic verses, Qiang and Yi poets create the imageries of the spiritual, determined, and dynamic peoples of their native communities, forging what I call a "transnational tribal solidarity" by building imaginary ties and affective connections with their "Native American brothers." In doing so, minority writers and poets rethink the very concept of the "tribe" as a historically denigratory term and reclaim the "tribe" as a place of indigenous solidarity. This global tribal literary imagination is powerful in helping Qiang, Yi, and many other ethnic groups in China to transcend their state-delineated status as minority nationalities and the cultural marginalization this "minority status" might entail, contending for a place of cultural centrality in our world of multicultural encounters.

By investigating the multicultural movements and influences within China's minority discourses, this book contributes to rethinking the paradigms of China studies, particularly its relationship to global multicultural studies. This book resonates with the call for examining the multilingual heterogeneity and diverse heritage of Chinese cultures in the field of Sinophone studies. Sinophone studies takes its inspiration from Francophone and Anglophone studies, decoupling "Chinese-ness" from the nation-state of China to explore the global dissemination and local variations of Chinese-language cultural productions.[21] Yet this book goes beyond Sinophone studies' presumption of the colonial legacy of dynastic China on its borderland peoples and the imposition of the Chinese language on non-Han groups. This book attends to what I call a "cooperative discursive relationship" between the Chinese state and the non-Han peoples: as Chapters 1 and 2 will reveal, modern China's state historians intently write non-Han peoples and their cultural traditions into the national narratives of China, which open up a precious discursive space for minority groups to articulate themselves as an integral part of Chinese history and culture. Admittedly, this is by no means an equal process for all of China's diverse minority groups, and some groups do experience more assimilations.[22] Yet, this discursive opening of a multiethnic Chinese-ness holds tremendous interpretive capacity: it allows minority groups to envision an "infinitely inclusive topology," incorporating "transcategorical conceptions of subjectivity"[23] to imagine their identities both along the conventional lines of national belonging and in more radical ways of transnational tribal solidarity and multicultural movements.

Race, Ethnicity, and the Signifying Power of "Qiang" in Chinese Cultural History

Among the myriad ethnic groups residing in China, this book chooses to focus on the Qiang because the evolution of the concept of the "Qiang" is perhaps among the most indicative of the dynamic, fluid, and mutually constitutive relationship between the Chinese political "center" and its ethnic "peripheries." As Pamela Kyle Crossley reminds us, "It is the construction (including mythologizing) of the past, not the past itself, that is at work in the formation of the modern 'ethnic group.'"[24] Perhaps among all of the racial and ethnic signifiers in China, "Qiang" is the one that has been most frequently constructed, mythologized, and reinvented from the earliest recorded history of China to the present day. Whereas many other pre-modern racial signifiers, such as "Fan" 蕃 and "Man" 蛮, have been gotten rid of in modern China for their derogatory meanings, "Qiang" has survived the historical turbulences and has continued to exert influence on China's national consciousness and multiethnic imagination.

In my discussion of the Qiang identity, I draw from a rich body of scholarly literature on identities, particularly cultural identities, in the modern world. I follow Stuart Hall's conceptualization of identity or identification as a discursive construction "always in process."[25] According to Hall, identity is not absolute or essentialist, but should be defined as a process of articulation, or a process of producing "articulated discourse" as a subject situates itself in conditional and contingent relationships to the "constitutive outside," or an "other" that consolidates the subject's sense of self.[26] In other words, personal or collective identity is not an object that an individual or group owns and simply passes down, but is a process through which an individual or a group forms consciousness about him/her/itself and articulates his/her/its relationship to others in relation to certain historical and social forces. Hall emphasizes both the connection between the "self" and the "constitutive outside" as well as the importance of representation in constituting identity; for Hall, representation does not merely *reflect* or express identity or subjectivity, but it is *formative* of identity—it is through representation that an individual or group articulates its sense of the self, deploying the "resources of history, language and culture in the process of becoming rather than being."[27]

The relationship between the Qiang and China enacts Hall's definition of identity as a process of discursive construction and articulated relationships: the imagery and concept of the "Qiang" as an indicator of an ethno-racial "other" have always been deeply embedded in China's national consciousness since the earliest period of Chinese history; the Qiang thus constitutes an important but "different" (non-Sinitic and non-Confucian) part of Chineseness: "Chinese culture"—however fluid and unstable the concept—has always imagined itself vis-à-vis the Qiang. On the other hand, many members of the contemporary Qiangzu imagine the Qiang identity in the broader cultural history of China—rather than asserting their "difference" or non-Chineseness, contemporary ethnic Qiang intellectuals and villagers endeavor to incorporate the Qiang into the narratives of the imaginary ancestry of Chinese civilization as an ethnically hybrid entity in which the Qiang have played a crucial part. The opening vignette of my Qiang host proclaiming the Qiang to be the "real ancestor" of Chinese people is a telling example of this imaginary ancestry. Chapter 2 of this book discusses how contemporary Qiang or Qiangzu cultural elites write the Qiang into the legendary ancestors of China, such as King Yu the Great (Da Yu), re-making the image of the historical Qiang as an indispensable contributor to the formation and flourishing of Chinese culture.

From the earliest period of Chinese history, "Qiang" has served as a symbol of the intertwined relationships between the Sinitic, Confucian cultural and moral "self" and its civilizational "others." Even though the "Qiang" in premodern literary and historiographic accounts can by no means by equated to the modern Qiangzu, "Qiang" has assumed important symbolic, cultural, and ethno-racial meanings in Chinese textual traditions over two millennia. The concept of the "Qiang" as a marker of ethnic and racial difference had long existed in China's pre-modern historiographical traditions and literary classics. For example, in canonical Chinese historiographical accounts and classical poetry, the image of the "Qiang" was repetitively evoked by Confucian literati as a lamentable reminder of the military and cultural threats posed by the alien racial groups occupying China's western margins, glossed collectively as the Qiang "barbarians."

In *The Book of Later Han* (後漢書), written in the fifth century by Confucian scholar Fan Ye (范曄), an entire section was entitled the "Biography of the West Qiang" (西羌傳). This section depicts the military interactions between China proper and various indigenous non-Sinitic groups residing in China's western peripheries, known as the "Qiang barbarians." Fan went to great lengths to portray the horrendous cultural customs of the West Qiang barbarians, such as the allegedly incestuous practice of marrying one's stepmother when the father has died.[28] An implicit moral judgement was ever-present in such writings, as the Confucius literatus deemed the Qiang's cultural practices as inferior compared to the ethical codes of the Sinitic self. In such historiographical writings, one can almost always identify a recurrent theme of the morally and culturally superior Sinitic group triumphing over the militant yet ruthless Qiang barbarians, as well as various non-Sinitic "savage" others. Many later canonical Chinese historical accounts inhered this tradition of casting non-Sinitic groups as inferior racial others in in need of the moral cultivation and civilizational acculturation from the Confucian political "center."[29]

What is more, classical Chinese poetry has no shortage of using the word and the concept of "Qiang" to reference a perceived cultural loss when the Sinitic cultural self came into often-unwarranted contact with its "racial others." Cai Wenji (蔡文姬, circa 132–192), a female poet from the Eastern Han dynasty who was abducted by the armies of the Southern Xiongnu to be the wife of a Xiongnu commander, grieved over her bitter fate of having to live with the Xiongnu barbarians as such:

> How poor my fate, alas, to meet such dismal times! . . .
> I was captured and abducted to beyond the western pass,
> The journey perilous and long to that *barbarian land* ("Qiang fang," 羌方) . . .
> And though I clung to life, I was dishonored and abased![30]

Cai's sharp sense of dishonor and abasement stemmed from her forced journey beyond the "west pass" into a bestial, uncultured land that laid outside of the pale of Chinese civilization, known as the "land of the Qiang." In this savage land, she was living with barbarians who "feed on rancid flesh" with their "speech gibberish."[31] This unbearable forced co-habitation with non-Chinese barbarians raped Cai of both her gender identity and cultural integrity as a noble, educated, and delicate Chinese woman. To salvage such extreme humiliation, the famous general Cao Cao (曹操, 155–220) eventually ransomed Cai Wenji from the hands of the Xiongnu nomads, restoring the cultural wholeness and political prowess of China embodied by a Han woman stolen from the bosom of her native land of "civilization."

From the above examples and numerous other similar passages and verses from classical Chinese historiographical and literary accounts, we can see that the word and concept of the "Qiang" served as a racial marker in premodern China. Rather than referring to one specific ethnic group, "Qiang" acted as a stock concept and stereotypical image in classical Chinese texts to represent racial others marked by their cultural, dietary, linguistic, and sartorial differences and deviations from the civilizational "center" of China. Even though "Qiang" mainly implied the non-Sinitic groups residing in China's western borderlands, it was sometimes used interchangeably with other "savage groups," such as the Xiongnu in Cai Wenji's poetry, to signify racial otherness and undesirable cultural differences for China proper.

Indeed, race or racism can be defined as a binary demarcation between "that which is known and familiar, deriving from the same culture . . . designated as 'civilized'" and "that which is not understood, or that which is hostile, deriving from a strange culture . . . designated as 'barbaric.'"[32] Both Fan Ye and Cai Wenji portrayed the Qiang/Xiongnu as alien racial groups that possessed peculiar cultural traits, such as feeding on stale meat and sharing a wife between father and son. Both Fan and Cai labeled the Qiang/Xiongnu as from a "strange culture." Moreover, Cai's accusation of the "gibberish speech" of the Xiongnu from the standpoint of a Chinese elite demonstrated the potency of language, or linguistic difference, in marking racial otherness: as someone well-versed in classical Chinese literary traditions, Cai did not conceal her contempt for what she considered to be an uncouth speech spoken by the racial others, much like how the ancient Greek despised the non-Greek-speaking slaves and labelled them as culturally and morally inferior, and thus "barbarian."[33]

Despite its power in governing the racial consciousness and cultural hierarchy of pre-modern Chinese thought, the concept of the "Qiang" experienced a significant, positive shift in modern China. As I will discuss in Chapter 1, during the Republican era (1911/1912–1949), urged by the need to construct the myth of a unified and multiethnic Chinese nation-state, ethnic Han historians and ethnologists excavated the Qiang's perpetual presence in Chinese textual traditions to argue for a shared origin between the Han and the non-Han groups as belonging to the same Chinese peoplehood or Chinese race (*Zhonghua minzu* 中華民族[34]). In various books with the same title, *The History of the Races in China* (*Zhongguo minzushi* 中國民族史), Republican-era scholars were eagerly creating textual genealogies of a shared origin of the *Zhonghua minzu*, articulating that the Qiang—together with many other non-Han groups, such as the Miao—were not of a different race, but were important and forgotten ancestors of the Chinese people. This discursive shift paved the way for the historical racial others like the Qiang to enter into a multiethnic modern Chinese national entity. It also testifies to the fluid and dynamic formation of nationhood: as Prasenjit Duara asserts, "what we call nationalism is more appropriately a *relationship* between a constantly changing Self and Other, rather than a pristine subject gathering self-awareness."[35] The historically demeaned Qiang racial other is turned into an ethnic group integral to the national self of modern China, as Chinese nationalists re-interpreted and re-invented the signifying practices of the "Qiang" to re-draw the ethic boundaries of China.

If the Qiang were mystified as a long-overlooked ancestor to multiethnic Chinese-ness during the Republican period, it was not until the Communist Ethnic Classification Project, which spanned the 1950s and 1980s, that the political and cultural contours of the Qiangzu as a modern ethnic group were definitively drawn. The Qiangzu (Qiang ethnic group) was constructed by the Ethnic Classification Project as an ethnic group in Sichuan's Aba Tibetan and Qiang Autonomous Prefecture at the eastern edge of the Tibetan-Qinghai Plateau (Figure 2). The Qiangzu share many linguistic, sartorial, and cultural traits with its neighboring Tibetan groups in Sichuan.[36] The Qiangzu speak various dialects of the Qiangic language, part of the Tibetan-Burman language family within the Sino-Tibetan language groups. In fact, in the Qiangic language, the Qiang people refer to themselves as *rme*, meaning "indigenous people" or "locals." This self-address reveals the strong sense of indigeneity the Qiang people exhibit, which exerts powerful influence on their contemporary cultural productions.

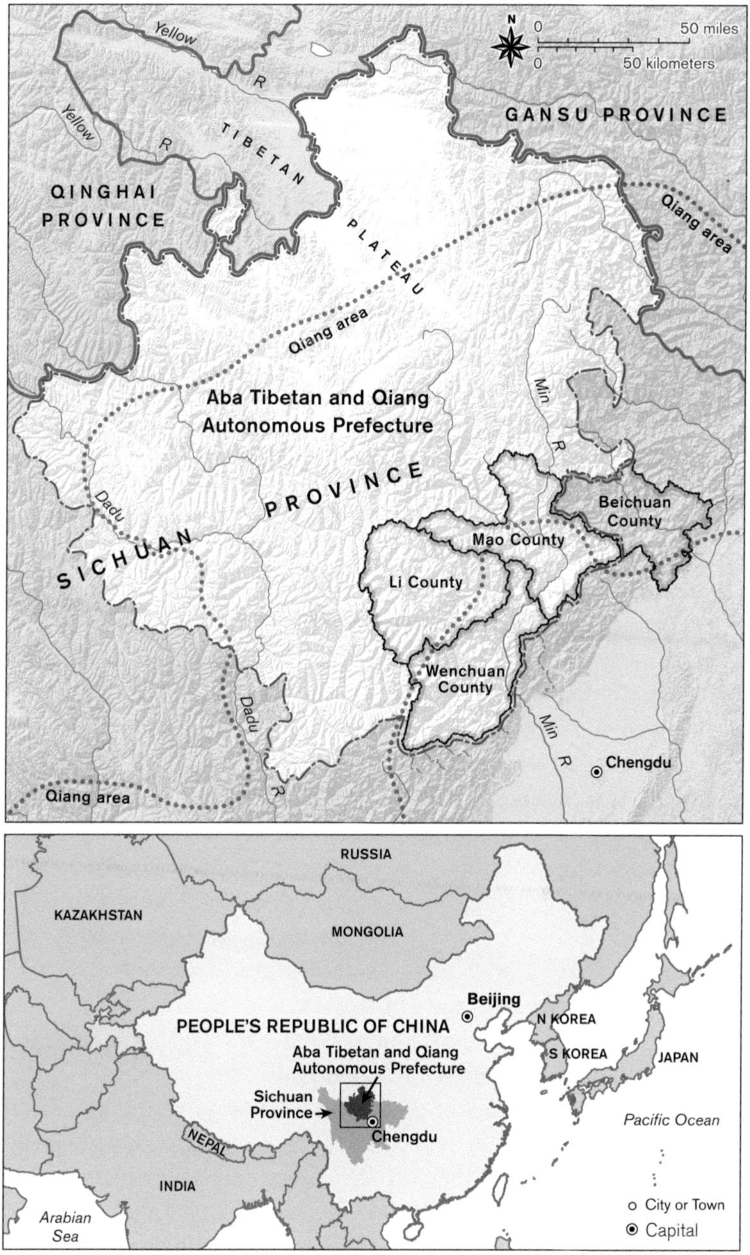

Aba Tibetan & Qiang Autonomous Prefecture map for Yanshuo Zhang
version 5, revised 1/23/2025

Figure 2. Map of the geographical distribution of the modern Qiang ethnic group in Sichuan.

Indeed, as modern China's prominent ethnologist Fei Xiaotong put it, the Qiangzu inhabit a highly hybrid "ethnic corridor" (*minzu zoulang* 民族走廊) in southwest China, a land home to a galaxy of ethnic groups with diverse cultural traditions, myths, as well as wide-ranging and overlapping indigenous origins.[37] As a preeminent scholar who participated in many ethnic investigation and classification efforts during the Communist era, Fei defined the mountainous regions inhabited by the Qiang, the Yi, the Tibetans, and many other minority groups in western China as the "Tibetan-Yi Corridor" (*Zangyi zoulang* 藏彝走廊).[38] Calling it an interethnic "contact zone," Fei wrote about the multiplicity and diversity of ethnic identities in southwest China: many ethnic groups were formed through constant cultural interactions, mutual influence, and even amalgamation with other ethnic groups.[39] Particularly, the Qiangzu straddles Tibetan and Sinitic Chinese cultural systems, developing a "hybrid" ethnic identity that absorbs multiple influences to expand the capacity of ethnic imagination in China, as the rest of the book will demonstrate.

The Qiangzu came to be even more intimately imbricated in China's national identity and global image in 2008, when the Wenchuan earthquake severely hit this small minority group. In May of 2008, the Wenchuan earthquake plagued numerous rural communities in Sichuan, and the Qiang were among the most severely impacted. At a moment of national crisis, the Chinese government tokenized the Qiangzu's cultural markers and practices, such as embroidery and architecture, as symbols of China's multicultural heritage, promoting the Qiang as an emblem of China's national identity on the international stage by registering many Qiang cultural practices on the highly-coveted UNSECO World Intangible Cultural Heritage List (Figure 3). The Qiangzu, a previously "noteless" minority group with about 300,000 in population, came to embody the Chinese state's global ambition of establishing itself as a vibrant multiethnic country under the capable political leadership and cultural stewardship of the Communist Party.

This sudden rise to fame of the Qiangzu attracted an influx of scholars, tourists, and filmmakers from both China and abroad to the monumentally fortressed Qiang villages, establishing ethnic tourism and visual practices as a new platform to imagine minority identity, re-inventing the "Qiang" yet again as a global ethnic group with rich visual spectacles and cultural implications. One important example of the new transnational fascination with the visual allures in Qiang villages is a film produced by a Chinese American crew, *Forbidden Kiss* (in Chinese 古堡之吻, *gubao zhiwen*, or "kisses in an ancient castle"). Chapter

Figure 3. Yanshuo Zhang interviewing Qiang embroidery master Li Xingxiu. Photograph courtesy of Jingui Zhang.

3 will discuss how this film, created by a Los Angeles-based Chinese American director, portrays the Qiang village as an imaginary site of pristine, pre-industrial Chinese culture through a romantic comedy that involves a smart local Qiang woman and an American architectural student who comes to study Taoping Qing Village's architectural wonders. Questions of cultural legitimacy, preservations of ethno-national traditions, and representational power are raised in this film, as the American student and the Qiang woman engage in heated debates about indigenous versus Western Enlightenment worldviews, experiencing both romantic attraction and sharp cultural conflicts. This film visualizes the monumental Qiang village as a metaphor for China's fraught encounter with globalization led by Western countries (Figure 4).

As Pamela Kyle Crossley points out, "it is the role of historical consciousness, rather than history itself, that is of significance in the contemporary minorities policy in China."[40] From a pre-modern marker of racial difference to a modern ethnic group central to China's national identity, and now a global indigenous group frequently featured in media representations, the conceptualizations of "Qiang" testify to the rich and dynamic historical consciousness of constructing ethnic belonging during different historical eras in

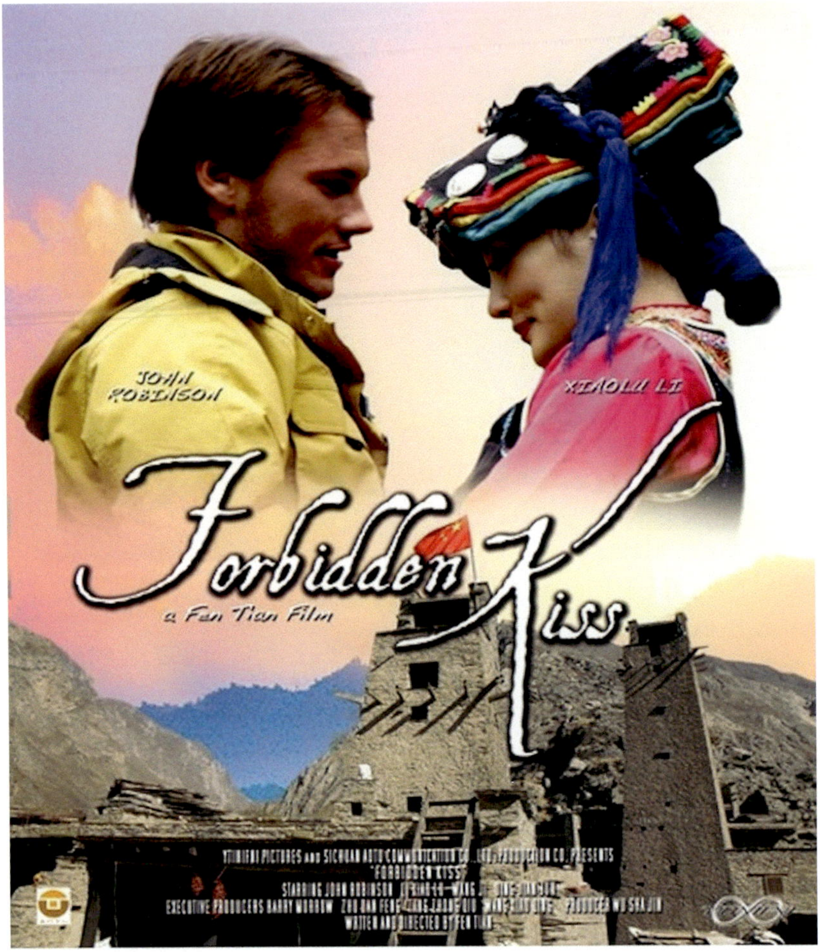

Figure 4. Film poster of *Forbidden Kiss*. http://www.1905.com/newgallery/hdpic/748274.shtml.

China. The imaginaries surrounding the "Qiang" bespeak the mutually constitutive relationship between the national and the ethnic in China. In other words, the "Qiang" is much more than a self-enclosed ethnic group, but a capacious site of signifying practices: as a signifier of ethno-national identities, the "Qiang" is subject to nationally and ideologically constructed myths, serving the changing needs of the nation and representing the dynamic and interactive relationship between the transnational, the national, and the local.

It is precisely this rich and complex history of the ethno-national imagination embodied by the evolving notions of the "Qiang" that this book taps into.

The evolving signifying practices surrounding the Qiang and the history of the Qiang's inclusion into China's national imagination also testify to the role race plays in ethno-national identity construction. Race is never a definitive concept, much less a stable process of social formation. Rather, it is a "system of social distinction" that arises from the interactions individuals or groups have with each other, usually with "competing ancestral, ethnic, and religious" interests.[41] As a result, racial distinctions afford certain groups with power and privilege and deprive others of them.[42] The Qiang's "evolution" from a racial other to an ethnic group endowed with tremendous cultural power central to the Chinese nation-state and *minzu* diversity in the modern era is a telling example of the socially transformative power of racial concepts. To understand how race, ethnicity, and the nation have become intertwined in modern China, I now turn to a brief history of the formation of the multiethnic Chinese polity in the twentieth century.

Ethnicity in Modern China: A Historical Journey

As James Leibold notes, "Minzu . . . provides the discursive parameters for defining national, ethnic and cultural identity" in modern China.[43] *Minzu* is a rich and informative concept that can tell us a lot about the interlaced ethnic and cultural identities of China's various ethnic groups and their relationships with the nation.

In recent years, many U.S. historians have offered insights into the making of the modern Chinese polity as a multiethnic nation-state since the late Qing era. At the critical transitional point from an empire to a nation, the question of who would constitute the new citizens of China became a prevailing concern for the nation's political leaders and intellectuals from the late nineteenth to the mid-twentieth centuries. As Benedict Anderson points out, modern nation-states, unlike former empires, tend to be imagined in "sovereign" and "limited" terms.[44] Anderson conceives of a "deep, horizontal comradeship" that unites citizens of a nation together on a limited landmass.[45] To do that, a nation needs to clearly demarcate its geographical boundaries and define the peoples of the closed national entity. The need to forge a legitimate nation-state propelled the different regimes in modern China to exclude, include, and co-opt the non-Han peoples, many of whom lived in the nation's geographical frontiers and have had differing relationships with the Chinese political centers since imperial times.

From the late Qing to the early Republican era (roughly the 1800s to 1910s), many non-Han groups that were formerly considered "barbarians" in imperial China—such as the Qiang—came to be regarded as essential populations for the imperial government and the emerging Chinese nation.[46] The enormous landmass inhabited by non-Han peoples from the Mongolian grassland to the Tibetan Plateau—and everything in between—held a special place for modern nationalist thinkers like Liang Qichao (1873–1929), who conceived of a vast Chinese nation composed of multiple ethnic groups revolving around the Han. Liang envisioned a modern nation whose geographical boundaries were to be mapped onto the immense lands inhabited by the Qing's multiethnic imperial subjects.[47] Liang also coined the term *Zhonghua minzu* (中華民族/中华民族) to represent these multiethnic peoples, including the Han, who were to form a Chinese race that would serve as the basis for the new Chinese nation.[48] Liang Qichao's *Zhonghua minzu* paradigm aligns perfectly with Anderson's conception of the modern nation as a "sovereign," "limited" entity: China was to become a nation limited within the geographical contours of the Qing empire and a sovereign for the Chinese race against the imperial encroachment of Western and Japanese powers. Liang's use of *minzu* thus denoted both a broader concept of the Chinese people as a whole and a narrower concept of the indigenous non-Han groups, such as the Miao, in China.[49]

The Republic of China was established on the premise of the unity of the five major ethnic groups, the Han, Manchu, Mongols, Hui and Tibetans, who together formed an important demographic basis of the Chinese race.[50] Yet beyond these larger ethnic groups, Republican-era scholars "discovered" the nation's many smaller indigenous ethnic groups residing in the mountainous hinterlands of southwestern and northwestern China, as well as along many other "borderlands" in the country. The development of such modern disciplines as ethnology and archeology enabled Republican scholars to scientifically study the ethnic "others" that were long relegated to the status of barbarians in imperial China and "[authenticate] myths of national belonging."[51] Chapter 1 unveils the photographic works and travelogues authored by one such scholar, Zhuang Xueben, who avidly joined the Republican government's expedition teams to journey into the Qinghai and Sichuan ethnic borderlands and conceived of the Qiang and Rong (Tibetans) as good-natured citizens that belonged to a greater Chinese nation. Zhuang wrote for an educated Han readership for the popular Shanghai-based *Liangyou Magazine*, stunning his readers with images and words never before associated with the concept of Chinese-ness. Indeed, non-Han peoples came to be imagined as part of the Chinese national self and were extensively represented in academic and expedition literatures and visual materials in the Republican era.

Upon the founding of the People's Republic of China in 1949, the Communist Party searched to define the ethnic make-up of the peoples of China and sought to institutionalize ethnic diversity. Such efforts culminated into the Ethnic Classification Project, which "gave shape, and, in some cases, existence" to the *minzu* categories of China.[52] The Ethnic Classification Project was a crucial project that helped the Communist Party construct the "unified, multinational People's Republic of China"[53] by conceiving of the broader *Zhonghua minzu* with both the Han and the non-Han minority *minzu*. The Classification Project created the paradigm of the unitary Chinese people as the fifty-five minority *minzu* plus the one Han majority *minzu*, a paradigm that has been ubiquitous and instrumental in understanding ethnic issues in the People's Republic.[54] In the 1950s, the Party also strove to enfranchise the non-Han peoples with political rights, such as giving them representative seats at the National People's Congress.[55] The government further established autonomous regions, prefectures, counties and *xiang*[56] to institutionalize the system of *minzu* self-governance (*zizhi*).

The Ethnic Classification Project and its corresponding institutions were an exemplar of the Chinese Communist Party's construction of China's multiethnic imagined community by way of politicization, or by emphasizing minority groups as political entities and giving them political power and representation in the nascent People's Republic.[57] At the same time, there has been another important strand in the state's efforts to construct minority identities in China, which is what Chinese scholar Ma Rong calls "culturalization." It is this idea of culturalization that has been largely overlooked in U.S. scholarship on ethnic issues in China.

According to Ma, culturalization entails "emphasizing the cultural characteristics of ethnic groups" and "treating ethnic relations as cultural relations."[58] If the politicization of minority groups affords them the political and social rights that ensure their status as the citizens of China on equal terms with the Han, then culturalization helps cultivate in minorities important ideas about their cultural identities and ethnic histories. As Chapter 1 will show, a state history-making project, *The Concise Histories of China's Ethnic Minorities*, which was started in the 1950s and finalized in the 1980s, has played an instrumental role in constructing historical narratives of China's fifty-five officially recognized minority groups. The Project imbricates imperial historiographies and Communist teleological historical visions with minority cultural traditions to create foundational narratives about minority groups' cultural identities. The Project firmly roots the diverse histories and cultural traditions of China's fifty-five minority groups within the core narrative of the *Zhonghua minzu* as a unitary, multiethnic national entity.

When the word *minzu* was first introduced into the modern Chinese political lexicon via translating the Japanese neologism *minzoku* in the late 1890s, it answered the call for the systematic conceptualization of the people(s) of China that preoccupied nationalist thinkers like Liang Qichao.[59] The word *minzu* has taken on a unique conceptual and political trajectory in modern China. Simultaneously encompassing the English notions of race, nation, people, ethnic group, and nationality,[60] the evolution of the meanings of *minzu* in modern China reflects the deeply interrelated and inseparable relationship between the non-Han *minzu* (ethnic groups) and the greater *Zhonghua minzu* (Chinese nation or race). The fifty-five *shaoshu minzu* (ethnic minorities), created by the Communist Party's Ethnic Classification Project, have become an inalienable part of China's imagination of itself as a unitary, multiethnic polity. The *shaoshu minzu* have been embedded into the very idea of Chinese-ness whenever the People's Republic evokes images of itself in both domestic and international settings.

It is important to note that, just as "Qiang" is a historically constructed and ever-evolving concept, so is the label and concept of "Han." As this book discusses the historical situatedness of the "Qiang" in China, I aim to also contextualize the changing boundaries and connotations of "Han." "Han" is a complex super-sign that has existed for a long time in Chinese history and has informed the formation of modern China's national consciousness. As Thomas Mullaney demonstrates, at various points in history, Han has served as a proxy for "Chinese civilization," a "biracial category of Chinese," and a "political-geographical category of China."[61] Whereas the idea of Hanren, or Han people, has existed in Chinese history for a long time, the compound word and conceptualization of Hanzu (Han ethnic group) as a coherent and self-contained ethnic group, just like that of Qiangzu, is a decidedly modern phenomenon.[62] The simultaneous antiquity of the ideas of "Han" and "Qiang," evidenced by the textual presence of these words in pre-modern Chinese literary, philosophical, and political discourses, and the recentness of the categories of Hanzu and Qiangzu as clearly-delineated ethnic groups, give rise to the intricate interplay that shapes the contour of ethno-national relations within China. As Chapters 1 and 2 will illuminate, the textual presence of "Qiang" in what is usually considered as "Han" culture, such as the mythologization of Da Yu (King Yu) as a Qiang hero in local tourism literature produced in Sichuan, does not dilute the mythic power of Da Yu as legendary figure. On the opposite, the interethnic interplay of the Qiang-Han origin of Da Yu reinforces the belief of the multiethnic ancestry of *Zhonghua minzu*, a powerful myth that can trace back to Republican era ethno-racial discourses and has continued to exercise influence on the minds of Qiang writers and scholars today.

Multiculturalism and Strategies of "Creative Belonging" in Reform-Era China

The bulk of the book deals with how the Qiang ethnic identity has been produced in the reform era in China (1980–present). The reform era is an important period in which ethnic minority groups have been actively inventing their identities by conversing with national discourses and international cultural influences. After the suppression of ethnic diversity and minority cultural expressions at the height of the Cultural Revolution (1966–1976), China has been embarking on a journey of "reconstituting of the ethnic," as "questions of minority empowerment and national belonging have been central to minority discourse in post-Mao China."[63] In other words, as the Chinese reform era has been characterized by an unprecedented speed of economic development and China's increasing power in global political and economic affairs, internally, the nation has been witnessing a revitalization of ethnic cultures under the banner of multiculturalism.

In the reform era, the Chinese government has been intent on encouraging the diverse expressions of ethnic cultural traditions. In 2012, the then-president of China, Hu Jintao, consecrated the importance of "culture" in "strengthening the socialist nation" at the Eighteenth National Congress of the Communist Party.[64] Hu highlighted the importance of allowing ethnic minority cultures to prosper.[65] China has made several laws to institutionalize the protection, inheritance, and carrying forward of ethnic cultural traditions, and there have been several nation-level scientific research projects aimed at rescuing minority languages at the verge of extinction.[66]

The Chinese state's promotion of ethnic cultural diversity transcends the terrain of political discourse and has resulted in various kinds of attempts to patronize, curate, and even consume minority cultures and cultural institutions at different levels of Chinese society.[67] In addition, with the administrative and financial help of local governments, ethnic tourism is flourishing in many multiethnic provinces of the country, such as Sichuan, Guizhou, Yunnan and Guangxi.[68] Local governments usually work with minority intellectuals and villagers to "brand" minority cultures and present minority traditions and natural landscapes to tourists while formulating articulations of minority identities and improving the living standards of minority populations. Certainly, this is by no means an even process and has produced inequalities across regions and among ethnic groups.[69] The development of ethnic tourism and representations of minority groups in national media often even have the effect of reducing minority cultures to consumable objects and exotic spectacles.[70] Yet one fact is undeniable: China's diverse ethnic cultures—particularly those smaller minority groups in southern and western China—are celebrated and presented in public, being recognized as distinctive and valuable. Moreover, minority literatures, cultures, and societies are closely studied in many national scholarly venues.[71]

In many ways, China is becoming a multicultural country that actively promotes its diverse ethnic cultures and sees such ethno-cultural diversity as important national assets. Some crucial dimensions of a multicultural society include that society's acknowledgement of the cultural diversity of its different groups, how that society encourages "creative dialogue" among its members from various ethnic and cultural backgrounds, as well as how the cultural groups within that society share their traditions and "strands of thought" while maintaining respect for each other.[72] The Communist Party's explicit call for the flourishing of minority cultures and the national and regional governments' efforts to champion minority cultures in scholarly discourses, public venues and tourism activities speak to contemporary China's eagerness to construct a multicultural society.

Multiculturalism—in its conceptual plurality and wide-ranging forms across the globe—is both the benchmark of any culturally heterogenous society and a way of governing diversity.[73] Stuart Hall reminds us that multiculturalism takes many shapes, such as liberal multiculturalism, which seeks to incorporate different cultural groups into mainstream culture and only allows private, particularistic cultural practices; pluralist multiculturalism, which locates a communal or communitarian political order within different groups' articulation of diversity; and commercial multiculturalism, which prefers the consumption and commodification of cultural difference.[74]

In other words, multiculturalism is not a singular theory that can be equally applied to any society, but is a perpetual process of making sense of and managing cultural difference in heterogenous societies with rich local variations and experiences. It is possible for a heterogenous society to possess more than one version of multiculturalism, as local actors and minority groups can form different relationships with the nation.

In the current global search for multicultural solutions to problems of race and ethnicity, it is essential for us to place China's multicultural experience within a transnational perspective. China's multiculturalism cannot be equated with liberal-style Western multiculturalism, for the latter emphasizes the respect for individual and group political rights and the ability to translate multicultural claims into movements for social justice.[75] In liberal Western countries, such as the United States, minority groups' lobbying efforts for recognizing difference can often develop into formal legalization procedures, such as the Civil Rights Movement's success in overthrowing racial segregations and the Affirmative Action's insurance of the (at least theoretically) equal treatment of people from different racial, gender, and national backgrounds in employment and schooling opportunities.

The Chinese state's advocacy for multiculturalism, centered on the expression of ethnic cultural diversity, is largely driven by the political purpose of fostering national unity and stability and is strongly motivated by the economic goal of developing some of the nation's traditionally impoverished minority regions.[76]

In fact, China's unique multiculturalism entails the articulation of localized cultural and ethnic identities as a means for ethnic minorities to practice their citizenship, as noted by political scientist Susan K. McCarthy.[77] McCarthy argues that citizenship practice in China can be viewed from a more "participatory, practice-based" perspective, as opposed to the "legal-juridical" and "right-bearing" concept of citizenship in the West.[78] This means that, by participating in the process of conceiving of and articulating ethnic traditions and identities, minority groups experience their status as the citizens of China, mediating their relationship to the nation with "local concerns, local institutions, and local cultural identities."[79]

It is within this context of a Communist multiculturalism that the Qiang identity is being invented and maintained, particularly through the mediating power of local intellectuals and cultural industries. As Chapter 2 will demonstrate, in today's Sichuan, there is a vibrant Qiang studies research circle (*Qiang xue yanjiu*) composed of both ethnic Qiang and local Han scholars.

These scholars actively participate in the invention of the Qiang identity by engaging in historical and cultural scholarship to excavate the multiethnic origin of the *Zhonghua minzu* that centers on the Qiang. They also produce epistemological claims about the Qiang's historical contributions to Chinese civilization by articulating the importance of Sichuan and the Yangtze River as the long-forgotten cradle of Chinese civilization. Most notably, many Qiang and Han scholars in Sichuan insist on the non-Han origin of some of China's legendary ancestors, such as King Yu (Da Yu) of China's mythic Xia dynasty, by arguing that King Yu was born into the ancient Qiang tribes in Sichuan, associating historical myths with local cultural sites to forge creative claims about the Qiang's Chinese-ness. Minority intellectuals and local scholars are well-versed in "orthodox"/Han-created narratives of Chinese history and culture, yet they innovatively appropriate these narratives to foreground their own ethno-regional claims.

Therefore, the formulation of minority identities for many smaller minority groups in contemporary China concerns itself with connecting the ethnic, the local, and the national. It involves minority intellectuals' mobilization and re-creation of national discourses and historical resources, as they "establish continuity with a suitable historical past."[80] Such a process is highly creative and demands the creative agency of the ethnic minority members of China, as they have to imagine themselves into Chinese historical, cultural, and literary sources that traditionally relegated them as "barbarians," as seen in the earlier parts of this Introduction. This creative process also establishes the Qiang and many other minority groups as a central part of a cultural membership that is Chinese-ness, expanding the ethno-racial and cultural capacity of what we conventionally think of as "Chinese." In this sense, "creative belonging" entails the creative interpretation, reinvention, and discursive fashioning of "Chinese-ness" not as a narrow ethnic or national marker, but as an inclusive cultural membership.

Rather than reacting against national discourses as "inauthentic" impositions upon their identities, smaller minority groups like the Qiang carve out precious discursive spaces to assert their ethnically distinctive Chinese-ness within such national discourses. In other words, the multiethnic interpretations of Chinese-ness permitted by China's current ideology of multiculturalism allows many ethnic groups to formulate innovative and imaginative notions of both their ethnic histories and their Chinese identities, merging the ethnic with the national rather than pitting one against the other.[81]

Admittedly, this ideological and discursive freedom to re-invent Chineseness is not equally distributed among all of China's minority groups.[82] Yet for smaller minority groups like the Qiang, it is possible to imagine an ethnic importance into the cultural symbols usually attributed to the Han, inventing new traditions and articulating ethnic identities without violating the nation's foundational political principles. A multicultural China tolerates and even encourages some flexibility and fluidity in the explanation of its long-upheld myths and symbols, as long as such new articulations fall within the political framework of an ethnically intertwined, unitary nation.

This brings us to the broader question of how ethnicity and cultural differences are produced, maintained, and managed in our globalized world. Many scholars have observed that, for neoliberal regimes characterized by a new relationship between the state and its diverse populations, multiculturalism and the acknowledgement of cultural difference are a necessary governmental technology. For example, Charles Hale contends that the granting of collective rights to marginalized cultural groups in Latin America is an "integral part of neoliberal ideology"—the neoliberal regime "shapes, delimits, and *produces* cultural differences rather than suppressing it."[83]

In many multicultural societies, "difference" becomes an important cultural and political capital for states to govern and manage their diverse populations. Rather than a simple erasure or assimilation of difference, many multicultural states nowadays encourage minority groups to actively manage their difference by working with the state, institutionalizing ethnic traditions and indigenous cultural expressions. In this process, the state recognizes ethno-cultural difference as essential components of a society and makes laws to protect minority heritage.

Such recognition is a double-edged sword. As Chapter 6 will demonstrate, on the one hand, the institutionalization of ethnic traditions, usually dubbed "Intangible Cultural Heritage" (非物质文化遗产 *feiwuzhi wenhua yichan*) in the Chinese context, increases the visibility of non-Han traditions and endows minority groups with abundant financial and social resources to carry forward their ethnic traditions. Yet, on the other hand, state-led institutionalizations of ethnic cultures sometimes result in a homogenization and commercialization of minority cultures, forcing minority groups to alter their traditions to cater to the taste of the Han public or mainstream media. Chapters 5 and 6 will unveil how both Qiang grassroots activists and cultural elites combat the homogenization and museumification of their traditions by engaging in cultural compilation projects—minority people question the exoticizing gaze of the Han and assert the dynamic subjectivity of their traditions in their cultural productions.

Structure of the Book and Chapter Outline

In order to reveal the dialogical process of ethnic identity-making in contemporary China, this book develops an innovative structure that investigates *both* how national policies and transnational cultural influences are shaping the Qiang identity *and* how the Qiang respond to such influences and engage in creative strategies to foster a sense of belonging within China. By developing this dialogical approach, this book presents how multicultural movements and interactions are essential in formulating minority identities in our globalizing world. In this regard, this book strives to go beyond a case study of one ethnic group in China, but aspires to demonstrate the rich history of the co-constitution of the national and the ethnic in China, bringing China into a global search for diversity and multicultural discourses.

In this sense, I treat historical, cultural, and artistic texts and discourses not as static objects of study, but as what anthropologist Erik Mueggler calls a "regime of reference."[84] According to Mueggler, what a society deems as "traditions" is an interleaved relationship between a social world and an "extrasocial world," or a "regime of reference in which the attributes of social practices were independent of place and one in which those attributes derived from the qualities of place."[85] In other words, social practices, including textual practices and cultural imaginaries that are formative to a certain group's self-identity, are products of perpetual interactions between different social and extrasocial worlds. As this book will demonstrate, these social and extrasocial worlds include both physical places of worldly interactions, such as minority villages, and cultural and discursive spaces where the physicality of space transforms into rich interactions between minority people and the world around them. One example of the latter case is how the physicality of the Da Yu (King Yu the Great) altars in Sichuan start to assume cultural meaning for the Qiang intellectuals eager to imagine the Qiang into China's multiethnic genealogy. Such interactions and worlds become a regime of reference, because they start to formulate traditions for the Qiang as a group of people, as members of the Qiang ethnic group make reference to these sites, texts, and ideas as symbols of their identity.

The six chapters of the book are divided into three parts: Chapters 1 and 2 focus on how the concept and idea of "Qiang"[86] has evolved historically in the poetic traditions, historical writings, and national discourses that are usually considered as canonical in the Chinese textual traditions. Chapter 1 and Chapter 2 also probe into the signifying power of "Qiang" in the formation of modern China's national consciousness and contemporary China's multicultural politics. Chapters 3 and 4 discuss how the "Qiang" has transformed into an active and creative modern ethnic minority group by demonstrating how the "Qiang" has been visualized in local and transnational cinema, tourism, and the built environment. Finally, Chapters 5 and 6 translate and introduce to the English-speaking world for the first time many literary works produced by contemporary ethnic Qiang writers. These final chapters examine how Qiang writers have expressed concerns about the changes that have profoundly reconfigured traditional Qiang village life. Among their concerns, the feminization of the Qiang native son as a symbol of the weakening power of ethnic traditions and the abandonment of the rural Qiang mother as a betrayal of indigenous lifeways have become important themes.

Chapter 1: From "Barbarians" to "Brothers" and Cultural Guardians: Race, Ethnicity, and the Invention of the Qiang in China's Textual Traditions and National Discourses

Starting at the pivotal moment of China's national rebuilding after the 2008 Sichuan earthquake, Chapter 1 asks the important but puzzling question: How have the Qiang, who were routinely cast as a racial other and cultural barbarian in classical Chinese poetry and historiography, come to assume the role of China's "cultural guardian" in the Communist official nationalist ideology since 2008? How do the shifting connotations of the "Qiang" embody the fluidity of ethnicity and the evolving relationships between the Chinese political-cultural center and its ethnic "peripheries?" Chapter 1 answers the above questions by offering a historicized intellectual genealogy on how the concept of the "Qiang" has evolved from a marker of racial otherness and ethnic estrangement in classical Chinese literature and historiography to a symbol of interethnic solidarity built upon a shared ancestry in modern Chinese political discourses. The chapter surveys important official ideologies and national narratives from imperial China to the twentieth century. By analyzing a range of state political discourses, national history-making projects, and China's contemporary multicultural politics in the global arena, Chapter 1 reveals how the "Qiang" occupies a unique ideological and cultural place in China's ethno-national imagination.

Chapter 2: "Da Yu Rose from the West Qiang:" Minority Scholarly Production and the Cultural Politics of Imaginary Ancestry in the Qiang Regions of China

Continuing with Chapter 1's discussion of how the "Qiang" embodies the intertwinement between China's national identity and multiethnic image, Chapter 2 shifts the focus from national discourses to the local invention of the Qiang identity. This chapter probes how contemporary Qiangzu intellectuals and entrepreneurs excavate the mythic presence of the "Qiang" in China's foundational myths to forge creative industries, mobilizing Han Chinese national cultural symbols to carve out an economic and political space for minority groups in reform-era China. This chapter examines how ethnic Qiang intellectuals and local scholars in Sichuan reinterpret the images of China's legendary sage king Da Yu (大禹 or King Yu the Great) and mythic founder Yandi (炎帝 the Fire Emperor or Emperor Yan) to reinvent the idea of *Zhonghua minzu*, placing the Qiang at the center of Chinese national imagination in local scholarly and touristic publications.

Chapter 3: A Village's Affair with the World: Representing the Qiang Native Village in Transnational Cinema and Tourism

Chapter 3 reveals how the Qiang ethnic culture has entered into the global visual circulation. This chapter investigates how Taoping Qiang Village as a native minority village spatializes China's fraught encounter with globalization. This chapter examines Chinese Six-Generation director Guan Hu's blockbuster *Design of Death*（杀生）and Los Angeles-based Chinese American director Tian Fen's（田芬）*Forbidden Kiss*（古堡之吻, 2014）, both of which were filmed in Taoping. The chapter supplements cinematic and artistic analysis with my ethnographic observations in Taoping Qiang Village to reveal how visual practices are organizing and redefining what it means to be ethnic minority or an indigenous community in globalizing China. The chapter illuminates the rich visual metaphors and diverse cultural imaginaries enveloped within the space of a small Chinese minority village (Figure 5 and Figure 6).

Chapter 4: The Run-Away Minority Bride: Fluid Indigeneity and Ethnographic Poetics in Qiang Indigenous Cinema

Pivoting the focus from transnational and mainstream cinema, this chapter takes the reader to the realm of indigenous cinema and theorizes about "ethnographic poetics" in contemporary Chinese indigenous cinema. By looking closely at two indigenous cinematic works, this chapter unveils the anthropological impulses and aesthetic innovations of contemporary Chinese indigenous filmmakers in reframing the "ethnographic" as a mode of identity-making. The chapter focuses on the mythological, shamanistic, and indigenous worldviews represented by contemporary indigenous Qiang cinema as a response to the industrialization and commercialization that have taken place in rural ethnic China.

Chapter 5: Between the Languishing Ethnic Mother and the Bewitching "Poisonous Cat:" Gender and Commercialization in Contemporary Chinese Minority Literature

Switching focus from the visual realm to the literary realm, this chapter focuses on how the question of gender shapes Chinese ethnic minority groups' experience with modernization. Particularly, I investigate how two prevalent images, the languishing, rural ethnic mother and the bewitching ethnic seductress, figure into Chinese minority writers' accounts of minority groups' fraught encounter with modernization. This chapter will offer readers a dynamic view of a range of literary genres, particularly autobiographical essays and fiction, produced by ethnic Qiang authors of southwestern China. Through a literary journey into the gendered landscape of these multiethnic groups, we will discover how minority communities experience the contradictory aspects of modernity exemplified by the complex relationships between the sexes.

Figure 5. Overview of Taoping Qiang Village. Photograph courtesy of Jingui Zhang.

Figure 6. Touristic promotion board of the cinematic representations of Taoping Qiang Village in domestic Chinese and international films. Photograph by author.

Chapter 6: Paradise Recrafted: The Problems of Secular Modernity in Chinese Multiethnic Literature and Village-Level Cultural Activism

In this final chapter of this book, I analyze the cultural and social impetuses for minority writers and activists in southwest China to critique secular modernity. I will reveal how minority writers and activists detail the spiritual traditions of their ethnic groups, combining their efforts to document culture with their search for ethnic subjectivity in China, a nation with an alleged atheist state ideology. I will present how minority writers and activists claim ownership to their cultures and formulate powerful discourses to advocate for a spirituality-centered, alternative cultural system. In fictional and memoir accounts, ethnic Qiang writers in China voice discontent with the basic tenets of modernity as they reconstruct ethnic traditions through writing and cultural activism. Eventually, Qiang writers and activists re-enchant what they consider to be an overly secularized Chinese society by unveiling the social and aesthetic values of the mystic beliefs, spiritual quests, and cultural wonders of indigenous ethnic groups.

In summary, this book does not study minority groups' literary and cultural traditions as self-contained entities; nor does it offer a conventional textual close reading of minority literary and cultural discourses. The greatest innovation of *Creative Belonging* lies in its dialogical approach and interdisciplinary methodology: the book looks into how minority identities are constantly invented and reinvented in the interactions between national political narratives and minority groups' articulations of their place in multiethnic China and the globalizing world. The book questions the boundary between the "national" and the "ethnic" by illuminating how minority identities are in dynamic flux and are products of China's changing national identity and situatedness in the globe.

The book demonstrates how minority identities are formulated and transformed in a variety of genres and practices. As the following chapters will reveal, these different genres and practices break down conventional boundaries between various cultural productions (such as the fictional and the documentary, the ethnographic and the imaginary), and they bear remarkable thematic resonances to each other—they embody a potent indigenous consciousness of Chinese ethnic groups to safeguard their imaginary or real heritage rooted in the topographical features and historical legends of their native lands; these cultural productions also bespeak the yearnings of smaller minority and indigenous groups to make global connections as they search for alternative accounts of the human past and indigenously-driven visions of the human future to forge creative ways of belonging in China and in the world.

In the end, *Creative Belonging* shows its readers how ethnic minority authors, intellectuals, and activists can expand our knowledge about China and Chinese-ness, and how ethnic minority groups interrogate and propose solutions to China's complex encounter with modernization and the world as creative agents. Through its engagement with various genres of cultural productions, this book reveals how ethnic groups in China—as well as many other parts of the world—creatively combine and re-invent cultural and historical sources from multiple indigenous, national, and global sites, producing new epistemologies to challenge the teleological, pragmatical visions of modernity and Western-led globalization.

PART I

Imagining the "Qiang" in Chinese National Narratives and Minority Scholarly Debates

CHAPTER 1

From "Barbarians" to "Brothers" and Cultural Guardians

Race, Ethnicity, and the Invention of the "Qiang" in Chinese Textual Traditions and National Discourses

In July 2008, two months after the devastating Sichuan earthquake that was soon consecrated as a "national trauma" (*guo shang* 国殇) by the Chinese central government, the then prime minster of China, Wen Jiabao, urged the public that the safeguarding of the Qiang ethnic minority culture was a matter of national importance.[1]

Feng Jicai, a renowned Chinese author coming out of the post-Mao "scar literature" school but championed for his recent efforts of rescuing China's traditional and folk cultural heritage, was entrusted with the task of documenting and preserving the Qiang ethnic heritage. In a news article detailing Feng's determination to spearhead the systematic safeguarding of the Qiang ethnic heritage, Feng remarked: "We absolutely need to rescue and protect the culture of Qiang at any cost, for the Qiang is like a brother—indeed, an *elder brother*—to the Han."[2] Feng went on to lament the destruction of the Qiang culture during the earthquake as a national calamity:

> Before we had a chance to sort out the Qiang heritage, it was faced with the destructive blow of the earthquake. This was not only a blow to the Qiang ethnic culture, but a blow to our Chinese culture (*Zhonghua minzu wenhua* 中华民族文化) as a whole, and a blow to our national life (*minzu shengming* 民族生命)."[3]

Indeed, the 2008 Sichuan earthquake was devastating for the Qiang's cultural well-being. The earthquake not only destroyed many vernacular Qiang villages and their architectural fabrics, but also killed many aged *shibi*, or

Qiang shamanistic ritual masters, and buried numerous cultural artifacts, including musical instruments and other treasured goods, of the Qiang regions of Sichuan province.[4]

The ethnic group known today in China as the Qiang or Qiangzu is a small ethnic minority group with a population of approximately 300,000, residing mainly in the Aba Tibetan and Qiang Autonomous Prefecture in northwestern Sichuan.[5] Straddled between the politically and economically dominant Han populations to its east and the ethnically distinct Tibetans to its west, the Qiang had, prior to the earthquake, been a lesser-known group even within China's contemporary multiethnic cultural politics. What political and cultural factors propelled China's political leaders and cultural elites, such as Wen Jiabao and Feng Jicai, to designate such a national preeminence to "Qiang cultural heritage?" Why did China's leading officials creatively deploy such rhetoric as "the elder brother of Han" to elevate one small ethnic group, contending that its well-being and cultural integrity are vital to the "national life" of *Zhonghua minzu* (Chinese nation or people) as a whole? Most importantly, how did the idea of the Qiang, which was historically a racial other and "barbarian" in classical Chinese poetry and historiography, come to shoulder the all-important task as the guardian of *Chinese culture* under the Communist multicultural politics in the twenty-first century?

These are puzzling yet important questions to ponder. Answers to these questions will shed light on how ethnicity, a fluid and ever-evolving term in different cultural contexts, is framed in China, one of the world's largest multiethnic nations. Ethnicity, taking heterogenous inspirations from various cultural and historical sources, continues to hold sway in our globalizing world and remains one of the most powerful organizing principles of people's identities. This chapter traces the evolution of the concept of "Qiang" in Chinese cultural history and textual traditions. Here, by "textual traditions," I refer to both historically established textual genres in China, such as poetry and historiography, and the modern inventions of ethnography and national narratives. As we will see in this chapter, the introduction of such modern Western disciplines as anthropology and ethnology into twentieth-century China not only expanded the ways in which ethnicity and ethnic groups were imagined, but also greatly enriched the Chinese textual and writing traditions, as empirically-based observations of frontier societies and peoples started to figure into the Chinese literary and cultural imagination. In this sense, the "metamorphosis" of the idea of the "Qiang" serves as an important site to understand the creative interactions between Chinese textual genres, modern academic disciplinary innovations, national identity formation, and the shifting connotations of ethnicity.

Following a historical trajectory, we will investigate how the concept and word of "Qiang" morphed from a signifier of racial and cultural difference in classical Chinese poetry and historiography to a marker of interethnic solidarity and a shared sense of citizenship in the multiethnic Republic of China by way of ethnographic writing and the construction of racial discourses. The early twentieth century, particularly the 1920s and 1930s, was a pivotal moment of the construction of modern Chinese nationhood as the Republic of China (1911/1912–1949) confronted Western and Japanese cultural and academic paradigms. The textual invention of "Qiang" stood at the center of a multifaceted national imagination of the former "barbarian" groups into the core of a multiethnic Chinese nationhood. Moving away from the Republican era, we will probe how a series of national history-writing projects spearheaded by the Chinese Communist Party from the 1950s to the 1980s continued the Republican-era national discourses and contributed to re-imagining the "Qiang" from a racial other to an integral part of a multiethnic, intermingled *Zhonghua minzu* defined by its shared musical and poetic heritage. Particularly, the Communist national narratives creatively re-interpreted classical Chinese poetry to reconstruct the image of the "Qiang" as an important contributor to China's great musical traditions, such as the Qiang reed pipe (*Qiangdi* 羌笛).

Through exploring the invention of the "Qiang" identity at critical moments in Chinese history and in China's key national discourses, I aim to not only theorize the fluid nature of race and ethnicity in China, but also investigate the historical and cultural contingencies that converge to transform certain racial and ethnic categories. Particularly, I will argue that the "Qiang" has not only been constructed as an ethnic group in China, but more importantly, as a cultural myth of the interethnic ancestry of the whole of *Zhonghua minzu* in China's modern national narratives. As this chapter will demonstrate, the "Qiang" is not simply a word or a historical entity, but a key conceptual framework through which modern Chinese intellectuals and national discourses imagine the Chinese national identity. Moreover, through a series of cultural, textual, and material constructions, the "Qiang" has become *a system of cultural symbolism and knowledge* to denote the changing relations between the political and cultural "center" of China and its ethnic "peripheries," even though such "centers" and "peripheries" were always unstable. This chapter serves as the foundation of the book, as the invented ideas and traditions of the "Qiang" have continued to influence how the modern Qiangzu (Qiang ethnic group) perceive of themselves, as well as how the modern Qiangzu have creatively interacted with the long textual traditions of imagining the Qiang in China's cultural history.

"Bestial" and "Fierce:" The Construction of Race and the "Qiang Barbarians" in Classical Chinese Poetry and Historiography

In his conception of the importance of writing in wielding cultural and political power in early China, historian Mark Edward Lewis proposes that "the use of written graphs to create or preserve 'artificial' or technical languages whose mastery distinguishes elements within society" was a prominent feature of traditional Chinese society.[6] Lewis argues that the power of writing usually "[outlasts] the moment of inscription," crossing many historical periods to endow power to the writing elites and to construct the imagined space of the Chinese empire around the written documents.[7] Written documents assumed ultimate moral and cultural authority and served to categorize human communities and organize knowledge in pre-modern China, providing important basis to the political rule of the imperial government.

In China's long textual traditions, the distinction between the Sinitic, writing "self" represented by Confucian literati and the often non-literate or non-Confucian racial and ethnic "others" residing in the borderlands of China was an important binary informing the poetry and historiography produced over a long span of time. Particularly, the Qiang was constructed as a racial alien and barbarian other in diverse historical periods and various textual traditions, especially in classical poetry and historiography, to accentuate a sense of cultural and political superiority of the Confucian Sinitic "self" in Chinese cultural history.

The Book of Later Han (*Hou Hanshu* 後漢書) is an exemplary historiography in which we can discern classical historians' textual constructions of the alien "others" on the peripheries of China. As one of the canonical historical books in traditional China, *The Book of Later Han* was authored by Fan Ye (范曄, 398–445) and aimed to present the historical facts and events of the Eastern Han dynasty (25–220 AD). *The Book of Later Han* contains various "biographies" (*zhuan* 傳) of the non-Sinitic (non-Chinese) groups surrounding China proper. These written documents served to construe the "textual double of the polity,"[8] or textual imaginations of the different demographic communities in China, and such writing had lasting influence on how non-Sinitic groups were regarded and administered in Chinese history.

Xiqiang zhuan (*The Biography of the Western Qiang* 西羌傳) is one of the six biographies on the non-Sinitic groups of China in *The Book of Later Han*. Instead of seeing "Qiang" as one singular or closed ethnic entity, Fan Ye conceived of "Xiqiang" (West Qiang) as a loose term with open borders and porous boundaries: Fan defined the peoples of Xiqiang as stretching from the northwestern frontier of China to the Shu Kingdom (ancient Sichuan). This region to the west of China proper had cultural customs that diverged significantly from the Confucian Sinitic groups. The peoples that were categorized as Xiqiang tribes resided in vastly different landscapes, from expansive and prohibiting deserts to steep mountain ranges.

As Edward Said argues in *Orientalism*, "space acquires emotional and even rational sense by a kind of poetic process, whereby the vacant or anonymous reaches of distance are converted into meaning."[9] In the writing of classical Chinese historiography, the distant and unfamiliar lands, because they laid outside of the reach of Chinese culture, were considered as home to barbarian peoples and racial others. *The Book of Later Han* was ridden with a sense of cultural and moral superiority in its depiction of the geographically distant Xiqiang peoples. Particularly, this book casts the Xiqiang, as well as the five other non-Sinitic groups, in dehumanizing and bestial terms. For example, Fan Ye states that the peoples of Xiqiang could "bear cold and heat like beasts," and that these peoples were of a "mighty and formidable nature," as they took in the "golden energy (*jinqi* 金氣) of the west."[10] The words "beasts" and "mighty and formidable" are used to connote what the author imagined to be an animalistic primitiveness that the Qiang embody.

The Biography of the West Qiang also manifests a clear demarcation of the "otherness" of the peoples of Xiqiang, as it compares the undesirable cultural customs of these peoples with those of the Sinitic/Chinese. Fan Ye laments that the people of Xiqiang "had no emperors or minsters," thus no political order or political organization. What is more horrible is the fact that among the Xiqiang tribes, "once the father perishes, [the son] would marry the stepmother; when the elder brother dies, [the younger brother] would marry the widowed sisters-in-law."[11] Marrying one's stepmother or sister-in-law would be considered as incest in the Confucian ethical code. For Fan Ye, these horrendous customs spelt the moral inferiority and cultural deficiency of non-Sinitic peoples as stateless, anarchic, and morally questionable savages.

Furthermore, *The Biography of the West Qiang* details the invasions and aggressions conducted by the Xiqiang tribes against China proper from the Shang dynasty throughout the Han dynasties, as peace and unrest replaced each other periodically. Notably, Fan Ye as an imperial historiographer used the terms Qiang, Rong (戎), and Rongdi（戎狄）interchangeably to gloss the diverse tribes collectively known as Xiqiang. In the mind of Fan Ye, the demarcation between the alien others and the Chinese self seemed more important than the distinctions among these alien groups themselves. Fan also used the term *zhurong*（諸戎 "various Rong/barbarians"）to refer to the eventual "pacification" of the southwestern alien others by Chinese cultural and military forces.[12]

The portrayal of the Xiqiang or Qiang as a bestial and fierce racial other in *The Book of Later Han* finds its echo in various poetic accounts of traditional China. The image of the "Qiang" occurred repeatedly in classical Chinese poetry to denote the barbarian existence of non-Sinitic groups feared by the Chinese from the central plains. For example, in the *Classics of Poetry* (*Shijing* 詩經), China's earliest poetry collection, a poem titled "Yinwu" (殷武) in praise of King Yinwu of the Shang dynasty evoked the Qiang. In this poem, the anonymous poet states:

> In the past, there was the [capable king] Chengtang [who established the Shang dynasty]; none of those from the [distant lands of the] Di and Qiang (氐羌) dared not pay tribute to him; none of them dared not make him their own king. Indeed, Chengtang was the king of the entire world.[13]

This poem glorifies how King Chengtang of the Shang dynasty defeated the otherwise belligerent Di and Qiang tribes, bringing them to pacification and rendering them subjects of his rule.

The military aggressions of the nomadic Qiang were seen as a force that continued to threaten the political rule, social stability, and cultural integrity of China proper, culminating in the lamentations of such poets as Cai Wenji (蔡文姬, 132–192) of the Eastern Han dynasty. At a chaotic time of warfare and divisions in China during the Eastern Han dynasty, Cai was abducted by the armies of the Southern Xiongnu (南匈奴) and made to be the wife of a Xiongnu commander. Cai grieved over her unfortunate fate of having to leave China behind and venture into the "Qiang's land:"

> How poor my fate, alas, to meet such dismal times! . . .
> I was captured and abducted to beyond the western pass,

> The journey perilous and long to that *barbarian land* ("Qiang fang," 羌方) . . .
> And though I clung to life, I was dishonored and abased![14]

Cai's sharp sense of dishonor and abasement stemmed from her forced journey beyond the "west pass" into a bestial, uncultured land that laid outside of the pale of Chinese civilization, known as the "land of the Qiang." In Cai's words, in this savage land, she was living with barbarians who "feed on rancid flesh" with their "speech gibberish."[15] Like Fan Ye, Cai also lamented the fact that "people from the plains [the Chinese] are vulnerable and weak," while the attacking soldiers were "all from Hu and Qiang."[16] To Cai, the belligerent image of the barbaric Hu and Qiang savages was only accentuated by their horrendous dietary habits and uncultured language. The unbearable cohabitation with non-Chinese barbarians raped Cai of both her gender identity and cultural integrity as a noble, educated, and delicate Chinese woman. To salvage such extreme humiliation, the famous general Cao Cao (曹操, 155–220) eventually ransomed Cai Wenji from the hands of the Xiongnu nomads, restoring the cultural wholeness and political prowess of China embodied by a woman stolen from the bosom of her native land of "civilization."

From the above examples and numerous other similar passages and verses from classical Chinese historiographical and literary accounts, we can see that the word and concept of the "Qiang" served as a racial marker in premodern China. Rather than referring to one specific ethnic group, "Qiang" acted as a stock concept in classical Chinese texts to represent racial others marked by their cultural, dietary, linguistic, and sartorial differences or deviations from the civilizational "center" of China. Even though "Qiang" mainly implied the non-Sinitic groups residing in China's western borderlands, it was sometimes used interchangeably with other "savage groups," such as the Xiongnu/Hu in Cai Wenji's poems, to signify racial otherness and cultural difference.

Both *The Book of Later Han* and the many examples of the "barbarian Qiang" in Chinese poetic traditions testify to how race and culture were entangled in traditional China. Frank Dikotter, in his study of imperial Chinese epistemology of racial distinctions, pinpoints some pivotal dynamics at work in texts like *The Book of Later Han*. Dikotter notes that in Chinese classics, alien groups were measured "according to a yardstick by which those who did not follow 'Chinese ways' were considered barbarians."[17]

Like all forms of racism, traditional Chinese elites defined race by using

Chinese culture and the Sinitic group as the standard by which all other groups were measured. Similar to racism in the Western context, traditional Chinese constructions of race implied a "process of differentiation," or the articulation of the undesirable physical and cultural traits of the racial "others" in the eyes of the dominant group.[18] Moreover, the textual constructions of the Xiqiang and other non-Sinitic groups as racially deviant betray the Confucian writing elites' efforts of using writing as a political and cultural instrument to internalize and exercise their power over ethnic and racial groups residing in the borderlands of China.

Alien groups such as the Xiqiang were deemed less civilized and glossed as the racial other due to at least three important factors: their physical traits and sartorial identities; their perceived moral inferiority and despicable social practices; and their less advanced cultural development and less sophisticated cultural norms in the eyes of Confucian literati.

Physical and sartorial traits can be given social meaning.[19] In *The Book of Later Han*, in addition to the Xiqiang tribes, many other peripheral peoples were depicted as bearing different bodily functions and alien sartorial identities compared to the Chinese. For example, in Fan Ye's depiction of the "southern barbarians and southwestern savages" (*Nanman xinanyi* 南蠻西南夷), the historian mentioned that these peoples were "fond of colorful attires," and they "practiced tattooing and body-piercing" and "bathed with the opposite sex in the same stream."[20] Both body piercing and bathing with the opposite sex were considered extremely inappropriate in the Confucian moral conduct. While one's body was seen as the ultimate seat of respect for one's parents and therefore calls for ultimate wholesomeness and care, Confucian moral code also dictated a strict distinction between men's space and women's space in society, never permitting something like bathing with the opposite sex in the same stream. Therefore, the physical traits of body piercing and cultural custom of bathing with the opposite sex were deemed undesirable by Confucian literati like Fan Ye. Fan concluded that the southern barbarians and southwestern savage "resembled beasts and did not distinguish between the elderly and the young," living in a disordered and stateless society similar to the Qiang.[21]

In addition to physical and sartorial identities, moral and social practices also factored into traditional Chinese historians' assessment of alien peoples and their perceived "backward" situations. For Fan Ye, tribes of the Xiqiang practiced such savage customs as marrying their stepmothers and widowed sisters-in-law, which were morally condemnable by the Confucian ethics of respecting the proper orders and hierarchies among family members. Not having their own emperors or ministers to govern these people, according to Fan, was one major reason why these people lived in such a pitiable social environment.[22]

One final but important aspect that classical Chinese historiographers believed set the racial others apart from the Chinese was their cultural backwardness. In *Biographies of the Southern Barbarians and Southwestern Savages*, Fan Ye pointed out that it was only after the Chinese had sent migrants, sometimes even criminals, into the land of the "barbarians," were the barbarians able to learn the proper ways of ritual and speak the human (Chinese) language, being uplifted from their culturally and morally despicable situation.[23]

Fan Ye ended most of his "biographies of barbarians" with a note that the alien peoples were eventually pacified: they submitted to Chinese culture and political rule, and they came to "know about [the proper orders of] marriage," and "schools were established to teach about rituals and righteousness," or Confucian morality.[24] In other words, as an imperial historiographer, Fan Ye exemplified many Confucian moral and political ideals of assimilating the alien groups with the forces of Chinese civilization and political conquest. It seems that his accounts of the "barbarians" were tainted with highly idealized and politicized attitudes, as barbarians were almost exclusively depicted as willingly submitting to Chinese rule and learning to acculturate themselves to Chinese civilization.

In *The Book of Later Han* and other classical historiography and poetry, whenever the Xiqiang or other geographically and culturally distant peoples were evoked, they were used almost exclusively to heighten the demarcation between the superior Sinitic self and inferior non-Sinitic others. Therefore, "imaginative geography and history help the mind to intensify its own sense of itself by dramatizing the distance and difference between what is close to it and what is far away."[25] Classical historiography distinguishes the Chinese from its barbarian others geographically, morally and culturally, as the distance between the Chinese center and the alien peripheries was stressed to reinforce the Chinese sense of moral and cultural authority.

As a book that accrued tremendous power in the Chinese textual traditions, *The Book of Later Han* invented stereotypes of the uncultured Xiqiang and other "barbarian" groups, stereotypes that would recur in subsequent historical writing in dynastic China. While it is not the goal for this chapter to provide a comprehensive survey of the historical lineage of writing about the cultural others in every single dynasty, examples abound if we were to look into the canonical historiographical writing in China: from *The Book of Tang* to *The Book of Ming*, major historiographical accounts in subsequent dynasties perpetuated the same stereotypes of demarcating the boundaries between the Sinitic "self" and the racial others. These historiographical accounts helped establish not only a textual, but also political and cultural order in the Chinese empire, informing the empire's social organization and its governance of the many ethnic and racial groups inhabiting the geographical peripheries of China.

Curious Gaze at the Borderlands: Republican-Era Epistemology of Ethnicity and the Qiang as Compatriots

The dualistic thinking between the Sinitic civilizational and cultural self and the non-Sinitic other in Chinese textual traditions that we saw in the first section experienced a dramatic shift in the early twentieth century, when the Republican-era witnessed epistemologically new understandings of ethnicity in China.

As historian James Leibold points out, it was during the late Qing dynasty's transition from an empire to a nation-state that the historical "barbarians" came to be viewed as an integral part of the Chinese national self.[26] This transition took place mainly in the late nineteenth to the early twentieth centuries. The political imperative to fend off Western encroachment of China's territories and resources drove Chinese intellectuals to reconsider the long-established political and cultural hierarchy between the Chinese self and its ethnic others, who occupied the vast and coveted frontiers of China. Faced with the grave aggressions of Western others, late Qing to early Republican politicians and scholars made room for the "internal others," or China's own ethnic others, in both political ideology and national policy. Leibold argues that the "territory question" (*lingtu wenti*) and "national question" (*minzu wenti*) in late imperial and modern China became intertwined: the search for China's national identity entailed both the bounding of the Chinese geo-body—to define a finite territory that included the frontier lands—and the incorporation of the historically alienated ethnic and racial others into the Chinese national self.[27] As a result, "frontiers and minority nationals" became instrumental in "constructing political and cultural narratives of Chinese nationhood" in the late ninetieth to early twentieth centuries.[28]

It was in this context that the Qiang first came to be recognized as a dis-

Figure 7. Book cover of *Qiangrong kaochaji*, original edition.

tinct *minzu* (ethnic group 民族) by Republic-era scholars. In 1934, a celebrated journalist and photographer, Zhuang Xueben (莊學本 1909–1984), set out for an expedition to southwest China following the Nationalist government's mandate to explore the frontiers of the nation.[29] Unable to travel to Tibet itself, Zhuang decided to venture into the little-known Sichuan and Qinghai ethnic frontiers. Zhuang became one of the first modern Chinese intellectuals who had done field research to identify the Qiang as an independent ethnic group, as opposed to being part of a collectivity of nomadic tribes known as the Xiqiang or Xifan in classical poetry and historiography.[30]

One of Zhuang's most prominent works is his *Qiangrong kaochaji* (*Expeditions into the Land of the Qiang and Rong* 羌戎考察記). The book was first published in 1937 in the heat of China's national anxiety due to its war with Japan. The author made it clear on the outset that his purpose of traveling to the northwestern and southwestern Chinese hinterland was because "the northeast [region of China] was lost [to Japanese occupation];" yet other frontier lands, such as the northwest and the southwest, remained vast and rich for *Chinese* exploration and exploitation.[31] The nationalist imperative to maintain the territorial integrity of China propelled scholars like Zhuang to investigate the frontier peoples and include them into the newly defined Chinese geo-national body—newly defined but under foreign threat.

In this book that resembles a travelogue with rich illustrations, Zhuang exhibited a friendly, curious, and scientific attitude toward his subjects of study, the Qiang and Rong (Tibetan) peoples of Sichuan. He not only applied the modern criteria of language, religion, shared customs, and history to categorize the Qiang as a distinct ethnic group, but also vindicated all frontier ethnic peoples of their "savage" reputation in classical historiography and poetry.

In the Preface to this book, Zhuang defended the frontier peoples as his "compatriots" (*tong bao* 同胞) against the convention of labeling them as barbarians in traditional China. Zhuang writes:

> Because of the natural barriers of the mountains and rivers . . . as well as the disorganized frontier political situations, [this part of China] has been alienated for a long time. That is why people's lifestyles and cultures remain as if they were in primitive times. If we, with our new insights of the twentieth century, observe our old-fashioned compatriots to be lagging behind the civilization of the current century . . . we might naturally think of them as barbarous and dangerous. Yet if we spent long enough time with them, we would know about their happiness and interesting nature and their ancient customs. We would realize how noble and pure their spirit is (*jingshen gaojie* 精神高潔), and how respectable and hospitable they are (*kejing keqin* 可敬可親). *Therefore, those who denigrate our compatriots as barbarians are gravely mistaken.*[32]

This passage is almost a direct refutation of the Qiang's "bad reputation" as an incestuous, disorderly barbarian group in the eyes of Confucian literati like Fan Ye, which we saw in the earlier section. Zhuang's claim that the frontier peoples were equal citizens ("compatriots") in the newly established Republic of China and admirable for their moral characters ("respectable and hospitable") are not only personal remarks, but also speaks about an important epistemological transformation in modern China to see the historically inferior racial others residing in China's borderlands as equal citizens to the nascent Republic of China. Rather than considering the Qiang and Tibetans as racial others, Zhuang actively talked about them as equals to the Han majority group of China and even criticized the mistreatment of the Qiang and Rong groups as "barbarians" in the past, a mistreatment rooted in the ideological biases that the Sinitic/Chinese group held against these frontier communities. Zhuang attributed the historical misunderstanding about these groups to the natural barriers that prevented equal interactions between the Sinitic groups and these groups, rather than the intrinsically questionable moral and cultural traits of these groups themselves.

It is notable that Zhuang's depictions of the Qiang and Rong groups, though still filled with somehow essentialized characteristics, were derived from his personal experience of visiting the frontier regions in Sichuan, rather than purely ideological projections such as those perpetuated by pre-modern Chinese scholars like Fan Ye. Moreover, throughout the entire book of *Qiangrong kaochaji*, there are many detailed descriptions of the cultural practices, religious customs, and local lore that Zhuang collected in the region, together with the many photographs that he took in the Sichuan-Qinghai borderlands. These observation-based depictions and visual representations of the region mark Zhuang Xueben's work a product of the ethnographic imagination of frontier societies rooted in the modern disciplines of anthropology and ethnology.

In fact, right around Zhuang's decade of expedition in the 1930s, ethnology (*minzuxue* 民族學) as a modern discipline emerged in China, characterized by a new emphasis on field work and direct, personal observations of ethnic groups. In 1926, China's prominent scholar Cai Yuanpei (蔡元培) published an important piece, "On Ethnology" (*shuo minzuxue* 說民族學), which delineated the methodological foundations of modern ethnology as an empirical science:

> What distinguishes modern ethnography from that of the past is that [modern ethnography] is based on investigative research (*kaocha* 考察). Sometimes this is combined with personal efforts, [as the researchers] go deep into the natural ethnic tribes, experience extremely harsh expeditions and endure great risks . . . Those who are lucky enough to reach their research destinations can then write up *detailed and accurate* (*xiangquede* 詳確的) reports.[33]

In this passage, Cai highlights the importance of investigative research and fieldwork as the reliable means to obtain "detailed and accurate" understandings of tribal communities. Cai even goes so far as to champion the personal sacrifices and risks endured by the researcher as the researcher embarks on a journey of pursuing truth. As I have argued elsewhere, Cai Yuanpei's conception of ethnology as both an empirically-based science and an embodied personal enterprise is characteristic of the May Fourth enlightenment discourse, which prizes reason and the rational pursuit of knowledge as the ultimate conduit to truth.[34] Undeniably, such "rational" pursuit of empirical knowledge is tainted with a strong nationalist flavor, as the birth of ethnology and anthropology in modern China went hand in hand with the nationalist desire to conceive of an independent, coherent, and multiethnic Chinese nation.

The title of Zhuang's book and Zhuang's decade-long physical expeditions into the Sichuan-Qinghai borderlands coincide with Cai's advocacy for investigative research in China's borderlands. When Zhuang visited the frontier societies in western China, many other Han ethnographers and scholars also set foot in regions ranging from the Northeast to the Southwest, documenting the cultural customs, histories, and current conditions of China's various ethnic groups, from the Hezhe (赫哲族) of the Northeast to the Miao (苗族), Lolo (羅羅), and Hui (回民) of the South and Southwest.[35] Therefore, Zhuang's textual and visual construction of the Qiang is part of a nation-wide trend of understanding frontier societies and border regions, an ethnographically- and ethnologically-driven enterprise deeply seeped in a nationalist agenda.

In Chapter 6 of *Qiangrong kaochaji*, Zhuang makes a systematic effort to identify the cultural and ethnic traits of the Qiang as a distinct group of people. In this chapter, he lists many ethnic cultural manifestations to "prove" that the Qiang was, like the Han and the Rong, a distinct ethnic group. For example, he writes about the Qiang's singing-dance, *guozhuang*, as being deeply influenced by the dance of the Rong, though the Qiang had yet to develop its own unique style.[36] Zhuang was also amazed by the Qiang custom of refraining from intermarrying other ethnic groups.[37] Most importantly, Zhuang is concerned with the survival of the Qiang language and religion, two criteria of ethnicity most sacredly held by modern ethnologists. In the last few sections of the chapter, Zhuang writes about the gradual loss of the Qiang (oral) language due to the Qiang's lack of a written script and the perpetuating force of the Han cultural influence:

> The common name for the Qiang language is "local talk" (*xiangtan* 鄉談), and it is the original language of the Qiang. Currently, people in their middle age and above still speak in *xiangtan*. Old people are very fluent in the local language, but those below their middle age need to use the official language [Sichuanese Mandarin] to talk about specific terms . . . Nowadays, the Qiang people have been seriously Sinicized (*Hanhua*), and they are happy to use the official language and embarrassed to use the local talk. Even young people are very fluent in Sichuanese Mandarin.[38]

Here, Zhuang exhibits an acute understanding of the power of language in demarcating ethnic boundaries. Language was the main criterion he used to distinguish the Qiang from the Rong, and he seems aware of the fact that the loss of the Qiang native language would entail an endangerment of the Qiang's nascent ethnic identity.

Similarly, Zhuang is concerned with the Qiang religious practice—shamanism—as a defining characteristic of the Qiang culture. He writes in detail about the shaman's costume and religious instruments, as well as the different purposes a shamanistic ritual would serve.[39] These detailed descriptions result from his direct observations of the Qiang cultural practices and are also the ideological products of his own time—the nationalist imperative felt by many Republican-era scholars to understand the ethnic groups of China grew out of China's increasing tension with Japan in the 1930s, when China's newly bounded territorial boundary was under threat.

Republican-era scholars like Zhuang used decidedly modern categories such as language and religion to demarcate the Qiang as an ethnic group. Language-based taxonomy of ethnic identity, as Thomas Mullaney points out, became prominent in the 1930s in China by way of Western ethnologists' advocacy. The model of delineating ethnic boundaries based on groups' linguistic differences became emic thanks to the epistemological innovations made by Western ethnologists such as British scholar H.R. Davies. The language-based ethnotaxonomy developed by Davies was viewed as more scientific and accurate than the imperial Chinese way of identifying ethnic groups based on their visible physical marks and cultural habits.[40] More importantly, language was seen as more "natural and meaningful" in identifying different groups, allowing modern ethnologists to advocate for the inclusion of the historically marginalized ethnic minority groups into the nation-state.[41] Furthermore, direct ethnographic knowledge of different groups, such as that obtained by Zhuang's adventurous expedition into the frontier lands, became revered in the search for the ethnically and culturally "authentic" Chinese nationhood and served as a scientific method to construct the knowledge about the nascent multiethnic Chinese nation-state.

The imagination of a multiethnic modern Chinese national identity in the early twentieth century not only involved empirically-based studies of ethnic groups like those conducted by Zhuang Xueben, but also a transformation of the ideology and concepts around non-Sinitic minority groups as a whole. Around the same time that Zhuang published his *Qiangrong kaochaji* in 1937, a prolific body of historical studies of ethnicity in China was blooming, which contributed to revising the cultural and political ideologies surrounding the historical "barbarian" others of China. At least three major studies with the title of *Zhongguo minzushi* (*History of the Races of China* 中國民族史) were published by scholars like Lin Huixiang (林惠祥 1936, 1937), Ren Qiu and Wang Tongling (王桐齡 first edition 1928, second edition 1934), and Song Wenbing (宋文炳 1935). These studies are an eclectic combination of Chinese imperial/traditional historiographical narratives with modern nationalist concerns and racial conceptualizations. All three studies follow the structure of imperial historiography in their chronological ordering of the dynasties of China, from the pre-Qin legendary times to the Republic of China; they also directly borrow the imperial terminology, such as Yi (夷), Di (狄), Man (蠻) (Ren Qiu and Wang Tonglin), Donghu (東胡) and Diqiang (氐羌) (Song Wenbing), and Baiyue (百越) (Lin Huixiang) to address the different racial groups and ethnic communities in and around China.[42]

Despite their direct borrowing of traditional terminology, these studies are by no means modern replicas of classical Chinese knowledge about race; rather, they try to reconcile the epistemological contradiction between Western Darwinist discourses of race and traditional Chinese cultural knowledge of race by using pre-modern Chinese textual materials (racial terms and chronological orders) to account for the modern need of establishing a racially and ethnically coherent Chinese nation.

Among these three historical studies of China's races, Lin Huixiang's is most exemplary of how Western racial discourses and Chinese traditional knowledge become enmeshed for modern Chinese intellectuals to carry out their own nationalist agendas. In Lin's *Zhongguo minzushi*, the author juxtaposes two kinds of classificatory systems of China's races: the traditional Chinese system and the modern Western system. Lin defines the former as a system "oriented toward the past" while deeming the latter as a system "targeting the present."[43] Lin does not invalidate the traditional Chinese system of designating different names for the "ethnic others" (such as Yi, Man, Rong, Di); yet he also introduces Western racial discourses into his understanding of China's ethnic and racial make-up. He cites Western-language sources such as British anthropologist A.H. Keane's categorization of the Mongolo-Tartar polysyllabic speech and Mongoloid races of Thibetan intermediate speech.[44] At the same time, Lin juxtaposes the Western system with both traditional Chinese system and modern Chinese intellectuals' understanding of race. He seems to find no contradiction in traditional Chinese and modern Western racial epistemology, a combination of which gave rise to modern Chinese ethnological and racial discourse of *Zhonghua minzu* in the early decades of the twentieth century.

Perhaps the most powerful claim made by Republican historians like Lin is the conclusion that, despite the changing ways of naming and classifying China's ethnic and racial groups, an assimilationist trend dominated how racial and ethnic relations in China had developed. Lin asserts:

> The Huaxia branch [of the races residing in China] is not only a major body of the Han stock today; other branches, upon coming into contact with the Huaxia and mixing with it, have usually become assimilated into it. But because it [the Huaxia] has absorbed much influence from other races, it is no longer the Huaxia when it first came into being. Therefore, it is more appropriate to name it Hanzu rather than Huaxia today.[45]

In this passage, Lin imagined China to be a racially unified and ethnically coherent country by designating the Han as the leading ethnic/racial group that had successfully assimilated, but not eliminated, the diverse racial and ethnic groups of China. Lin imagined the modern Hanzu to be the core of the historical Huaxia group, with the Sinitic group at its core. At the same time, non-Han groups were considered as enriching and expanding what it means to be Chinese by historians like Lin. This fundamental idea of a unitary and multiethnic Chinese racial-national identity would later have profound influence on how modern China's nationhood was constructed for the most part of the twentieth century.

Yet when it first came into being in the 1930s, the theory of China as an ethnically diverse nation contradicted itself with the earlier narrow understanding of Chinese-ness and ethnic Han centralism (*Dahan zhuyi*) advocated by intellectuals like Zhang Binglin (章炳麟 1869–1936). For political activists like Zhang, it was necessary to draw a boundary between the ethnic Han and other—potentially foreign and threatening—ethnic groups of China, such as the Manchu, the ruling ethnic group of Qing China. The anti-Manchu sentiment was largely fueled by certain ethnic Han intellectuals' wish to restore Han superiority and political power after almost three hundred years of the rule of a non-Sinitic group in China; this sentiment was fermenting much of China's nationalist discourse at the turn of the nineteenth and early twentieth centuries.

The leap from Han-centralism and purism to the acknowledgement of the diversity and hybrid nature of China's ethnic groups was a crucial turning point in modern China's ethnic discourse. This leap further marks Republican intellectuals' turning away from the binary, oppositional imagination of China's ethnic integrity exemplified by the pre-modern racial discourse of the Chinese self pitted against ethnic others, which I discussed in the first section of the chapter. Rather, the new ethnic discourses in the Republican era were imbued with elements of what the contemporary world deems as multinationalism or multiculturalism, with a desire to include and give name to the formerly despised "barbarian" groups of China and consider them as part and parcel of a multicultural China centered around the "Han." In this sense, the idea of "Han" has transcended the idea of a narrow ethnic category according to Zhang Binglin, but has morphed into a "political-geographic category of China:" the term "Han" functioned as a concept that mobilized ethno-national consciousness in early to mid-twentieth-century China, while deriving "political and symbolic power from its deep connection to the Chinese geo-body."[46] For historians like Lin Huixiang, "Han" came to be understood as the core of the historical Huaxia/Sinitic people of China and should be applauded for its cultural and ethnic inclusivity, as other ethnic groups were seen as continuously interacting with and mingling with the Han to give shape to the *Zhonghua minzu*. Together, these multicultural and multiethnic groups were considered as owners and creators of the Chinese nation-state and Chinese civilization in the eyes of Republican-era scholars.

As such, Republican-era intellectuals and historians "[shifted] the focus of investigation from internal constitution and history of separate groups to ethnic boundaries and boundary maintenance."[47] In other words, categories such as "Han" and "Qiang" became fluid sites of ethno-national construction. It was this creative boundary-making and mobilization of ethno-cultural imagination that constituted a new trend of ethnic imagination in early to mid-twentieth-century China.

Zhuang Xueben, one of the first modern scholars setting foot on the land of the Qiang, was part of that ideological transformation to acknowledge the diversity and equality of China's indigenous peoples. If historians like Lin Huixiang and Wang Tongling drew their conclusions from a textual understanding of Chinese and Western racial discourses, ethnologists and anthropologists like Zhuang set the model of modern ethnographic fieldwork by conducting numerous expeditions into the Sichuan's frontier lands. Zhuang's *Qiangrong kaochaji* is full of rich, personal details of his adventurous journeys in a land traditional historiography named as "Qiangrong."

In this book, Zhuang exhibits a keen awareness of distinguishing the traditionally ambiguous alien groups residing in the land of Qiangrong. Particularly, he makes great efforts to separate the Qiang from the Rong (戎). In fact, one of the main purposes of Zhuang's expedition into West Sichuan and part of Qinghai was to understand and document the demographic make-up of this last frontier of China. Zhuang ruminates over the differences between the Qiang and the Rong (Tibetan) populations. Among the many differences, language remained as Zhuang's top consideration in distinguishing between the two. He documents that Qiang people used Sichuanese Mandarin as their spoken language but they possessed no written language; contrarily, Rong people used the Tibetan language as their official language, even though the vast majority of Rong were illiterate.[48]

In his book, Zhuang seems to be much more fascinated with the cultural customs and ethnic traditions of the Qiang than the Rong, even though he stumbles upon ambiguities from time to time and admits about his confusion about the two groups. In a chapter titled "Weizhou, the Place Where Qiang and Rong Co-exist," Zhuang writes that he could not quite tell the Qiang spoken language apart from that of the Rong.[49] Elsewhere, he mocks himself for being unable to identify the people on the street as to which group they belonged, the Qiang or the Rong. He excuses himself by saying, "Without being able to tell the Qiang from the Rong, I had to go with the convention and identify all [of those idling on the streets] as 'barbarians' (*manzi*)."

Like the term "Qiang," the concept of "Rong" in imperial Chinese historiography denoted many fluid and not-clearly-defined groups of people. Rong in classical historical writing referred roughly to the "barbarians" west to China proper who were described in imperial Chinese historiography as people who "spread their hair and clothed animal skins," demonstrating "barbarian" cultural and sartorial customs.[50]

Republican-era scholars like Zhuang not only exhibited deep fascination with the Qiang and the Rong, but also constructed a historical genealogy of the interethnic relationship between these groups and the Han. In Republican-era historians' account of the racial and ethnic make-up of China, such as those composed by Lin Huixiang, Ren Qiu and Wang Tongling, it is widely believed that the Qiang, or Diqiang (氐羌) were one of the ethnic ancestors of the Tibetans, who were referred to as Rong in Republican-era scholarship.[51] In Lin Huixiang's *History of the Races of China*, he states that the Tibetans originated from both the Tibetan lineage (*Zangxi* 藏系) and the Diqiang lineage (*Diqiangxi* 氐羌系).[52] The construction of the interethnic ancestry and consanguinity of the Qiang and the Tibetans reveals Republican-era scholars' larger political goal of imagining a diverse but ultimately unitary and coherent Chinese peoplehood to fend off Western and Japanese encroachments of Chinese territory.

In the above passages, the Chinese term *minzu* (民族) was used to refer to both race and ethnicity. According to Pamela Kyle Crossley, the term *minzu* itself has an intellectual genealogy. Any understanding of the concept of *minzu* should not be taken out of its historical context. In the nineteenth and twentieth centuries, while the term *minzu* was the Chinese equivalent of the Japanese neologism *minzoku*, denoting special meanings of national and ethnic boundaries in the formation of modern nation-states, in classical Chinese corpus, *min* simply meant common people, and *zu* evolved from a signifier of "a small group of people within a locality or a larger organization, and over time acquired the sense of kinship."[53] In other words, the words *min* and *zu* did not have the ethno-nationalist connotation in pre-modern Chinese ideology as they did in modern nationalist movements.

The modern concept of *minzu* or *minzoku* has a strong association with the popularist national revolutionary discourse of East Asia. East Asian nations fought for national independence in the late nineteenth and early twentieth centuries.[54] The modern term *minzu* in China came to incorporate the historically peripheral peoples, or the ethnically non-Han peoples, in the conceptualization of *Zhonghua minzu*, a unitary, multiethnic Chinese people. Under the racial-nationalist framework developed by modern nationalist thinkers like Liang Qichao, the term *minzu* has both a broader meaning referring to a nation and a narrower meaning referring to the nationalities or ethnic groups within a sovereign nation.[55] For modern thinkers like Liang, the Han ethnic group formed the main body of the Chinese race/nation, while various ethnic "others" constituted important parts of this nation.

As a Republican-era scholar, Zhuang was under the influence of *minzu* discourses to conceptualize both the grander *Zhonghua minzu* and the specific ethnic groups within *Zhonghua minzu*. Interestingly, Zhuang's depiction of what he considered to be a social custom of the Rong, where many people drank from the same jar of a barley wine called *zhajiu*, shown on the cover of his book, is widely touted by ethnic Qiang writers and scholars in the twenty-first century to boost their community spirit of sharing good things with others, according to my field research in the Qiang regions of Sichuan province. Therefore, it is evident that the so-called Qiang and the Rong ethnic groups had much cultural overlap, despite Republican-era scholars' desire to set the two groups apart from each other. The very desire of distinguishing between the two and tracing their ethnic and discursive genealogies speaks about modern intellectuals' eagerness to construct a multiethnic Chinese nationhood by creatively deploying historical sources and bounding people within the sovereign nation-state yet designating clear boundaries among them. It also testifies to the fluidity of ethnic boundary-drawing and how the categorization of ethnic groups may reveal more about classifiers' perceptions of the world than objective criteria regarding different groups themselves.

As Foucault contests in *The Order of Things*, "the process of naming will be based, not upon what one sees, but upon elements that have already been introduced into discourse by structure."[56] The eagerness of Republican scholars like Zhuang Xueben to name the Qiang as a unique ethnic group through observing its cultural customs and linguistic traits reflects the epistemological influence of modern Western ethnological and racial discourse on early twentieth-century China's national and ethnic thought. For this reason, naming China's hitherto undistinguished ethnic others, such as the Qiang and the Rong, became "a matter of constructing a secondary language based upon that primary, but certain and universal, language."[57] The Foucauldian notion of "secondary language" pinpoints how naming can naturalize epistemological assumptions and observed facts and turn them into something as powerful as language itself, giving out a sense of "naturalness" in categorizing, ordering and differentiating different communities of people. Indeed, even though the term "Rong" gradually disappeared in modern Chinese ethnic discourse because of its pre-modern "barbarian" cultural baggage, "Qiang" stays intact and has been utilized and "recycled" in both China's national discourses and the contemporary ethnic Qiang people's self-identities, as the rest of the chapter and this book will reveal.

Moreover, naming entails the establishment of structures and characteristics that serves a certain purpose: by selecting a set of characteristics as the defining features of a classified group, naming and structuring human difference "deliberately ignores all differences and all identities not related to the selected structure."[58] As we have seen, in writing his *Qiangrong kaochaji*, Zhuang deliberately attributed certain linguistic and cultural traits to the Qiang and other traits to the Rong. The "Rong" was classified as the Gyalrong Tibetans (嘉絨藏族) unique to Sichuan by Chinese ethnologists in the latter half of the twentieth century, reclaiming a new place in China's national discourses and cultural consciousness.

Republican-era ethnic thought has left an indelible mark on how twenty-first century Qiang and its neighboring rGyalrong Tibetan identities are understood. In a 2007 re-publication of Zhuang Xueben's 1937 *Qiangrong kaochaji*, Alai (阿来 b. 1959), a celebrated and award-winning ethnic Tibetan writer from Sichuan, prefaced the re-publication of the book by praising it as a work that allows him to "journey into [his] homeland."[59] In his preface, Alai sees himself as an "insider" to the exotic and enticing frontier regions Zhuang depicted and elevates the book as a guide to the ethnic and cultural origins of those seeking their roots, especially Gyalrong Tibetans like himself. Alai writes:

> Over forty years ago, I myself was born in the land described as the land of the Rong in [Zhuang's] book. I became one member of the Gyalrong branch of the big Tibetan family . . . Yet for a young boy who grew increasingly curious [about his roots], I lived in a world of silence and chaos where nothing was explained . . . Where do we come from? This is a question . . . about my entire ethnic community and culture, one that demands close scrutiny of the broad geographic landscape and dimmed history. This re-publication of Mr. Zhuang Xueben's book describes [my ethnic origins] with the eyes of the "other." For our present and future writing about ourselves [as ethnic minorities], this book provides a precious model . . . Therefore, I say, I am journeying into my homeland within this book.[60]

In this preface, Alai claims that Zhuang's *Qiangrong kaochaji* provides important clues to the ethnic origins and history of his native Gyalrong Tibetan ethnic community. He praises Zhuang for his detailed descriptions of the ethnic culture and history of the "land of the Rong." Alai also seems to concur with the theory of consanguinity when he acknowledges that his Gyalrong Tibetan group is part of a larger "Tibetan family" within Sichuan and China. It is notable that a Gyalrong Tibetan author, rather than one that is classified as Qiang today, should preface a book and claim it to be a guide to his "homeland," when the book was originally more concerned with depicting the customs of the Qiang and establishing its ethnic difference from the Rong. Alai's words and sentiments once again speak to the idea of consanguinity and interethnic solidarity that was first broached by Republican-era scholars like Lin Huixiang and Zhuang Xueben.

The ambiguities and uncertainties lying between the Qiang and the Rong observed by Zhuang in the 1930s seem to be downplayed and replaced by a visual emphasis on the distinct ethnic imageries of the two groups in this new edition. This 2007 re-publication is much more richly illustrated and filled with many of Zhuang's photographs taken in the same region, albeit in their enlarged formats. The 1937 original publication only included thumbnail photographs taken by Zhuang, and the photographs were usually collective portraits of people in the villages surrounded by the natural landscape of the region. By contrast, the 2007 version includes many detailed and close-up portraits of individual Qiang and Gyalrong girls and young women to accentuate the exotic cultural customs and borderland societies of the Qiang and the Rong.

As we can see from Figure 8, the front and back cover images both feature a frontal portrayal of a Rong girl in her elaborate ethnic attire, and the girl is playing the mouth harp (*kouxian*), a traditional music instrument usually played by young women and girls in the region. With no background and no social context, this photograph creates a sense of timelessness as it proffers up the close-up image of indigenous women for the consumption of the Chinese reading public.[61] This new formatting and re-editing of Zhuang's book projects the image of the land of the Qiang and Rong as a treasure house of exotic beauty and pronounced cultural difference within China. The prominent visual display of borderland society and indigenous women constructs the land of the Qiang and the Tibetans as mysterious, charming, and inviting.

The disconcerting difference between the original version of Zhuang's scholarly-informed and textually-oriented account and the 2007 visually-rich

Figure 8. Book cover of *Qiangrong kaochaji*, 2007 edition

new edition of the book *Qiangrong kaochaji* reveals the different social and ideological agendas of studying about ethnic differences in China then and now. The 1930s witnessed the ideological transformation from imperial historiographers' derogatory portrayals of China's peripheral peoples as racial others to the modern ethno-nationalist construction of these peoples as compatriotic citizens and diverse symbols of the nascent Chinese nation-state. In the 1930s, non-Han groups like the Qiang and the Rong/Tibetans became the subject of modern academic disciplines, such as ethnology and anthropology. It was a time when the social scientific desire of understanding China's demographic make-up was entwined with the political necessity to bring the nation's diverse ethnic groups into unity to defend China against Japanese and Western colonial encroachments. In twenty-first-century China, ethnic minorities tend to be conceived as the aesthetic and ethnographical representations of China's multicultural society, as some later chapters of this book will tackle. As we will see in the rest of the book, the words and images generated by ethnic Han intellectuals like Zhuang Xueben have created lasting social memories on both the ethnic frontier societies and Chinese nationalist thought in general. For now, let us turn to the Reform era (early 1980s to the present), another pivotal moment of constructing multiethnic Chinese identities in modern history.

Constructing Minority Histories in the Debris of History: Communist Multiculturalism and History-Making Projects in Reform-Era China

As China left the Republican era, it was left with that era's invention of the ethnic consanguinity and interethnic ancestry of the different ethnic groups of China. In this section, we enter the final important moment of twentieth-century China's construction of ethnic discourse, the 1980s. Since the late 1970s and early 1980s, China has been undergoing a systematic socio-economic reform. This era is commonly known as the Opening-up and Reform era. The Reform has not only brought forth socio-economic transformations for China, but has also introduced profound changes to how ethnic traditions are written into China's cultural histories in official national narratives. In other words, ethnic cultural symbols, such as the Qiang's musical traditions, have been narrated into the core of not only a minority, but more importantly, a *Chinese* cultural identity, as the beginning of this chapter demonstrates. In this last section of the chapter, I will probe how minority cultural traditions have been established in Reform-era China's official historical narratives to expand the very notion of Chinese-ness beyond the centrality of the Han majority group.

While during the Cultural Revolution (1966–1976), ethnic cultural traditions were relegated as feudal, superstitious and backward *luohou* practices, in the post-Mao era starting in the late 1970s, suppressed memories of the past and minority groups' traditional cultural manifestations were allowed to re-emerge. According to cultural anthropologist Ralph Litzinger, "memory work"—the practice of remembering and forgetting selective parts of the past—has been a "constitutive element in [ethnic minorities'] cultural politics," as minorities are now freer to infuse their ethnic subjectivities with the post-Mao rhetoric of socialist modernization.[62] Notably, given the special role the state plays in China's Reform-era society, minority cultural politics starts not as self-bounded indigenous movements but with the central state: it is the ideological apparatus of reviving "traditional culture" and re-evaluating cultural diversity created by the state that afforded minority peoples the possibility of imagining their identities anew.

In Reform-era China, in both the cultural and administrative realms, the Chinese state has been practicing multiculturalism and espousing ethnic diversity, though the degrees to which multiculturalism is practiced may vary from time to time.[63] After the high socialist period from the late 1950s to the late 1970s, a period in which the study of ethnic diversity was regarded as a "capitalist bourgeois enterprise," post-1980 China has witnessed a revival of an official fascination with China's ethnic cultural diversity and ethnically distinctive "traditional cultures."[64] Many ethnic literature journals have been flourishing in different provinces and regions of China. Minority cultural heritage, such as architecture, foods, traditional dances and medicine, have been inscribed on provincial, national, and international lists of "intangible cultural heritage," a topic that this book returns to in Chapter 6. Different minority groups have been able to reclaim and showcase their traditions, including their "distinctive ways of life," "worlds of sentiment, belief, and feeling ingrained within the [ethnic] subject and deep within the history of the Chinese nation."[65]

Indeed, scholars of Reform-era China seem to concur that a general trend of cultural pluralization and a return to China's indigenous cultural traditions have found their legitimations as China has become an important force in global modernization since the 1980s. Arif Dirlik, in his discussion of how culture and history are interpreted in postrevolutionary China, argues that native cultural traditions are now consecrated as expressions of "alternative modernities" for countries like China, where the nation's rich heritage is no longer seen as a sign of backwardness—as in revolutionary times—but as an indisputable marker of the nation's unique strength.[66] Dirlik remarks that cultural differences are vindicated as nations compete for claims of modernity outside of the Euro-American cultural hegemony.[67] The Euro-American model of modernity, marked by the universal values of Enlightenment liberty and rationality and the superiority of Western culture, is no longer beholden by "Third World" countries as the one and only valid manifestation of progress and modernity. Even though these countries are still searching for modernity, they have been pondering how Western ideals can be married to native values and produce a unique experience of national modernity.

Similarly, Jason McGrath, in his assessment of Chinese modernity in the post-socialist market era, identifies four basic characteristics of Chinese society during this period of reform: *shichanghua* (marketization), *duoyuanhua* (pluralization), *gerenhua* (individualization), and *fenhua* (division, differentiation).[68] McGrath notes that a significant social transformation took place in post-socialist China, namely the structural transformation of Chinese society from a unified social system in which "the political, the economic and the cultural are all intimately intertwined" to a market society in which "the economic differentiates itself and in turn drives diversification and pluralization of many other aspects of society and culture."[69] The rapidly growing Chinese market economy and increasingly diversifying Chinese social structure, together with the relative autonomy of cultural and consumerist sectors, now afford individuals and communities with a myriad of personal and collective choices, which in turn lead to abundant opportunities for them to assert their identities.

The 1980s, the dawning era of China's neoliberal reform, was also characterized by a renewed ethnic discourse and ideology that emphasized the "plurality in unity" (*duoyuan yiti geju*) theory advanced by China's prominent ethnologist and sociologist Fei Xiaotong (费孝通 1910–2005). Fei theorized about the ethnic conglomeration that happened throughout Chinese history, maintaining that the Han was the core ethnic group that assimilated and combined many diverse ethnicities to form a diverse but united *Zhonghua minzu*, or Chinese people.[70] With the open-door policies of its economy, Reform-era China also set out to define the strength of the nation as lying in the plurality of its own ethnic groups. In national narratives, such plurality was seen as rooted in the crucial role played by the Han and a historically continuous process of ethnic assimilation and acculturation (*minzu ronghe* 民族融合) toward becoming one multiethnic national entity.[71] Apparently, Fei's theories bear remarkable similarities to the Republican-era ethnic discourses that the earlier section of this chapter introduced.

It is within this context that the Qiang, as well as many other ethnic minorities, have been portrayed as the guardians of China's national culture and indispensable to the national integrity of China as we saw with the incidence of the Wenchuan earthquake at the beginning of this chapter. The construction of contemporary Qiang identity arguably began with the publication of the *Series of Concise Histories of Chinese Ethnic Minorities* (*Zhongguo shaoshu minzu jianshi congshu* 中国少数民族简史丛书) in the mid-1980s. The *Series* was part of a state-commissioned project that set out to offer a comprehensive account of the cultural and socio-economic histories of China's fifty-five officially recognized ethnic minorities. Even though the research of the series had begun in the 1950s, according to its authors, this book series was interrupted by the Cultural Revolution until the central government resumed its National Ethnic Affairs Committee (*Guojia minzu shiwu weiyuanhui* 国家民族事务委员会) in 1978. The freer ideological climate for respecting ethnic diversity in the late 1970s and 1980s allowed the editors and authors of the Series to officially publish the *Series*, constructing the diverse historical narratives of China's different *shaoshu minzu* (ethnic minorities).[72]

In the preface to this series, the authors stated: "In order to invoke a sense of pride for their own ethnic histories, to promote a spirit of patriotism and to strengthen China's ethnic solidarity, and to march into socialist modernization together, we have decided to publish the *Series*."[73] From this, we can see that the *Series* has the political purpose of constructing a diverse but unitary national community in which every ethnic group feels like an integral part of China. Notably, beyond touting the political ideology of China as a "multiethnic and united nation" (*tongyi duominzu guojia*), the goal of "marching into socialist modernization together" was cited by the authors as a major intention for publishing the series.[74] This shows that the anxiety to develop China economically and usher in growth for its minorities was lying at the core of an otherwise largely ideologically inspired compilation of ethnic histories.

In the *Concise History of Qiangzu* (*Qiangzu jianshi* 羌族简史), a collective history-making effort spearheaded by scholars of the Han, Qiang, and other ethnic origins (such as Tujia), the Marxist ideology of historical progress prevails in the first half of the book. The Qiang were portrayed as a brave and rebellious people that had historically resisted the feudal oppression of imperial China, the tyranny of the Kuomintang (KMT), and the invasion of foreign missionaries such as the Americans.[75] The *Concise History* depicts the Qiang as having an eventual "rebirth" (*xinsheng* 新生) under Communist governance, and it asserts: since the founding of the People's Republic in 1949, "the Qiang have deeply felt the warmth of our socialist country and have developed a growing bond with the Communists and the People's government, paving their way to the upcoming social reform and ethnic regional autonomy."[76]

Evidently, the first half of the *Concise History of Qiangzu* is tainted with a class ideology central to the Communist-Marxist political discourse: ethnic minorities such as the Qiang were depicted as part of the "people" who, under the progressive political guidance of the Communists, had the potential of overthrowing China's older regimes and establish a liberating people's government together. The fact that the research and writing of the *Series* started in the high socialist period of the 1950s under Mao Zedong's rule explains this class-oriented Marxist undertone.

Indeed, as a core thinker of Communist nationalism, Mao "defined nation as anti-imperial, and democracy as both anti-feudal and 'in the interest of the broad masses of people.'"[77] Ethnic minorities, who were often marginalized or subjected to the imperial government's assimilationist policies, figured prominently into the Communist conceptualization of the Chinese people (*renmin* 人民). Furthermore, the term *minzu* was a central term that Mao used to represent the Chinese nation. *Minzu* in Mao's terminology denoted both the narrow sense of an ethnic group and the broader sense of a people sharing the same destiny, such as in the compound word *Zhonghua minzu*. The concept of *minzu* was a major component in Mao's formulation of the *renmin*.[78] For the authors of the *Concise History*, the Qiang, along with other ethnic minorities represented in the *Series*, belonged to the anti-imperial, anti-feudal class of people: in the Communist historical narratives, it was minority people's continuous political struggles against China's reactionary regimes and foreign encroachments that helped shape their historical identity as a rebellious and progressive people.

If the first half of the *Concise History of Qiangzu* carries the conventional political mentality of Mao's China and its theory of a revolutionary regime aimed at liberating the *renmin*, then the last part of the book, "The Customs, Religion, Literature, Art and Technology of the Qiang," is surprisingly scant with political judgments. It is this last portion that establishes the Qiang as the guardians of China's ancient traditions and elevates Qiang's ethnic culture as an integral part of China's national culture. It is also history writings like the *Concise History* that marked a watershed in Reform-era China's ethnic discourse: from the political portrayals of ethnic minorities as part of the revolutionary classes, China's state historians were gradually shifting toward depicting minority groups as the guardians of unique cultural assets shared by *all peoples* of China.

The authors of the *Concise History of Qiangzu*, from the outset, portray the Qiang as an integral part of Chinese civilization, possessing long and proud ancient traditions. In the Introduction of the book, the authors claim: "Qiang is one of China's oldest ethnic groups, widely distributed [all over China] throughout history."[79] Echoing the Republican-era discourse of ethnic consanguinity, the authors continue the tradition of constructing the myth of the interethnic ancestry of the Qiang, the Han, and other ethnic groups. They state:

> Since the Tang and Song dynasties, the cultural integration between Qiang and Han—and other ethnic groups—has never ceased . . . The Qiang have not only absorbed the great elements of other cultures, but also have maintained their own traditional culture (*chuantong wenhua*), presenting an ethnic make-up [of China] that is harmonious yet different (*he'er butong*), united but diverse (*duoyuan yiti*).[80]

The above passage falls under the important historical and intellectual genealogy of constructing the Qiang in China's textual traditions. While the assertion of the Qiang as one of China's oldest ethnic groups may ironically stem from the long textual history of defining the Qiang "barbarian" that we saw in the first section of the chapter, the depiction of the Qiang as a vital part of China's interethnic origin is reminiscent of the Republican-era scholarship on the shared ancestry of China's ethnic groups. As such, textual traditions and national discourses are recycled, re-invented, and made to bear on new political and cultural significance in the Reform-era under the banner of Communist multiculturalism.

In the last section of the *Concise History of Qiangzu*, the authors detail the "traditional culture" that they assign to the Qiang. The Qiang's traditional culture is divided into several categories: matrimonial and familial customs; religious customs; Qiang shamanistic traditions and the rituals of spiritual healing; lastly, folk literature, folk songs, folk dance, and most importantly, the famous Qiang reed pipe, *Qiang di* (羌笛).[81]

Qiang di, the Qiang reed pipe, is perhaps the most powerful cultural symbol deployed by authors of the *Concise History* to legitimatize the historical place of a people that were otherwise deemed as "barbarians" in earlier Confucian historiographical and poetic traditions. In the section titled "Ethnic Musical Instruments" (*minzu yueqi*), the authors devote several pages to *Qiang di* as an important component of *Chinese civilization*. The authors of *Concise History of Qiangzu* construct a historical lineage of *Qiang di* by invoking the presence of this musical instrument in Chinese poetic traditions:

> Among the folk instruments of Qiangzu, the most distinguished and most famous may be *Qiang di*. It is said that *Qiang di* was invented by the ancient Qiang people who were herders of the Northwest Plateau. *Qiang di* was not only widely circulated on the ancient land of *Zhonghua minzu*, becoming the celebrated musical instrument depicted by Han, Tang, Song, and Ming dynasties' literati, but it is still a beloved instrument among the Qiang people distributed along the Min River and Pu River [tributaries of the Yangtze River] today, after more than a thousand years' time.[82]

In the above passage, the authors imagine a historical continuity and cultural endurance of *Qiang di* by citing its presence in China through different dynasties. Importantly, the authors regard *Qiang di* not simply as a musical instrument that belongs to the Qiang, but as a token of the musical history of the whole of China, as they asserted that the Qiang flute was "widely circulated on the ancient land of *Zhonghua minzu*," or the Chinese people.

Two pages later, the authors go to great lengths to break down the appearances of *Qiang di* in classical Chinese poetry. They cite the works by such canonical Chinese poets as Li Bai (701–762), Wang Zhihuan (688–742) and Gao Shi (ca. 704–765) during the High Tang period to assert the cultural relevance of *Qiang di* to the musical and poetical traditions of ancient Chinese civilization:

> Many of the musical scores of ancient *Qiang di*—despite their historical prominence—have not made their way to the present day. Wang Zhihuan's verse 'What use of the *Qiang di* to play resentfully of the *Yangliu* melody? Spring breeze will barely cross the Yumen Barrier.' (羌笛何須怨楊柳，春風不度玉門關) and Li Bai's poem of 'Hearing the *Zheliu* melody [of sorrow and departure] tonight, who would not be evoked of yearnings for the homeland?' (此夜曲中聞折柳，何人不起故園情) are all references to the *Zheyangliu* (折楊柳) ancient melody of *Qiang di* [that sang of the pains of departure] . . . Unfortunately, we have not had the luck of hearing these ancient *Qiang di* pieces anymore today.[83]

Lamenting that the ancient melodies of *Qiang di* are a dying art today, the authors go on to cite an entire poem by the renowned Tang dynasty frontier poet Gao Shi titled "Listening to the Flute on the Frontiers" (塞上聞笛):

Clouds are clear on the nomads' sky and the herded horses have returned.	雲淨胡天牧馬歸
The bright moon and Qiang flute[84] accompany the garrison buildings.	明月羌笛戍樓間
I venture to ask where the plum blossoms have fallen.	借問梅花何處落
After one night's blowing of wind they have covered Mountain Wu.[85]	風吹一夜滿吳山

The authors of the *Concise History*, by citing well-known verses of Chinese poetry during the Tang dynasty, construct the myth that the modern Qiangzu—as descendants of the ancient Qiang—have been important contributors to China's poetic and musical traditions. They do so by showing evidence of how *Qiang di* was repetitively invoked by classical Chinese poets to refer to the great musical tradition of the Qiang as a people.

Even though the textual evidence deployed by the *Concise History* seems highly compelling at arguing for the historical continuity of the cultural traditions of the Qiang, a closer examination of how such key terms as "Qiang" and *Qiang di* were used in their actual historical contexts will reveal a serious cultural anachronism. For one, the authors of the *Concise History* confuse the ancient historiographical and literary use of "Qiang" with the modern construction of Qiangzu, betraying their eagerness to establish historical continuity and invent traditions for the Qiang.

According to Ming-ke Wang, and evidenced by the numerous poetic and historiographical accounts of the Qiang shown in earlier sections of this chapter, the idea of "Qiang" in pre-modern China did not denote a fixed and well-defined ethnic group. Rather, it signified the Chinese way of referring to a *generic* alien "other" or "others" west to the Chinese cultural sphere.[86] The earliest mention of the term "Qiang" in the Chinese language appeared in Shang dynasty oracle scripts around the thirteenth century B.C.E, and the Chinese in the Shang used it to name the peoples west to themselves, seeing these peoples as less human and less cultured.[87] Tracing the records of the Qiang in classical Chinese historiography, Wang further contends that the term "Qiang," rather than evoking the history of a continuous and coherent people known as the modern Qiangzu, revealed the Chinese desire to demarcate between the self and the other as the territory of the ancient Chinese empire expanded. Wang notes:

> As the ethnic entity of the Chinese was forming, the *Qiang* came to denote a shifting ethnic boundary. While Chinese territory expanded westward [to the Qinghai-Tibet Plateau], continually assimilating western populations, this ethnic boundary also shifted farther westward . . . Thus, the *Qiang* was not necessarily a 'people' that had continuity in time and space; instead, it was an ethnic boundary of the Chinese in constant flux.[88]

Wang remarks that during the Warring States period, Chinese historians used the term Di-Qiang (氐羌) for a foreign people "living in the far west" of China proper; during the Tang dynasty, the implications of the term "Qiang" became further complicated.[89] The concept of the "Qiang" in Tang dynasty historiographical writing referred to the inhabitants residing in the "belt zone" on the eastern fringe of the expanding Tibetan Kingdom, or Tubo (吐蕃).[90] Rather than denoting a small group of people known today as the Qiangzu, the Qiang in Tang dynasty referred mainly to the many "tributes and confederacies" who were glossed with the term "Qiang" in historical records such as the *Old Book of Tang* (*jiu tangshu* 舊唐書) and *New Book of Tang* (*xin tangshu* 新唐書).[91] Therefore, instead of being a closed ethnic entity with a set of well-defined cultural traits, the "Qiang" in Tang China and beyond denoted the shifting boundaries between different human groups, highlighting the construction of the Chinese cultural "self" vis-à-vis non-Sinitic groups embedded in the signification of "Qiang."

The fact that "Qiang" in pre-modern Chinese historical writing carried a connotation different from the "Qiang" in modern China can be further corroborated by careful contextual readings of Tang dynasty poets such as Gao Shi, who are heavily cited by authors of the *Concise History*.

Gao Shi (高適 704–765), a poet of the High Tang period who took on a military post on the northeastern frontier in the year 737, wrote prolifically of his experience of being in the Chinese army in the ethnic borderland.[92] By examining a few verses composed by Tang poets such as Gao Shi and Wang Zhihuan, we will see that these poets were more concerned with pacifying the ethnic frontiers and expressing the bitterness of life in the borderlands than lauding the musical tradition of their belligerent Qiang neighbors.

In Gao Shi's famous "Song of Yen" (燕歌行), he wrote:

Now gloom settles on mountains and rivers all through this borderland;	山川蕭條機邊土
Nomad horsemen press our ranks hard, Blending with wind and rain . . .	胡騎憑陵雜風雨
Haven't you seen on those tracts of sand The pain of marching and battle?[93]	君不見沙場征戰苦

In this poem, the bitterness of the army's military life on the northeastern frontier as the army combatted against the Khitan, or Huren (胡人), was revealed to its bare bones. Gao expressed the hardship of a military life against the nomads, as they "press our ranks hard." Gao also expressed his concern over the recurrent invasions of the northern nomads, or *hulu*, as he sighs:

So somber and grim, these border ramparts	邊城何蕭條
Where the bright sun darkened in clouds of brown.	白日黃雲昏
Each time I come to some site of battle,	一到征戰處
I grieve that the nomads may return."[94]	每愁胡虜翻

As a military official, Gao Shi was worried about pacifying the frontiers and stopping the nomads' invasions, and his poems refused to romanticize the borderland life precisely because of his personal experience of having lived in the harsh environment for several years. This is why he expressed his grief as he worried that "the nomads may return," as the Chinese army languished at the "site of battle."

In another poem, "The North Tower of Golden Fort" (金城北樓), Gao echoes Wang Zhihuan's evocation of the sorrowful melodies of *Qiang di*:

Should you ask me of these borderlands, what else there is out here—	為問邊事更何事
Ever and now the nomad flutes Sing bitterness without end.[95]	至今羌笛怨無窮

The line that the "nomad flutes sing bitterness without end" is an unequivocal depiction of the bitter life in the military camps in the borderland embodied in the melodies of *Qiang di*. The *Qiang di* was a "barbarian" musical instrument appropriated by Chinese soldiers as a cultural entertainment but also a reminder of the borderland anxieties lamented by poets like Gao Shi: the Qiang nomads were fiercely invading China proper, particularly China's northwestern border regions, causing China's perpetual anxiety over lost territories and lost lives in the harsh and barren borderland regions. These northwestern borderland regions roughly overlap with today's Qinghai and Gansu provinces of China.

Qiang di as a cultural symbol of the political, military, and interethnic conflicts in China's Northwestern borderland regions was a recurrent image in Tang dynasty poems, such as the ones we saw above by Gao Shi. Notably, in the poem above, Stephen Owen's translation of *Qiang di* is not "Qiang people's flute," but simply "nomad flutes." Owen employs the same translation for Wang Zhihuan's "Lyrics of Liangzhou" (涼州詞), which is also cited in *The Concise History of Qiangzu*:

Yellow sands rise far away on high among white clouds	黃沙遠上白雲間
Silhouette of a lonely fortress on a thousand-foot mountain.	一片孤城萬仞山
Why should this nomad flute be playing wrath at the "leaves" of willow,	羌笛何須怨楊柳
Since the wind of spring will never cross Jade Gate Barrier?[96]	春風不度玉門關

The Tang poets—and the translator—summon *Qiang di* plainly as an instrument of the "nomads" that were interchangeably known as Qiang or *hulu*. This flute was often played in the military camps, singing the sorrows of military life and the vast, deserted frontier lands. The Jade Gate Barrier, located in present-day Gansu province, separated China proper from the northwestern borderlands—thus the "lonely fortress" in Wang's poem. In both Gao Shi's "The North Tower of Golden Fort" and Wang Zhihuan's "Lyrics of Liangzhou," the poets use the word *yuan* (怨, bitterness or resentment) to express the negative emotions trigged by the nomad flute, or Qiang flute: the Qiang nomads posed perpetual military threats to China proper, and the playing of their flute accentuated the sense of anxiety and fear that Tang poets felt about

Figure 9. The Jade Gate Pass (Yumenguan) as a tourist spot in Gansu Province. Photograph by author.

China's borderlands, which were perpetually under the threat of the Qiang nomads (Figure 9).

The Tang poets did not sing praise of the "great tradition" of *Qiang di* as our contemporary commentators do, and this was most likely because the military and political threats of the nomads overshadowed the great musicality of the instrument. Whenever the *Qiang di* was invoked, it was almost exclusively accompanied by sentiments of the lamentations, sadness, and loneliness of frontier military life. Therefore, the *Qiang di* depicted in Tang dynasty "frontier poems" is more of a cultural symbol of China's perpetual anxiety over its territorial sovereignty, as well as a signifier of the bitter frontier military life, rather than an embellishment of an ethnic musical tradition.

Yet, in the eyes of the state historians who authored the *Concise History of Qiangzu*, the *Qiang di* bespeaks the diverse and long-standing traditions of China's music and poetic history. The *Qiang di* is interpreted by contemporary China's state historians as a testament to the enduring interethnic relations in China and a sign of the cultural exchanges that took place between different ethnic communities in pre-modern China. In this sense, twentieth-century historians glossed over the interethnic conflicts and warfare between China proper and its nomadic Qiang others by creatively re-interpreting Tang-dynasty poems to connote the great "shared" history of the various ethnic groups in China, inventing a shared ancestral memory in order to construe a coherent and unitary *Zhonghua minzu* for the book's modern audience.

It becomes obvious that the contemporary authors of the *Concise History of Qiangzu* are engaging in a discursive practice of "cultural nationalism"[97] when they creatively re-interpret pre-modern poetic images to construct ideas of the great cultural traditions of China. The authors of *The Concise History of Qiangzu* "create, support and foster national (or supraregional) integration by means of marshaling forth cultural and historical symbols,"[98] such as *Qiang di*. In the imagination of contemporary state historians, this ancient symbol of military conflicts and border anxiety became a laudable part of Chinese civilization under the banner of multiethnic unity.

At this point, we may ask: What propelled China's state historians to construct multiethnic cultural symbols by going to great lengths to discover and re-create narratives of China's cultural history? To answer this question, we need to understand how ethnic cultures are invented in post-1949 China under the Communist multiethnic national policies.

Somewhat like their predecessors who engaged in systematic studies and classifications of China's vast ethnic minorities in the first half of the twentieth century, Communist intellectuals in the 1980s shouldered the task of constructing a *cultural* national community by offering a place for the historically alienated "others" in the political and discursive terrains of China.

In the 1950s, the newly established People's Republic desired to make sense of the diverse peoples under its governance and to effect democracy to all members of its multinational state by engaging in a systematic Ethnic Classification Project (*minzu shibie* 民族识别), as suggested by Thomas S. Mullaney's study.[99] Under such imperative, the Ethnic Classification Project set out to document and classify *all of* China's minority nationalities.

Chinese Communist Party's (CCP) effort to recognize the ethnic diversity of China and grant different nationalities equal political rights demonstrated the regime's unique ways of imagining and constructing the Chinese national community. As Mullaney observes, the CCP's classification enterprise distinguished itself from the Nationalist Party's advocacy for a mono-*minzu* China and the former Qing empire's "indirect rule" when it came to the governance of China's vast and regionally different ethnic groups.[100] For Communist intellectuals of both the 1950s Classification project and the 1980s *Concise History* project, great ethnic traditions (*minzu chuantong* 民族传统) were invented, evoked, and consecrated. While the 1950s Classification project emphasized the recognition of the *groups and communities* of what would later be enshrined as China's fifty-five ethnic minorities, the history-making projects in the 1980s aimed at legitimizing the *cultural identities* of these already-categorized groups.

As a result of Reform-era China's efforts of establishing the cultural pasts of its minority groups, traditions are being invented and textualized. This is best illustrated through how the ancient image of *Qiang di* as an instrument of frontier bitterness and territorial anxiety was redefined as a manifestation of China's multiethnic musical and poetic tradition in the 1980s.

As Eric Hobsbawm points out, when a tradition is invented in a modern society, it usually serves three purposes: (1) to establish and symbolize "social cohesion or the membership of [both real and artificial] groups;" (2) to establish and legitimize institutions, status, and relationships to authorities; and (3) to foster socialization and beliefs, as well as to inculcate acceptable values and behaviors.[101] If the 1950s Ethnic Classification Project aimed at establishing social cohesion and membership for China's otherwise vast and ambiguous ethnic communities, then the 1980s *Concise Histories* project had the effect of inculcating beliefs and constructing values to be instilled on these post-classified groups. The 1980s history-making projects, particularly the *Concise Histories of Shaoshu Minzu* series, succeeded in constructing the cultural identities of the former "barbarian" groups of China by creatively reinterpreting canonical historical and literary images in China's long textual traditions, such as Tang-dynasty poetry.

As we will see in the rest of the book, ethnic minorities such as the Qiangzu have imparted this state-invented cultural history to imagine who they are. A lot of members of the Qiangzu that I have interviewed proudly invoke the Qiang's long duration in Chinese cultural history by alluding to the historical and literary sources that inspired the *Concise History of Qiangzu*. Therefore, the *Concise History of Shaoshu Minzu* series are vital history-making projects in modern China that have inculcated a sense of ethnic pride and cultural integrity for China's diverse and historically denigrated non-Han groups. This important *Series* reverses the image of the non-Han as uncultured others in pre-modern Chinese textual traditions. The *Series* establishes non-Han groups as indispensable contributors to China's historical integrity and cultural richness.

Around the same time when *The Concise History of Qiangzu* was published, a similar book, *The History of Qiangzu* (*Qiangzu shi* 羌族史), was authored by three of Sichuan's own Qiang-studies scholars. In *The History of Qiangzu*, the evocation of the *Qiang di* as a prestigious instrument of the Qiang people is also evident.[102] In addition to lauding the poetic nature and popularity of the *Qiang di* among the Qiang themselves, the authors also spoke highly of the Qiang's creative genius and artistic finesse, such as their folk dances and spiritual and ritual practices. Authors of *The History of Qiangzu* used such terms as "elegant folk literature," "unpretentious folk songs," and "colorful dances and musical instruments" to categorize Qiang cultural heritage.[103] Evidently, local historians in Sichuan have been influenced by the national narratives of the long and enduring history of the Qiang in China constructed in *The Concise History of Qiangzu*.

Therefore, ethnic traditions were invented in the 1980s at a time when China was eagerly transforming its historical identity and proactively redefining its ethnic diversity. The 1980s rhetoric of establishing ethnic minorities as guardians of China's traditional culture has exerted a powerful influence on the subsequent re-conceptualization of ethnic history and China's cultural past in the 1990s and beyond.

Reflections: The Qiang as People, Myth, and Cultural Symbol-The Contemporary Reincarnation of the Textual Construction of "Qiang" in Qiang Villages

More than ten years have passed since Weng Jiabao's speech at the 2008 Wenchuan earthquake, which marked the beginning of a new wave of institutionalizing Qiang cultural heritage in the twenty-first century. In May of 2018, Xinhua Net, one of the major national official news outlets in China, featured a story of how Qiang people are proudly reviving and passing down various Qiang traditions after a decade of rebuilding the Qiang homeland. The reporter of this news story observes that, from Qiang embroidery, Qiang theater, to Qiang medicine, a diverse range of Qiang cultural heritage manifestations are blossoming in schools and in the Qiang communities in Sichuan.[104] Most notably, this story highlights how a local Qiang math teacher teaches students the skills of playing the *Qiang di*, as the teacher remarks: "Today we are learning to play 'The Song of Harvest' (*fengshou ge*). This is a joyous song. Do not use drawn-out notes; [use short notes to] try to convey the conviviality of this song."[105]

If Tang-dynasty poets like Wang Zhihuan and Gao Shi lamented the high-pitched quality of the *Qiang di* as an embodiment of border anxieties and military conflicts, contemporary Qiang people are reinventing this tradition yet again by creatively adding their own understandings, skills, and emotions to this old instrument. No longer blamed as a symbol of interethnic warfare in the Tang dynasty and less frequently mystified as a token of the shared ancestral memory of *Zhonghua minzu*, the *Qiang di* of today has become a creative instrument of the Qiang people to deploy their imagination and express their own sentiments for their daily lives.

This contemporary cultural re-making of *Qiang di* by the Qiangzu people themselves is confirmed by my ethnographic research in Taoping Qiang Village in the Aba Tibetan and Qiang Autonomous Prefecture in Sichuan. In the summer of 2019, as I strolled through the "tourist new village" that was built to accommodate tourists in order to preserve the historical Taoping Village, I encountered a souvenir stand managed by a Qiang man. As Figure 10 shows, this Qiang man was making, selling, and showcasing *Qiang di* for visitors. In addition to *Qiang di*, he also made and sold *kouxian*, the mouth harp that we saw in Zhuang Xuben's book in an earlier section of this chapter. Interestingly, the *Qiang di* that he displayed was thoughtfully ornamented with a colorful *Zhongguo jie*, a knot-tie decoration that had been popular among ordinary Chinese people and appeared in many national and international events, such as the Beijing Olympic Games in 2008, as a popular symbol of Chinese culture. Behind the man, a larger-than-life replica of the double-eared jar was installed as another tourist attraction. The double-eared jar has been unearthed in many Qiang regions of China and touted as an archeological testimony to the ancient relics and continuity of the Qiang culture in many local and national scholarly publications.

This scene is a creative manifestation of the multifaceted construction of *Qiang di* as simultaneously a sign of the interethnic ancestry for *Zhonghua minzu*, an ethnic instrument that belongs to the textually mythologized ancient Qiang people, and a profitable vehicle for tourist income. This scene is a transhistorical juxtaposition of the textual and material imagination of the "Qiang" as a people, a myth, and more importantly, *a system of cultural symbolism* in China's long and convoluted history of dealing with its borderland societies and peoples.

Figure 10. Qiang flute maker in Taoping Qiang Village. Photograph by author.

In this chapter, we have journeyed through a long history of imagining and constructing the "Qiang" in China's textual traditions and national narratives. We have witnessed how race, ethnicity, and culture are intertwined in Chinese history as the concept of the "Qiang" has transformed from a pre-modern signifier of otherness to a modern token of national pride. The "Qiang," as one of the longest-standing ethno-racial categories in China, has been perpetually constituted and re-constituted as shifting political and cultural factors demand the re-conceptualization of what it means to be Chinese. As such, race and ethnicity are not fixed categories but denote the changing relationships between different groups of people at different historical periods. From pre-modern historiographers and poets to modern ethnographers and state-historians, the writing elites of China have created the "Qiang" vis-à-vis the broader interethnic social landscapes in China. In turn, those classified as the modern Qiangzu in Reform-era China have spoken back to this long and rich tradition of constructing the "Qiang" in Chinese cultural memory. In this sense, the construction of "Qiang" is vital for understanding not only a small ethnic minority group, but also the very motivations and changing definitions of "Chinese-ness."

In the rest of this book, we will explore the dynamic exchanges and mutual influences between local scholarly communities, minority intellectuals and villagers, as well as national and transnational factors. These factors converge to continually re-fashion the conceptual contours of the "Qiang," particularly as China is in the thicket of its economic reform and social transformation, finding itself at the crossroads of multiple competing forces of "globalization."

CHAPTER 2

"King Yu Rose from the West Qiang"

Minority Scholarly Production and the Cultural Politics of Imaginary Ancestry in the Qiang Regions of China

In the middle of the labyrinth of Taoping Qiang Village, a Qiang village in the Li County (理县) of Sichuan Province nestled in the eastern Himalayas, long before tourists started gracing this now-crowded area, a local Qiang villager, Mr. Wang, began running a private museum in his own backyard. For over two decades, Mr. Wang, who calls himself a "peasant" (*nongmin* 农民) because of his agricultural work, has been collecting artifacts unearthed in the Qiang regions of Sichuan and showcasing his collections with a guided tour for curious tourists—mostly free of charge. Mr. Wang named his museum Taoping Qiang Ethnic Culture Museum. A quick stroll into this museum, and your eyes will meet with a rich variety of objects and instruments that Mr. Wang has meticulously collected and thoughtfully cared for, all on his own funding. From two-eared pottery jars to the monkey-skin hats worn by Qiang shamans; from metal agricultural instruments and fur coats to the careful arrangement of the fireplace (*huotang* 火塘), a centerpiece of the traditional Qiang household, Mr. Wang curates a comprehensive range of artifacts and objects related to Qiang culture (Figure 11).

Amid the two-thousand objects and artifacts in Mr. Wang's museum is a wall with a calligraphic letter, silently summoning the visitor:

> We are a group of retirees from Chengdu [the capital city of Sichuan province] and are deeply moved by Mr. Wang's consistent efforts to protect and spread Qiang culture with his individual power . . . We call for everyone to help out and turn this one man's project into a collective project through which people from all ethnic backgrounds develop and expand this Qiang culture museum. This would contribute to the preservation of the precious historical heritage of *Zhonghua minzu* (Chinese nation or Chinese people).

Figure 11. Mr. Wang in front of his Qiang culture museum in Taoping Qiang Village. Photograph by author.

Perhaps a subtle letter calling for donations, this walled text, hand-written on red rice paper, is symbolic of the marginalized conditions of Mr. Wang's grassroot cultural project. Despite the letter writers' urging that Mr. Wang's museum contributes to the preservation of Chinese culture as a whole, Mr. Wang's museum receives little to no official support. There is no state funding and resources supporting Mr. Wang's museum. During my many field trips to Taoping and the many conversations I had with Mr. Wang in his museum, hardly anyone else came in for a tour. Even though the museum had its heydays, culminating in Mr. Wang's moderate media coverage and the small awards he had garnered, in the current era of ethnic tourism, Mr. Wang's museum, like himself, is like a quiet giant standing at the far eastern corner of Taoping.

As a self-trained expert of Qiang culture, Mr. Wang and his museum project are exemplary of the grassroots cultural activism in twenty-first-century China, particularly the constraints and creativities of minority cultural productions in the political economy of tourism and regional development in China. Even though different minority groups have different experiences with China's state discourses and national policies, all minority groups are grappling with the question of how to carve out spaces of political, cultural, and ethnic belonging within the parameters of multiculturalism in China.

In Chapter 1, I looked at how the "Qiang" was constructed as a system of cultural symbolism in China's textual traditions, simultaneously embodying the ideas of a group of people, a myth of the interethnic ancestry of China, and a signifier of the expanding notions of Chinese-ness in twentieth-century national narratives and official political discourses. In this chapter, I will turn to how local activists and intellectuals in Sichuan respond to this national trend of mythologizing the Qiang in scholarly and cultural productions. If the "Qiang" was constructed as the "constitutive other" of China's national identity in the twentieth century, in the twenty-first century, local intellectuals and minority scholars are actively engaged in an enterprise of creating minority-centered narratives of Chinese culture, particularly by foregrounding the importance of non-Han peoples in the origin and development of China's cultural past.

In this chapter, we will journey into the fascinating world of minority scholarly productions in Sichuan province, the province in China with the largest number of the ethnic group categorized as the Qiangzu today. Particularly, I will investigate the entanglements between regional development, the cultural industry of "ancestral tourism," and the ethnopolitical desire for minority groups like the Qiang to engender social and political spaces of creative belonging in the backdrop of twenty-first-century China's rapid social transformations. I argue that minority scholars and local intellectuals are invested in a process of "discursive self-fashioning" as they construct the Qiang identity by deploying various national, historical, and contemporary discourses and cultural rhetorics foundational to China's national imagination. I will reveal the representational tactics and cultural tropes employed by ethnic Qiang intellectuals and local scholars of Sichuan as they engage in creative projects to foster the mythologization of the Qiang as an important ancestor to China's civilizational prosperity and interethnic consanguinity. Even though, as Chapter 1 reveals, the mythologization of the Qiang started in early twentieth-century national discourses, in the twenty-first century, ethnic Qiangzu scholars and local intellectuals in Sichuan have claimed the creative agency of crafting the historical narratives about the Qiang by challenging the entrenched hierarchy between the "civilized" Han and the "barbarian minorities" that was prevalent in Confucian ideology and classical Chinese textual traditions.

Particularly, I examine how ethnic Qiang intellectuals and local scholars in Sichuan reinterpret the images of China's legendary sage king Da Yu (大禹 or King Yu the Great) and mythic founder Yandi (炎帝 the Fire Emperor or Emperor Yan) to reinvent the idea of *Zhonghua minzu*, placing the Qiang at the center of Chinese national imagination. I will also study a unique genre of contemporary minority writing, or what I term "tourism literature." Tourism literature is semi-literary, semi-promotional writings composed by local authors who paint vivid pictures of the Qiang regions of Sichuan as a pristine, mythic source of Chinese culture awaiting the discovery of the outside world. In combining historical speculations, local legends and a textual excursion into pre-modern Chinese cultural myths, tourism literature contributes to the "ethnicization" of Da Yu and Yandi as ethnic Qiang heroes. This creative process of remaking the national legendary figures of China allows minority groups like the Qiang to create their cultural identities in the context of regional development in neoliberal China, unsettling the historically established hierarchy between the Confucian Chinese cultural "center" and its "peripheries."

In this chapter and beyond, I develop the concept of "discursive self-fashioning" to urge students and scholars of China to understand China's *shaoshu minzu* not simply as happy singing and dancing groups with an exotic flavor—as *shaoshu minzu* are often portrayed in China's popular media and TV programs—but as active producers of serious scholarly and cultural discourses. Importantly, as the rest of this chapter will bear out, minority scholarly discourses usually question the "canonical" or Han-centered narratives of Chinese culture and history in China's well-known texts and legends, challenging the discursive power wielded by the cultural and political dominance of the Han/Huaxia/Sinitic ethnic group.

This chapter presents local cultural and scholarly productions generated by scholars and writers of both Qiang and Han ethnic origins in Sichuan, including an important local journal, *Xiqiang wenhua* (*The Culture of West Qiang* 西羌文化), published by the Sichuan Provincial Qiang Studies Association (*Sichuansheng Qiangxue xuehui* 四川省羌学学会) and the Aba Prefecture Qiang Studies Association of Sichuan (*Abazhou Qiangxue xuehui* 阿

坝州羌学学会), two local scholarly associations. Particularly, I foreground local Qiang and Han intellectuals as the core producers of cultural knowledge related to ethnicity and Chinese-ness. Instead of seeing minority and local scholarly productions as supplementary to or derivative of a more "established" scholarly canon maintained by elite Han scholars, I shift the focus to how minority and local scholars re-define the very notion of Chinese-ness by centering the Qiang in China's cultural history.

Xiqiang Wenhua: Reconstructing King Yu as a Qiang Ethnic Hero

Xiqiang wenhua is a journal published formerly by the Sichuan Aba Prefectural Qiang Studies Association and now jointly by the prefectural and provincial Qiang Studies Associations of Sichuan. Founded in 1996, the journal is published once a year (sometimes more or less frequently) and serves as an important platform for Sichuan's local scholars to showcase their research and voice their cultural opinions for the various Qiang regions of the province. The journal has an advisory committee that consists of writers, cultural workers, scholars, as well as citizen historians from various Qiang regions in Sichuan. For example, Mr. Wang of Taoping Qiang Village, the citizen historian and scholar introduced at the beginning of the chapter, is listed as a "committee member" (*weiyuan* 委员) for this journal and is a frequent contributor.

The journal prides itself on upholding "academic (*xueshuxing* 学术性), ethnic (*minzuxing* 民族性), and regional (*diyuxing* 地域性)" features. As a regional scholarly journal, *Xiqiang wenhua* centers around the excavation and preservation of Qiang cultural heritage as it is defined and reinvented by contemporary minority and local scholars. The keyword in the title, Xiqiang, or West Qiang, famously comes from the *Book of Latter Han*, an important pre-modern Chinese historiographic account that I discussed in Chapter 1. The reader may recall from Chapter 1 that the term Xiqiang (West Qiang) connotes the peripheral cultural status of the Qiang in classical Chinese texts: the "Qiang" was glossed as many non-Sinitic people collectively known as the "Qiang barbarians" inhabiting the western badlands of China. *The Book of Later Han* devotes an entire biography about the Xiqiang peoples and their peculiar marriage customs, sartorial traditions, and rebellious nature in its "Biography of Xiqiang." *Xiqiang wenhua*, a contemporary regional journal, turns the derogatory connotations of the term Xiqiang on its head by reclaiming "Xiqiang" as a new center of Chinese civilization through the journal's discursive fashioning of the "Qiang" identity both in China's historical past and in the present day.

Every issue of the journal is divided into several sections: a section on historical research, a section on the study of the folkloristic, religious and cultural customs of the contemporary Qiang people, and one section on the interpretation of classic Qiang literary texts (including the oral and pictorial *shibi* shamanistic texts). Sometimes the journal features ethnographic writings on the various Qiang villages and original literary works by contemporary Qiang writers. In recent issues, especially issues published after the 2008 Sichuan earthquake, sections such as "Development and Deliberation" (*Fazhan yu sikao* 发展与思考) have been prominently featured in the journal, as local scholars and intellectuals increasingly feel the need to debate about the best strategies to promote Qiang cultural heritage and preserve Qiang ethnic traditions to stimulate regional economic and social development.

Beyond the surface of a regional scholarly journal, *Xiqiang wenhua* is a multiethnic site for contemporary minority imagination, as it straddles ambiguous epistemological and cultural worlds: the journal intentionally plays with the myths of the "Qiang" in Chinese history and textual traditions, mobilizing the creative agencies of local scholars to re-write these myths into the construction of the knowledge about the modern Qiangzu as an important ethnic group integral to the civilizational prosperity of China.[1]

The first prominent aspect of *Xiqiang wenhua*'s construction of the Qiang identity in Chinese history is its play with the multilingual Xixia (West Xia) empire. For example, some of the earlier issues of the journal boldly uses the now-extinct Tangut script for the title of the journal on the cover (Figure 12). As shown in Figure 12, the cover of the 2010 issue of the journal, as in many other issues, juxtaposes the Tangut script with the pinyin romanization for the Chinese characters for *Xiqiang wenhua*, yet the Chinese characters themselves are absent.

In today's Sichuan, many ethnic Qiang scholars believe that the Tangut Xixia Empire that existed between 1038 and 1227 and swept across many regions of West China—such as Ningxia, Qinghai, and Gansu—was founded by the ancient Tangut Qiang people (*Dangxiang Qiang* 党项羌). The Tangut Qiang are in turn believed to be the direct ancestors of the modern Qiangzu ethnic group by many ethnic Qiang scholars. This belief has now entered into the domain of textual production and is utilized by Qiang villagers as an imaginative token of the Qiang's cultural ancestry tracing back to the stronghold of the West Xia dynasty. For example, some guesthouses in certain tour-

Figure 12. Cover image of the journal *Xiqiang Wenhua* (The culture of West Qiang).

istic villages in the Qiang regions of Sichuan proudly display red couplets written in the Tangut script. These couplets infuse the ethnic Han cultural tradition of producing and hanging couplets at the door with the myth of the Tangut language as an "ancestral language" to the Qiang.

Not only do ordinary Qiang villagers mobilize the Tangut script as a textual symbol for their connections to the West Xia dynasty, but ethnic Qiang scholars have also created a discursive space for asserting the centrality of the Tangut script in contemporary Qiangzu oral literature. During my field research in Sichuan, I came to know Professor Zhang Shanyun (张善云), a well-recognized ethnic Qiang scholar in China. In 2019, Professor Zhang happily gifted me a book of Qiang folk songs from Feng County in Shaanxi province, which he compiled and edited. Titled *Three Hundred Qiang Songs from Feng County*, Prof. Zhang's book is a compilation of folk love songs from Feng County. The lyrics of each love song are printed both in modern Chinese and in the Tangut language. In the preface, Prof. Zhang asserts that this book is the "first and to this day, the only book of Qiang folk songs that uses both the [Han] Chinese script and Tangut script—the script of the Qiang—that has been published in China and in the world" (Figure 13).[2]

Prof. Zhang's assertion of the Tangut script being the script of the modern Qiangzu and the bilingual nature of this book reflect the deep desire for contemporary Qiangzu scholars to claim the historical continuity of the "Qiang" as a long-standing ethnic group in China and Asia. These textual efforts of "reviving" the extinct Tangut language also embodies contemporary Qiangzu villagers' and scholars' discursive construction of the modern Qiangzu's deep ties to the distant but, in their eyes, awe-inspiring Xixia (West Xia) dynasty.

As a contemporary Qiang studies journal, *Xiqiang wenhua* taps into the rich historical memory and imaginative tropes afforded by the Tangut script and the Xixia dynasty to construct the historical continuity for the Qiang in China's cultural past. In addition to creating a discursive realm of the contemporary Qiangzu's connection to the Xixia dynasty, another important strategy for contemporary scholars and authors of *Xiqiang wenhua* to assert the historical importance of the Qiang in China is through constructing an imaginative ancestry of Chinese people that centers around the Qiang. This is a collective project where "[minority] scholars, writers, officials and entrepreneurs are forming an 'entrepreneurial ally' in China today."[3] Furthermore, as I argued elsewhere, "[through] such an entrepreneurial ally, [minority and regional scholars] mobilize and capitalize on a host of cultural symbols, historical narratives, and canonical figures in 'orthodox' Sinitic-Chinese culture to both develop regional economies and challenge the historical hierarchy between the 'civilized Han center' and its 'uncultured' non-Han 'peripheries.'"[4] By constructing the legendary history of Da Yu (King Yu the Great) as an ethnic Qiang hero, regional and ethnic minority scholars in southwest China achieve the double goal of both stimulating local tourist economy and contesting for the epistemological authority to re-center ethnic minority groups in canonical Chinese historical narratives.

Figure 13. Cover image of *Fengzhou Qiangge Sanbaishou* (Three hundred Qiang songs from Feng County).

For many different issues of *Xiqiang wenhua* published to this date, the topic of Da Yu, or King Yu the Great, a well-known ancient sage king of China, appears in almost every single issue. Even though Da Yu is a household name in China, prior to *Xiqiang wenhua* and similar scholarly productions generated by the Qiang intellectuals of Sichuan, there seemed to be no connection between Da Yu and the Qiangzu. Yet the essays and articles published in *Xiqiang wenhua* exhibit a strong desire to attach both an ethnic label—Qiang—and a regional label—Sichuan—to this ancient mythic figure that once "belonged" to canonical classical Chinese texts. The numerous articles and essays written by Qiang and sometimes Han ethnic scholars and historians of Sichuan in celebration of Da Yu can be broken down into three general categories: the geographic origin of Da Yu as a great Qiang figure born in the mountains of West Sichuan; the familial genealogy of Da Yu as the descendent of the Yellow Emperor, a common ancestral symbol for the Chinese people, and thus bridging the ethnic origins of the Han and the Qiang as stemming from the same ancestors; lastly, Da Yu as an ancient sage king known for his selfless love for the people and his diligence as a governor, making him a much-admired hero of the Qiangzu today and a contributor to China's national spirit.

Where does this desire to attribute both an ethnically Qiang and regionally Sichuan origin of Da Yu derive from? What are the cultural, ideological, and social implications of "localizing" a national mythic figure? To answer these questions, we need to look beyond the immediate concerns of the Qiang scholars of Sichuan and explore the broader socio-cultural contexts for the rising phenomenon of monumentalizing and capitalizing on ancient mythic figures in different parts of China in the age of China's economic and social reform.

In his study of the creative frenzy of forging monumental parks of the mythic king Da Yu in Hubei and Zhejiang provinces and the numerous temples devoted to another sage king, Shun (舜), in various regions of China, Robin McNeal argues that ancient mythological sources can be mined for both their financial and cultural capital in regional developmental agendas. He maintains: "Through the construction of new monuments celebrating legendary figures or events and, at the local level, the promotion of distinctive regional customs and traditions, [regional identities] can be integrated into the larger national narrative of 'five thousand years of Chinese history.'"[5] McNeal observes that there is an ongoing trend for many divergent regions in contemporary China to embrace China's common national mythic symbols, most often the sages kings Yao (尧), Shun and Yu (禹), as each region exploits the different historical memories embedded in these figures in order to "forge meaning, identity, and power today as in the distant past."[6]

McNeal's detailed study of the Shun temples and Yu monuments in provinces ranging from Anhui and Shanxi to Hubei reveals how ancient legendary figures can be localized and capitalized on, as each province strives to claim its own association with these unifying cultural symbols of China since imperial times, and, in the process, to transform local community through cultural tourism while "maintaining or reasserting some sense of historical identity."[7]

The Qiang regions of Sichuan are no exception to this contemporary enterprise of repackaging China's historical or legendary figures for the purpose of foregrounding regional identity and stimulating regional economy. In the era of neoliberalism on a global scale, the cultural heritage of any given people—both tangible heritage like ancient monuments and architecture and intangible heritage like collective memory, legends and oral traditions—fall under a "heritage regime" in which the state and various other public and private stakeholders join efforts in managing traditional expressions of life. In other words, within the rubric of neoliberalism, a new form of cultural governance has emerged. This is a form of governance in which power decentralization and multiple players shape a nation's socio-economic life, and "cultural heritage" becomes a focal point where different levels of governments, together with provincial experts and indigenous groups, interact to create narratives about a people's past and bring about regional development.[8]

Notably, contrary to the Han-dominated provinces studied by McNeal, the claims to Da Yu's legacy made by the Qiangzu intellectuals of Sichuan exhibit an ethnic consciousness for minority scholars to elevate themselves to the equal cultural and economic status as their historically more powerful Han counterparts. Therefore, in our study of contemporary China's reimagining of its historical past, we would run the risk of getting only a partial picture if we were to skip the study of the endeavors carried out by minority peoples. For, as anthropologist Rosemary Coombe points out, "[heritage] resource management," just as other forms of neoliberal governmetanlity, "legitimatizes new relations of power and knowledge, as it creates new subject positions for individuals and social groups, while fostering the articulation of collective subjectivities holding possessive relationships to culture."[9] The role of *local and provincial scholars* in managing heritage resources and legitimatizing new relations of power and knowledge vis-à-vis the nation is crucial: these scholars mediate between nationally circulated myths (heritage resources) and local needs for cultural visibility and economic development. It is illuminating, as the following passages will show, how Qiangzu scholars have come to claim a new "possessive relationship" to Chinese culture through the leadership of local intellectuals. Minority intellectuals serve as cultural brokers as they re-appropriate cultural symbols that had historically belonged to the Confucian Chinese textual canons to re-invent the cultural and ethnic identities of minority groups in an era of neoliberal cultural governance in China.

Geng Shaojiang (耿少将) is one of the many prominent ethnic Qiangzu scholars who espouse the idea that Da Yu was of Qiang ethnic origin. In a chapter titled "Qiangzu in the Xia-Shang Period" in his book, *A Complete History of the Qiangzu* (*Qiangzu tongshi* 羌族通史), Geng quotes from classical Chinese sources as diverse as *Mencius* (*Mengzi* 孟子) and *The Records of the Grand Historian* (*Shiji* 史记) to support his claim that Da Yu was born a Qiang person. According to Geng, both *Mencius* and *The Record of the Grand Historian* show textual evidence that "Yu was born in Shiniu, and he was a person of the Xiyi."[10] Geng concludes that these sources all point to Da Yu's birthplace as the Shiniu County of West Sichuan.[11] Da Yu's birthplace, Geng further argues, was part of the land of West Qiang (Xiqiang, or Xiyi) as referred to in classical historical documents, making him evidently a Qiang hero.[12] Later in the chapter, Geng argues that the Xia dynasty established by Da Yu and his son was a Qiang-centered era of China, and it is impossible to separate the Qiang from the Xia dynasty.[13]

Geng's belief that Da Yu was a Qiang king is widely shared by other scholars and writers in Sichuan. For example, *Xiqiang wenhua*'s 2007 issue includes many articles on the topic of Da Yu and his relevance to the Qiang ethnic and cultural identity. Da Yu, an immensely familiar legendary figure to the Chinese cultural imagination, is widely known for his feats of controlling the floods in ancient China and for choosing his nation over his family. Legend has it that around the twenty-first century B.C.E., Da Yu succeeded in managing the floods of the major rivers in China where his father and predecessors had failed.[14] Legend also has it that in order to tame the ravenous rivers of China, King Yu passed by his own home three times without entering it, putting his people before his family and exemplifying sagely virtues as a king.[15] He became a beloved figure in both elite, "canonical" historical writing, such as *The Records of the Grand Historian*, and popular Chinese religion. Many provinces, from Sichuan, Zhejiang and Anhui to Shanxi, have had memorial temples for Da Yu since imperial times for people to pay homage to this legendary sage king.[16]

Even though the Chinese admiration for Da Yu is by no means a contemporary invention, but rather, with roots dating back to pre-modern times, the idea that Da Yu was a Qiang king and that he embodied the ultimate virtues of a king because of his Qiang identity is decidedly tainted with contemporary ethnic cultural consciousness. In other words, many contributors to *Xiqiang wenhua* deploy the historical prominence and cultural richness of the legendary figure Da Yu as a national hero of China to articulate for the subjective positions of the Qiang in contemporary China's multiethnic cultural politics and to "legitimatize new relations of power and knowledge"[17] in China.

Several articles in the 2007 issue of *Xiqiang wenhua* weave together the image of the sage king Da Yu as a crucial figure for China's historical progress and ethnic unity. In an article titled "New Explorations of the Culture of Xia Dynasty and Da Yu," co-authored by two locally prominent scholars (Tan Jihe and Wang Chunwu), the authors argue that Da Yu was an exemplar of such Confucian virtues as "great benevolence" (*daren* 大仁), "great wisdom" (*dazhi* 大智), and "great courage" (*dayong* 大勇).[18] Quoting other scholars in a recent academic convention on Da Yu and his legacy, Tan and Wang suggest that the Xia dynasty established by Da Yu serves as "the root of Chinese civilization."[19] The authors, informed by a Marxist teleological perspective of history, make a strong case for the importance of Da Yu and his contribution to China's national progress and cultural integrity:

> Xia dynasty was an era when China progressed from a pre-historical society to a civilizational society, from tribes to a nation. Da Yu, the first and foremost king of Xia dynasty documented in *ancient records*, was the transitional figure who brought such progress to completion . . . As scholar Feng Guanghong points out, "With Da Yu's success in controlling the floods of China, he introduced agriculture to China, and the Xia calendar was invented, helping people settle down with an agricultural lifestyle. The Xia language and rituals . . . provided the same national consciousness for the Chinese people." Therefore, [we can conclude that] "The culture created by Da Yu of the Xia dynasty was the root of civilization for China" (emphasis mine).[20]

Evident from the above quote is the authors' desire to establish that the legendary Xia dynasty, said to have been founded by an equally legendary Da Yu, laid the civilizational foundations to China. The authors also assert that, because historical sources point to Da Yu's birth in the ancient Qiang regions of Sichuan, we need to then relocate the "origin" of Chinese civilization geographically westward to Sichuan, a western province in China. Through this effort, the scholars redefined the "Qiang barbarians" in classical Chinese texts to be the embodiment of China's legendary Xia dynasty.

In the same issue of the journal, there is another article titled "Yu Rose from the Land of Shu All of China." In this article, the author Long Xianzhao makes an elaborate argument on the regional and ethnic origins of Da Yu as a Qiang king originating from Sichuan, which was known as the Kingdom of Shu during certain historical periods in China. Like Tan and Wang cited above, Long makes references to many "ancient records" to provide evidence for his point:

> Sima Qian of the Former Han (Western Han) dynasty said, "Yu rose from the land of Xiqiang." Then Yang Xiong (扬雄 53 BCE–18 AD) in his *Chronicles of the Kings of Shu* (*Shuwang benji* 蜀王本纪) maintained that "Yu was originally a person of the Guangrou County of the Wenshan Prefecture, born in Shiniu." This is *trustworthy history* (*xinshi* 信史) and serves as precious historical documents with high historical value. Since the Western Han [dynasty] government had newly established prefectures and counties along the Min River Valley (*Minjiang liuyu* 岷江流域), the imperial court obtained oral historical materials from the Qiang people of that region, thereby providing reliable references for book-writers to document *history* (emphasis mine).[21]

In this passage and the passage cited immediately preceding this one, the authors go to great lengths to provide historical links between what they claim to be the case (that Da Yu was a Sichuan-born king of Qiang ethnicity) and what has been documented in imperial historiographies. It seems that the authors believe that historical writings are the most powerful proof that Da Yu was indeed a "native" hero of Sichuan, despite his prominence all over China.

Yet by emphasizing the power of historic documents to prove Da Yu's ethnic and regional origins, the scholars have bypassed the fact that a lot of the "trustworthy historical" documents they cite are themselves mythological in nature. By perpetuating the ancient myth of the king Da Yu and insisting that such myth should be treated as history, native scholars of Sichuan are actually participating in a millennia-long tradition in China where mythological beliefs and figures are intertwined with historical messages, and where the blurred lines between history and mythology serve both political and socio-cultural purposes in different eras.

As McNeal points out, in many of imperial China's authoritative historical books, such as *The Records of the Grand Historian*, the mythical qualities of legendary figures, such as sage kings Shun and Da Yu, "have not been completely effaced."[22] McNeal notes the tendency for the authors of orthodox Chinese historical records in imperial times to keep intact the mythical aura of certain figures.[23] The tendency to mythologize China's founders had propelled literati and local governors in China to pay homage to these figures throughout history by way of renovating local temples and making stone inscriptions to celebrate the legendary figures' acclaimed virtues.[24]

Da Yu was an epitome of this mythologizing tendency in both national and local history. According to Mark Edward Lewis, Da Yu as a wise and benevolent conquer of the floods that plagued China enjoyed continuous celebrations and an unequivocally positive reputation since as early as the Zhou dynasty and throughout Chinese history.[25] This is so because the conquering of floods denoted the ordering of human space and the legitimatization of political institutions and political power in early China.[26] From an early time on, mythological accounts and literary writings in early China helped heighten the sagely image of Da Yu as not only a conqueror of floods and thus a manager of human spaces, but also an "instructor" who taught people about agriculture and helped establish a proper political order in early China.[27]

For example, "Tribute of Yu" from *Shangshu* is a classic account of Da Yu's miraculous management of the floods in the late Warring States period; it "constituted a mythology of origins that justified the state through literally demonstrating its role in water control," while at the same time "figuratively [dramatizing] the role of the ruler as the one who maintained crucial distinctions that defined human society."[28] In other words, the image of Da Yu as a sage king who successfully controlled the floods in China, delineated the territories of the empire, and brought prosperity to people made him a laudable figure in the imperial Chinese imagination of national order and political authority.

Throughout Chinese history, this established image of Da Yu became a recurring theme in major historical documents. More importantly, Da Yu's legacy and authority have been appropriated by different regions since ancient times, including Sichuan. As Mark Edward Lewis reminds us, Sichuan has historically maintained a prominent cultural relationship to the legacy of Da Yu.[29]

Shuwang benji and *Huayang guozhi* (*Chronicles of Huayang* 華陽國志), two of the most widely circulated imperial historical sources cited by twenty-first-century scholars from Sichuan, were produced by Sichuan's native scholars Yang Xiong (扬雄) and Chang Qu (常璩) in the West Han and Jin (晋) dynasties, respectively. Lewis notes that both Yang and Chang evoked the myth of Da Yu in their otherwise "historical" writing of the chronicles and geography of Sichuan.[30] By doing so, Yang Xiong and Chang Qu became some of the first mythologizers of official Chinese history, creating a millennia-long tradition of idealizing China's civilizational founders that successive dynasties and regimes, including the modern era, have built their national imagination upon.

In the article, "Yu Rose from the Land of Shu, Nourishing All of China," which was discussed a few pages ago, the author Long Xianzhao cites Yang

Xiong to prove that Da Yu's legendary birth in Sichuan is "trustworthy history." Long participates in the mystification of Da Yu by invoking imperial historical sources that are already mystical in nature. Moreover, Long finishes the article by referring to another figure widely known in Sichuan for his feats of conquering the floods in the province: Li Bing (李冰) of the Warring States period. Li Bing is a well-known and deeply respected historical figure who helped the people of Sichuan build the Dujiangyan Irrigation System and brought the honor of Sichuan as the "Country of Heaven" (*Tianfu zhiguo* 天府之国) by turning it into a rich and fecund land.

In his article, Long makes an explicit connection between Da Yu's legacy and the Dujiangyan Irrigation System in Sichuan: "The spiritual wealth of Yu of the Xia dynasty is crystalized in Dujiangyan. The principle of guiding the water (*daojiang*) [that was utilized by Da Yu] became the major principle of Dujiangyan."[31] Indeed, in Zhou dynasty songs praising the feats of Da Yu, Da Yu was said to guide the water naturally, instead of suppressing the course of the waterway, which had led to his success.[32] Similarly, Li Bing himself was also known for his wise take on the managing of floods: he believed that the flood tamer should respect the nature of the water and allow it to flow its own course, instead of trying to suppress it or stop it.[33]

Long cites ancient documents, such as *Huayang guozhi*, to argue that Li Bing as a later embodiment of Da Yu's spirit was worth paying homage to. For Long, Li Bing exemplified Da Yu's wisdom and selfless love for the people. Long maintains:

> The wisdom of guiding the river when managing floods [was epitomized by Li Bing]. It not only nourished Ba Shu [Sichuan], but also nurtured all of China. Li Bing's experience was popularized in different parts of our nation and it was developed further according to the different topological features of different regions.[34]

Indeed, as Lewis shows, in imperial Chinese cultural imagination, both Da Yu and Li Bing shared important mythic traits as capable governors who brought order to China and the local region.[35] Furthermore, while Da Yu became a patron sage in Sichuan, Li Bing became one of the most celebrated exemplary local officials and was attributed with the characters of Da Yu, as Sichuan had boasted a long history of both official and popular worship of Li Bing since as early as the Han dynasty.[36]

In the conclusion of his article, Long further elaborates on the historical, geographical and cultural affinities between Da Yu and Li Bing, both of whom are depicted as prominent figures rising from Sichuan's Min River Valley:

> The mountains and rivers along the Min River Valley were pregnant with beauty and productive of talents (*zhongling yuxiu*). It gave birth to Da Yu and, thanks to the blessings of heaven and earth, attracted such talents as Li Bing . . . who controlled the floods and made the people rich [and] created a brilliant river civilization [along the Yangtze], nourishing all of China. The magic charm (*shenqi meili*) and unique landscape (*dute fengguang*) of the mountains and rivers of the Min River Valley will surely exist with glorious China forever.[37]

Apparently, authors like Long are establishing a strong correlation between national cultural symbols (Da Yu and, to an extent, Li Bing) and the regional identity of Sichuan. Such an endeavor is both spatial and temporal: spatially, it places Sichuan, a province in the western borderland regions of China, at the core of Chinese civilization; temporally, it connects the otherwise disparate eras and dynasties to form a coherent narrative about Chinese history that the author believes is indispensable to understanding the future of "glorious China." Long also demonstrates a strong desire to underscore the regional importance and distinctiveness of Sichuan when he attributes the province's rich cultural history to its "magic charm" and "unique landscape."

At this point, we might ask: if Da Yu has been a crucial symbol of Chinese national cultural imagination since antiquity, what propels *contemporary ethnic minority and regional scholars* to re-appropriate this symbol and re-interpret it as a heritage for minority people themselves? In the age of neoliberal development, what does minority peoples' claim of their ownership over "orthodox" Chinese cultural symbols suggest about the efforts they make to reinvent their ethnic identities?

In contemporary China's ethnic cultural movements, it is not uncommon for ethnic minorities to utilize the cultural symbols and invoke the historical resources conventionally associated with the Han, however unstable and problematic the very notion of Han is. Post-Mao China provides a fertile ground for different groups to exercise their subjectivities and re-claim their identities vis-à-vis China's national narratives. As Stevan Harrell and Li Yongxiang observe, for another minority people of southwest China, the Yi, the revisionist writing of Chinese history places the Yi at the core of Chinese civilization: Yi scholars have extensively appropriated the Chinese cultural repertoire and declared that such well-known Chinese cultural sources as

Daoism, the Supreme Ultimate (*taiji*), and the yin-yang system all originated from the primitive Yi religion.[38] Just like the Qiang studies scholars in Sichuan, not only do Yi scholars claim their indigenous and long-standing relationship to the land of southwest China, they have also tried to reverse the Chinese cultural imagination of the Sinic self pitted against the "barbarian" other that had perpetuated most of imperial Chinese historical representations by insisting that it was the Yi, rather than the Han, who were the major contributors of Chinese civilization.

Similarly, Ralph Litzinger's study of the Yao minority scholars' rewriting of Chinese history reveals that "[all] attempts at historical reconstruction must wade through the thicket of Chinese terms for those labeled the noncivilized and the noncultured," or "those not converted to Chinese modes of speaking, dressing, dwelling, and thinking."[39] Litzinger's research on the Yao of Guangxi suggests that elites of the Yao minority group, like those of the Yi, endeavored to establish a coherent narrative of their ethnic group by insisting on its historical duration and uniqueness, questioning both the imperial and Marxist ideologies that relegate non-Han peoples to the categories of aliens and barbarians or occupants of the lower rungs of human history. As such, Harrell and Li conclude that ethnic minorities have spoken back to this Han-centrism by asserting "minority-centrism" based on their contemporary reinterpretation of existing cultural beliefs in Chinese civilization.[40]

Minority scholars' eager construction of ancestral memory by way of re-centering non-Han groups as the core of Chinese civilization testifies to Ming-ke Wang's conception of "historical mentality" (*lishi xinxing*). According to Ming-ke Wang, historical mentality refers to "a kind of psychological self-awareness made popular among a group of people about how individuals and collective identities are situated in historical time."[41] Particularly, a group of people engage in a process of "collective imagination of what constituted important historical pasts (historical constitution/*lishi jiangou*)."[42] Through this process of collective imagination, that group of people then engage collectively in a kind of "historical practice" to construct facts and behaviors that are meaningful to them.[43]

Minority scholarly writing is a process of constructing historical mentality and engendering historical practice in contemporary China. The stories and legends of Da Yu, with their mythological undertones, have taken on the importance of historical mentality for ethnic Qiang and Han scholars of Sichuan. The mythological aura of Da Yu's legends lends itself well to continuous reinterpretation and reincarnation. By "excavating" the historical presence of Da Yu in ethnic Sichuan through a Foucaultian process of constructing intellectual genealogy and relying heavily on textual inventions of the Qiang's historical past in Chinese civilization, the Qiang and Han scholars of Sichuan produce a collective identity for the contemporary Qiangzu. In the eyes of local scholars, it is the Qiang's heroic connection to the transformative legendary figure of Da Yu that should determine the Qiang's place in China's past and present.

Like the Yi and the Yao, the Qiang of Sichuan are preoccupied with a discursive enterprise of remaking history and claiming their ethnic heritage. In the remainder of the chapter, I will demonstrate how contemporary Qiang intellectuals have gone beyond the figure of Da Yu to conjure up the myth of a hybrid ancestry with the Han in both scholarly and popular cultural writings and how, rather than resisting the influence of the Han, Qiang elites have made creative efforts to fit the history of ethnic assimilation into their ideal image of the Qiang. I argue that in doing so, ethnic Qiang scholars have found a niche to both guard the Qiang ethnic identity—however constructed it may seem—and to welcome the socio-economic development that they have long desired, just like the mountainous minorities Yi and Yao described by Harrell, Li and Litzinger.

Relocating the Cradle of Chinese Civilization Westward and Imagining a Multiethnic Hybrid Ancestry through Ancient Sage Kings

The Qiang's contestation of Han cultural supremacy is first and foremost manifested in how local scholars' writing has challenged the established geo-cultural center of Chinese civilization and "relocated" it from the Yellow River Valley to the Yangtze River Valley, particularly the Min River Valley of Sichuan. For example, at the beginning of the article "Yu Rising from West Sichuan, Nourishing All of China," Long contests the long-entrenched idea that the Yellow River of northern China is the cradle of Chinese civilization. As a local scholar, he introduces the regional significance of Sichuan province by re-centering China's cultural focal point from Central China, where the Yellow River flows, to a vast region that extends to West China covered by the Yangtze River. He writes:

> Many think that the ancestors of China originated from the land where the Yellow River flows by . . . Yet the birthplace of Chinese civilization is not that straightforward. For example, the decedents of the Yellow Emperor resided in the Jiangshui River [Yangtze River] and the Ruoshui River, and the Yellow Emperor's descendent Da Yu was born in the Guangrou region, all which belonged to Sichuan. These indisputable facts tell us that the cradle of Chinese civilization is not a single point, but the intersections between the Yangtze River and the Yellow River.[44]

Against the prevailing idea that Chinese civilization stems from the Yellow River, an idea popularized by the twentieth-century nationalist discourse, scholars like Long Xianzhao put forward an alternative articulation that unsettles how Chinese history and civilization have been interpreted in the twentieth century. They do so by arguing that "the cradle of Chinese civilization is not a single point," or the Yellow River alone, but should include the Yangtze River.

As early as the first decade of the twentieth century, nationalist thinkers such as Liang Qichao popularized the idea that the geographic origin of the Han people can be located in the Yellow River Valley, following the migratory path of the legendary ancestor of China, the Yellow Emperor.[45] On the contrary, the Yangtze River flowing through southern China was considered as "weaker" in terms of cultural prominence, and many historically alienated "savage" groups, particularly the ethnic others, were seen as associated with the Yangtze River. To refute the long-established presumption of the superiority and orthodoxy of Chinese civilization as lying in the north, particularly the Central Plain, contemporary scholars of Sichuan province set out to argue for the cultural eminence of the Yangtze River. They claim that the Yangtze River should be considered as another origin of Chinese civilization and that the Yangtze River is by no means inferior to the widely-accepted "cradle" of China, the Yellow River. By doing so, local scholars are re-centering the geopolitical prowess of a region—southern and southwestern China—that had been traditionally associated with exotic, unruly, and marginalized communities in imperial historical imagination and modern nationalist sentiments.

In China's current era of neoliberal transformation, a strong tendency of regionalization and the flourishing of regional knowledge and contestations for cultural power are growing. Regional diversity, ethnic distinctions and cultural differences seem to become increasingly hailed as assets of the nation, even though the claim to be different is still strictly contained within the ideological framework of the Party-state. Harrell and Li point out that "the rise of local economic power and consequent appearance of a limited degree of local political maneuvering room" have contributed to the rising creative freedom for regional elites to reinvent regional identities.[46]

Indeed, it seems to be a common governmental move for neoliberal regimes around the world to allow for a limited degree of expressive freedom for various groups of people to assert their differences and exercise their autonomy. As Charles Hale observes, the granting of collective rights to disadvantaged cultural groups is an "integral part of neoliberal ideology"—the neoliberal regime "shapes, delimits, and *produces* cultural differences rather than suppressing it."[47] Various ethnic minority groups in China today are actively engaging in a discursive enterprise of reversing their marginalized status by re-conceptualizing their relationships to "orthodox" Chinese culture, or the culture created by the historically dominated Han Chinese group. But this enterprise is only possible under the rubric of endorsing ethnic diversity for national unity as an official ideology in China.

What this means is that, on the one hand, the Chinese state has produced ethnic "difference" in the first place by freeing up some ideological space for minorities to assert their particularistic ethnic and regional identities. On the other hand, minorities' contentions for difference and cultural prominence, such as the Yi's re-writing of Chinese cultural symbols and Sicuanese scholars' claim of Da Yu as a Sichuanese hero, still fall under the general ideology of China as a unitary multiethnic nation. Moreover, the important transition from the Maoist tendency of reducing ethnic diversity to class difference to the acknowledgement of ethnic and cultural distinctions in post-Mao China is crucial to understand reform-era China's minority cultural revival movements. Such movements of reconstructing the knowledge of Chinese culture testify to Stuart Hall's notion that knowledge is always contextual, situated and positioned: "the term ethnicity acknowledges the place of history, language and culture in the construction of subjectivity and identity."[48] As we have seen, the changing discourses surrounding "ethnicity" from imperial to modern and contemporary China has been powerful in creating histories, shaping ethnic cultures, and determining the languages used to make sense of ethnic identity. Consequently, neoliberal China's ethnic cultural revival movements appropriate rich historical sources and the changing political languages regarding "ethnicity" to form ethnic subjectivity and identity.

In addition to contending for the regional importance of Sichuan, ethnic Qiang scholars and Han scholars who are occupied with the study of Qiang history have also engaged in a process of deploying cultural symbols like Da Yu and the Emperor of Fire (Yandi 炎帝) to claim their relationship to these otherwise pan-Chinese mythic figures. In Long's article, for example, Da Yu is portrayed as an ethnically hybrid king who embodied both Han Chinese and Qiang ancestry, and he exemplified the ethnic prominence of the Qiang as one of the two important tribes that gave birth to the Chinese people. Long writes:

> The origin of Chinese civilization is very diverse but coherent, and very colorful. The Yellow Emperor flourished along the Ji River (姬水), and the Yan (Fire) Emperor (Yandi) flourished along the Jiang River (姜水) . . . Da Yu was born in the land of West Qiang [part of West Sichuan], and his mother's tribes belonged to the Jiang tribe. The Yan Emperor had the surname of Jiang, the Yellow Emperor with the surname of Ji. The perennial intermarriages between the Ji and the Jiang tribes are evidence that the Yan Emperor and Yellow Emperor continued to intermingle with each other.[49]

Here, Long is constructing an imaginary genealogy of the Chinese people (*Zhonghua minzu*) by asserting that the Yandi (Fire Emperor) "flourished along the Jiang River" while Yellow Emperor was active along the Ji River. Yang argues that the Jiang (Qiang) tribes and the Yellow Emperor (Han) tribes "[intermingled] with each other" to give rise to the *Zhonghua minzu* as a multiethnic people.

Indeed, it is a belief widely held by scholars in Sichuan that legendary ancient sage kings like King Yu (Da Yu) and Emperor Yan connected the Qiang with the Han, and that they exemplified the great Chinese spirit by being ethnically hybrid and creative. For example, Yang Guangcheng (杨光成 1938–2011), the former editor-in-chief of *Xiqiang wenhua*, also one of the most active Qiang scholars who had promoted the Qiang culture in Sichuan during his lifetime, produced a prolific body of writing that articulates the ethnic hybridity of the Qiang as sharing close ancestral kinship with the Han.

In a short biography-style piece about Emperor Yan titled "Yandi—Ancestor of China's Qiang-Yan Culture and Agriculture," Yang clearly assigns a Qiang ethnic identity to Emperor Yan, an imaginary ancestor of ancient China. In his article, Yang describes the historical cults among Chinese people to worship Emperor Yan for agricultural harvests, and he describes Emperor Yan as the forefather of agriculture in China and a great contributor to China's ethnic and national unity:

> The Yandi, or the Divine Farmer (Shennong), was active five hundred years before the Yellow Emperor . . . Emperor Yan was truly the ancestor of the *Zhonghua minzu* and the creator of the Qiang-Yan culture. How he deserves the title of the Great Emperor of Divine Farmer![50]

In this passage, Yang lauds Emperor Yan as "truly the ancestor of the Chinese people." Yang not only equates Yandi with the ancestor of *Zhonghua minzu*, but also assigns to him the status of the "creator of the Qiang culture."

Why do ethnic Qiang scholars like Yang Guangcheng feel the urge to claim their ownership of cultural symbols, such as Yandi (Emperor Yan), one of the most important legendary ancestors of China, that were never before directly associated with the Qiang? Under what circumstances would minority peoples initiate ethnic movements like this and establish real or imagined connections to national "traditions?" In the twenty-first century, as nation-states loosen their authorial grip on the claims of culture, local communities and indigenous groups have engaged in endeavors of articulating their past as an act of empowerment. James Clifford reminds us that "assertions of priority and ownership, in a world of movement and exchange, are always claims to power."[51] Here, "power" can be understood broadly as not only political power, but also the power of discourse and cultural imagination. By asserting that they "own" such mythic figures as King Yu and the Emperor Yan, which have always been important to the Chinese cultural imagination, Qiang scholars of Sichuan are exercising the cultural power of Clifford's notion of "indigenous articulation."

In the neoliberal world, to advance their identity politics, indigenous groups tend to articulate their past by "[retrieving] and [activating] traditions that are grounded in particular ancestral places."[52] In the case of the Qiang, various Qiang historians and scholars regard northwestern Sichuan province as the ancestral place of the Qiang, and through contemporary scholarly endeavors, they retrieve and activate legendary figures that have even the slightest connection to their ethnic native land to claim ownership to the civilization of China. In this sense, the "articulated tradition is a kind of collective 'voice' but always in [a] constructed, contingent sense."[53] In other words, ethnic Qiang scholars are re-articulating a tradition that has already been constructed by their Han counterparts and re-appropriating certain cultural sources for their own empowerment. The Qiang's articulated tradition, such as the claim that Emperor Yan was the ancestor of the Qiang, is contingent upon the creative freedom afforded by China's neoliberal regime that regards cultural difference as important assets for minority groups to participate in the discursive construction of a multiethnic, unitary Chinese nation. It is within this context that Qiang scholars like Yang take the creative leap to claim that the pan-Chinese Yandi was of an indigenous Qiang origin.

If Clifford's model of "indigenous articulation" is based more on his work on North American native populations who want to reclaim their ancestral memories prior to their modern contact with Western colonizers, the traditions articulated by China's ethnic "indigenous" groups like the Qiang are different: their claimed "traditions" are often entangled with a long history of perpetual cultural assimilation and mutual influence between minorities or peripheral peoples and China's political cultural "centers" from imperial to modern times.

According to Stevan Harrell, there are three types of typical response by China's peripheral peoples to the historical "civilizing missions" conducted by China's political and cultural centers: that of fierce rejection and resistance; that of wholesale adoption, and that of partial compliance and adoption.[54] In late imperial China, different peripheral groups in China's southwestern frontiers operated in distinctive and potent political and military institutions, such as the *tusi* or chieftain system, which endowed local religious-political leaders with tremendous power over local affairs. The imperial court in Beijing made painstaking efforts to govern this ethnically and politically contentious region of southwest China in an effort to assimilate its peoples and strengthen imperial rule in China's multiethnic frontiers.

Many indigenous groups in Sichuan have been subject to assimilation and civilizing projects from China's Confucian centers since the imperial times, and more severely in the late imperial Ming and Qing dynasties. As early as the Tang and Song dynasties, Confucian education came to the ethnic frontier regions of Sichuan, particularly the regions known as the Qiang regions today, as Chinese-style schools were being built, local elite families sent their children to these schools, and some local students excelled in the civil service examinations to serve the imperial administrative system.[55] In Ming and Qing dynasties, a more forceful and violent process of suppressing Qiang identity was evident, as the majority of indigenous peoples that were considered as Qiang changed their family names to Chinese ones and started to adopt Chinese customs for fear of persecutions resulting from military conflicts between frontier regions and the imperial court.[56] As a result, the Qiang regions of Sichuan went through a "Sinicization"[57] process and became more assimilated into Confucian Chinese culture. Eventually, in the Qing dynasty, "Han cultural features, such as ancestral halls, use of Chinese script, Han surnames and general names, began to be seen" in the region.[58] Rather than staging fierce resistance against the Qing court's effort of assimilating them, the indigenous peoples of Sichuan known today as the Qiang adapted or were made to adapt many Han Chinese customs and cultural norms, which have become deeply embedded in the Qiang cultural memory to this day. Ironically, some of these marks of ethnic and cultural assimilation, such as the Han Chinese legendary ancestors that were perpetuated in people's minds through a Confucian education and local officialdom, have become the "ethnic heritage" that the Qiangzu today are proud of reclaiming.

This long history of cultural assimilation has more or less contributed to contemporary Qiang scholars' familiarity with and creative re-appropriation of prominent Chinese cultural symbols and legendary figures, especially King Yu, the Yellow Emperor and the Emperor Yan, in an effort to claim the Qiang's roots in Chinese cultural history. The power of mythic figures such as Da Yu has exerted an influence on the Qiang cultural landscape since the late imperial era, as local steles with carvings of Da Yu's legends were made by imperial officials in the Qiang regions of Sichuan, dating back to the Qianlong era of Qing dynasty roughly 1736 to 1795.[59] It is evident that the imperial court and cultural centers of China used mythic figures and China's imaginary ancestors to tighten the imperial rule and foster a unifying system of cultural imagination in their management of ethnic frontier regions.

This tendency to mystify China's past and consecrate a few key legendary figures to "unite" China became heightened in the early twentieth century, when the creation of the concept *Zhonghua minzu* propelled nationalist thinkers to appropriate imperial mythic figures once again, yet for the purpose of forging a national consciousness for China's emerging nation-state. Nationalist thinkers such as Zhang Binglin (1869–1936) conjured up the image of the Yellow Emperor as the true ancestor of the Han lineage-race, which eventually came to be imagined as the ancestor of all the peoples of China.[60] In this sense, both imperial officials and modern nationalists became what Paul Cohen calls "mythologizers:" they masked their present needs and political intentions as narratives about the past, letting the agendas of imperial governance and modern national imagination govern their explanations of the past.[61]

Yet, also as Cohen has argued, "[once] assertions of the past enter deeply into people's minds (and hearts), they acquire a truth of their own."[62] Despite—or precisely because of—a long history of cultural assimilation and ethnic unification from late imperial to modern China, minority groups like the Qiang have developed distinctive ethnic consciousness and have re-appropriated cultural materials of the dominant Han group to forge new senses of their ethnic identities and claim new truth for themselves.

In addition to formal historical and academic writings published in journals like *Xiqiang wenhua*, there is another kind of writing that embodies the local anxiety of elevating the cultural prominence and proving the historical richness of the minority regions of Sichuan. This kind of writing is what I term as "tourism literature"—literary and cultural accounts composed by local authors and intellectuals with a popular audience in mind, usually produced with the explicit goal of promoting local tourism and establishing a "tourism imaginary" for a certain place.[63] The creation of tourism imaginary is crucial for the intellectuals in Sichuan to exercise their ethnic and regional subjectivity, as they get to practice an entrepreneurial spirit not only in the field of regional tourism, but also in making new cultural and political discourses. By combining long-accepted myths of Chinese culture with regionally distinctive memories, provincial scholars construct what I call a "place-bound cultural politics." That is to say, provincial experts play up the natural and cultural appeal of their homeland in Sichuan and engage in spatial imaginations that serve to bring in tourist development for the region and assert a certain region's unique place in China's contemporary cultural landscape.

Ethnic tourism has been fast developing in China since the 1980s. The Chinese government encourages ethnic tourism to both stimulate regional economic development and strengthen the image of China as a multicultural nation-state.[64] The development of ethnic tourism in various multiethnic provinces in China has meant that ethnic identity has assumed economic value in addition to political and cultural value.[65] As Bai Zhihong observes in Yunnan, a multiethnic province in southwest China neighboring Sichuan, the development of ethnic tourism has motivated minority people to "appropriate state-defined categories and re-shape them into the repertoire they desire."[66] In other words, the development of ethnic tourism in contemporary China has produced a fertile socio-economic ground for minority groups to re-articulate their cultural traditions and create discursive spaces to assert claims of their ethnic identities and reinforce their ethnic consciousness.

One way minority groups in China make claims of their ethnic identities through tourism is by creating "tourism imaginary," or the images and ideas "that people have in their minds about places as tourist destinations."[67] As a rich interdisciplinary concept, "tourism imaginary" is the result of multifaceted representational processes that produce the images of targeted tourist destinations. Graburn and Gravari-Barbas note that the production of "destination image" through the generation of tourism imaginary involves representational strategies as variegated as literary tropes (mythology, plays, fictions) and visual methods (films, paintings); moreover, destination image-branding usually requires cultural entrepreneurs to mediate between the indigenous or destination populations and the tourists.[68]

Graburn and Gravari-Barbas have offered some critique of the production of destination images, as it more often than not entails a political and commercial process, and the resulting image "is a simplified construction of iconic and hopefully memorable features aimed to attract the particular range or type of tourists that is desired."[69] While Graburn and Gravari-Barbas, as social scientists, have put more weight on the socio-economic factors surrounding the production of tourism imaginary and destination images, my study of tourism literature focuses on how Qiang writers remake the Qiang *cultural identity* in the process of building the tourism imaginary of their homeland. Instead of glossing the production of tourism literature as simply a process of commodifying local historical and cultural resources, I inquire into what these allegedly historical writings mean for local people themselves, as well as how myth-making can be a powerful way of not only generating tourism imaginary, but also shaping the cultural identity of the contemporary Qiang rooted in the landscape of Sichuan.

Qiang tourism literature is published either in bounded volumes or local cultural magazines; they are mainly authored by Qiang scholars and writers and are widely disseminated in the bookstores, museum stores and souvenir stands in the Qiang tourist regions of Sichuan. Most Qiang tourism literature is composed of cultural essays (*wenhua suibi* 文化随笔) and vivid descriptions of famous local tourist destinations of cultural and natural significance (*minsheng guji* 名胜古迹). Unlike the majority of the academic and historical essays published in journals such as *Xiqiang wenhua*, Qiang tourism literature is richly illustrated—often in full color. Furthermore, Qiang tourism literature contrasts with the formal historical writings discussed earlier in this chapter in its anecdotal references to local celebrities and insiders' views on "local legends" to tantalize the imagination of tourists. Yet, far from being intended as a product for casual mass consumption, tourism literature in ethnic regions like the Wenchuan Prefecture of Sichuan speaks unmistakably of the desire of local elites to construct a distinct place-bound cultural imaginary. By doing so, minority elites and writers both promote local economic development and potentially challenge the established orders of cultural hegemony in China.

Taoping shihua (Historical Accounts on Taoping 桃坪史话) is such a book. It was authored by the late prominent Qiang scholar Yang Guangcheng (杨光成, 1938–2011) in 2007, one year before the Sichuan earthquake. This slim volume was published in full color with brief accounts of the Taoping Qiang Village and other Qiang-related historical tourist sites of Sichuan. This is a book of sixty pages and priced at a very affordable 10 RMB (under two U.S. dollars). This book can be purchased in various tourist stands in Wenchuan. This book weaves together the image of Taoping Qiang Village and its nearby Qiang cultural sites as places deeply seeped in history. It does so with a highly imaginative narrative of the history of the people of Qiang in relation to the history of Chinese culture as a whole. Like the academic and historical journal essays examined earlier in this chapter, *Taoping shihua* endeavors to articulate the regional identity of Taoping/the Qiang into the grander narration of Chinese civilization. It positions the Qiang not as a backward or antithetical ethnic other to China's modernizing nation-state, but portrays the Qiang as a major contributor to Chinese culture throughout history, making the Qiang regions of Sichuan "must-see" tourist sites for visitors from all over China and some places in Southeast Asia.

In this book, the author Yang Guangcheng writes in an inviting and anecdotal way about the traditional cultural customs of the Qiang to offer readers glimpses into this otherwise "archaic" ethnic group in the eyes of many Han tourists. For example, when Yang mentions the importance of fire in the traditional lifestyle of the Qiang, he emphasizes:

> Fire played a vital role in the development of human civilization. The ancient Qiang were the forerunners [of inventing and using fire]. The ancestor of the Qiang, the Fire Emperor (Yandi), was known as the master of fire. The Qiang have a tradition of admiring the color red: the wedding gown and bride's veil of a girl are in red; heroes and the well-accomplished are honored with a red scarf . . . The worship for the color red and fire helped form the unique "culture of fire" (*huohong wenhua*) for the Qiang.[70]

Through the depiction of the use of the color red, the author invites readers into the life-world of the Qiang without overwhelming them with an exceedingly exotic ambience. In fact, since the color red is familiar to Han

Figure 14. Cover image of *Taoping shihua* (Historical accounts of Taoping).

Chinese tourists, the cultural affinity they would feel by reading this passage would become a positive asset in establishing an appealing tourist imaginary of Taoping Village. It is important to note that, the evocation of "sameness" and "similarity" between Qiang and Han cultures is used by author Yang Guangcheng as a literary trope to familiarize Han readers and tourists with the Qiang cultural customs.

Throughout the book, Yang is intent on enhancing the positive tourism imaginary of Taoping—as well as many nearby Qiang ancient villages and sites—by proudly describing both historical and recent cultural and media endeavors of capturing the attractiveness of these places. Such endeavors, according to Yang, are carried out by both Chinese and international agencies: film productions made by Communist state directors in the 1950s and 1990s; academic research about the Taoping Qiang Village conducted by both American missionaries in the 1930s and Japanese academics in the 1990s, as well as the effort made by the Aba Tibetan and Qiang Autonomous Prefecture in Sichuan to list Taoping as a UNESCO World Heritage site, even though such effort did not entirely come to fruition.[71] All of these textual and visual evidences testify to Taoping's rich history of interacting with the outside world and being at the center of tourism imaginary in southwest China.

The book *Taoping shihua* is richly illustrated throughout, and there are ten pages of full-color photographs of the artifacts unearthed by archeological undertakings in the region, placed side by side with ancient tombs and even pictures of the famous Terra Cotta Warriors that went into the tomb of the first emperor of the Qin dynasty, which seem to suggest that the archeological findings of Taoping and its nearby Qiang villages are as important to Chinese civilization as other well-recognized sites. The author Yang's tireless documentation of the cultural events and discoveries that have taken place in Taoping and its neighboring Qiang regions testifies to Graburn and Gravari-Barbas' notion that the construction of tourism imaginary—the imagery and ideas of a tourist destination—involves many creative narrative and visual tropes.

In this book, Yang has deployed several different creative devices to conjure up the tourism imaginary of Taoping Qiang Village. They include literary devices—highly poetic and mythic accounts of the Qiang and their customs (for example, the importance of fire in Qiang daily life); historical devices—the evocations of Qiang throughout history, even though such "history" itself is a product of ethnic imagination aimed at empowering the Qiang people and articulating their long presence and ethnic solidarity in China (for example, the claim that the Qiang was an ancient "international ethnic group" crossing over the Euro-Asia continent[72]); and finally, visual devices—the photographs of archeological findings and important Qiang ethnic tourist sites in the Aba Prefecture of Sichuan. Therefore, as a piece of tourism literature, *Taoping shihua* exemplifies a highly imaginative process in which multi-sensorial, multi-disciplinary creative devices are used in the name of writing about ethnic culture.

Yet beyond Yang's immediate desire for promoting the tourism of his Qiang homeland by writing flatteringly about local tourism lures, some other claims he makes in the book regarding the ethnic origin of the Qiang show that the conjuring up of tourism imaginary is sometimes more than a pursuit of economic return, but can also be an active process of gaining cultural capital in the contemporary world through reinforcing local cultural beliefs and enabling a sense of cultural ownership. In a section titled "Taoping Today" (*Jinri Taoping*), Yang Guangcheng includes a detailed genealogy he compiles about Chinese kings of high antiquity according to his study of Sima Qian's *Shiji* (*The Records of the Grand Historian*) in the Han dynasty:

> The genealogy of China's Qiang ethnic kings and emperors are as follows: the Yellow Emperor (黄帝), Gao Yang (高阳, 颛顼), Gao Xin (高辛-Fang Xun (放勋，帝尧), Zhong Hua (重华，帝舜), Xia Yu (夏禹) [What is more,] Fu Xi (伏羲), Nü Wa (女娲), and Yan Di (炎帝) all originated from the ethnic tribes and groups of Xiqiang (西羌族团). The Three Sovereigns and Five Emperors (三皇五帝) were all people of Xiqiang; that is why the Chinese call ourselves Descendants of the Yellow Emperor and Fire Emperors (炎黄子孙) today.[73]

While the names Yang lists here—China's ancient sage kings and legendary rulers—are all familiar terms in Chinese culture, the ethnic origin he assigns to these figures—that is to say, they all came from the ancient West Qiang (Xiqiang) ethnic tribes—seem to be a new epistemological declaration. By claiming that the Three Sovereigns and Five Emperors (*sanhuang wudi*) were without exception Qiang in origin, Yang is declaring that the Qiang, together with or even in place of, the Han, are the true ancestors of the Chinese people. Yang therefore asserts the central role the Qiang people played in Chinese civilization.

At first glance, one may wonder why a piece of tourism literature would be concerned with the ethnic genealogy of China. Yet when read side by side with other academic writings discussed earlier in this chapter regarding the legendary foundation of the Xia dynasty by a "Qiang" king Da Yu and his historical legacy in China, it is not hard to discern that, by concerning themselves with making myth about the ethnic origins of the Chinese people, contemporary Qiang intellectuals are not only trying to boost local cultural prominence, but are also engaging in a process of challenging established cultural hegemony of the ethnic Han as the only legitimate heir of ancient Chinese civilization.

The search for origins, especially the writing of the myth of origins, is almost always accompanied by a politically or socially contentious intent. Judith Shklar suggests: "The myth of origins has been a typical form of questioning and condemning the established order, divine and human, ethical and political."[74] Just like Harrell's study of contemporary Yi scholars' effort of attributing such Chinese traditions as Daosim and the yin-yang system to the Yi, myth-making can be a powerful form of identity-building, as it evokes memories of a certain group's real or imagined past, re-articulates that past, and possesses the potential of reigning over people's belief systems and gaining its "potency from [its] ability to persuade."[75]

In evaluating contemporary ethnic minorities' attempts at claiming their historical integrity and challenging established cultural orders, the important question is not whether or not the claims they make are factually based or empirically sound but why they feel the urge to question established systems of knowledge in the first place. Re-appropriating the myths constructed by the Han Chinese cultural center seems to reveal the tendency for minorities to claim ownership of a cultural system that had historically subjugated them as peripheral, unimportant, or backward. Qiang writers and scholars are drawn to the persuasive power of re-imagining "orthodox" Chinese legendary figures, such as the Three Sovereigns and Five Emperors, to be of Qiang origin. By doing so, Qiang intellectuals and local scholars make the claim that the Qiang regions are the forgotten cradle of Chinese civilization, for these regions gave birth to the "ancestors" of the Chinese, who were long associated with the Han. This process of re-imagination endows minority writers and scholars with a sense of ethnic agency and pride, overthrowing the negative images attached to them in imperial historiography and the label of "backwardness" put on them, as examined in Chapter 1.

Some previous studies of contemporary minority groups' assertions of their ethnic cultural integrity, such as Harrell's study of the Yi in contemporary China, neglects to emphasize that these ethnic movements often go beyond proclaiming the ethnic centrality of different groups, but are also intertwined with these groups' deep identifications with the locality or locale of their physical homeland. In fact, place and place identity are key in constructing or reinforcing ethnic identities: place produces "a richly textured sense of the ways in which space is grounded by distinctive ways of life.[76] Moreover, place supplies a "symbolic guarantee of stable, continuous, cultural patterns" that generate a sense of kinship and familial ties to groups of people."[77] In other words, culturally and topographically specific places act as powerful loci to form familial binding among a group of people and help them imagine their belonging to a fixed location, serving as stable or stabilizing signifiers of ethnic identities.

Indeed, "land" and "native place" serve as important tropes for Qiang elites to construct their historical relations to Chinese civilization and to foster an ethnic identity rooted in the Qiang's indigenous status in Sichuan province, the place that most Qiang consider to be their home place in China.

Topophilia, or the affective ties humans form with their material environment, are powerful motives that recur in contemporary Qiang cultural writing.[78] Natural landscapes, more than indicators of the beauty and abundance of a certain region, can be evoked as "handiwork of ancestors" from whom a certain individual or groups of people have originated, even if such ancestry is constructed mythically.[79] The myth of Qiang's origin as descendants of such legendary figures as Da Yu and Yandi is decidedly marked with indigenous scholars' imaginative references to the landscapes of western Sichuan. In fact, both the academic and popular literature authored by Qiang and Han scholars of Sichuan takes pride in the Qiang homeland as the birthplace of China's cultural and natural wonders.

For example, Gu Yunlong (谷运龙 b. 1957), one of the most renowned contemporary Qiang writers, has authored a succinct piece, "Ode to Min River" (*Minjiang fu*) in the 2011 issue of *Xiqiang wenhua*. In it, Gu expresses his deep attachment to the "beautiful, sublime and magnificent" Min River, a major river in Sichuan, by evoking topographical symbols familiar to many people residing in the Min River Valley. Gu also labels the Valley as the cradle for the Qiang:

> The Min Mountain has a mountain ridge called Gongkang. A river flows out of Gongkang and is called Minjiang. The river traverses thousands of *li* and excites singing and invites dancing, cleansing history from time immemorial with incredible ease. [The Min River] nurtures Tibetans and Qiang in the mountains and rivers, pregnant with Bashu civilization (*Bashu wenming*) at the corner of the Country of Heaven (*Tianfu zhirang*).[80]

Even though Gu uses an almost formulaic literary style to depict the Min River by referring to some of the most widely known facts of Sichuan, such as Sichuan being the home of Bashu civilization and its nickname *Tianfu zhiguo*, he is nonetheless trying to evoke a collective longing for the homeland for the people of Sichuan, especially minority peoples such as the Tibetans and

Qiang. Or perhaps we can say that the evocation of well-known cultural symbols can serve the purpose of constructing a "totemic ancestor" suggested by scholar Yi-fu Tuan, as the Qiang now portray themselves as the important descendants of this mythic ancestor known as Da Yu, who is believed by Qiang intellectuals to be an indigenous hero born into the Min River Valley.

One paragraph later, Gu depicts the lovely landscape and charming scenes of the Min River Valley in an even more picturesque and alluring tone:

> [The Min River Valley] boasts ten thousand acres of grassland; its earth is colorful, and its sky blue. It embraces the "fairyland" (*tonghua shijie*, a common term used to reference the famous Jiuzhaigou natural sightseeing spot) with various charms . . . In the summer there is Dagu Glacier, while in the winter there is Gu'er Hot Spring . . . Giant pandas move awkwardly but are cute, golden monkeys are mischievous but can feed themselves . . . Every step one takes, one would find a wonderful scene; every journey one embarks upon is like a song, and each journey is splendid.[81]

The list of natural wonders, including the "fairyland" Jiuzhaigou, the Dagu Glacier, and the Gu'er Hot Spring and the wildlife of Sichuan, such as the "awkward but cute" pandas, are depicted with a poetic language that exhibits the Qiang writer's topophilia for a land he proudly proclaims as his home place. The Qiang writer Gu Yunlong claims the Qiang's sense of geographical and spatial belonging in this splendid land of West Sichuan and calls it home. For Gu, West Sichuan is the "locus of memories" and "means of gaining a livelihood"[82] for the Qiang, as many of those categorized as the Qiangzu in post-1949 China have led an agricultural lifestyle and lived their daily lives in the mountains and valleys of West Sichuan. Most of the rural Qiang communities are familiar with the images and scenes depicted in the essay. In this sense, the minority writer Gu Yunlong nails the Qiang ethnic identity by attaching a place-bound value to this identity, expressing his affectionate feeling of being at home in the charming topographic features of Sichuan.

Later in the essay, Gu further evokes Da Yu and other natural and cultural wonders of Sichuan in his writing:

> The Dujiangyan Irrigation System nourishes ten thousand *li* of fecund land . . . We pay homage to Da Yu and his father, who tamed the rivers and mountains of China to enable people to live a peaceful life; we admire Li Bing and his son for attracting [admirers] from many places and prevented famines from happening under heaven.[83]

As discussed previously, Dujiangyan, Li Bing and Da Yu have been deeply embedded in the regional consciousness of the peoples of Sichuan. But now these places and figures have been evoked again to testify to contemporary Qiangzu scholars' attachment to and "ownership" of this land of great natural and cultural productivity. To summarize his essay, Gu praises: "How beautiful the Min River (*meizai Minjiang*); how splendid the Min River (*zhuangzai Minjiang*); how grand the Min River (*weizai Minjiang*)."[84] Here, Gu plays the role of an enthusiastic poet who passionately lauds the land of his personal and ethnic origin, making the land at once an embodiment of his love for the Min River and a collective reference to Sichuan's diverse landscape as a life-giving homeland for its ethnic Qiang inhabitants.

Indeed, the construction of space, both physical and symbolic, is instrumental in revitalizing the identities of different groups of people and challenging the horizontal, homogenous time-space of the totalizing nation-state. Homi Bhabha argues that the discursive space of the nation can be multivalent and ambiguous due to the "performance of narrative" carried out by the "heterogeneity of its population."[85] Bhabha points out that as pedagogical objects of the nation's ideological and historical projects, the "people" can also engage in performative narratives by exercising their agency and forming counter-narratives of the nation "that continually evoke and erase its totalizing boundaries."[86] In other words, despite being constantly subject to the pedagogical discourses of the unifying nation-state, minority people perform their own identities by narrating their lived experiences and constructing a "space of the nation-people"[87] that questions the Han cultural hegemony of the nation-state. By doing so, minority people like the Qiang juxtapose their own identities and experiences with the pedagogical subjection of the singular, homogenous nation.

This construction of minority people's space can be best seen through the example of how Qiang scholars of Sichuan geographically re-center the cradle of Chinese civilization from the conventional Yellow River Valley to the Yangtze River Valley (particularly the Min River Valley in Sichuan) and its vast hinterlands. Such symbolic re-ordering of the national space is supplemented by these writers' strong identification with the physical space of the Min River Valley as a regional center. At the margins of the nation, minority scholars such as Yang Guangcheng and Gu Yunlong and other local scholars in Sichuan problematize the Han-centered cultural hegemony of modern China by asserting their own perceptions of the national past. For example, they have repetitively emphasized the vital role played by the often mythologized Qiang ethnicity since antiquity as the major contributor of Chinese culture and nation, needing no further "salvation," "liberation" or "civilization" from anyone. Minority and regional scholars and writers also claim ownership of a nation rooted in the local centers—Min River Valley rather than the Yellow River Valley—by resorting to the cultural and affective sources, such as the legendary figures Da Yu and Yandi, that have been constructed and enacted in China's foundational mythological narratives since imperial times.

In addition to Bhabha's theorization of the space of the people, we can also see that Qiang scholars have formulated what Henri Lefebvre calls "representational space" to reimagine their ancestral past and remake their future. According to Lefebvre, the "representational space" is a "space which the imagination seeks to change or appropriate. It overlays physical space, making symbolic use of its objects."[88] As Lefebvre emphasizes, the representational space represents a certain kind of reality—a knowledge, an ideology, or an ideal—higher than the enfolded physical space itself.[89]

The representational space conjured up in the rich literary and historical writings by Qiang authors examined in this chapter is powerful in constructing the knowledge of the imaginary ancestry of the Qiang: such pan-Chinese cultural symbols as the Three Sovereigns and Five Emperors are mystified as ancestors of the Qiang people and born into the mountains of Sichuan. This imaginary ancestry is deeply embedded in both Qiang writers' affective attachment to the cultural and natural landscapes of Sichuan and a strong desire to foreground regional identity in neoliberal China. Such representations make use of the topographical features of Sichuan, such as the Min River Valley, to construct knowledge about a naturally abundant and culturally rich ethnic home place. Literary and historical representations thus establish the "ideal" of the Qiang as they imagine themselves to be within the lineage of China's most important legendary ancestors and proudly proclaim their rootedness in a culturally rich Sichuan province.

Conclusion

In reform-era China, locally produced scholarly and historical representations have reinforced the twentieth-century-manufactured knowledge of the cultural distinctiveness of the Qiang ethnic group (seen in Chapter 1). Yet beyond a simple reinforcement of minority identities formed in twentieth-century China, local intellectuals and minority scholars in the twenty-first century have initiated a creative enterprise of self-representation and discursive self-fashioning by participating in the long tradition of mystifying China's legendary ancestors. Particularly, they turn pan-Chinese cultural symbols into markers of ethnic and regional integrity. With a spirit of "enterprising" the rich historical memories and cultural imaginations formulated in China since imperial times, which are dubbed as "cultural heritage" in the age of neoliberal multiculturalism, local intellectuals and Qiang scholars and writers engage in a discursive process of re-inventing their ethnic and regional identities.

Despite being in the guise of historical scholarship, this process of constructing an ethno-regional identity in local journals and tourism literature is highly imaginative and mythologizing: the "Qiang" has been constructed by local and minority scholars as a mythic presence in Chinese history. The "Qiang" has also been defined as a central presence in the civilizational development and formation of a multiethnic Chinese peoplehood in the discursive projects undertaken by local scholars, manifested in the imaginative connections these scholars make between the Qiang and China's legendary ancestors.

This invention of a Qiang-centered, Sichuan-based "Chinese" identity expands the cultural and ethnic capacity of "Chinese-ness:" it dislodges Chinese-ness from the ethnic Han and the myriad cultural and historical symbols usually attached to the Sinitic/Huaxia/Han group throughout Chinese history. As such, the local production of a Qiang-centered interpretation of Chinese history diversifies the cultural membership and ownership of such loaded concepts as "Chinese culture" and "Chinese history." Local and minority scholars mobilize and appropriate cultural symbols such as Da Yu and Yandi to fit their construction of the Qiang identity into the national rhetoric of ethnic unity; at the same time, they problematize the Han-centered notions of Chinese history. This process is invaluable in empowering the traditionally marginalized ethnic groups of China and instilling in them a sense of ethnic pride and national belonging.

If state-history projects such as *The Concise History of Qiangzu* published in the 1980s aimed at portraying ethnic minorities like the Qiang as somewhat static guardians of China's "traditional culture," then locally-initiated scholarly and touristic writings in the twenty-first century challenge this "pedagogically" singular version of the national past by asserting the Qiang's creative genius and dynamic contributions to Chinese civilization. These local discursive projects re-write minority peoples into the core of Chinese culture by reversing the peripheral, passive, and backward images that imperial Chinese historical discourses attributed to China's non-Han groups. Local scholarly projects assert the central role the Qiang played in Chinese civilization and keep producing new narratives of ethno-regional cultural integrity. Contemporary minority scholars are only able to challenge established notions of Chinese history and culture after they have immersed themselves in imperial and modern historiography *and* become well-versed in state-sanctioned versions of history in contemporary China. Therefore, as this chapter has demonstrated, minority intellectuals and local scholars and writers have manifested great imaginative and discursive mastery of state discourses and local cultural histories to successfully turn narratives of marginalization into a declaration of cultural ownership in a neoliberal China that valorizes ethnic diversity.

PART II

Visualizing the "Qiang" in Cinema, the Built Environment, and Tourism

CHAPTER 3

A Village's Affair with the World

Visual Culture and Representing the Qiang Native Village in Transnational Cinema and Tourism

Taoping Qiang Village (Taoping Qiangzhai 桃坪羌寨) is a small but famed village located about 100 miles away from Sichuan's provincial capital Chengdu. Tucked in the mountains in West Sichuan's Aba Tibetan and Qiang Autonomous Prefecture, the village is home to over a hundred ethnic Qiang households. The fortressed, monumental stony village is easily recognizable for its distinctive Qiang-style architecture, imposing watchtowers, and an extremely intricate spatial structure that puzzles the visitor's gaze (Figure 15).

Taoping Qiang Village, together with a host of Qiang and Tibetan villages known for the same *diaolou* (碉楼) architectural structure in the neighboring regions, has been inscribed on the UNESCO Tentative List of World Heritage.[1] On an ordinary day, Qiang villagers in their ethnic attire set up their souvenir booths early in the morning to welcome tourists, who pay approximately 60- RMB (approximately 10 US dollars) admissions fee to enter the historic village. Tourists from all over China and other Chinese-majority countries in Asia, such as Singapore, follow local tour guides to visit the unique Qiang architecture. Many of the tourists marvel, in different Chinese dialects, at the intricate inner spaces of Qiang residences and excitedly declare their discovery of the "cultural wonders" in Taoping as they climb up the towering Qiang castles. Away from the tourists, on the central square, the place where the community comes together for weddings, evening parties, and other collective activities, an artist or two always sits down quietly in front of the main watchtower, portraying the panoramic scene of the village with brushes on the one hand and a small cloth on the other, wiping sweat as they endure the scorching sun typical to a fine day in Taoping Qiang Village.

Widely hailed as a "Mysterious Oriental Castle" (*shenmi de dongfang gubao* 神秘的东方古堡) in both touristic imagination and serious scholarly

Figure 15. Overview of Taoping Qiang Village. Photograph courtesy of Jingui Zhang.

portrayals in China, Taoping Qiang Village has become an iconic site for many official and popular media productions in China and transnationally. In 2016, a national official documentary series aimed at presenting and reviving village cultures in China, *Remembering Home* (*Jizhu xiangchou* 记住乡愁), prominently featured Taoping and labeled it a model village that "roots itself in its foundations" (*Shougen guben* 守根固本). Animating *Remembering Home*, China's current President Xi Jinping made the mandate to "remember home and protect our feelings of homesickness," which has become a central governmental policy to revive rural environments in China.[2] Each episode of the *Remembering Home* series features a culturally and historically prominent village in China, and Taoping Qiang Village is one of the handful of ethnic minority villages that made their way to national stardom, as the documentary series was aired and watched all over the country.

Beyond official media, Taoping has become a favorite site for popular Chinese-language cinema. In 2012, China's Sixth Generation director Guan Hu (管虎) shot his blockbuster *Design of Death* (*Shasheng* 杀生) in Taoping Qiang Village, conjuring up a modern moral tale of a primitive village. Guan Hu's film won the 2012 Taiwan Golden Horse Award of Best Artistic Design

Figure 16. Movie poster for *Design of Death*. https://movie.douban.com/photos/photo/1513799776/

for its solemn and awe-inspiring representation of the Qiang village's spatial features. The film sparked heated discussions among China's cinephile community about how it metaphorically revealed the trappings of Chinese history and culture in the setting of a minority village.[3] The film also helped inspire a new wave of ethnic tourism, attracting more tourists to Taoping, enhancing the village's mythic aura in the minds of millions of China's middle-class Han consumers, who take delight in both the popular cinematic portrayals of and a tangible "exotic" tourist experience afforded by Taoping (Figure 16).

How did one minority village become such a darling of national and transnational popular media? How did Taoping come to both represent China's developmental triumphs and its eagerness to discover its alternative and pre-industrial cultures? And what has been the symbolic effect of filmmakers' and media makers' productions, which deploy and appropriate "ethnicity" as a conceptual category to serve different ideological and social purposes? This chapter seeks answers to these important questions. I particularly focus on the post-socialist period (1980–present) and probe how popular cinematic works, such as Guan Hu's *Design of Death*, contest the coherent imagination of the national community in their satirical, postmodern depictions of the "other" cultures of China, unveiling the intrinsic crisis and moral incongruence of a fast-transforming nation.

My approach in this chapter is as highly ethnographic as it is cinematographic. Drawing on my decade-long intermittent fieldwork in Taoping Qiang Village, I investigate how local villagers have interacted strategically with the images of Taoping created by a transnational network of cinema and media. By taking readers into the lifeworlds and physical spaces of Taoping Qiang Village, I demonstrate how visual technologies, such as photography and cinematography, transform the ways minority villagers imagine who they are in China, as well as how images travel and circulate to increase the social mobility and visibility of minority villagers in multicultural China.

The cinematographic and the ethnographic are intimately intertwined in the space of Taoping. As I will demonstrate in this chapter, the cinematography of the two films under discussion (*Design of Death* and *Forbidden Kiss*) creates ethnographic spectacles for a mainstream Han audience eager to consume the carefully packaged exotic Qiang village as paradoxical sites of moral contestations and interethnic romantic tensions. Meanwhile, Qiang villagers in Taoping take advantage of the media spaces generated by visual technologies to create what I call an "image solidarity:" Qiang villagers are forming new social and ethnic bonds and even meaningfully competitive relationships over their shared memories and experiences in the process of producing images about a stereotypical Qiang village. The production of image engenders new social relations and imaginaries both among the Qiang villagers themselves but also between Taoping and the world surrounding it.

Through both a visual/cultural and an ethnographic analysis of the different forms of spaces and spatial interactions in Taoping Qiang Village, I reveal how the cultural and historical environments inhabited by non-Han peoples can bear a special relationship to the Chinese nation. In such spaces, ethnic minorities negotiate with the modernizing nation by creatively employing mainstream cultural productions and adjusting to the developmental agendas of the nation. Instead of being passive recipients of the intentions of Han artists and tourists, minority peoples participate in the Chinese nation's political and economic agendas with deep self-reflections, as they create touristic spaces in the minority village by leveraging the power of visual technologies. Image-making mediates the self-awareness of minority groups, helping them articulate their experiences into a densely interconnected web of multicultural encounters. The ethnographic reflections in this chapter will reveal that minority communities in today's China are actively engaged in creative processes of producing images of and about themselves, constructing their place in the nation and navigating complex cultural contact between the local, the national, and the global.

Seeing the "Self" through the "Other:" The Qiang Village as Site of Post-socialist Cultural Anxiety

In the post-socialist era, minority-themed cinematic works in China have assumed new symbolic and cultural meanings that usually question the very logic of a coherent "national culture," particularly in the context of marketization and globalization.

This section will focus on how Taoping Qiang Village is represented in popular cinema in contemporary China. I examine how Taoping Qiang Village has become a prototypical, symbolic minority village that embodies post-socialist China's cultural anxiety when the nation is straddled between its traditional values and Western cultural influence. I will show how two films that feature Taoping Qiang Village, Guan Hu's *Design of Death* and Chinese American director Tian Fen's (田芬) *Forbidden Kiss* (*Gubao zhiwen* 古堡之吻, 2014), engage in critique of post-socialist Chinese modernity as China finds itself at the intersections of the local, the national, and the global. Particularly, I examine how the Enlightenment ideals of progress and science, which had long defined twentieth-century China's search for nationhood, are parodied on the site of a minority village, as post-socialist Chinese cinema seeks to deconstruct revered ideas about the Chinese nation with aesthetic and cultural tropes referring to the ethnic and geographic "other."

Design of Death: A Trans-Temporal Moral and Cultural Tale

Design of Death is Sixth Generation director Guan Hu's 2012 blockbuster. The film was shot in Taoping Qiang Village, and the crew spent three months in the village.[4] The film has accumulated many accolades in the Chinese-language cinema community: it won six awards from the 2012 Taipei Golden Horse Film Festival and three awards from the Beijing College Student Film Festival in 2013.[5] It has also received over 30,000 favorable rankings and commentaries by China's cinephile community on Douban Film (*Douban dianying* 豆瓣电影), one of China's most popular and influential online film forums.[6] Later, film stills from *Design of Death*, together with other films shot in Taoping Qiang Village, were installed in the village by a local tourism development company as promotional materials to brand this minority village (Figure 17). All of these phenomena help create and circulate images of Taoping Qiang Village both in popular cultural imagination and in the built environment of the village itself, which has been opened up for touristic and aesthetic gaze in an increasingly globalized, consumerist China.

The timing of the production of *Design of Death* is crucial to understand how images of this minority village have been manufactured and circulated in China. When the film was shot in 2012, it was four years after the 2008 Sichuan earthquake that had profoundly changed the cultural and natural landscape of the Qiang regions of Sichuan—many Qiang people had lost their homes during the earthquake and were relocated to newly built villages. Taoping, like many other Qiang villages in Sichuan, has experienced a burgeoning tourist economy, as the earthquake destroyed much farmland of the Qiang people and local governments have been ardently promoting tourism to improve the livelihoods of minority people and boost economic growth. Even though Taoping opened up to tourism as early as the 1990s, it is the post-2008 era that has permanently fixed the village in the imagination of Chinese popular culture due in large part to the popularizing effects of tourism in making visible minority communities.

Design of Death is a moral and cultural tale of how an imaginary village by the name of Longevity Village (*Changshou zhen* 长寿镇) in southwest China confronts a pervert who constantly upsets its well-established social and moral order. The story is set in the Republican era, in the 1940s. Longevity Village seems to be a perfectly peaceful and orderly village on the surface, with its long-established moral codes, ritual traditions, as well as social and gender hierarchy. The village has been operating under these traditions and codes for thousands of years and is widely regarded as a model village by people near and far. However, the order of the village is profoundly unsettled by a young man called Niu Jieshi (牛结实), who was born into this village to a peddler who happened to pass by the village many years ago. As the son of an outsider (a man not originally from the village), Niu Jieshi has caused continuous chaos and brought unexpected surprises to his fellow villagers, and he constantly challenges revered traditions of the village. Niu Jieshi comes to be hated by almost everyone in the village, and the community has been planning to get rid of him. His only genuine connection to the village is through a mute widow with whom he has fallen in love and had a baby. Eventually, the

Figure 17. Tourism board at the entrance of Taoping Qiang Village. Photograph by author.

pervert Niu Jieshi is punished by the collective will of villagers who design his death with a conspiracy.

Seen as a whole, the film offers a localized metaphorical representation of some of the most profound challenges experienced by modern China, such as the crumbling of traditional Confucian values and the battles for gender and social equality. The fact that the film was not shot in a film park or staged village but in an actual natural village, especially an ethnic minority village, is telling. My analysis of *Design of Death* will focus on the dialectics between the local and the national to reveal how one minority native village comes to embody "the divided [national] self" by evoking images and perceptions of the "other."[7]

As Prasenjit Duara points out, in twentieth-century China, the local, especially the native place, had always been an important site that embodied values of the nation.[8] Rather than being a static, fixed locale that passively indexes or registers a set of values, the local should be more properly categorized as a "type of knowledge" or a "genre"—various academic disciplines and artistic representations work together to produce the "local," which is a place that "temporalizes this space [under discussion] as belonging to another time."[9] In other words, the local, particularly the native place or village, embodies the changing epistemological and political situations of modern China and also serves as a testing ground for the possibilities of the nation by signifying national transformations within the limited space of the native place.

Design of Death epitomizes Duara's conceptualization of the local as a site of knowledge production vis-à-vis the nation. Particularly salient in the film's representation of the local is its use of an ethnic minority village to construct local knowledge and identity. The film not only features the visually stunning and complex architectural environment of Taoping, but it is also produced almost entirely in the Sichuan dialect (*Sichuan hua* 四川话), creating a sense of an alternative tempo-spatial order. As Gina Anne Tam argues, *fangyan*, or dialects, in modern China imply a diversity of local experiences and expressions that are deemed as non-standard, and *fangyan* as a cultural construct entails the need for linguistic unification and standardization in the service of nation building.[10]

The predominant use of Sichuan dialect in the film accentuates a sense of locality, if not insularity: most people in Longevity Village live in its self-enclosed environment and have never come into contact with any outside forces or cultures. The only two figures in the film who speak Mandarin are the two medical doctors; one of them is a Longevity Village native who is trained overseas and comes up with a plan to kill Niu Jieshi. The other is a doctor who chances into the village when he is trying to save Niu Jieshi in Niu's coffin. Language implies power, as the two Mandarin speakers are the most educated and scientifically savvy in the film—they talk eloquently, in Mandarin, about the human body, pathology, and health. The two doctors are regarded by the Sichuanese-speaking locals as authorities of life and death.

Yet the film also reveals the vulnerability of the epistemological power manifested by the use of Mandarin. The prowess of Mandarin as the national language and the language of knowledge becomes futile when one doctor fails to kill the spirit of Niu Jieshi as a courageous rebel who is later remembered by people, and the other doctor fails to identify the true cause of Niu Jieshi's death despite his articulate questioning, in Mandarin, of the first doctor.

As the film's dialogues in Sichuanese dialect utilize many vernacular expressions (such as *laozi* 老子, a colloquial expression used by men to arrogantly address themselves and show their contempt of others), the Sichuanese dialect creates a sense of humor to entertain the audience. According to my interview with a Qiang person in the village, *Design of Death* featured many local non-professional actors, who are genuine native speakers of the Sichuanese dialect. The Sichuanese dialogues require subtitles for a Mandarin-speaking audience to be legible. The film features Mandarin Chinese and English subtitles to help the audience interpret the complex Sichuan dialect. This gesture of downplaying Mandarin and elevating *fangyan* in contemporary Chinese cinema is characteristic of post-socialist Chinese art: the nation is no longer the consecrated locale of meaning, nor is the state the main producer of art and literature as in earlier periods, particularly during the high socialist period of the 1960s and 1970s. Rather, a tendency of pluralization (*duoyuanhua*) and disaggregation (*fenhua*) has defined Chinese art and literature in the post-Reform era.[11] Here, pluralization means the representation of a plurality of cultural and linguistic values, and disaggregation means the separation of art and literature from state heteronomy.[12]

The film's profound questioning of the "center" and the "standard" is symbolized by the reversed hierarchy between *fangyan* and Mandarin. The geographic insularity and linguistic "otherness" of Sichuan are not regarded by the filmmaker as in need of reformation or standardization—China's *fangyan* themselves have been subject to reform and standardization during many historical moments in the twentieth and twenty-first centuries.[13] In this film, linguistic and cultural "deviance" is used as a contestation against the hegemonic power of cultural dominance wielded by Mandarin: the Mandarin-speaking doctors, despite their knowledge and intentions, are incapable of saving the people of Longevity Village. By contrast, the Sichuanese-speaking locals in the film eventually come to the realization of the value of a rebel like Niu Jieshi to keep the village alive and to change its rotten traditions. The Sichuan dialect in the film thus functions as an assertion of the resilience of local cultures in post-socialist China, as ideas of the singular, uniform, and omnipresent nation are contested in contemporary Chinese cinema.

Beyond the linguistic dimensions, *Design of Death* asks profound questions about the local and the national by presenting the spatial and architectural features of Taoping Qiang Village in a satirical and metaphorical way. By maximizing the visual impact of the unique spatial features of Taoping, the film portrays Longevity Village as simultaneously mysterious, primitive, and strikingly familiar to anyone acquainted with Confucian Chinese culture.

The unique Qiang-style castles and watchtowers in Taoping and their solemn grey and brown colors are appropriated by the filmmaker to conjure up the image of Longevity Village as an insular and primitive place. In the film, the oldest and most revered patriarch of the village passes away. According

Figure 18. Film still from *Design of Death.*

to local traditions, the patriarch's wife has to serve as a human sacrifice and be "buried" with the old dead man by sinking into the river. A medium long shot reveals the horrendous scene when the young Widow Ma, dressed up in a white gown, is being carried by male members of the village to the river for the funeral (Figure 18). While the black gowns worn by the young males resemble apparitions and the white dress worn by Widow Ma expresses desperation, the grey stony houses on the back of the scene create a breathless, suffocating atmosphere of spatial trapping. This scene is a symbolic revelation of the entrapment women experience in Confucian China: they are imprisoned in the walled world of the inner chamber and unable to escape what a patriarchal system subjects them to.

Earlier in the film, a panoramic shot of Taoping Qiang Village's awe-inspiring castles creates an even more striking sense of spatial authority: the massive Qiang architecture extends endlessly in the scene, and no human figure or trace of life can be found except at the center of the scene, where Widow Ma is being carried in the funeral parade (Figure 19). Widow Ma becomes invisible and is symbolically erased from the scene. This long shot powerfully reveals the architectural details and spatial make-up of Taoping as the setting of the story. The formidable and extensive castles, together with the background sound of young males chanting, unmistakably communicate a sense of authority: the imposing spatial features of the village serve as visual signifiers of the authoritarian patriarchal rules of Confucian moral values, which minimizes women's value.

Figure 19. Film still from *Design of Death.*

In this film, Widow Ma typifies the traditional Chinese woman subject to patriarchal kinship and Confucian morality. She is mute and unable to speak for herself. Moreover, she submissively accepts her fate of being used as a human sacrifice. She is a prototypical "patrilineally related kinswoman" who is expected to enact "normative performances" by correctly playing her roles in inhuman rituals and traditions that reinforce the patriarchal rules in the village.[14]

The turning point comes when Niu Jieshi breaks the rules of the patriarchal traditions. As people send Widow Ma into the water and she sinks in the river, Niu Jieshi jumps into the river and saves her. To everyone's surprise, Widow Ma reemerges from the water and Niu Jieshi laughs at people: "What a wonderful and pretty woman (in Sichuanese dialect, *poniang* 婆娘)! Anyone want her for a wife? No? I'll take her and play with her on my own!" Despite his remark of "playing with her," by saving the woman from widowhood and death, Niu Jieshi breaks the thousand-year-old Confucian tradition of real or symbolic female sacrifice. Later, Widow Ma learns to love Niu Jieshi and the two are soon to have a child. Niu Jieshi essentially salvages a female sacrifice and gives her new life. His unruliness and boldness pinpoint the perils of traditional Chinese culture, and his fellow villagers do not realize his value until he is put to death. Eventually, the child of Niu Jieshi is saved, even though Niu himself is punished to death when villagers conspire to give him a poisonous powder to swallow.

By narrating the story of a social pervert and a widow in visually impactful ways, *Design of Death* provides symbolically powerful critique of Confucian culture and localizes an otherwise universal tale of the victimization of women and social perverts in a small minority village in Sichuan. Ethnic minority villages, such as Taoping, are used by post-socialist films as imaginary locales to symbolize the primitiveness and backwardness of certain misogynistic elements of Confucian culture.

If the film sets out to critique the inhumanness and backwardness of some of China's most revered traditions and to reveal the pitfalls of Chinese civilization, the important question to ask is: Why is an ethnic minority village, rather than a regular Han village, made to bear the brunt of such social critique? What imaginative and cultural capacity does a minority village offer for the critique of national culture in post-socialist China? The geographical location of Taoping at the southwestern borders of China and its distinctive Qiang architecture are appropriated by a Han director, Guan Hu, to achieve two purposes: first, to conjure up exotically tantalizing spectacles to attract Han viewers; second, to disguise the director's critique of Han culture in the ideologically "safer" space of a minority village.

The exoticization of Taoping is prevalent throughout *Design of Death*. As the foregoing analysis shows, the film features the architectural and spatial make-up of Taoping with many visually astonishing techniques, such as presenting a panoramic image of the extensive buildings in the village. The film also includes many "exotic" objects unrelated to Qiang culture, such as the head of a Buddha and animal totems, to conjure up the atmosphere of Taoping as a primitive, insular, and tantalizing location. The effect of such visual exoticization is evident when we look at online tourist platforms in China, in which many travelers write about their trips to Taoping by referring to the village as a "mysterious Oriental castle" (*shenmi de dongfang gubao* 神秘的东方古堡).[15] We can infer that many Han tourists are attracted to Taoping for its exotic architecture thanks to the film's visual impact. The film, widely watched by China's middle-class viewers from around the country, helps create spectacles of Taoping that accentuate the reputation of the village as a "mysterious Oriental castle" to satisfy Han viewers' and tourists' curiosity and consumerist desires about non-Han cultures.

Yet the exoticization of Taoping as a minority village achieves something more than entertaining Han viewers and tourists. In fact, by resorting to the seemingly alien location of a minority village, director Guan Hu disguises his deeper critique about Han Chinese culture and society as a whole. In post-socialist China, the pluralization of values and diversification of cinematic and artistic expressions make it possible to portray the minority "other" in order to reflect on the national culture itself. This tradition goes back to the 1980s, when the Root-searching literary and artistic school focused on revealing the earthliness and "authentic" state of being of the ethnically and geographically peripheral peoples and societies of China, in response to the cultural void and national identity anxiety caused by the Cultural Revolution.[16]

In the twenty-first century, as China's economic and social reform deepens, market forces and global influences have encouraged diverse cinematic styles and expressions to emerge. Meanwhile, radical changes in both the urban and rural living environments have created another form of anxiety for neoliberal China: when the nation's social and built environments are constantly evolving, the very idea of a coherent, communal socialist nation is crumbling.[17] As the idea of the nation or national culture is no longer stable, minority villages come to bear the brunt of Han film directors' critique of Chinese culture and society as a "safer" choice than Han villages. While the national film censorship system makes it extremely hard to project the critique of Chinese culture into a Han village, the country's peripheral non-Han peoples, because they were long regarded as barbarians and less civilized in imperial Chinese historiography (examined in Chapter 1), once again become the "reasonable" choice for Han directors to engage in critique of Chinese culture.[18] Therefore, by choosing a Qiang village rather than a Han village for his film, Guan Hu achieves both commercial success by presenting visually exotic images of Taoping to his audience *and* critical depth as the film reveals the social and cultural anxieties of reform-era China.

Guan Hu has been widely acknowledged for his avant-garde cinematic depictions of the lower social classes of contemporary China, such as migrant workers and the rural populations. Guan Hu started his cinematic career when he was a student at the Beijing Film Academy in the 1990s.[19] Even though *Design of Death* may seem like a timeless tale about the historical, Confucian China, the film is in line with Guan Hu's care for the marginalized groups in contemporary China: the miserable conditions of social outcasts, women, and the disabled are performed by Widow Ma and Niu Jieshi in the film. While Widow Ma is mute and deprived of her ability to articulate for herself, Niu Jieshi is considered to be a pervert and alienated by his fellow villagers. These two figures resonate with the migrant workers and marginalized population that Guan Hu strives to portray in his other cinematic works.

Therefore, *Design of Death* has become a trans-temporal moral and cultural tale in which a contemporary Chinese film director voices his criticism of not only China's past but also China's present. *Design of Death* borrows the village-scape of Taoping to mystify Qiang culture and achieves commercial and critical success by presenting a myriad of exotic elements in Taoping. At the same time, Taoping Qiang Village becomes a symbolic surrogate for Longevity Village to mirror the problems of Confucian culture and the conditions of marginalized populations in contemporary China.

Taoping plays a fascinating double role in this film. As an actual Qiang village, Taoping has witnessed a considerable growth of popularity among middle-class Chinese tourists and film lovers, becoming a renowned tourist destination partly thanks to the spectacular rendering of its images in *Design of Death*. As an imaginary locale for Longevity Village, Taoping also references the cultural and social problems of China that the director sets out to critique. This shows us how minority cultures and village spaces are deeply embedded in China's national imagination and reveals the symbolic power of a minority village in indexing national problems. The minority village has come to embody the increasingly divided Chinese society and culture in the post-reform era, when China's rapid social transformations have left many cultural and moral chasms that may be filled by the alternative space of the minority village.

Forbidden Kiss: When the Ethnic Encounters the Global

The second film I will analyze in this chapter echoes the tradition of using the alternative space of the minority village to index national problems represented in *Design of Death*. More importantly, it extends the critical representational capacity of the ethnic minority village into a transnational framework of cultural encounters between China and the West. The second film under analysis is a romance based in Taoping Qiang Village titled *Forbidden Kiss*, directed by Chinese American director Tian Fen.

Despite the stereotypical image of Taoping as an antiquarian and stagnant space perpetuated in popular media and cinema, Taoping and the Qiangzu as a modern ethnic group are no strangers to global cultural contact. The earliest Western scholarly and cultural depictions of the Qiang as a modern ethnic group date back to the nineteenth century. In the 1800s and first half of the 1900s, American and British missionaries set foot on the Qiang regions of Sichuan. For example, Thomas Torrance (1871–1959), a British missionary and amateur archeologist, made the zealous claim that the Qiang belonged to a lost tribe of ancient Israel, connecting the Qiang to Judeo-Christian worldviews and reinforcing his religious fervor to convert the Chinese into a West-led spiritual and political world order.[20] Similarly, an American Baptist missionary and scientist named David Crockett Graham (1884–1961) was active in Sichuan from the 1910s to the 1940s, helping establish disciplinary archeology in China,[21] collecting natural history specimen for the Smithsonian Institution, and eventually publishing *The Customs and Religion of the Chi'ang (Qiang)* in 1958.[22] At a time when modern academic disciplines such as archaeology and ethnology were being formed in China, Western religious, scientific, and imperial forces intersected in the Qiang regions to conceive of China's minority groups' place in the world.

The Qiang's entanglement with global cultural and political influences have continued into the twentieth and twenty-first centuries. Since the 1990s, the Qiang and Taoping have witnessed a new wave of international scholarly attention. During my fieldwork in Taoping, I was often reminded by villagers that many Japanese scholars have been enthusiastically studying Qiang languages and cultures (there are many diverse variations of Qiang languages and cultures), claiming that the Qiang language shares important traits with the Japanese language. A quick glimpse into current international scholarly productions would indeed reveal that Japanese, American, and other international scholars are regularly conducting research about Qiang life and society.[23] Particularly, after the 2008 Sichuan earthquake, many international researchers have come to the Qiang regions to study the reconstruction of the Qiang homelands.[24] In 2013, the Qiang and Tibetan *diaolou* buildings that we saw at the beginning of the chapter were inscribed on the UNESCO World Heritage Tentative List, an endeavor spearheaded by the National Commission of the People's Republic of China for UNESCO.[25] Taoping is among the nominated representative *diaolou* structures for this particular inscription.

Therefore, contrary to popular imagination that characterizes Taoping as a "mysterious Oriental castle," Taoping and the Qiangzu have long been a part of a global circulation of ideas and cultural exchange—Taoping is far more known to the outside world than many tourists and artists imagine it to be. Yet Taoping's contact with the outside world does not always entail a smooth or equal exchange. It is precisely the tensions and conflicts of a minority village's encounter with the global world that *Forbidden Kiss* explores.

Like *Design of Death*, *Forbidden Kiss* was shot in Taoping Qiang Village in 2012. It was written and directed by Tian Fen (Jennifer Ten), a Chinese American film director based in Los Angeles. Ms. Long, a native to and long-time resident in Taoping, told me that the director Tian Fen became fascinated with Qiang culture after she learned about this ancient minority village from some media productions, so Tian decided to make a feature film about the Qiang. The film tells the fictional story of how Jack, an American architecture student, comes to Taoping to study the wonders of Qiang architecture, which survived the 2008 Sichuan earthquake. Enthusiastic as Jack is, he blunders often in the village and violates its many traditions and rules as an ignorant foreigner. The most fatal mistake Jack makes is to kiss local Qiang young women and make them fall in love with him, when it is a (imagined) taboo for unmarried Qiang women to kiss their lovers.

The transnational production of the film itself, in addition to the story it is trying to tell, is metaphoric and representative of the contact between the ethnic and the global in China today. For this reason, I will supplement my analysis of the film's theme and style with interviews and conversations with local Qiang people, who witnessed and participated in the process of filmmaking.

The making of *Forbidden Kiss* involved deploying local people and resources and assembling Qiang cultural symbols and images to conjure up an imagined "heterotopia" of China in the age of neoliberal globalization. According to Foucault, a heterotopia is "a sort of place that lies outside all places and yet is actually localizable."[26] A heterotopia is an "other" space that remains at a certain distance from mainstream society and yet is not separate from that society: heterotopias are spaces that are "outlined in the very institution of society, but which constitute a sort of counter-arrangement . . . in which all the real arrangements [of society] are . . . represented, challenged and overturned."[27] *Forbidden Kiss* imagines Taoping Qiang Village as a cultural and social heterotopia in China: the Qiang people in the village are portrayed as faithful observers of pre-industrial social norms, particularly sexual mores: young women are imagined as being forbidden from kissing their lovers, lest they lose their chastity and acquire a stigma that prevents them from having a good marriage prospect in the future. Taoping is depicted as a culturally and sexually pristine land precisely because of Qiang people's unwavering adherence to these norms.

This equilibrium is broken when Jack, the American young man, receives the kiss of a Qiang woman named Yuanni, the heroine of the story, in a trance, as Yuanni delivers with her lips the juice of a life-saving grass to Jack when Jack mistakenly tastes a poisonous plant near the village.

As we have seen from the previous section, it is common for Han-produced literary and cinematic works to conjure up the images of minority regions as heterotopias because of the geographically and culturally peripheral status of non-Han areas. As Yuqing Yang, a scholar of minority cultures in China, argues, "the construction of heterotopia both capitalizes on and revolutionizes the stereotypical image that has predominantly presented the ethnic other as ancient."[28] In *Forbidden Kiss*, just like in *Design of Death*, the spatial features of Taoping are portrayed as central to the cultural insularity of the place, which contributes to its tenacious retaining of "ancient" customs in a fast-developing China. The poster of the film presents a frontal look of the watchtowers of Taoping with no other human figures but the superimposed image of the two protagonists, Jack and Yuanni "(See Figure 4 from Introduction). The entire film is shot in Taoping and features different angles of the village without any visual reference to any other locations near Taoping, creating a sense of cultural self-closedness to reinforce the imagined antiquarian atmosphere of the village.

The spatial features of Taoping are translated into its cultural otherness, especially its sexual mores governing women. As Louisa Schein notes, in the Chinese imagination of its ethnic and cultural others, the minority other is usually gendered.[29] Southwestern minority groups like the Miao have historically been gendered as feminine, as they were subject to the assimilation policies of late imperial China and were almost universally imagined by imperial historiographies and ethnographic depictions as occupying a feminine, submissive, and exotic place in China, not too threatening and inviting romanticized imagination.[30]

In post-socialist cultural productions, southwestern minority groups such as the Qiangzu are imagined as feminine in Han cultural productions. This image of the submissive, exotic Qiang contrasts sharply with the militant, masculine image of the "Qiang" as a bellicose other in classical Chinese poetry and historiography, which I examined in Chapters 1 and 2. Moreover, minority others are also almost always perceived as "sexually nonnormative or deviant" in Han representations.[31] In *Forbidden Kiss*, the filmmaker portrays Qiang women as sexually submissive and inexpressive: even when Yuanni and Jack have confirmed their feelings for each other, Yuanni pushes Jack away when the latter is trying to kiss her. When Jack tries desperately to find the woman who saved his life by feeding him the life-saving grass juice, everyone in the village turns him down for fear of discovering that a woman in their own household did the forbidden deed. The imagined sexual submissiveness and passiveness of Qiang women are projected by the Han Chinese American filmmaker as important attributes to the sexual and cultural pristineness of a minority people: when Majia, a Qiang man, suspects that his own sister kissed Jack to save his life, he becomes so enraged that he accuses his sister of "ruining the purity of us Qiang people!"

The film's obsession with cultural and sexual purity is telling of post-socialist China's anxiety over its cultural integrity in the face of rapid national reform and globalization. In post-socialist China, the Marxist state ideology has lost its cohesive power to hold the national community into a coherent, teleological singular entity as it did during the high socialist era (1950s to 1970s); as a result, China is eager to fill the moral vacuum left by the fading importance of Marxism in ordinary people's lives.[32] The market economy has created more social strata and a diversification of values. The rapid economic and social transformation has further undermined the traditional lifestyles of many communities and relocated numerous urban and rural residents for urbanization and industrialization projects.[33] Under these circumstances, like in many advanced capitalist countries, Chinese modernity tends to search for authenticity and meaning in another time and space: it "constructs and appropriates a distant non-modern world and puts it on display in museum-like fashion," reclaiming a gradually vanishing identity, or traditional values and cultural authenticity.[34] In *Forbidden Kiss*, the distant non-modern world of Qiang people is romanticized as a "museum" that preserves the purity of Chinese culture, as women there try hard to guard their chastity and people hold fast to old traditions with all their will.

Therefore, the acceleration of the spatial and temporal transformation of post-socialist China has been compressed into the imaginary space of one minority village: the minority village is imagined to be frozen in time and serves as a rich reservoir of China's real or fictional moral and cultural values. Despite Taoping Qiang Village's proven long contact with the outside world and the relatively "free" courtship styles exhibited by villagers—young Qiang people frequently engage in social gatherings to find their mates and date just like their Han counterparts—the village is romanticized as a culturally and sexually pure land to countervail the forces of modernization and development, as such forces plague China's very sense of cultural integrity.

Here, "purity" bespeaks the representational capacity of ethnic minorities to perform the spatio-temporal and gendered "other" of modernity: if modernity is characterized by a masculine progressiveness, aggressiveness, and forward-looking spirit, then minority people and culture in cinematic representations complement modernity with their feminine submissiveness, adherence to old traditions, and their preservation of an uncontaminated self-enclosed space.

This complementary role of modernity performed by ethnic minorities is complicated when the force of the global is introduced into this film. In the remainder of this section, I will analyze how Taoping is depicted as a locale of conflicts and tensions when the ethnic encounters the global, and what such conflicts and tensions mean for a China caught between diverse forces in the globalizing world.

Various cultural critics have pointed out that in China's modern history, there are always two "others" the nation has to face: the internal others of China's non-Han peoples, and the external others of foreign countries, or foreigners.[35] In the age of Western and Japanese colonial occupation in China from the mid-1800s to the mid-1900s, the foreign "others" made urgent the question of the territorial integrity of China, while the domestic/internal "others" inspired Chinese nationalist thinkers to draw the boundaries of the ethnic make-up of the Chinese nation. In the reform or post-socialist era, while Western colonial concerns in China have faded, the nation's increasing business and cultural interactions with Western countries have created a new sense of crisis: by encountering the foreign, China "swerves among territorial, historical, cultural, linguistic and ethnic registers of nationhood," negotiating not one, but several forces of influence as it attempts to maintain and, at times, re-create its national identity.[36]

This complex encounter is depicted in *Forbidden Kiss* through the American student Jack's uneasy interactions with Qiang villagers and the clash of values experienced by both parties. Despite Jack's intention of doing research on Qiang architecture, he frequently violates ethnic traditions and intrudes upon both the physical and cultural spaces of the minority village. One of the most crisis-ridden encounters between Jack and local villagers is when he and Yuanni dispute the legends and religious beliefs of the Qiang people. When Yuanni enthusiastically tells Jack about how the Qiang worship the stone because all their houses are built in stone and local people believe that an ancient deity made stones fall from the sky to help the Qiang construct their homes, Jack laughs it off by saying "Unfortunately, scientists do not think in the same way." Jack then launches into a lecture about how tectonic shifts created the mountain ranges on earth, trying to correct Yuanni's "naïve" understanding of the natural environment that she lives in. This greatly enrages Yuanni, who turns her back to Jack and says to him: "You keep your belief; I keep mine. I'm done!" (Figure 20).

Elsewhere in the film, Jack blunders and offends villagers many times: he insists on finding the girl who kissed him to save his life, making everyone

Figure 20. Film still from *Forbidden Kiss.*

nervous and embarrassed, as kissing a man before marriage would have serious consequences for a young woman; he exchanges gifts with a local Qiang young woman Caiyun, misleading the latter into his romantic inclinations and steals a kiss from her; he also upsets the men in the village when he freely flirts with or befriends Qiang women, causing distrust and jealousy among villagers and breaking their hitherto harmonious relationships with each other. In all of these instances, Jack is portrayed as reckless and ignorant, and the Qiang are always on the right side: they are offended by Jack's callousness and punish his violation of local rules when they alienate him or prevent him from going to community gatherings. Finally, the villagers banish Jack and Jack leaves the village.

In this film, Jack is a symbolic representative of the foreign other who bullied China for a hundred years and finally experiences China's revenge. As Louisa Schein observes, the internal others, or ethnic minorities, can represent the "hope for recovery" for the Chinese national self threated by many decades of fraught encounters with Western cultures in modern history.[37] In the modern era, mainly during the twentieth and early twenty-first centuries, whenever China encounters the West, it is almost always the West's rules that China must obey. From entering the WTO and agreeing to the rules of the free market to numerous other encounters, China seems to follow the order established by the liberal West. Yet in *Forbidden Kiss*, this political and cultural hierarchy is reversed. The internal other (the Qiang) is malleable and serves not only as a surrogate of China's hundred years of humiliation in the face of a Western-dominated world order but also offers hope for recovering

China's dignity. By playing the role of a moral authority who punishes the foreign other, the internal other (the Qiang) provides an ideologically convenient solution and redeeming value to the complex and multifaceted encounters between China and the West in modern history.

Instead of portraying Jack, the Westerner, as an epistemological and cultural authority, *Forbidden Kiss* reverses the hierarchy between the ethnic and the global by depicting the Qiang as the cultural superiors: Jack is disliked and becomes almost an outcast in the village, when people of all ages start to question his intentions and resent him for challenging the sexual and cultural codes of the village. No one in the village is willing to accommodate Jack by changing existing rules and traditions; rather, Jack must constantly adjust to Qiang people's beliefs and preferences, which proves difficult and painful for this American young man. Jack's fate in the village bears striking resemblances to Western missionaries like Thomas Torrance and David Crockett Graham mentioned earlier in the chapter—both Torrance and Graham were arrested in Pengshan County, Sichuan, for grave robbing and excavating artifacts in the province.[38] The didactic tone of punishing foreigners for violating ethnic cultural rules in *Forbidden Kiss* therefore strikes a postcolonial chord, even though the romantic union between Jack and Yuanni by the end of the film flattens an otherwise deeply historical critique of Western imperialism in southwest China.

From Figure 21, we can also see that when Yuanni and Jack engage in their dispute, Yuanni stands above Jack and criticizes him for his positivist, deconstructionist explanations of Qiang myths. Yuanni occupies a cultural and moral high ground, as Jack has to look up to her and admit his mistake. Here, Yuanni, the Qiang woman, is depicted as an authoritative figure defending ethnic traditions by articulating the historical and cultural richness of what Western researchers like Jack deem as "unscientific." As she stands at the gate leading into a Qiang house, she becomes a symbolic guardian who carefully protects not only the cultural beliefs but also the physical spaces and territories of a small minority village. The spaces and territories in Taoping represent the cultural values and physical territories of China itself—the narrator of the film, the Old Papa of the village, mentions that the conflicts between Jack and the Qiang are "conflicts between Western and Eastern [Chinese] culture," unequivocally referring to the Qiang as a surrogate for China itself.

By portraying Jack as a helpless and powerless man and Yuanni as an authoritative and courageous woman, the film reverses the power hierarchy between the ethnic and the global by letting Yuanni occupy an epistemologically and morally advantageous place when she encounters the foreign other. In portraying minority women as powerful guardians of valuable traditions and unflinching contestants of the foreign other, *Forbidden Kiss* challenges the stereotypical image of minority women as socially submissive and culturally and sexually exploited in previous cinematic and cultural productions in China. This earlier image is well discussed by scholars like Dru Gladney and Louisa Schein. While Gladney believes that the exoticization and eroticization of minority women serve to commodify them and feed the Han voyeuristic and consumerist desire, Schein analyzes the "infantilizing and trivializing" tendency of both artistic depictions and real-life Han encounters with minority women, which often lead to the objectification of the latter.[39]

My analysis of Yuanni in *Forbidden Kiss* shows that newer cinematic productions have transcended this stock image of minority women as exoticized and erotized objects in Han cultural imagination and have endowed minority cultures and minority women with more subjectivity and cultural articulateness. The submissive status of minority women is transformed into a powerful and generative force that helps defend the cultural integrity and moral wholesomeness of not only the ethnic, but also the national. Yuanni in *Forbidden Kiss* epitomizes this new cinematic tendency in post-socialist China and creates a new image of minority women in Chinese cinema: minority women like Yuanni embody China's strong desire to guard its own traditions, defend its values, and challenge the foreign other after a hundred years of humiliation and subjugation by Western rules. Despite its romanticization of Qiang traditions, *Forbidden Kiss* opens up a new discursive space where the ethnic speaks through the national to challenge the global. This film thus broadens the representational power of ethnic minorities in Chinese cinema and art: minority peoples are imagined as the guardians of "traditions" in China. Yet traditions no longer stand for backwardness and evoke a sense of shame; rather, they form powerful articulations of the national identity and help the nation negotiate with the global.

Ethnographic Reflections: Visual Culture and Image-Making in a Minority Village

The fact that *Forbidden Kiss* was made in Taoping Qiang Village in consultation with local villagers contributes significantly to its cinematic perspective and empowering tone. In this last section of the chapter, I will discuss how the media-created images of Taoping interact with minority people's daily lives to forge a new relationship between people and place in contemporary China, particularly in ethnic minority regions. We will delve into the power of visual media, particularly photography and cinema, in reconfiguring ethnic awareness and constructing a sense of shared identity for Taoping villagers.

The story of how the transnational production team made *Forbidden Kiss* was narrated to me by Ms. Long, a well-respected and influential Qiang entrepreneurial and cultural figure, also a native of Taoping Qiang Village. Ms. Long has been ardently promoting her village and Qiang culture in China for the past twenty years.

According to Ms. Long, *Forbidden Kiss* bases its storyline, particularly that of the heroine Yuanni, on Ms. Long's own life experiences and her legacy among the Qiang people (personal communication). Like Yuanni, Ms. Long is bilingually fluent in the Qiang language and Mandarin and is extremely articulate. Ms. Long occupies a relatively privileged space as one of the most educated in the village and serves as a "cultural broker" who mediates between the local, the national, and the global in promoting minority cultures.

Now in her mid-forties, Ms. Long was born and raised in Taoping Qiang Village and was regarded as the "Beauty of the Village" (*zhaihua* 寨花) in her twenties and thirties. She first introduced this village to tourists in the early 1990s when she organized a group of Qiang young women to sing and dance on the roadside to draw the attention of tourists. Ms. Long later represented the Qiang in the National Communist Youth League Representatives Congress (*tuandaihui* 团代会) in 1995 and was met by the then-president of China, Jiang Zemin (personal communication). Ms. Long's home is full of enlarged, framed photographs showing her meetings with both China's national leaders and international cultural officials, such as UNESCO representatives who came to Taoping (Figure 21).

Ms. Long told me how she accompanied Henry, the UNESCO official, to tour Taoping and explained to him the architectural wonders and two-millennia history of her native village. This story is somewhat adapted into *Forbidden Kiss* as Yuanni helps Jack conduct his research. For both Yuanni and Ms. Long, being minority women entails a sense of pride and empowerment, as they can use their cultural competency and linguistic talents to engage with the global and articulate for the political and cultural place of their home village both on the national and international levels.

Ms. Long and other Taoping villagers provided important help for the production of *Forbidden Kiss*, such as lending their Qiang festive costumes to

Figure 21. Photograph from Ms. Long's traditional Qiang home. Ms. Long (*far left*) meets with Jiang Zeming, the former president of China, with other ethnic minority representatives. Photograph by author.

the crew. In turn, the production of this and other films have helped construct Taoping residents' identity as the ethnically, culturally, and entrepreneurially conscious minorities in contemporary China. As Jenny Chio, an anthropologist of Chinese ethnic tourism, suggests, mass media images play a key role in shaping contemporary minority villagers' perspectives on place, tourism, and, I argue, minority identity itself.[40] Chio suggests that ethnic minorities, especially those in southwest China, have increasingly resorted to visual means, such as taking photographs and shooting short documentaries, to record their life and express their relationship to the places they inhabit.[41] The minority villagers that Chio studies in Guizhou and Guangxi also manage the images of local landscapes to ensure the perfect photographic potential of different scenes, catering to the tourist gaze and showing their "civilized (*wenming*) behavior and modern attitudes."[42]

In Taoping, we can discern a similar phenomenon of how minority villagers are trying to make their village look good to the tourists and the world. But instead of examining how villagers manage the look of natural landscapes as does Chio, I focus on how minority villagers learn to look at and appreciate the cultural landscape by participating in and observing film productions in the village.

Ms. Long said she and other Taoping residents marveled at how the cinematography of films such as *Design of Death* and *Forbidden Kiss* revealed the beauty of their native village to them:

> When the film crews were working in Taoping, we all went to watch. I was amazed at how wonderfully the cinematographer captured the allure of Taoping: the architecture, the underground water system . . . everything appeared more charming in the video cameras of the crew. The villagers were saying, "How come we never saw our village this way? How did the film crews make our village look so attractive?" (personal communication)

In Taoping, visual practices such as filmmaking have shaped minority people's perceptions of their spatial and cultural surroundings, allowing them to imagine "possible lives" lived with the power of media.[43] By observing the making of films and videos by outside artists and directors, villagers are gradually trained to look at their surroundings from the eyes of an observer—more precisely, from the eyes of the artist or the tourist who sees the village from an aesthetic perspective.

This learned awareness of the cultural and aesthetic value of their native villages[44] has been transformed into part of the Qiang villagers' self-identity and has become a viable part of their lived reality, particularly as a way for villagers to stimulate a visually-driven local tourism economy.

In Ms. Long's home, as well as the homes of many other Taoping residents, villagers have photographic galleries where they hang the photographs of themselves with various film crews, local or national political figures, or simply family portraits and festival captions. Villagers use these photographs to entertain both themselves and their visitors, as they are eager to share the stories behind the photographs with tourists (Figure 22).

Ms. Long told me that photography became a popular means of self-expression in the village after some Han photographers first started to capture the beauty of Taoping and shared their photographs with villagers in the 1990s. "Sometimes these Han photographers would ask us to pose for them. After we saw their work, we were pleased. More and more people wanted to have themselves and their homes photographed, and photography gradually became a vogue in Taoping." Ms. Long remembered with delight how

Figure 22. Tourists sitting inside a Qiang house open for tourism. Photograph by author.

photography became a major method to record life and express identities for Taoping villagers. Photography as a modern visual media facilitates the villagers' new relationship with their village: for a people saturated in a rich oral tradition, photography allows Taoping villagers to "furnish instant history, instant sociology, instant participation,"[45] as it helps them visualize their environment and their experiences, making and recording quotidian history and participating in their own life-worlds with a keener sense of presence and cultural ownership. In other words, photography and cinematography have endowed minority villagers in Taoping with an ethnic pride and "image solidarity" that was previously unknown to them.

For Qiang villagers, visual technologies like filmmaking and photography help them perceive their village and its visual appeal as modern observers. Such images and spectacles are then transformed into the kind of cultural capital that is desired in the minority regions of China: these images and spectacles please the tourist gaze and draw tourist revenue, with landscapes of aesthetic beauty and exotic experience."[46] The photo galleries, together with other visual materials, such as the billboard featuring different films produced in Taoping shown earlier in the chapter, have attracted many tourists and conveyed the aesthetic allure of the village to visitors. The images have also helped Taoping villagers articulate and narrate their cultural traditions to visitors. In other words, visual media such as photography and cinematography have chiseled a sense of tempo-spatial togetherness for Taoping villagers, ushering in a sense of solidary around image-making and image-management that was never before possible in a previously remote village.

Unlike purely commercial images circulated on the internet, images and photographs in minority people's homes are not devoid of content and meaning. Guy Debord criticizes the alienated, often commercialized images floating in the "society of the spectacle," which are decontextualized, impersonal, and serve to negate real-life experience.[47] Because minority people's photographs are rooted in the environment in which they were produced and are often accompanied by personal stories and explanations, they create a "fascinating, ancient and mysterious intimacy between presence and representation," between the presence of villagers and their lived reality and the representational power of portrait photography to retain the aura and authenticity of such lived experience.[48]

In Taoping Qiang Village, I often see tourists curiously gazing into the photographs in Qiang villagers' homes, asking questions about the context of the photographs, and eliciting stories and episodes of contemporary minority life when villagers sit down to talk about these photographs. Enlivened by narration, these portrait photographs create a social space where tourists and residents engage not in purely commercial transactions but meaningful conversations and interactions. Tourists ask villagers where and when the photographs were taken, who the photographed were, and the relationship among the people photographed. Sometimes, a story about the photographs would morph into a more in-depth exchange about the recent history and changes of the village, and villagers and tourists engage in thought-provoking conversations about Qiang culture and life. Even though such interactions may be fleeting, and they end the moment tourists leave the Qiang village, such interactions allow minority villagers to articulate their life stories and experience. These interactions also allow tourists to go beyond consuming the images for their aesthetic value, allowing tourists to learn about minority life and traditions, being educated about the lived reality of the non-Han peoples of China.

Therefore, on the site of Taoping Qiang Village, visual media such as portrait photography and film stills retain the ritualistic value of art that Walter Benjamin argues for in "The Work of Art in the Age of Mechanical Reproduction." Because they are deeply embedded in a historically rich and socially meaningful environment, photography and film images in Taoping re-enact the earliest ritualistic function of art, creating a space of sacredness, reverence, and authentic existence for both villagers and tourists.[49] This is not to say that such space is devoid of commercial activities—after all, tourists have to buy a ticket to enter the historic Taoping village and many of them stay and shop for souvenirs in the recently built New Taoping Village after visiting the historical Old Taoping Village. Yet, by eliciting stories and experiences from the villagers and enacting interactions between villagers and visitors, the visual media in Taoping creates affective environments that facilitate minority communities' articulation of their identities. As minority villagers tell visitors their stories, they construct a narrative world that connects their past, present, and future, enfolded in but ultimately transcending the walled space of the Qiang residences. The visual materials, mainly photography and film stills, in Qiang villagers' homes help combat an otherwise more rampant pace of commercialization and a consumerist appropriation of minority cultures in contemporary China.

The rich interpersonal environments created by visual technologies in Taoping betray the double-edged effect of tourism on ethnic identities in China today. Ethnic tourism has been fast developing in China since the 1980s. The Chinese government encourages ethnic tourism to both stimulate regional economic development and strengthen the image of China as a multicultural nation-state.[50] The development of ethnic tourism in various multiethnic provinces in China has meant that ethnic identity has assumed economic values in addition to political and cultural values.[51] As Bai Zhihong observes in Yunnan, a multiethnic province in southwest China neighboring Sichuan, the development of ethnic tourism has motivated minority people to "appropriate state-defined categories and re-shape them into the repertoire they desire."[52] In other words, the development of ethnic tourism in contemporary China has produced a fertile socio-economic ground for minority groups to re-articulate their cultural traditions and create discursive spaces to make claims about their ethnic identities and reinforce their ethnic consciousness in the nation.

One way minority groups in China make assertions about their ethnic identities through tourism is by creating "tourism imaginaries," or the images and ideas "that people have in their minds about places as tourist destinations."[53] As we have seen, visual media, especially photography and filmmaking, helps Taoping villagers create the tourism imaginary of Taoping as a historically rich, culturally complex, and aesthetically appealing locale not too far from metropolitan China. The fact that several critically acclaimed and commercially successful blockbusters have been shot in Taoping makes this village a desired destination for China's urban middle-class tourists seeking to experience a different culture not too far from home. In other words, by working with filmmakers and various visual media, Taoping villagers have created the right amount of "exoticness" and crafted profitable images for the tourist imaginary of Taoping—such images are attractive to Han tourists without invoking too much geographical or cultural strangeness.

By taking advantage of visual media, villagers in Taoping enact and affirm their ethnic identities. Images and image-making help mediate a minority village's relationship to a fast-changing nation and the outside world, and they facilitate minority villagers' renewed relationship with both national and global cultural and economic forces. Yet, the development of visually-driven tourism is not an equalizer: we can observe many class differences and wealth gap within and beyond Taoping, and tourism only exasperates the gap.

In recent years, more Qiang elites and entrepreneurs exhibit a strong desire to record their villages in photography and cinematography, and they sometimes hire Han directors and local filmmakers. Qiang elites like Ms. Long frequently travel back and forth between their native villages and Chengdu, Sichuan's provincial capital, to do business and leverage financial and political resources for the development and representation of their native villages.

In addition to Ms. Long, another prominent example of successful bilingual, bicultural Qiang elites who traverse major cities and their native villages is Mr. Zhou, a respected and well-to-do Qiang entrepreneur. Mr. Zhou is well respected both in his home village and in the culture industry in Sichuan. He relayed to me that he worked as a main editor in an official TV channel in Chengdu for years, gaining experience and insights in branding different cultural and natural sight-seeing spots in Sichuan. This background has enabled Mr. Zhou to form an extensive professional network with the culture industry in Sichuan. Mr. Zhou gradually morphed into an entrepreneur himself. He has been funding many Qiang-related cultural and educational causes in Sichuan and was gathering a film crew in Chengdu to make a documentary for his native village.[54] Mr. Zhou believes that making a documentary would help his home village become visible and help advance his plan to develop his village into a cultural hub for future tourism purposes. "This is my village. It is culturally prominent. I want to preserve its beauty and make it seen," asserts Mr. Zhou. Like Ms. Long, Mr. Zhou has strong professional and business ties in Chengdu and is well known in the world of cultural productions in this provincial capital. Ms. Long and Mr. Zhou travel comfortably between two worlds—one of rural ethnic Sichuan and one of the urban center of Chengdu, a major metropolitan area in west China.

The minority native village thus becomes a space of imagination, re-creation and negotiation in media productions and villagers' daily lives. The translocal tendency for minority elites like Ms. Long and Mr. Zhou to simultaneously occupy more than one social and geographical space testifies to "the native place as a fluid place of identification" in contemporary China.[55] Rather than being a static and fixed place, the native village becomes a web of spatial and social relations both within and beyond its immediate space: translocality means that "home itself becomes complicated, its roots to a single locality multiplied to a network of localities."[56]

Taoping Qiang Village has become such a native village that allows minority elites to travel back and forth between the village and the metropolitan centers, being highly mobile as they navigate an extensive web of professional and business networks to bring resources, opportunities, and visibility to their home regions. These minority elites epitomize a "translocal China" where the roots of home extend into a wider geographical and political space and where personal, professional, and ethnic identities traverse the boundaries of fixed locations. Translocal minority elites make the boundaries between the urban and the rural, mainstream and minority porous and volatile. Indeed, translocal minority elites challenge existing boundaries and draw new ones as they shape new realities of ethnic representations in China.

Yet image-making, by empowering some of the minority communities and giving them more social capital, also disempowers others. As Faye Ginsburg points out, the question of who controls the "production and distribution of imagery" is central to the question of power.[57] In Taoping, some of the families and individuals less apt at the technologies of image-making and image-management have not been able to partake of the economic and social opportunities afforded by Taoping's growing tourism. For example, even though many households have opened guesthouses in Taoping, certain guesthouses are more popular than others. Some households I visited with fewer tourists were plain-looking and devoid of the photographic allure that makes Ms. Long's home popular. Villagers who run guesthouses must learn to present aesthetically appealing and artistically tasteful spaces to attract Han tourists. They also need to be business-savvy and good at entertaining urban guests.

As such, we can conclude that image-mediated mobility—that is, social mobility and geographic mobility generated by one's ability to manage and create desired images of ethnicity—is profoundly shaping minority life in China today. By traversing between the local and the national (and sometimes even international) spaces, minority elites such as Mr. Zhou and Ms. Long enjoy a significant degree of mobility and form a new class of ethnic entrepreneurs in China. These ethnic elites should not be simply regarded as China's "other"—they are linguistically, entrepreneurially and culturally savvy and live comfortably both as ethnic minorities and successful Chinese entrepreneurs and professionals. They are active practitioners of modern technology and eagerly constructing multiethnic, multicultural spaces of human interactions to dislocate ethnicity from the home village, creating multiple nodes of professional, economic, and cultural identities that challenge the image of minority groups as passive recipients of national transformations and modernization projects.

Conclusion

In this chapter, I have explored how minority villages such as Taoping Qiang Village embody the cultural anxiety of a fast-transforming China and the crisis-ridden encounters between China and the West. By privileging the ethnic and the local, post-socialist cinema challenges "Chinese culture" as a coherent and singular concept and manifests a diversity of cultural, linguistic, ethnic, and regional values. Taoping Qiang Village, as an actual minority village, takes on symbolic meanings in national and transnational cinematic representations. It becomes a site where contested ideas of the nation and China's encounter with the global are articulated. The village is at times exoticized (like in *Design of Death*) and at times symbolized (like in *Forbidden Kiss*). The minority village is sometimes represented as the alternative space of the nation and sometimes portrayed as the very embodiment of the nation. The rich representational capacities of Taoping Qiang Village show us how deeply embedded China's national imagination is in minority spaces. Such imagination is multi-dimensional and intricate, and minority villages like Taoping will likely continue to figure into the Chinese nation's reflective search for its contemporary identity in a globalizing context.

I have ended this chapter by offering ethnographic insights into how image-making, initiated by Han Chinese and international artists and directors, have become a viable way for minority villagers to imagine and construct their identities in the tourism space of Taoping Qiang Village. This ethnographic account supplements earlier sections of cinematic analysis and engages with minority people as the *producers and creators* of images to mediate their relationships to both their own living environment and globalization. I have demonstrated that representation does not stop at the level of discourse and the media, but permeates minority people's daily lives. In tourism activities, villagers in Taoping carve out a space of articulation, social engagement, and mobility in their narration and re-creation of the images of themselves and their home village. By contrast, this process has left out villagers who are not good at producing "charming" images and has created new class divides in Taoping. For readers interested in learning more about the perils of commercializing minority cultures and the class and gender ramifications of turning minority villages into touristic spectacles, Chapter 5 of this book provides literary accounts of the dramatic transformations in rural ethnic China penned by minority writers. For now, we have witnessed how the technologies and abilities to craft desired images of the minority village, particularly through photography and cinema, have both produced solidarity among Qiang villagers and created uneven social power structures, particularly as minority villagers seek to re-imagine their symbolic and real place in contemporary China. As China continues to encounter the West, divergent forces converge to shape what it means to be both ethnic minority and Chinese. Visual culture and visual technologies will continue to shape the imaginary contours of ethnic identities in China and beyond.

CHAPTER 4

The Run-away Minority Bride

Fluid Indigeneity and Ethnographic Poetics in Qiang Indigenous Cinema

In Chapter 3, we journeyed through the world of representing the Qiang "native village" in popular cinema: the Qiang village is constructed as a site of romantic and ethnic contestations in cross-cultural encounters and as a locus for the imagination of an "alternative" Chinese culture in the eyes of ethnic Han directors across the Pacific. The end of Chapter 3 tapped into the visual representation of ethnic, familial, and local identities through the medium of photographic galleries popular in Qiang villagers' homes. The construction of these identities on the walls of local villagers' homes presents itself as an emergent domain of indigenous consciousness: the ability to curate aesthetically appealing images of minority lifeworlds has allowed many Qiang villagers to develop tourism right at home and to represent themselves to Han visitors and render their life experience in visible and meaningful ways.

This chapter shifts the focus away from the Han or mainstream representation of Qiang culture to examine how indigenous cinema produced in the Qiang regions negotiate ethnic identities through navigating the visual and social spaces of "cultural hybridity." Particularly, this chapter joins anthropological theories with insights from cultural studies and cinema studies to understand the cultural motifs, community concerns, and stylistic innovations of twenty-first-century Qiang cinematic productions. I unveil the anthropological impulses of contemporary indigenous filmmakers in negotiating minority traditions vis-à-vis state-led modernization projects and developmental agendas in China.

By looking closely at two recent cinematic works—one documentary and one feature film—produced in the Qiang region of Sichuan, I develop the theory of "ethnographic poetics" to understand the aesthetic elements and social messages of minority cinema in today's China. Unlike the romantic and utopic imagination of the Qiang village as a pristine site of "other Chinas" with antiquated customs and exotic spectacles, which we saw in *Forbidden Kiss* and *Design of Death*, both examined in Chapter 3, Qiang indigenous cinema is characterized by an ethnographic urge: by engaging in detailed visual and cultural representation of Qiang traditions in flux, indigenous and local Han filmmakers strive to reconstruct ethnic communities by critically examining the conflicts and promises of intercultural and interethnic encounters. Instead of launching into wholesale attack against "external" forces, such as national and regional developmental projects, indigenous Qiang and local Han filmmakers in the Qiang regions display nuanced understandings of the trends of cultural interactions, analyzing both the lure and the danger of development and globalization with an inventive visual language and acute cultural sensibilities.

In this chapter, I theorize "ethnographic poetics" as the visual, cultural, textual, and affective engagement with ethnographic methodologies and narrative powers. It has become an important mode of expression for indigenous artists, filmmakers, and activists. As this chapter will reveal, the expressive power of ethnographic modes of narration goes beyond the conventional association between "ethnography" and "documentary." In other words, in addition to recording culture ("film as data or evidence"[1]), ethnographic poetics can be deployed in feature films and imaginary accounts. Ethnographic poetics can transcend the realist stamp of ethnography and ethnographic documentary and be highly lyrical, explorative, and suggestive. It is important to recognize indigenous artists' creative use of "ethnography"—no longer reserved as an epistemologically privileged site for outside researchers to make sense of local communities, ethnographic modes of expression are flexible artistic and cultural vessels that empower minority communities to contest notions of culture and ethnicity.

The development of ethnographic poetics among indigenous artists and filmmakers is not an overnight or single-handed phenomenon. Rather, it involves complex processes of identity negotiations, innovative use of local ethnic elements, and most importantly, an inventive mixing of cultural inspirations. This last dimension of cultural hybridity—creatively and freely drawing cultural elements from different traditions—are characteristic of both contemporary Qiang life and the artistic creations of indigenous film in the Qiang regions.

In the rest of the chapter, we will immerse in the world of Qiang indigenous cinema in the broader context of global multicultural and indigenous cinema. I will demonstrate how Qiang indigenous cinema exemplifies ethnographic filmmaking as "relational practice"[2]—it is a process of real and symbolic collaborations, mutual (mis)understandings, and negotiations between indigenous Qiang and Han actors and factors. In this sense, "ethnographic poetics" becomes more than just an artistic medium and morphs into a site of cultural "thought experiment" as indigenous filmmakers and communities construe the future of ethnicity and identity. It is the aesthetics and ethics of collaborative filmmaking that contributes to the formation of indigenous discourses in China's ethnic minority regions today.

Collaborative Documentary and Fluid Indigeneity

As the Qiang communities are coming into increasingly multifaceted contact with other groups in and outside of China, it is important for us to place the study of Qiang indigenous cinema in the global trend of indigenous visual culture. In their innovative study that shifts the scholarly attention from Hollywood's representation of Native Americans to how Native Americans themselves engage in film watching and filmmaking, Eric L. Buffalohead and M. Elise Marubbio broach the critical concept of "visual sovereignty." Buffalohead and Marubbio argue:

> Indigenous communities and filmmakers globally respond through film against representations of them as exotic and vanishing peoples, as innocent or dangerous, or as colonized by more advanced settler cultures.[3]

Buffalohead and Marubbio suggest that indigenous communities use film as a response to external cultural representation and an assertion of minorities' self-representation, particularly as minority groups combat stereotypical and static images of themselves in mainstream media. The idea of film as cultural response goes hand in hand with these scholars' concept of "visual sovereignty." Buffalohead and Marrubbio establish the concepts of "cinema of sovereignty" and "visual sovereignty" as follows:

> Both terms promote the belief in Indigenous people's right to represent themselves and their histories in ways that reflect their cultures, needs, and ways of knowing and telling . . . They focus on reversing the effects of colo-

> nialism by reclaiming land and resources, cultural knowledge, languages, and Indigenous governance locally within countries and globally across nations.[4]

In other words, cinematic and visual sovereignty constitutes a cultural, epistemological, and even political realm for indigenous communities to assert their voices and articulate indigenous worldviews, reversing the cultural stereotype of indigenous groups as the passive and quiet other receiving the gaze and influence from external, often dominant, forces.

Similarly, scholars of indigenous cinema in Canada have observed that "[at] the same time as they work with narrative and aesthetics," indigenous creative and artistic forms "are an active part of transformations taking place on the level of know-how and knowledges."[5] Indigenous creative forms are not simply artistic innovations, but carry with them epistemological powers that transform indigenous groups' relationship to other communities and facilitate the articulation of indigenous groups' ancestral memories and epistemic contestations.

Echoing the flourishing trend of indigenous cinema elsewhere in the world, in the Qiang regions of Sichuan province today, there has emerged a new wave of collaborative documentary filmmaking. Here, "collaborative" means collaborations between ethnic Han and Qiang artists, villagers, and cultural workers. Collaborative filmmaking emphasizes the narrative priority of indigenous experiences and stories. Furthermore, indigenous storytelling and worldviews shape the narrative structure and aesthetic choices of films, even though both minority and Han people may participate in the process of filmmaking.

In this section of the chapter, I will investigate an important recent documentary produced in the Qiang regions of Sichuan, *Ten Years in Search of the Qiang* (*Shinian xunqiang* 十年寻羌).[6] This is a documentary directed by an ethnic Han artist, Gao Tunzi (高屯子). In this film, Gao traces the migratory journey of over 700 villagers from Xige and Zhitai Qiang Villages, who were mobilized by the local government to relocate from their home villages to a tea-growing area in western Sichuan following the devastating 2008 earthquake. This 82-minute-long film was initially released in 2019 and has been widely disseminated in many international film festivals, such as the Shanghai Film Festival and the Fifth West Lake International Documentary Film Festival in 2021 held in Hangzhou, China. Since its initial release, *Ten Years* has garnered many international accolades: it became the winner of the Cultural Heritage Award of the 16th Universe Multicultural Film Festival held in Los

Angeles in 2019 and received the Golden Award from the Third Beijing Ethnographic Film Festival in China (*Zhongguo minzuzhi jilupian xueshuzhan* 中国民族志纪录片学术展), organized by the Chinese National Museum of Ethnology.

Even though *Ten Years* was directed and realized by a Han artist, it demonstrates what I call "fluid indigeneity," as the conception, production, and reception of the film involves extensive collaborations between the Han director Gao Tunzi and the Qiang villagers that he filmed. Gao was born and raised in Sichuan's Aba Tibetan and Qiang Autonomous Prefecture and considers himself an indigene, as he expressed to me during an interview. Gao not only grew up in the Qiang religions of Sichuan, but he has worked as a photographer and writer in the Prefecture for over three decades, widely publishing photographic and journalistic accounts about the natural landscape and ethnic traditions of the Prefecture.[7] In this sense, he is an indigenous artist whose aesthetic practice and social consciousness are profoundly shaped by the land and history of the minority religions of western Sichuan. Moreover, this film exemplifies a strong indigenous aesthetics and indigenous consciousness that embodies the spirit of the ethnographic film as a "relational practice"[8]—the film not only reflects the collaborations and relations between the director and the locals, but also highlights the Qiang villagers' changing relations to their living environments, socio-cultural-religious worlds, and a fast-developing China.

Before we delve into the content of this film, I would like to say a few words about using the concept of "indigeneity" in the context of China Studies. An earlier generation of scholars in China Studies tended to regard "ethnic indigeneity" as irrelevant or unproductive to the study of China's *shaoshu minzu*, because the Chinese state rarely uses the concept of indigeneity to refer to China's ethnic minorities, and China's *shaoshu minzu* hardly had an official presence in global indigenous events and causes.[9] Indeed, as Chapters 1 and 2 of this book discussed, modern China's longstanding policy of a unitary, polyethnic nationhood denotes that the different *shaoshu minzu* are all part and parcel of a larger *Zhonghua minzu* (Chinese people) sharing the same territory. This national policy and the historically intermingled (real or imaginary) relationship among many of China's ethnic groups makes it hard to directly apply contemporary Western concepts such as indigeneity to the experience of China's *shaoshu minzu*.

Despite the lack of an official language and state policies to address them as "indigenous groups," the *shaoshu minzu* of today's China are undoubt-

Figure 23. Poster for *Ten Years in Search of the Qiang*. https://www.westlakeidf.com/en/movie/604

edly engaged in cultural and economic practices akin to those exercised by many indigenous groups of the world. As I have argued elsewhere, Qiang cultural entrepreneurs and writers resort to "the topographical features and cultural landmarks in Sichuan [to] articulate the geographical rootedness of the Qiang, pronouncing the Qiang to be the originary (indigenous) residents of . . . Sichuan and China."[10] Moreover, as Michael Hathaway notes, "indigeneity" in China is less of a rigid political classification and more of a "social fact" characterized by the dynamic connections the *shaoshu minzu* create with "land, wealth, [and] political power."[11]

Hathaway's idea of indigeneity as a social fact and social relation is complicated by the fact that sometimes ethnic Han actors participate in minority cultural causes, such as the case with *Ten Years*. Han artists' and cultural workers' participation in minority causes creates a porous space of indigeneity and engenders sites of cultural hybridity. In light of these recent developments, I propose the concept of "fluid indigeneity" to refer to how the concept and practice of indigeneity traverses established ethnic boundaries to allow for fruitful collaborations, unexpected discoveries, and ultimately, creative identity-making strategies as minority and majority forces join hands.

Ten Years in Search of the Qiang opens with the Qiang's origin myth by introducing the discussion between a young man and a Qiang elder regarding the origin of the human species. The opening, as well as the entire film, foregrounds indigenous episteme. The young man tells the elder that according to Darwin, "man comes from monkey." The elder mistakes Darwin for a local schoolteacher. When asked about how the Qiang shaman accounts for the origin of humans, the elderly Qiang man recounts the origin myth in the Qiang shamanistic traditions. The camera spins through a long scroll of the colorful and vivid Qiang pictographic epic, which narrates the legendary story about the marriage between a celestial goddess (Mujiezhu 木姐珠) and a monkey-headed man, Dou'anzhu (斗安珠). Douanzhu helps spread the seeds of crops and thus agriculture in the human world. The scroll takes up the entire scene for over two minutes, immersing the viewer in the visual symbols of the Qiang indigenous worldviews (Figures 24 and 25). This long take culminates in a final scene of the Qiang shaman, known as the *shibi* in the Qiang language: an immensely important figure in transmitting medicinal and social knowledge and in healing, blessing, and exorcising for the Qiang communities, the *shibi* is portrayed as performing rituals with a monkey-skin hat and a goat-skin drum, which are customary ritual vessels.

The unconventional opening of this documentary in omitting real human figures and landscapes and focusing exclusively on the mythic time-space of the Qiang pictographic and shamanic worldviews is telling of the aesthetic sensibilities and cultural messages of ethnographic poetic films: ethnographic poetics probes the deeper lyrical beauty, spiritual experience, and sentimental dimensions of community life, rather than technically recording a cultural phenomenon. For example, from the film stills, we witness the seemingly unlikely intimacy and expression of love between the goddess and

Figure 24. Film still from *Ten Years in Search of the Qiang*. Image courtesy of Gao Tunzi.

Figure 25. Film still from *Ten Years in Search of the Qiang*. Image courtesy of Gao Tunzi.

a monkey-headed man, conveying the Qiang cosmological view. Like many animistic traditions, the Qiang religious system “holds that every aspect of nature is inhabited by spirit and that some natural features such as springs, rivers, mountains . . . are specially loaded with cosmic power.”[12] It is from this indigenous cosmology that the marriage between a celestial woman and a half-animal human becomes possible, mocking the modern binary that separates humans from the rest of the natural world.

The fact that the film opens with a two-minute-long immersive view of the Qiang shamanistic scroll with no visual interventions or props is also a homage to the importance of pictographic traditions in shaping the Qiang belief systems and social structures. Indeed, pictographic traditions and spiritual practices are deeply entwined and are key to understanding many of southwest China's ethnic minorities. The pictographic scrolls (*tujing* 图经; in Qiang language, *shualeri*) used by the *shibi* have a long history that some scholars date back to approximately the Tang dynasty.[13] The *shualeri* are elaborately painted by hand and are widely considered by scholars as encyclopedic representations of traditional Qiang life: they cover topics as far-ranging as hunting and animal husbandry, and they illustrate the customs for weddings, funerals, and ritual ceremonies and worships.[14] The *shualeri* scrolls are foldable guides painted on paper or silk for portability, as the *shibi* carry them and pull them out during ritual ceremonies, chanting long ritual songs and texts based on the pictographic instructions on the *shualeri*.[15] The *shualeri* is a sacred object in the Qiang religious traditions: only well-respected *shibi* can take possession of them, and they can only be unfolded during important rituals and ceremonies.

The Qiang *shualeri* pictographic scrolls are also decidedly a product of cultural hybridity. As the film stills show, Chinese characters are a regular presence on the scrolls—as there lacks a standardized Qiang script, Chinese characters provide textual aids for the shamanic chants. Moreover, some scholars speculate similarities between the orally transmitted Qiang shamanic traditions and Daoist spiritual practices originating from ancient Sichuan.[16]

In addition to its potential connections to Han/Daoist traditions, the Qiang shamanistic tradition also shares important traits with both Han and other ethnic minority religions in southwest China. For example, Christine Mathieu, a scholar of the Dongba (东巴) religion of the Naxi (纳西) people of Yunnan, suggests that "the Jang and the ancient Qiang tribes who came to Lijiang [in Yunnan] may have possessed a script based on ancient Chinese characters."[17] Similar to the *shibi* traditions, the Dongba religion relies heavily on pictographic instructions and practices a shamanistic priesthood. The Dongba pictographic scrolls borrow widely from Tibetan Buddhist traditions, Bonpo traditions (an indigenous Tibetan shamanic practice), and have even been influenced by Mongol words and concepts.[18] What is known as the modern Naxi ethnic group is also a composite entity tracing its origin to several ethnic categories and lineages, including the Qiang,[19] or the historically constructed category of the "Qiang" as a collection of ethnic and indigenous tribes in China's western borderland, a topic Chapters 1 and 2 of this book addressed.

These scholarly insights about the mutual influences between the Qiang and the Naxi are echoed by my fieldwork observations. When I was doing field research in the Qiang regions of Sichuan, during casual chats with Qiang locals, there were several times when it was mentioned to me that the Qiang and the Naxi in Yunnan share linguistic and religious characteristics. Qiang locals have a strong awareness of their cultural and religious affinities with other ethnic minority groups in southwest China; these affinities exist outside of the Sinocentric and Sinographic imagination of China as a multiethnic country revolving around the Han. The minority-to-minority connections recenter indigenous motifs and interethnic affiliations as an important thread of ethnic identity.

Therefore, by presenting the Qiang indigenous spiritual and pictographic traditions, *Ten Years* elicits a rich and multifaceted world of cultural hybridity in southwest China. The minority-to-minority connections we can glean from this film also reaffirm the concept of fluid indigeneity that I broached earlier. Whereas in many other national and cultural contexts, "indigeneity" is almost always practiced with a group's explicit claims to its historical land, resources, and a strong desire to assert autonomy and ownership to certain ancestral practices, in southwest China, "indigeneity" implies shared histories, *interconnected* traditions, and a pride in the mutual influences and interethnic intelligibilities among different groups. These more relaxed attitudes and inclusive outlooks toward indigenous traditions allow China's minority groups to make important contributions to the global study of indigeneity, offering new experiences and unique insights that will broaden the discourse of indigeneity internationally.

Beyond its depictions of the foundational spiritual worldviews and religious practices of the Qiang, *Ten Years* unveils many internal conflicts and debates among different generations of Qiang villagers. The film reveals the uneasy transitions to a new urbanized lifestyle and the shifting generational attitudes toward indigenous traditions experienced by the Qiang migrants. For example, in order to relocate to the tea-growing region of Qionglai and move into modern apartments, the villagers have to give up their farming animals and abandon their ancestral tombs and worship shrines, all of which are attached to their land and form their attachments to their native homes. We see images of the older villagers bidding farewell to their beloved horses and cattle. One male villager pets his ox, which quietly surround him, and bemoans the sadness of the ox: "They are angry and frustrated now. They won't chew the thaw." Another villager caresses his horse, which sheds tears upon hearing about the upcoming separation from its owner. The film offers a close-up image of the dripping of the tears of the horse. During another scene, an older Qiang woman is portrayed as weeping over the fact that "we will die in other people's land and lose our ancestors," as the ancestral tombs will be left unattended. Whereas the young people in the villages celebrate the promises of this new move, the older villagers mourn together and whisper to their ancestors buried near the villages, pleading for the ancestors' forgiveness and understanding. The film presents these images and scenes in a non-intervening way, as the camera captures the daily-life scenarios in their original village settings, avoiding any visual or aural ornaments and following the villagers' movements with calm medium-long shots. In this sense, *Ten Years* assumes an observational mode, rather than eagerly jumping to a participatory mode.

Years after settling into the modern apartments in Qionglai, three elders from the villages try to persuade local officials and the young people to help them move the religious worship shrines from the original villages to their new neighborhood. The elders emphasize that they had made a promise to the Mubita, a god from the Qiang indigenous religion, that they would "invite him to the new village" and build a new worship shrine. For the elders, the worship shrine for Mubita serves as a tangible landmark for the Qiang identity and cements the togetherness of the villagers in diaspora. One young man, indulging in entertaining majiang games, despises the elderlies' request. He questions: "What kind of era are we living in? Why do you still believe in the things that your eyes can't see?" Feeling deeply misunderstood and frustrated, the elder responds: "Do you only believe in the things your eyes can see? How many things can your eyes see?" For the young man, the new urbanized lifestyle is cozy, as one can easily buy rice and vegetables from the market across the street, instead of toiling in the farmland for months. The elderly challenges the young man's thinking, asking him: "Yet where do the rice and vegetables you buy come from?" For the elderlies who grew up farming the native land, food is a blessing from nature and the gods. But for the young men, food is a mundane consumer product for exchange.

The debate between the young man and the Qiang elder reveals the generational gap and shifting beliefs in the Qiang communities. The elders' belief that humans are only part of the cycle of cosmic life embodies what Mark Bender calls a "cosmographic eye:" by revealing older Qiang villagers' attachment to their land, animals, and ancestral memories, the film demonstrates the traditional Qiang cosmological views that are "inclusive of both the human and the nonhuman, providing spaces for animals, plants, landscapes and waters, and all that perceivably makes up the cosmos."[20] Bender maintains that the "pluriverse" of indigenous communities is comprised of a rich sense of "place-competency:" indigenous communities are concerned with preserving the knowledge about and connections to a particular land, its flora and fauna; this "cosmopolitical" perspective profoundly critiques the human-centric views of industrializing, mainstream societies.[21] In *Ten Years*, the elders calmly narrate the cosmopolitical perspectives of the Qiang to the viewer, such as the custom of forbidding hunting in early spring, when animals and the forests are coming back to life. To many younger villagers, such cosmopolitical worldviews, deeply rooted in the elders' knowledge about the ecological systems of the place, have lost their sacred power, as younger villagers tend to view their relationship to nature as a transactional and pragmatic one. In this sense, the cosmopolitical and cosmographic perspectives in ethnographic films such as *Ten Years* challenge the encompassing power of the human in our anthropocentric era: the film presents alternative worldviews and ecological perspectives that question the transactional logic that dominates many younger Qiang villagers' understanding of their relationship to the land and nature.

By engaging extensively with the multiple aspects of Qiang villagers' life and probing their changing relations to their own community ethics, *Ten Years* exemplifies what film scholar Faye Ginsburg calls an "aesthetics of accountability." According to Ginsburg, an aesthetics of accountability emerges as "a new category in works that prioritize the relationship of the film to the subjects who appear in it."[22] In other words, contrary to how the minority village is usually represented in popular cinema, which tends to either romanticize the minority village as a site of pristine moral and sexual paradise or exoticize it as a land of cultural peculiarities, collaborative documentaries such as *Ten Years* present the minority village unsentimentally, as villagers experience it, taking accountability in revealing and reconstructing the ethics of indigenous communities in flux.

During my interview with the director, Gao Tunzi, Gao recounts the story of how he treated himself as part of the indigenous communities that he filmed. "I am not a photographer, but I am part of the native land (*xiangtu* 乡土)," Gao stated.[23] Days and weeks after the 2008 Sichuan earthquake, Gao entered the Qiang regions despite the looming danger of the afterquakes. At the encouragement of his wife, Gao started an embroidery project that helped Qiang female villagers use their embroidery skills to make a living in the face of the hardships presented by the loss of farmland.[24] Gao also revealed to me during our interview that as he spent more time with the villagers, there were moments when "film-worthy" accidents and events took place in the community. Yet, instead of rushing to record these events with his camera, which he deemed would be inappropriate and disrespectful to the community, Gao participated in the events as a community member himself and lent a hand to the villagers. Gao told me that because he deliberately missed a lot of film-worthy moments, he later wrote a book, a volume of non-fiction accounts, about the stories and figures that he encountered in the two villages that he filmed.

In his book, Gao reaffirms the aesthetics of accountability that he deploys in his film. "I came here to . . . use a language that I develop on my own to tell the stories of the *shibi* who communicate with their ancestral spirits and ghosts, and to account for the minds and hearts and realities of the Qiang people."[25] As with his film, Gao foregrounds the Qiang villagers' indigenous experiences, perspectives, and worldviews in his book. Gao also shared during the interview that some of the scenes in the film were staged because the original events had already passed. But he believes that these staged scenes are equally authentic because they are based on or reflective of the actual lived experiences and lifeworlds of the villagers.

Gao's understanding of the ethnographic film not as a technical documentation of community life but as a creative rendering of the relationship between himself, the Qiang villagers, and the land testifies to the power of collaborative documentary and ethnographic poetics. Gao collaborated with the villagers to help them rebuild their homeland after the earthquake. He shared with me that he helped the Qiang villagers to sell tea in Qionglai. He also collaborated with the villagers during all processes of filmmaking and prioritized the villagers' stories, experiences, and contributions over his own interpretations or personal tastes. In the closing credits of the film, there is a line of "thanking all villagers."

Probing the deeper roots of the contemporary Qiang identity grounded in indigenous cosmopolitical views, Gao folds the pictographic and mythic time-space of the Qiang shamanistic world into an otherwise realist chronological film about the migratory path of a group of Qiang villagers. In doing so, Gao evokes the affect of yearning for the home and creates contemplative, poetic portrayals of the Qiang elders' quest for spiritual roots against the tide of urbanization and secularization. The film's poetic mode can be seen in the close-up portrayals of the tears of the horse, the slow but steady unfolding of the colorful and vivid pictographic book of the shamanistic hymns, and the atmosphere of lamentation of the villagers upon the loss of their homelands. The dimensions of poetics and poesis—the lyrical rendering of ethnographic details—allows for the creative incorporation of indigenous spiritual traditions and social life into an otherwise "documentary" film. It is precisely the creative power of ethnographic poetics that enables an ethnographic documentary to open up to the realm of mythic imagination and cultural hybridity, as we witnessed in *Ten Years in Search for the Qiang*.

Even though Gao Tunzi as a director is of Han origin, he is epistemologically influenced by Qiang cosmopolitical worldviews and artistically indebted to the shamanistic, mythic time-space of the Qiang spirituality. His cinematic practice is exemplary of the community-driven impulse of indigenous cinema, which places community at the center of the filmmaking process and treats the community as "an active voice" as well as a methodology[26]—it is through contextualizing the Qiang communities in transition that Gao examines the dynamics of ethnic identities and experiments with the film language.

The successful collaborative and "hybrid" nature of *Ten Years in Search of the Qiang* as a two-way creative process between the director and the villagers also contributes to a new aesthetics and ethics of "fluid indigeneity," a theory that I broached earlier in this chapter. As the realization of *Ten Years* shows, ethnic Han or majority artists and activists can have a stake in indigenous cultural causes. In this sense, we should not limit our discussion of indigeneity (in China and globally) to the discussion of minority peoples alone. Majority artists who respect the history and traditions of minority groups can participate in the formation of indigenous discourses. This creates a space of fluid indigeneity where "indigeneity" is freed from an essentializing set of rules and traditions imputed to a particular group and becomes a living tradition and a dynamic space of interethnic and multicultural exchange. This fluid space of indigeneity may eventually contribute to "de-marginalizing" those at the geographic and political margins of a nation, endowing minority traditions and histories with new meanings in the process of re-inventing the images of minority groups and eventually redefining the national or mainstream culture through indigenous lens.

Exiles at Home: Contested Interethnic Romance and Cultural Performance in Erma's Wedding

If *Ten Years in Search of the Qiang* exemplifies the collaborative processes of ethnographic filmmaking in the Qiang regions, then the genre of indigenous "docufiction"[27] experiments with the possible futures of interethnic encounters through its imaginary play with "reality" and "fiction." In this section of the chapter, we will investigate a film that I categorize as an indigenous

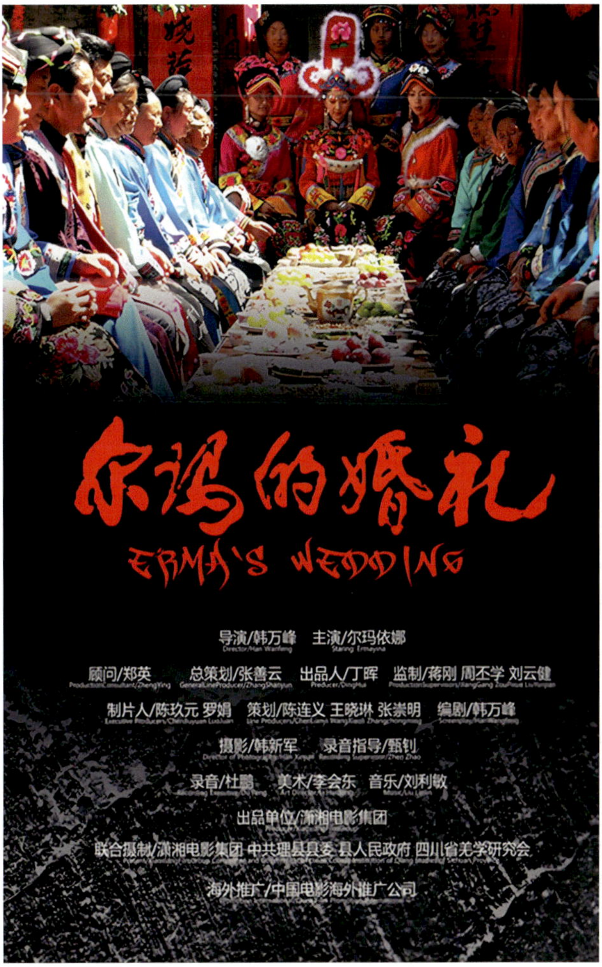

Figure 26. Film poster of *Erma's Wedding.*

docufiction, *Erma's Wedding* (*Erma de hunli* 尔玛的婚礼). Similar to *Ten Years*, *Erma's Wedding* presents Qiang villagers' fraught interactions with the fast-changing environments surrounding them. Particularly, by conjuring up the visually rich world of Qiang cultural symbolism and community rituals, *Erma's Wedding* begs the question of the value of indigenous cultural systems in the twenty-first century as it unveils a young Qiang woman's struggle to preserve the integrity of her culture.

Erma's Wedding was released in 2008. Like *Ten Years in Search of the Qiang*, *Erma's Wedding* embodies the collaborative spirit of ethnographic filmmaking in contemporary China. A renowned ethnic Qiang scholar, Professor Zhang Shanyun, serves as the main advisor for this film. Moreover, it is co-produced by the Li County (理县) Government and the Sichuan Provincial Qiang Studies Association, an academic organization comprised of mainly ethnic Qiang scholars, writers, and entrepreneurs. Li County is a Qiang-majority county and many of its leaders are of Qiang origin. My fieldwork in the Li County has allowed me to meet some political leaders in this region, most of whom are very sympathetic toward or active in Qiang cultural preservation causes. The participation of the Li County Government was likely mostly focused on drawing out Qiang cultural elements in the film, as the film does not fall into any preconceived political ideologies. On the contrary, the film poses many critical questions about the future of ethnic identities at the intersection of commercialization and globalization.

The director of the film is Han Wanfeng (韩万峰), an ethnic Han filmmaker widely known for his extensive engagements with minority-themed films. Prior to taking up *Erma's Wedding*, Han served as the literary director of the award-winning arthouse film, *Postmen in the Mountain* (*Nashan, naren, nagou* 那山, 那人, 那狗), which recounts the interethnic romance between an ethnic Han man and a Dong minority woman, as well as the beauty of the architecture and singing ceremonies of the ethnic Dong (侗) villages. In 2006, Han Wanfeng directed another film, *Flavor of the Green Betelnut* (*Qing binglang zhiwei* 青槟榔之味), about the Li ethnic group (黎族) of Hainan province, tackling the issue of the crisis of the Li ethnic language and the life choices of the younger generation of Li communities.

Even though Han Wanfeng is an ethnic Han director, unlike the Han directors studied in the previous chapter, who projected their moral and cultural imagination of minority groups onto the site of the Qiang village, Han deploys a strong documentary aesthetics and foregrounds indigenous expressions in his minority-themed films. In an interview that he conducted with the journal *Film Review*, Han Wanfeng confesses that he is merely an "observer who records" the minority communities.[28] Not only does Han use many nonprofessional actors who are villagers and locals, but he also insists on making room for the actors to talk in the Qiang language and act out his loosely designed plots based on the locals' own interpretations. Han highlights the importance of using the indigenous language to authenticate the acting and validate the emotions in his minority-themed cinematic works: indigenous actors are encouraged to speak naturally and carry out dialogues in the film as they would in their daily interactions, rather than following a strict script. Han Wanfeng suggests that in his filmmaking process, "if the rhythm [of the indigenous mother tongue] does not match the atmosphere [that I designed], I would recede to the back and let [the actors freely] talk."[29] Therefore, from its extensive Qiang advising team to Han Wanfeng's choice of foregrounding the Qiang language and highlighting the daily encounters of Qiang villagers, *Erma's Wedding* exemplifies a strong indigenous consciousness.

The plot of the film follows the romantic conflicts between Erma, a young Qiang woman, and her ethnic Han sweetheart, Liu Dachuan, who is an English teacher in the local school. The naming of the female protagonist is the first symbolic gesture in the film: Erma, or *rrmea*, means "locals" or "indigenes" in the Qiang native language. According to Maotao Wen, a scholar of Qiang language and culture, the Rme-language speaking people of southwest China straddles those classified as Qiang and those classified as Tibetans.[30] In other words, the ethnic group classified as "Qiang" or "Qiangzu" only represents one part of the Rme-speaking indigenous communities in the Himalayas. Wen argues that the Rme language is an indigenous language within the Sino-Tibetan language family and should not be equated with what is today known as the "Qiang" language—Rme is an indigenous linguistic marker that transcends the ethnic marker "Qiang," which has only recently been constructed as a separate ethnic category since the 1960s.[31] The contested nature of the ethnonym "Qiang" and its ambiguous relationship to a cross-ethnic indigenous identity transforms "Erma" into a rich discursive space and a site of cultural hybridity to understand the dynamic interethnic encounters that take place in the Eastern Himalayas.

Indeed, language plays an instrumental role in shaping the relationships among the characters and in revealing the interethnic social politics in *Erma's Wedding*. In the film, while most of the conversations among the Qiang villagers are carried out in the indigenous language, whenever there is a negotiation between different parties, such as conversations between different families and members from different villages, the Sichuanese dialect is used as the lingua franca. Mandarin, the official language of China, serves as a language of political command and the transmitter of official policies: many times, as Erma's family sits down together for dinner, the TV in the background broadcasts national news and events in Standard Mandarin and interrupts the family's conversations and gossips with a homogenous tone, reminding the family of the existence of a national socio-political space that seems faraway yet is omnipresent.

In the film, Erma is originally engaged to another Qiang man, Duoba, and the two families are in the process of planning their wedding. However, Erma starts to develop feelings for Liu Dachuan, a handsome English teacher in her younger brother's school. As an ethnic Han person, Dachuan is the only character in the film who does not speak either the Qiang language or the Sichuanese dialect. While he woos Erma and wins her heart with his half-baked English skills, his perpetual use of Mandarin throughout the film marks him as an outsider to the indigenous world of Qiang culture: having neither the linguistic abilities nor the cultural empathy to enter into the emotional world of the Qiang villagers, Dachuan later insists on having a modern Western-style wedding with Erma when Erma ends her engagement with Duoba and decides to marry him.

For Erma, a young minority woman who has rarely traveled outside of her immediate surroundings, Dachuan's English skills present themselves as an alluring ticket to a world beyond her imagination. In Erma's eyes, Dachuan is cosmopolitan, smart, and funny. By contrast, Duoba, an honest Qiang man who is about to inherit a seamstress shop from his parents, comes across as too rustic for Erma. Erma is completely uninterested in owning the seamstress shop with Duoba. She is attracted to the refreshing and expansive world represented by Dachuan. Yet Dachuan's cosmopolitan allure comes with a price tag: when Erma and Dachuan decide to get married, Dachuan, ever-so-eager to please his aunt, who is an influential local official, dictates with his aunt to hold their wedding in the county seat for the grandeur of a Western wedding and for the convenience of other local officials to be present.

Despite her fascination with her fiancé's multilingual talents, Erma yearns for a traditional Qiang wedding that involves elaborate shamanistic traditions, colorful gatherings, and exciting ceremonies attended by the entire village. Erma's parents, who are Qiang farmers, also feel strongly about holding a traditional wedding in order to honor their ethnic heritage. It is this conflict over the format of the interethnic couple's wedding that culminates into a powerful cultural critique in the film.

In order to persuade Erma and her parents to hold the wedding at the county seat, Dachuan's aunt, the director of the local educational bureau, comes to visit Erma's village. As the villagers warmly welcome Dachuan's aunt with freshly-picked plums and other local delicacies, the aunt offers many bribes to both lure and pressure Erma's family into accepting a Western-style wedding. The aunt not only promises to "recommend" Erma's brother to the best middle school in the area,[32] but also showers Erma's families with expensive gifts: she brings a huge TV set and a dazzling necklace to Erma's parents' house, in addition to giving Erma's brother a red envelop packed with money.

The aunt's generosity stems from her political prowess and social clout: rejecting her gifts and promises would be an open challenge to the political institutions and educational opportunities that she represents; it would also marginalize Erma's family, as the other villagers would probably resent that Erma's family shuns future opportunities for other Qiang women to "marry up." Erma's father, who has previously insisted on having a Qiang-style wedding because the Qiang "are not any lesser than anybody else," finally gives in to the power of the aunt. Meanwhile, Erma escapes from the village and hides on top of a hill, singing a folk song to remember her home as her grandma combs her hair. Earlier in the film, we see that it is Erma's grandma that paints the picture of the colorful Qiang wedding, which captivates Erma's imagination and leads her to rebel against a dull Western-style wedding. While other villagers are cheering the material promises of Erma's marriage, Erma's "exile" from her own village for a moment of reconnection with her ancestral traditions is telling of the poignant experience of minority communities under the sway of commercialization and development: caught between the desire to preserve her traditions and the need to gain material wealth, Erma as a minority woman protests with her absence. In this sense, Erma's escape from the home village—however temporary—becomes an ironic act of reaffirming her roots. When she can no longer fully be herself and maintain her ethnic identity in her own village, a moment of willing exile makes the whole village pause and contemplate the price of giving in to the material temptations of a developing nation.

Instead of glorifying Erma as the absolute heroine that salvages her culture, the film unexpectedly presents two alternative endings to reveal the ambiguities and contradictions of minorities' confrontation with cultural challenges. In one ending, Erma gets on a bus to go to the county seat to have a Western-style wedding, accompanied by her parents. She appears impatient and ill-tempered, as the long-winding road takes her on a journey of repetitiveness and ennui. Meanwhile, the groom, Liu Dachuan, is enthusiastically calling up his friends, many of whom are powerful local politicians and successful overseas Chinese businessmen. For Liu, the wedding is more an occasion for accumulating political and economic capital and growing his social network.

Stylistically, this ending echoes the beginning of the film, where we see the same bus following a never-ending, winding road. This ending enhances the documentary flavor and realist critique of the film, as the viewer is offered a slice of Erma's life without any climatic happy ending or a redemptive hero that comes to Erma's rescue. The film refuses to sensationalize minority life. Instead, it presents the internal struggles and uneasy compromises of a young minority woman who gives in to her fiancé's familial pressure and political influence. The identical scenery of the beginning and ending of the film with a bus slowly going on a country road symbolizes the circularity of Erma's life: Erma feels trapped on the never-ending road of trying to find her identity, as this "road" only leads to her immense loneliness and separation from her parental home, further breaking her apart from her Qiang heritage.

In another ending, Erma succeeds in persuading Liu Dachuan to have a Qiang-style wedding. It is in this ending that the film presents cultural exhibitionist, panoramic images of various aspects of Qiang indigenous heritage to combat cultural homogenization. In an almost five-minute clip with medium-long takes, we see the unfolding of a traditional Qiang-style wedding with hybrid cultural markers and interethnic signifiers.

After a series of collective festivities, such as open-air feasts, women's singing and men's dancing parties, a Qiang shaman begins the solemn ceremony of blessing the couple. The film's painstaking efforts to represent Qiang culture in its ritual settings is manifested in the ethnographic details carefully designed throughout the entire process of the wedding. For example, the *shibi* (shaman) is dressed up in a full ritual regalia, including a monkey-skin hat, a cloud-patterned colorful jacket, and a stick (Figure 27). Faithful to the film's commitment to a documentary poetics, the *shibi* in the film is an actual *shibi* who was still practicing in several Qiang villages, rather than an actor.

As Han Wanfeng relays in an interview, the original *shibi* that he filmed was dismissed as "unauthoritative" (*buquanwei*) by the Qiang experts that he consulted, because the *shibi* failed to wear a monkey-skin hat, which is traditional of Qiang shamanistic ceremonies.[33] Han retook this scene in order to present the "authentic appearance" (*yuanmao*) of a traditional Qiang wedding.[34] Here, the Qiang experts' insistence on the "unauthoritative" nature of the first *shibi*'s preparation testifies to the epistemological power of indigenous experts, who frame the parameters of authenticity in cultural representation. Even though a culture is always in flux and ethnic cultures today are in increasingly dynamic exchanges with other cultures, the articulation of "authenticity" is not without its merits: by correlating the solemnity and

Figure 27. Film still from *Erma's Wedding.*

ritual function of the *shibi* tradition with authentic cultural representation, the ethnic Qiang consultants of the film are restoring what Walter Benjamin would call the "aura" of a work of art. Benjamin maintains that "the existence of the work of art with reference to its aura is never entirely separated from its ritual function."[35] Benjamin further notes that the unique value of a work of art lies in "ritual, the location of its original use value."[36]

To indigenous Qiang communities, the *shibi* ceremony is a unique ritual that functions in a socially and spiritually meaningful context—*shibi* habitually blesses weddings and funerals and serves as the intermediary between the spiritual/supernatural realm and the human realm. He heals the community and exorcises evil spirits to restore peace and order in the Qiang village. As my conversations with a few *shibi* in the Qiang regions reveal, the *shibi* ritual is considered a solemn practice and many *shibi* intentionally withhold esoteric *shibi* performances from commercial or touristic settings in order to not violate the will of the deities and to preserve the sacred function of the ceremonies. *Erma's Wedding* embodies the ritualistic function of the *shibi* performance. The film's almost iconographic evocation of the image of the *shibi* as the main mobilizer of Qiang community life testifies to Clifford Geertz's idea that "sacred symbols function to synthesize a [people's] ethos," including the "tone, character, and quality of their life."[37] The *shibi* serves as a sacred symbol in the Qiang community. Particularly, on special occasions such as at weddings, the *shibi* evokes a solemn, spiritually-inspired, and collectivity-centered ethos for the community. He directs the procedures of the wedding, endowing it with a religious veil and performs the mythological poetics of the Qiang wedding. Because of his utmost importance in governing community ethics and representing both the spiritual and the worldly order for the Qiang community, the *shibi* is invoked not simply as a static token of traditional culture, but as a performance/performer of Qiang worldviews and the organizer of community rituals in *Erma's Wedding*. In this sense, the film's exhibitionist urge to meticulously present the visual details and ritual significance of the *shibi* performance transcends the realm of the spectacle: the icon of the *shibi*, as well as many other traditional Qiang cultural aspects shown in the film, are employed *not* to Orientalize the Qiang, but to restore the social context and perform the cultural meanings of many ethnic symbols that are easily taken out of context as mere aesthetic objects in mass media or mainstream cinema.[38]

In addition to its careful representation of the *shibi* traditions, *Erma's Wedding* also reveals the hybridity of contemporary Qiang culture and its creative combination of multiethnic and multilingual sources in imagining what it means to be "Qiang." For example, in one ending of the film, where Erma succeeds in persuading Liu Dachuan to have a Qiang-style wedding with her, Erma is accompanied by two bridesmaids as she steps away from the gate of her parents' house and crosses the threshold from girlhood to womanhood. She breaks a bowl by foot to symbolize the dissolvement of evil spirits as she enters into a new stage of her life. Notably, the gate is decorated with red couplets rendered in calligraphic formats in the Chinese language, resplendent with poetic verses that sing praises to life in the Qiang fortressed villages (Figure 28).

The red couplets and Chinese calligraphy are a common sight in the Qiang villages that I visited. During a wedding that I was invited to in Taoping Qiang Village in 2015, the Chinese character for "double happiness" (*hong shuangxi* 红双喜) was prominently displayed on the wall, as young Qiang women came up to the stage to perform dances for the festive occasion. Just as in the film, in the actual village wedding, Qiang villagers joyously celebrate the multiethnic sources of their identity: the Han Chinese script and its linguistic symbolism are proudly appropriated by Qiang villagers, who inhabit the kind of "third space" theorized by Homi Bhabha: the third space is a "creative space that lies between the discourse or position of the ruling subject and the discourse or position of the subaltern subject."[39] The Chinese character for "double happiness" is a coined word that does not appear in a standard Chinese dictionary,

Figure 28. Film still from *Erma's Wedding.*

but rather functions culturally as a folk symbol for celebrating matrimonial unions. The linguistic "deviance" of the character for "double happiness" and its usage by Qiang villagers testifies to the ambiguous relationship between the Han majority and the minorities of China: the character of double happiness lends itself well to the cultural imagination of Qiang villagers, who creatively draw from the Chinese language to enliven the celebratory mood of a wedding. In this sense, the Qiang villagers utilize the linguistic unruliness of certain Chinese characters to articulate their own relationship to "Chinese-ness." Just as how the extinct Tangut script was reimagined as a language of poetry by certain members of the Qiangzu, which I discussed in Chapter 2, Qiang villagers negotiate their own Chinese-ness as they become creative agents that bear a multifaceted, rather than submissive, relationship to what is conventionally known as "Chinese culture."

In *Erma's Wedding,* the joyous occasion of Qiang villagers' celebrations culminates in a moment of silence when the groom is left dumbfounded as he observes the *shibi* ceremonies. The unfolding of a series of celebratory festivities climaxes into the intoxicated smile on Erma's face. In the next scene, a perspective shot reveals the groom Dachuan's awkward situation as an outsider: he looks sideways to his bride, who is completely absorbed into the ceremonies. Meanwhile, Dachuan is left in total awe and seems to be at a loss, as the *shibi* ceremonies are completely alien to him (Figure 30).

Figure 29. A traditional Qiang wedding. Photograph by author.

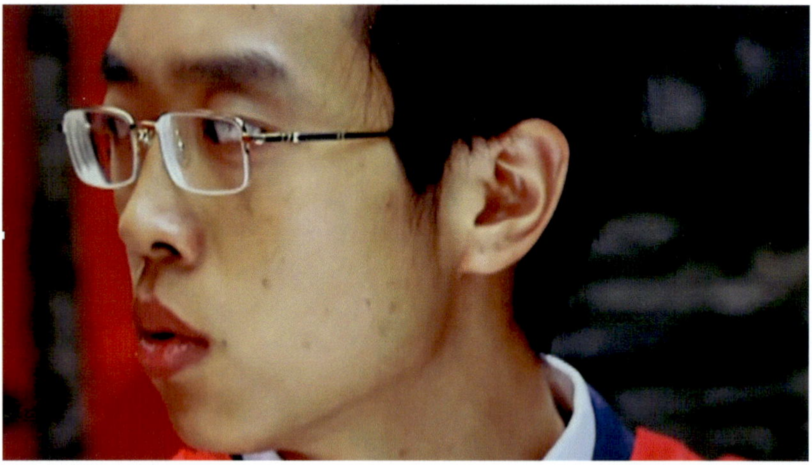

Figure 30. Film still from *Erma's Wedding*.

This is a significant scene that reverses the conventional aesthetic logic of rendering minority traditions as purely exotic spectacles in many cinematic works. Instead of dwelling on the visual appeals of Qiang cultural heritage and proffering it up as an object of consumption for the viewer, the film creates a critical space of inquiry: Dachuan's gaze can be characterized neither by sympathy nor curiosity, which are two common types of gazes cast upon minorities in many cinematic productions. Rather, it is a gaze of awe and reverence, tinged on both fear and confusion. In the rich symbolic world of Qiang shamanism and wedding ceremonies, Dachuan is a total stranger and portrayed as naïve, if not ignorant. While for him, a wedding is just a pragmatic occasion of uniting two people, for the Qiang villagers, it is a complete series of rituals defined by communal ethos, spiritual pathos, and a collective evocation of ancestral memories. As someone who is neither interested in these traditions nor knowledgeable about them, Dachuan appears as a total outsider and serves to heighten the integrity and coherence of Qiang cultural heritage itself: even without Dachuan's validation or participation, the wedding ceremonies are still in full swing. The religious, cultural, and artistic symbols in the ceremony constitute an organic entity that demands nothing but Dachuan's reverence.

In this sense, *Erma's Wedding* presents a strong indigenous consciousness as it questions the aesthetic and narrative conventions of cinematic representations of minorities: from the indigenous perspective, Dachuan is an outsider whose presence in the community can either potentially diminish the community spirit (in the first ending) or strengthen it (in this second ending). While Dachuan contributes to redefining the relationships and dynamics between the family members and community members, he can never erase the villagers' tenacious connections to their collective sense of belonging, which exists outside of Dachuan's epistemological and social imagination. In this sense, Dachuan functions symbolically as an outside or dominant culture: Erma and her fellow villagers refuse to be objectified or defined by Dachuan's behaviors, or the influence of external cultures. Rather, the Qiang villagers insist on performing their cultural identities in a socially meaningful context (such as the wedding that involves the entire village and becomes a festive occasion for all). It is this insistence on contextualizing rituals and restoring the social function of ceremonies that marks *Erma's Wedding* as an important film that creates spaces of critical inquiry: the minority-majority (or Qiang-Han) relationship is rendered in multidirectional and multifaceted ways. The film resists the simplifying tendency to reduce minority culture or minority-majority relationship in neatly categorized boxes, but displays the multiple possibilities, alternative endings, and contradictory sentiments in the lived situations of minority villagers confronting a more powerful culture and way of life.

Conclusion

In this chapter, I discussed the emerging indigenous cinema in the Qiang minority regions of China by probing into the aesthetic and cultural motifs of "ethnographic poetics." As the two films in this chapter demonstrate, ethnographic poetics is a creative mode that blends a documentary urge of preserving minority groups' vanishing traditions with visual representations of the cosmopolitical, mythical dimensions of indigenous worldviews that transcend specific historical periods. Ethnographic poetics is both ethnographic in terms of engaging in realist depictions of minority traditions and lived realities but also highly lyrical and poetic: it absorbs multiethnic and multicultural sources of inspiration, evocative of the spiritual roots of minority groups from time immemorial. Ethnographic poetic modes of cinema create a sense of myth that is essential to the collective identities of indigenous groups like the Qiang: rather than Orientalizing or mystifying the Qiang as an exotic spectacle for the visual consumption of the outsider, ethnographic poetics preserves the myths, or time-honored spiritual truths and community ethos, of indigenous groups confronting external changes. As both a stylistic innovation and a carrier of social messages, ethnographic poetic modes of cinema serve as a powerful critique of the developmental agendas of the nation and offers indigenous views on the modernizing, homogenizing trends that are overtaking minority regions in China. The spiritual truths and community myths that are invoked in ethnographic poetic modes of cinema can generate an empowering creative space that reaffirms the longevity of indigenous identities beyond the parameters of the modern nation. In this sense, the mythic portrayals of shamanistic traditions, solemn ritual ceremonies, and other indigenous activities also serve to poeticize such traditions, articulating their aesthetic and spiritual importance beyond their utilitarian functions. In both *Erma's Wedding* and *Ten Years in Search of the Qiang*, community ceremonies and spiritual beliefs are being ridiculed by those who do not understand or appreciate them (Liu Dachuan in the first film and the younger generation of the Qiang community in the second). By engaging in a poetic mode of depicting the beauty and aesthetic values of community traditions, the two films question the pragmaticism of the dominant culture intruding on the spaces of the Qiang village.

Finally, the collaborative nature of ethnographic poetic cinema enables indigenous communities to foreground their worldviews, epistemes, and aesthetic sensibilities, forging a space of "fluid indigeneity" as minority and majority artists and actors join hands to explore what it means to be indigenous in twenty-first century China.

PART III

Reconstituting the "Qiang" in Literary Voices and Cultural Activism in the Himalayas

CHAPTER 5

Between the Languishing Ethnic Mother and the Bewitching "Poisonous Cat"

Gender and Commercialization in Contemporary Chinese Minority Literature

As an interdisciplinary scholar of Chinese ethnic cultures, I routinely engage in ethnographic field research in the Qiang and other minority regions of China. One summer, I was staying in a guesthouse in the Longxi Qiang People's Valley in Wenchuan County, Sichuan. One evening, as I finished the dinner prepared by my Qiang hosts, we started our casual chats as usual. Both the male host and the female hostess told me the stories of the "Poisonous Cats" (*duyao mao* 毒药猫), or a small number of local women whom Qiang villagers believe to have bewitching and dangerous powers over their fellow villagers. In vivid detail, my hosts warned me of the risk of taking a bowl of rice from strangers, especially certain suspicious women, as these women can make one ill by "poisoning your bowl of rice with their fingernails when they serve you the rice." As the night grew darker, the mysterious stories of these Poisonous Cats lingered in the crisp evening air. Even though I had never encountered one single Poisonous Cat, I found these stories both bemusing and unsettling.

According to the Qiang traditions, the Poisonous Cats are women who have magic power to assume the shape of cats or other domestic animals. These women can use their special power to punish those they do not like or spread diseases and disasters. But who endows these women with said special powers? Why would these women cause calamity in their own kinship group and among their fellow villagers at the cost of being marginalized? Above all, what do the stories of the Poisonous Cats tell us about the gender imagination within ethnic minority communities, when minority groups themselves tend to be imagined in gendered terms in mainstream Chinese culture and media?

This chapter probes these problems by focusing on how the question of gender shapes Chinese ethnic minority groups' experience with modernization. Particularly, I investigate how two prevalent images, the languishing, rural ethnic mother and the bewitching ethnic seductress, figure into Chinese minority writers' accounts of minority groups' fraught encounter with modernization. On the one hand, as depicted by many Qiang essayists and poets, the rural ethnic mother is portrayed as a nurturing yet conservative force incapable of holding back the enterprising ethnic son, who is eager to leave the caring bosom of the mother in search of a masculine identity in urban China. On the other hand, modernizing projects, such as tourism developments, are critiqued as delusional feminine charms with the power to corrupt the virility of minority cultures by Qiang authors. Notably, in contemporary Chinese multiethnic literature, the dangers of modernization are usually embodied in the image of a seductive minority woman, often in the form of the Poisonous Cat, who possesses alternative powers and refuses to fully submit to any gender or social institutions. Therefore, the question of gender occupies uneven cultural, ideological, and material spaces as minority groups navigate the deeply ambiguous process of modernization, a process that upsets many time-honored moral values and social organizations of minority groups.

This chapter will offer readers a dynamic view of a range of literary genres, particularly autobiographical essays and fiction, produced by ethnic Qiang authors of southwestern China. Through a literary journey into the gendered landscape of multiethnic groups, we will discover how minority communities experience the contradictory aspects of modernity exemplified by the complex relationships between the two sexes. Particularly, we will see how modernity assumes a feminine gender in the images of the ethnic mother and the dangerous indigenous seductress: minority writers lament the commodification of ethnic traditions as the alluring "Poisonous Cat" (indigenous seductress) is complicit in turning the virile Qiang culture into touristic spectacles. At the same time, minority writers call for a return to ethnic traditions embodied by the mother as a healer of the malaises and alienations caused by the relentless modernization projects that are transforming minority communities. By reading a selection of previously understudied and untranslated Chinese minority literary works, I hope to enrich the general scholarly understanding of gender in contemporary China and reveal minority writers' critique of modernity from the angle of gender imagination.

The Unwanted Ethnic "Mother:" The Abandonment of Ethnic Homelands in Minority Autobiographies

Many of China's ethnic minority writers and intellectuals have unique bicultural and bilingual educational and personal backgrounds. Minority writers' bicultural/bilingual educational and personal backgrounds not only endow them with knowledge of the nation and national discourses, but also inform their literary creations with a "bifocality," or "reciprocity of perspectives,"[1] which makes their literary works concern simultaneously the ethnic *and* the national. In other words, many minority writers deploy perspectives that situate the ethnic experience within national circumstances and reveal national problems through the prism of minority lifeworlds.

In the world of letters in multiethnic China, autobiographical and memoir-style essays (*geren suibi* 个人随笔 and *huiyixing suibi* 回忆性随笔) are popular genres among Qiang and other ethnic minority writers. Writing at a time of rapid social transformations in contemporary China, multiethnic Chinese writers are eager to construct ethnic genealogies through the narratives of their own childhoods, youth, and familial histories. According to Michael M.J. Fischer, individual autobiographical writings can be a powerful vehicle for voicing and constructing ethnic identities. Because the autobiographical writings authored by a nation's ethnic minorities are usually grounded in particular moral visions and mediate between a sense of self and an ethnic community, autobiographical searchings often reveal a minority people's traditions and become "re-collections of disseminated identities."[2]

Fischer's conception of "disseminated identities" is crucial for our understanding of minority autobiographies. As many members of ethnic minorities in China are leaving behind their rural homelands to search for new livelihoods in the nation's urban centers, minority migrants form small diasporas and mingle with other ethnic groups, particularly the Han, in urban China. As we will see in this section, minority writers and migrants often experience dramatic—sometimes even tragic and traumatizing—culture shocks in metropolitan China. These experiences introduce disruptions and fragmentations into the lives of minority writers and migrants, as they can no longer hold onto the whole/wholesome cultural systems and social values practiced by their ancestors in their rural ethnic homelands. As such, minority writers reconstruct their ethnic consciousness by piecing together competing cultural values in the form of "disseminated," or fragmented and re-invented, identities. In other words, beyond personal accounts, autobiographical writings become important literary instruments for multiethnic writers to make sense of their collective experiences and memories.

In contemporary Qiang literature, many autobiographical writings are penned by bilingual/bicultural authors who have left their native villages permanently to take up professional work in various towns and cities in China. These authors later reflect on the events, experiences, and sentiments of their youthful years in their native villages. Similar to the May Fourth generation of writers of early twentieth-century China who left their villages to become urban intellectuals and later re-visited their hometowns only to find themselves bitterly estranged from their native regions, the minority writer's return to and remembrance of the native soil is never easy. In many ways akin to their May Fourth predecessors, contemporary Qiang writers with rural roots engage with the topic of the native soil (*xiangtu* 乡土) with a profound sense of intellectual wandering.[3] With their elite education and prestigious social status and many years of living away from their home villages, minority writers almost inevitably find themselves alienated from their native environments when they return for a visit. More significantly, such returns or remembrances are almost always entwined with a deep desire to "articulate and reenact the trauma of destruction and loss—of a sense of home, identity, and belonging—that [accompanies] the process of modernization."[4] Qiang writers document the traumas and destruction of the young ethnic son who departs from his home region and later comes back to the native village in search for a sense of cultural belonging.

In the autobiographical writings of three Qiang writers, Yang Zi (羊子, b. 1969), Wang Yong'an (王永安, b. 1954), and Ren Dongsheng (任冬生, b. 1978), the motif of an ethnic son rebelling against and eventually returning to the bosom of his ethnic native land in the image of the ethnic mother is salient. All three writers are representative of the bicultural minority elites who re-visit and remember their ethnic homeland and experience a shocking and traumatizing emotional journey. Such a journey propels the writers to rethink the relationship between ethnic identity and modernization, as well as their relationships to the land that nurtured them. Particularly, the question of gender comes into play, as the ethnic homeland is usually depicted as the "feminine" counterpart to a progressively forward yet pragmatic nation by male minority writers.

As Rita Felski reminds us, gender does not only affect the factual content of knowledge produced in the modern era, but more importantly, "[gender] affects . . . the philosophical assumptions underlying our interpretations of the nature and meaning of social processes."[5] In other words, gender and the understanding of gender help organize knowledge about the modern, which is an era characterized by disruptions, dynamic changes, and a forward-looking spirit in most societies. In the autobiographical and memoir-style essays that are popular among contemporary Qiang writers from Sichuan province, the image of an unwanted and languishing ethnic mother is a prototype that recurs in many writers' works. Reading the autobiographical writings produced by a range of Qiang male writers, one can easily decipher how the rural ethnic mother is associated with the "dead weight of tradition and conservativism that the active, newly autonomous, and self-defining [male] subject seeks to transcend."[6]

Qiang male writers like Yang Zi vividly bring to life the image of the ethnic mother as the carrier of the weight of traditions in the minds of freedom-seeking young minority men. Yang Zi (original name Yang Guoqing 杨国庆) is a prominent Qiang poet and writer who has achieved national fame. As the chief editor of *Qiangzu Literature* (*Qiangzu wenxue* 羌族文学), one major professional literary journal devoted to the Qiang people in China, Yang Zi is also the president of Wenchuan County Literature and Art Association (汶川县文联) in Sichuan.[7] In 2008, after Wenchuan and other Qiang regions in Sichuan were struck by a catastrophic earthquake, Yang Zi was invited by the Chinese Writers Association to publish an epic-style long poem titled *Wenchuan Qiang* (汶川羌).[8] In 2011, the National Museum of Modern Chinese Literature in Beijing hosted an academic conference exclusively for *Wenchuan Qiang*, making Yang Zi one of the first ethnic Qiang writers with such national honor and recognition.[9] In 2010, Yang Zi further joined eight other eminent Chinese writers to participate in the prestigious International Writing Program at the University of Iowa, making his first step toward becoming a "global minority writer."[10]

Similarly, Wang Yong'an and Ren Dongsheng are Qiang intellectuals who have obtained prestigious social status. Though not a nationally prominent writer like Yang Zi, Wang Yong'an boasts two degrees, one in Chinese Language and Literature from Southwestern Nationalities (Minzu) University and the other in Law from Sichuan University.[11] Wang has served the courts and legal bureaus in Li County, another important county with a concentrated Qiang population in Sichuan. He writes extensively in his free time and his essay won the First Sichuan Provincial Tianfu Literary Prize in 2005.[12] Ren Dongsheng, a prolific ethnic Qiang writer, is a member of the China

Essayists Association and won the 2010 West China Essays High Ranking Nomination Award.[13] In short, Yang Zi, Wang Yong'an and Ren Dongsheng are all prominent Qiang writers who have achieved provincial, national, or even international recognition.

Despite these writers' rising fame in the community of letters, they pen their poignant interactions with their mothers and their betrayal of their ethnic heritage and ancestral memories in their autobiographical essays. Yang Zi's "Mother in the Mountains" (*Shanzhong de muqin* 山中的母亲) is a memoir-style piece in which the poet remembers how he disappointed his mother through his unsuccessful attempts to leave behind his native village and his mother. In this essay, the image of the languishing and hardworking mother is enlivened through the poet's memory, and the extremely diligent mother is symbolized as the land that nourished the young poet:

> I suddenly remember my mother raising a hoe [on the farmland] in the mountains. Having lived her life for sixty years, she is still hoeing up weeds at midday. The scorching and endless sun is like tens of thousands of whips lashing her . . . When I was young, Mother's eyes were filled with various kinds of exhaustion and sufferings, one after another, with no end no matter day or night.[14]

Yang Zi's description of the "scorching sun lashing [his mother]" unambiguously reveals the toil suffered by an older rural Qiang woman. He sympathetically portrays the mother as someone who silently swallows up the bitterness, "exhaustion and sufferings" of the endless cycles of work. The mother's image is accentuated by her identity as a rural Qiang woman who has never left the mountains, deeply rooted and trapped in the land that she trudges on:

> Mother is a native Qiang person. [She always wears] long robes and wraps the "cloud headwear" around her head and [wears] a goat fur vest. She lives halfway up the hills but not once in her life has she climbed to the top of the Lotus Mountain in my hometown; nor has she ever left the ridged mountains that block her eyesight . . . Mother eventually doesn't know that the river [the Min River] flows out of the towering mountains and sculptures the Western Sichuan Plain, nourishing the famed abundance of West Sichuan.[15]

By never leaving the mountains that "block her eyesight," the mother remains ignorant about not only the outside world, but also her own surroundings: she does not even know that the river that runs through the mountains gives shape to the "famed abundance of West Sichuan."

The image of the unsophisticated yet hardworking mother is used by the writer to signify Qiang female peasants, many of whom are too attached to their farm work to leave the mountains. When Yang Zi and his siblings traveled afar and went back to tell the mother about what they had seen in the wider world, the mother finally became more aware of "the stunning and envy-provoking urban culture."[16] Yet she also grew more despondent and began feeling at a loss, for she could not leave behind her farm work to see such "stunning urban culture." The mother's yearnings for her children also grew, as the children kept wandering further away from home and became emotionally unavailable to the mother, occupying themselves with "digging for food [survival] in the colorful world."[17]

The plain but diligent rural ethnic mother toils on the unchanging fields to support her children, who eventually leave her behind and cruelly deem her undesirable in their search for a dazzling urban life. In the same essay, Yang Zi remembers the incident of how he "drifted" to Shenzhen, a major economic hub in southern China, to search for new opportunities but soon used up his money. His mother traveled back and forth between their home village and the urban center many times, trying to help her son. After many painstaking efforts, the mother finally gathered enough money to send to Yang Zi in Shenzhen, as her son had requested. When Yang Zi eventually went back to the village to visit his mother, instead of being warmly welcomed back as he had imagined, the mother became wildly enraged and desperate, grilling the son about the tortures that he had brought her:

> Tears silently trickled down from the goat-like face of Mother. Logs were burning briskly in the fireplace . . . the house was strangely quiet. "Didn't I give you a bowl of rice to eat? Why did you go to that faraway place to become a beggar and torture my heart? I have been saving and tightening my belt for you, but you have kindly repaid me this way. This is how you kindly repay my kindness?!" . . . Mother had been lovingly raising me up, but today she hit me on my head. It was only then did I realize her overwhelming disappointment in me.[18]

The traumatic encounter between the returning son and the desperate mother is poignantly rendered in this passage, as the hardworking and suffering mother finally broke down and blamed the son for making himself a "beggar" in that "faraway place," or the dazzling urban center of Shenzhen in

China. Not being able to persuade her son to remain in the mountains—as the mountains prove too poor and backward to appeal to the ambitious son—the mother tragically swallows up her own pains until this moment of emotional outbreak. The son's abandonment of his home village in exchange for a failed attempt to establish himself in urban China is deemed an act of betrayal of the mother. The son's callous action not only brings about financial burdens, but also a sense of humiliation to the mother: the mother's many years of hard work are only enough to pay off her son's debts and failures as a minority man in urban China. The mother's self-sacrificing spirit to help her son gather enough money to return to the village only erases her own identity as an industrious Qiang woman. This tragic interaction between the mother and the son means that the self-effacing ethnic mother functions "as a sacrificial victim exemplifying the losses which underpin the ambiguous, but ultimately exhilarating and seductive logic of the modern."[19]

In his autobiographical writings, Yang Zi enlivens the emotional dramas and ideological conflicts between the adventurous ethnic son, who is preoccupied with the "masculine" aspects of modernity characterized by "dynamic activity, development, and the desire for unlimited growth,"[20] and the seemingly feminine attachment to a piece of land and its time-tested traditions exemplified by the mother. Like many young people from rural China, Yang Zi the young Qiang man was lured by the opportunities in Shenzhen, a city in Guangdong that was designated to be an experimental economic hub in 1980 at the advent of the Chinese economic reform.[21] For many years, the city had the top GDP among cities in China with an average annual growth of 28%[22], and it represented wealth, opportunities, and upward mobility for Chinese youth eager to embrace the economic reform and change their lives. Yet for the Qiang mother, her son's unannounced departure to this faraway city spelt a terrible betrayal to his rural upbringing, and his being stripped of financial abilities in that city brought intolerable shame and torture to a hardworking mother, who had to "tighten [her] belt" to help her adult son. The mother's traumatized response to the son's return further traumatizes the son himself, as he is "staggered and stupefied, unable to feel [his own] existence."[23]

In this essay, Yang Zi reenacts a heightened emotional experience and articulates, in memory, the traumatic encounter between the rural ethnic mother and an urbanizing, adventurous son who tries to escape the mother's nurturing and safe bosom. It is important to note that throughout the essay, the author eliminates the possessive noun "my" and addresses his mother directly by the unmodified "Mother" (*muqin*). This form of address endows the mother with a universal aura and makes her a prototype of the toiling, suffering rural minority mothers who are unable to change the course of their children's assimilation into a modernizing nation. In this sense, Yang Zi's essay provides insights into the symbolic departure of the ethnic child from the rural space into an industrializing, modernizing national space.

At the end of the essay, Yang Zi reminds us that it is memory that mediates his relationship with his mother, as he seems unable to provide any real comfort to his mother:

> In a room, a person affectionately misses his mother, who bends her back in the distant, mighty mountains, giving her utmost efforts in her farm work . . . When will the heavens allow you to sit tranquilly in your son's room filled with gentle music and let your son . . . relax the strings of your heart that have been tight for a lifetime?[24]

In this paragraph, the first-person narrative of the essay suddenly transforms to a third-person narrative ("a person affectionately misses his mother"), distancing the narrator from the story and offering a birds'-eye-view of the image of the mother deeply attached to the rural homeland. Then, the writer calls his mother with second-person address and asks a question he cannot answer, namely, when can the mother truly rest her tired heart? Here, remembrance plays a contradictory double role. On the one hand, it offers what Svetlana Boym calls an "emotional topography of memory,"[25] as Yang Zi's remembrance of his mother articulates the emotional journey of a rural ethnic son's complex relationship with his native land and his mother, allowing the writer to critically reflect on his crisis-ridden coming-of-age. On the other hand, remembrance and memory only serve to distance the writer from the subject of his remembrance—his mother—as he finds it impossible to directly communicate his emotions to his mother, nor can he identify a reliable source of comfort to soothe his mother's worried heart. Thus the narrator escapes to memory in the form of writing and leaves unanswered and unanswerable the question of where his mother's heart can rest.

The motif of the languishing and unwanted mother occurs repeatedly in contemporary Qiang autobiographical and memoir-style writing to signify the quandaries of ethnic minority groups undergoing modernization. As Michael M.J. Fischer notes, in the increasingly complex and interdependent contemporary world, ethnicity can no longer be captured by the conventional understanding of "group process (support systems), a matter of transition (assimilation)," or an identity resulting from "straightforward transmission from generation to generation (socialization)."[26] To the contrary, ethnicity requires a conscious self-definition, and ethnic identities are often reinvented through remembering.[27] When minority groups, such as the Qiang, are constantly exposed to the modernizing impetuses and expanding market economy of a fast developing country like China, ethnicity is no longer simply an intergenerational transmission of some essential traits, such as language and ancestral memories, as these "traits" themselves are facing the danger of vanishing or being forgotten. This is evident in the fact that as an ethnic son, Yang Zi refused to take up the farm work of his mother and rejected the transmission of a rural identity from his mother. In the autobiographical writing of Qiang authors like Yang Zi, ethnic identity is reconstituted and reassembled when the writers critically reflect on how they betray their ethnic heritage and native land but later choose to return and anchor themselves emotionally and spiritually in their formerly abandoned ethnic past. Therefore, writing becomes an important discursive and cultural activity that helps minority groups redefine their identities in the format of reconstituting abandoned and fragmented pasts, stitching together that which is shattered by the rural minority subject's encounter with urban life.

Like Yang Zi, Wang Yong'an traces his rebel against his mother and native place in his essay "Homeland" (*Laojia* 老家). "Homeland" is a memoir-style essay in which Wang describes his return to his native village: the author takes his son to visit his native village and reclaims his roots in the village. In the essay, Wang remembers how his younger self had forsaken his ethnic and rural identity. Similar to Yang Zi, the younger Wang dreamed about leaving behind his home village and becoming a modern. In "Homeland," Wang recalls his poignant experience of fulfilling the dreams he had at the unexpected cost of renouncing both his mother and his ethno-rural identity:

> Thirty years ago, I left Zengtou Village at an age full of dreams. At first, under the dazzling light I could not tell day from night, in the coach of cars I could not tell if I was in movement or stillness. I let myself go and enjoyed and praised everything in front of me; meanwhile I cursed and betrayed everything from my past.[28]

For a Qiang youth like Wang, the city's abundant material wealth, as well as the tantalizing urban life represented by "dazzling light" and "coach of cars" were so appealing that he wholeheartedly embraced them without begrudging what he had to give up for these gains, namely, his homeland and his past. The materialistic sensations of such an urban life not only seduced Wang to forget his native place and curse his past, but also caused him to deny his mother outright. When his mother came to see him at work, Wang was too ashamed of admitting that the women in rags was his mother, that he told his colleagues that she was only his aunt. Only later did Wang realize the traumas and scars this denial had caused for his mother, who "wiped her sweat and trudged with her exhausted body, disappearing on the misty winding road in the mountains.[29]

Like Yang Zi's depiction of the mother's profound disappointment upon seeing the returning son, Wang Yong'an details the destructive effect that the "unexpected betrayal of her own son" had on a rural Qiang woman: she can only cover up her son's lie with her "tender smile," trudging away as the unwanted mother.

In another essay, Wang remembers a similar instance of denying his mother's love when he refused to wear the new linen clothes his mother had made for him, as his classmates in his high school laughed at him for wearing linen, Qiang people's favorite fabric.[30] For Wang the young Qiang man, rejecting the mother and her love symbolized a renouncement of both his rurality and minority status. The mother, an unrefined rural woman in the eyes of her son, embodies the unwanted marginality and material impoverishment that young minority men were quick to denounce. She is a token of backwardness and shame that the young and robust minority men made every effort to escape from.

In the Qiang autobiographic and memoir-style essays we have seen, the image of the earthbound, uneducated, and insular mother signifies the ethnic traditions and slowness to change that young Qiang men rebel against, particularly at a pivotal moment of China's economic reform and booming opportunities in the late 1900s and early 2000s. The minority young man enacts his masculinity through constantly performing masculine actions, achieving both horizontal and vertical mobility: he moves up the social ladder by receiving a college education; he goes beyond the bounds of his small rural home community to reinvent himself in urban China; he traverses the boundaries of ethnolocal relations by proving himself in Han-dominated cities and towns. Through all such actions, the minority man transgresses the socio-economic and ethno-regional limits represented by the ethnic mother, carving out a masculine space of ethnic identity in China. Yet, all these worldly gains come at the cost of traumatizing the rural ethnic mother, plaguing her with emotional catastrophes and financial debts that the son only regrets later.

The rural minority mother bears the brunt of the symbolic and material dichotomy between the fast-developing, "masculine" nation and the rural ethnic regions. This dichotomy is reconciled only when the adult male minority writer consciously mediates between his abandoned past and the crude realities of the present after a shocking return to the ethnic homeland. We will examine how an eagerness to return to the abandoned ethnic motherland is depicted by the mature Qiang male writers and even inspires female minority writers to re-establish the image of the Mother as the healer of the malaises of modernity in the final section of this chapter. For now, let us turn to another important gendered image in contemporary Chinese minority literature, the ethnic seductress, to understand how women's sexuality and feminine charms are symbolized as the poisons of modernity by minority writers.

The Uncontained "Poisonous Cat:" Combatting the Bewitching Feminine Powers of Modernity

If the memoirs and autobiographic writing of Yang Zi and Wang Yong'an reveal minority men's sentimental and poignant experience of renouncing the "feminine" native homeland in order to embrace the "masculine" urban centers of China, Qiang fiction writer Yu Yaoming's (余耀明 b. 1963) story "The Fragrant Key" (*Fenfang duoyowei* 芬芳朵哟喂) reveres this gendered hierarchy. In this story, Yu creates the vivid image of a Qiang seductress, whose entrepreneurial spirit, worldly calculatedness, and dangerous charms are almost the polar opposite of the timid, insular, and self-deprecating ethnic mother.

Yu Yaoming was born in 1963 in the Keku Township of Wenchuan County, Sichuan. With a degree in Chinese Literature from the Southwestern Minzu University in Chengdu, the cradle of many minority writers and scholars in southwest China, Yu has taken up the job of being a journalist, writing fiction, and authoring books and documentaries on Qiang culture for the past twenty years.[31] Originally published in an important Qiang literary magazine, *Caodi* (Grassland, 草地) in 2006, "The Fragrant Key" was later included in the *Selected Literary Works of Ethnic Minority Groups*, a national minority literature publishing project spearheaded by the Chinese Writers Association (*Zhongguo zuojia xiehui* 中国作家协会) in an effort to "develop ethnic minority art" by encouraging diverse expressions of ethnic life.[32]

In this story, Yu illuminates how modernity castrates the otherwise virile and wholesome minority cultures through its deceptive feminine charms. The story skillfully combines the indigenous gender legends of the Qiang with a profound critique of the delusive lures of modernizing discourses and practices, which bring emotional catastrophes and physical disintegration to minority groups. In this story, an indigenous Qiang woman, Adaying (阿达婴), and a Qiang man, Black Egg (*Hei luanzi* 黑卵子) originally occupy the lowest social ladder in Peach Blossom Qiang Village because both are the poorest in the village.

Despite Adaying's beauty and charms, no one dares to marry her, because she is considered as a woman with a destructive but enchanting power, known as a "Poisonous Cat" (*duyao mao* 毒药猫) in the Qiang indigenous traditions. As we saw at the beginning of this chapter, a Poisonous Cat is considered by Qiang villagers as a source of disorder for both her family and her community, and men in Peach Blossom Village all avoid Adaying like a poison, even though many of them have harbored secret desires for her. Among all the men in the village, only Black Egg openly expresses his desire for the bewitching Adaying. Black Egg himself is destitute and ugly with no marriage prospects in sight, and he thinks Adaying and himself can make a great pair.

Adaying shatters Black Egg's sexual fantasies for her—she destroys Black Egg's sexual organs when Black Egg flirts with her in a public restroom. Adaying also soon becomes wealthy after she opens up her home as a guesthouse to welcome Han tourists. Black Egg's name is suggestive of the sexualized nature of his experience in his own village: "egg" (*dandan* 蛋蛋) is an idiomatic, if somewhat profane, way of referring to the male sexual organs in the Sichuan dialect. Being a man without proper resources to survive in an increasingly touristic minority village, Black Egg feels further belittled by the business-savvy indigenous woman, Adaying, who deprives him of both his sexual potency and financial abilities. In the story, Adaying is portrayed as both sexually alluring/dangerous and socially powerful—she outsmarts and punishes minority men like Black Egg, taking advantage of mainstream society's voyeuristic desire to peek into Qiang culture as she keeps proffering up Qiang cultural symbols in exchange for the money and attention from tourists.

Not minding her village being labelled as a "living fossil" and "primitive culture"[33] by mainstream Chinese media, Adaying is unscrupulous about selling out the Qiang cultural objects passed down and entrusted to her, such as the Qiang's unique key-making techniques that helped this ethnic group survive many years of warfare.[34] With the help of a Han photographer, Adaying even patents the Qiang key as a unique ethnic tourism souvenir and becomes the wealthiest person in Peach Blossom Village after earning a fortune from it. Meanwhile, Black Egg feels ashamed of the contrast between the smart and popular Adaying and his own lack of resources to advance himself financially and romantically in his native village. Black Egg suffers from alienation and social oblivion, eventually dying from extreme poverty and humiliation.

The author Yu Yaoming's juxtaposition of Adaying's sexual prowess with her unsurpassed ability to fetishize Qiang cultural symbols touches upon women's complex relationship with consumption in modern societies. In the story, Adaying epitomizes the ultimate fetishization and commodification of Qiang culture: apart from patenting Qiang keys for sale, she even capitalizes on the legend of the Poisonous Cat for tourism profits. She overturns the negative connotation of the Poisons Cat as the *femme fatale* in Qiang communities by branding it as another spectacle in Peach Blossom Village. We have a very telling exchange between tourists and local villagers from the story:

> "Can you please tell us where Adaying lives?" [some tourists inquire]
>
> "What Adaying? There is no Adaying in Peach Blossom Village—only a Poisonous Cat." [the resentful villagers reply.]
>
> "What do you mean by Poisonous Cat?"
>
> "You don't know anything about the Poisonous Cat? She harms people and is very cruel. You will only know how cruel she is when she harms you."
>
> "We are not afraid of it. Please tell us where she lives."
>
> The tourists are always smiling. The more villagers talk about Adaying as the Poisonous Cat, the more mysterious and alluring her *diaolou* [fortressed, towering Qiang vernacular building] becomes. More and more tourists are coming for Adaying's *diaolou*. After a while, tourists just ask upfront: "Where does the Poisonous Cat live?"[35]

Much to the resentment of her fellow villagers, Adaying has become the wealthiest and most powerful woman in Peach Blossom Village precisely *because of*, not despite, her otherwise lamentable label as the Poisonous Cat. Adaying's ability to turn an indigenous gender taboo into a new site for symbolic and capitalistic profitability is closely tied to her seductive allures as a charming and intelligent minority woman, capable of inspiring consumptions from tourists: she exemplifies a "fetishized, libidinized, and commodified femininity produced through . . . the modern forms of desire."[36] Adaying taps into tourists' desire of consuming exoticized and eroticized versions of minority cultures by objectifying her gender identity and commodifying her *diaolou* and her ethnic background, fetishizing them as sellable experiences in exchange of tourist dollars. In this sense, Adaying also represents the scapegoating role[37] of the Poisonous Cat in Qiang communities: when faced with larger problems—such as modernization projects and their looming harms to local communities—Qiang villagers project their fear for such external "others" onto the smaller "other" of one village woman, scapegoating her for all the troubles modernization introduces into the village.

As an ethnic seductress, Adaying's power reaches beyond her local community: she is critiqued by author Yu Yaoming as possessing the "castrating effects of an ever more pervasive commodification"[38] that appeals to tourists yet reduces her ethnic community to consumable sites and sights. Adaying is complicit in constructing the minority village as a spectacle for cultural voyeurism and touristic pleasure at the cost of feminizing minority men, such as Black Egg, and depriving them of their sexual and financial abilities.

The almost legendary rise to fame and fortune that Adaying enjoys as a minority woman experiences a dramatic and gendered turn at the end of the story. Despite Adaying's wealth and social status, she lives alone in a dark Qiang house that does not see light very often, and she is subject to social alienation from her fellow villagers—a woman who is considered as a Poisonous Cat is usually seen as a threat by her villagers and lives almost like a social outcast in the Qiang community. On the evening of Black Egg's funeral, Adaying dreams about Black Egg and how she and her dog triumphally destroy Black Egg's penis, which Adaying deems too ugly and black to be attractive. Before Adaying can indulge in her triumph for too long, she smells a pleasant fragrance, and for the first time in a long while, she experiences light in her house, as "a pipe of sunlight penetrates the scar on the wall, and she sees the traditional Qiang key with nine nails given to her by an old shaman . . ."[39]

The words "pipe of sunlight" and "penetrate" are symbolic of the restoration of the virility of Qiang culture represented by Black Egg and the old shaman. The shaman is usually the most respected male figure in Qiang communities and is the ultimate patriarchal authority in Qiang villages, responsible for ensuring the harmony and order of Qiang communities through his power to communicate with the spiritual world and to bestow blessings to Qiang people. If Adaying's feminine power has brought about the physical destruction and humiliation of Qiang men like Black Egg in exchange of her own fame and fortune in the capitalistic world of tourism, the phallic image of "a pipe of sunlight" and the penetration of sunlight into the scarred holes of Adaying's dark home suggest the revival of the virility and wholesomeness that Qiang men have lost to the deceiving charms of modernization.

This story embraces a sharp feminist critique of modernity by revealing how Adaying, as a minority woman, becomes subject to the rampant consumerism in modernizing China as she thoughtlessly and greedily turns her feminine charms into tourist capital and severely distorts the integrity of her own culture. In this story, Adaying has not only caused the sufferings of Qiang men, but has also exacerbated the social inequality in her community: she monopolizes the touristic resources and profits in the village and remains the center of attention for Han tourists for her beauty and her ability to render her house aesthetically appealing to please tourists. By contrast, Black Egg's shabby home and his ugly appearance attract no tourists, and he lacks the ability to extract the exchange value of his Qiang culture, dwarfed by Adaying's superb skills of turning all things Qiang into touristic commodities. Therefore, the development of tourism and the introduction of capitalistic exploitations into Qiang villages are depicted as seemingly promising but eventually corruptive feminine forces in the story, as such forces threaten to deprive minority cultures—particularly minority men—of their masculinity and potency, rendering minority men useless in the competitive world of tourism characterized by relentless cultural exhibitionism and materialistic indulgence.

In this sense, "The Fragrant Key" is a gender allegory and a profound critique of the gendered logic of consumer culture in modern societies, as "the modern becomes aligned with a pessimistic vision of an unpredictable yet curiously passive femininity seduced by the glittering phantasmagoria of an emerging consumer culture."[40] As a minority woman, Adaying is seduced by the destructive forces of commodifying minority cultures; she exploits her own culture and her feminine beauty to gain glittering material profits in her village. In so doing, Adaying becomes simultaneously an object for consumption and an inciter for consumerism.

Importantly, Yu's choice of letting the "Poisonous Cat" Adaying embody the dangerous forces of consumerism is both heir to and mocks the traditional gender imagination in Qiang culture. According to Ming-ke Wang, a scholar of Qiang culture, the designation of certain women as Poisonous Cats betrays Qiang villagers' fear of the "pollution" of a village's bloodline and the potential moral impurity that women may introduce into Qiang villages.[41] The Qiang have a long tradition of othering and marginalizing a sst-mall number of women—particularly young and charming women—as the carriers of "poisons" that can cause illness and temporary disorders in their villages. Capable of transforming into the shapes of domestic animals, such as cats and horses, these women play the role of tricksters to seduce and scare village members, usually males, and to exercise their sexual powers and other abilities; the women labeled as Poisonous Cats are often scapegoated for the disasters a village encounters, yet they are almost always tamed and turn back into their human shape to conclude episodes of temporary social disorder.[42] Even though these women are usually disliked by their fellow villagers, they are considered essential to fend off greater "poisons"—such as the Qiang's powerful neighbors, the Tibetans and the Han—as these women help resolve internal discords to consolidate Qiang communities.[43] In other words, the legend of the Poisonous Cat represents the desire to simultaneously "domesticate" or suppress women and the need to marginalize and scapegoat a selected group of women to maintain the social stability and male supremacy in Qiang communities.

In "The Fragrant Key," we see an incarnation of the Qiang's traditional gender imagination as Adaying is being othered as a Poisonous Cat that causes disharmony in Peach Blossom Village. However, departing from the conventional trope of the tamable Poisonous Cat, Adaying's power grows so wildly that she eventually brings permanent physical harms to Qiang men and introduces irrevocable disruptions to her village's equality and harmony.

How does an otherwise "domesticable" woman transcend the gender norms of her community to become its biggest malady? In the story, we can find clues that despite being labelled as a dangerous woman, Adaying is bewitched by the even more consuming power of modernization and development, which in turn exoticizes Qiang culture: tourists ask for the Poisonous Cat, or Adaying's house, as a sight-seeing destination, not caring for local villagers' warnings that the Poisonous Cat can cause them harm.[44] Moreover, Adaying rationalizes her monopoly of the touristic resources in Peach Blossom Village by comforting herself that she does so to help feed and clothe her blind grandmother.[45]

Despite the potentially emancipatory power of touristic development in bringing prosperity to formerly impoverished minority women, minority women are portrayed as falling prey to the spellbinding power of the cultural exploitation that underpins the developmental projects in minority villages by authors like Yu Yaoming. The gender hierarchy in this story—minority women being a site of sexual prowess and financial capabilities yet also a source of threat to local men—invites us to rethink the gender landscape of China's modernization.

Previously, many scholars have discussed how minority groups are subject to gendered imaginations in Han Chinese literary and cultural representations. For example, Dru Gladney has analyzed how China's official and mainstream media often eroticizes and objectifies minority people—particularly minority women—as the colorful "others" for the consumption of Han spectators.[46] Similarly, Yuqing Yang writes about how southwestern Chinese minority groups with strong matriarchal traditions, such as the Mosuo, have become the subject of both romanticization and moral judgements among Han scholars and tourists, as the Mosuo's unique matrimonial and social customs center around women and inspire Han critics to reflect on the patriarchal pitfalls of Han culture.[47]

Yu Yaoming's story "The Fragrant Key" shifts our critical attention away from painting minority groups simply as passive gendered others awaiting the consumption and exploitation of Han people and mainstream Chinese media. Rather, the story explores the fraught question of gender *within* minority communities themselves, revealing the heterogeneity and uneven nature of gender in multiethnic China. The story unveils how minority men like Black Egg struggle to claim a masculine space, combatting a sense of "self-feminization and anxiety"[48] that usually ensues from interethnic contact within China.

As Ben Hillman and Lee Ann Henfry's study of minority masculinity in China demonstrates, as different ethnic groups come into contact with each other throughout China's long history, a perpetual anxiety of emasculation characterizes the cultural interactions between men from diverse ethnic groups.[49] On the one hand, certain northern and western minority groups, such as the Mongols and Tibetans, tend to be masculinized as militant, physically capable, and attractive in Chinese literary and cultural representations; on the other hand, many southern minority groups are feminized as submissive and passive.[50] Minority men's gender imagination is confined in the space of interethnic contact and domination. During the process of rapid modernization and the transformation of rural minority communities, capitalistic forces introduced by Han-centered tourism push minority men like Black Egg to reconceptualize their masculinity vis-à-vis minority women—they have to countervail the all-consuming power of national development as they navigate the drastically evolving social relations, financial resources, and interpersonal relationships in the compressed space of a minority tourism village.

Through following the tumultuous journey of Adaying's rise to the top of social ladders and the failure and emasculation of Black Egg as the price for Adaying's success, author Yu Yaoming questions the convenient and simplistic formula of portraying minority groups as a quiescent gendered "other" onto which (Chinese) modernity can project its own agendas. Instead, we witness the complexity and ambivalence of the question of gender on the site of Yu's fictional Peach Blossom Village. Peach Blossom Village bears uncanny familiarity with the real social and gender problems in many Chinese minority villages: while Adaying symbolizes the self-Orientalization and self-exoticizations that many minority communities partake of in exchange for economic profitability, Black Egg accuses the self-feminization of such endeavors and strives to rebuild a masculine vibrancy in minority villages, even though he fails in his endeavors and is completely castrated by the bewitching forces of touristic development embodied by Adaying.

Eventually, it is the old shaman, who has passed the age of virile masculinity yet remains powerful for his traditional role of restoring social order, that cautions minority groups of the beguiling danger of sexualizing and romanticizing the minority self in a fast-developing China. Toward the end of the story, Adaying dreams about how the old shaman once entrusted the Qiang key to her as a token of her ethnic history; it is only then that she realizes that ethnic traditions are to be inherited and respected, not reduced to their exchange value in the tourism marketplace.

In contrast to the masculine images of the exciting spaces of urban life in China that we saw in the autobiographical writings of Qiang writers in the previous section, Yu Yaoming's fiction offers a sharp feminist critique of Chinese modernity. He combines the description of the deceiving charms of modernity with the Qiang's indigenous beliefs of the lure and danger of the "Poisonous Cat" to caution readers of the danger of falling into the traps of the tempting but destructive promises of consumerism and the materialistic exploitation of ethnic cultures. Therefore, the question of gender is not one-directional and static (the passive, gendered minority groups vs. the normative, dynamic Han), but entails multi-layered interactions, performance, and social relations between minority men and women within the space of minority communities, especially as such communities go through radical transformations in the face of overwhelming modernization projects.

Return to the Mother's Bosom: Reconciling with Ethnic Traditions

After journeying through the contrasting gender imagination of the dangerous "Poisonous Cat" and the languishing mother in contemporary Qiang literature in the first two sections, in this final section of this chapter, let us return to the nurturing bosom of the ethnic mother with minority writers.

Rita Felksi reminds us that the maternal image is usually considered to be an "authentic point of origin" and a "mythic referent untouched by the strictures of social and symbolic mediation."[51] This is especially true when the so-called progressive modern society introduces scars, traumas, and a divided sense of the self into minority communities, as we saw in the first two sections. Writing becomes a process of reconciliation and an act of reclaiming the ethno-rural identity for Qiang writers who realize, later in their lives, how a personal denouncement of the mother and the native land spells a collective amnesia and dangerous abandonment of ethnic heritage.

This realization is particularly fleshed out in Qiang essayist Ren Dongsheng's memoir-style writing. In his 2014 essay collection *Qiang Wind All Over the Wilderness* (*Qiangfeng bianye* 羌风遍野), Ren pens many pieces of his personal remembrance and critiques of the declining social mores in his native Qiang region in Sichuan. In an essay titled "Secrets on the Top of the Min Mountain" (*Minshan zhidian de mimi* 岷山之巅的秘密), Ren offers critical reflections on the alienation between people and land in the Qiang regions in contemporary China, revealing his own journey of abandoning and later returning to the ethnic homeland.

In his essays, Ren Dongsheng uses many metaphors pertaining to the mother to call for a return to ethnic heritage. The homecoming Qiang intellectual is no longer content with the material comfort and professional success afforded by a life in the cities, but questions the alienation between himself and his native ethnic land:

> Some of them [the Qiang people], including me, truly reached a separation from the native land (*gutu*). Traveling too far, we could not go back. Yet, this departure caused us to lose ourselves . . . *we cut off the source of milk/nurture (naiyuan) from the soil and from our ethnic origins.* "Qiang" appears nowhere in our lives except as a character printed on our ID's and on our resumes. We boast nothing, understand nothing, and have nothing to do with our ethnic origins and with soil. We are a flock of migratory birds flying between two places, caught in a dilemma and trapped in an impasse (emphasis mine).[52]

In this passage, Ren reveals the emotional and cultural quandaries of the Qiang people who depart from their native land and live like "migratory birds" that belong nowhere. The cultural uprooted-ness experienced by the Qiang people who migrate to the cities is described by Ren as a radical separation from the "source of milk/nurture," or their ethnic traditions and land. Here, Ren likens ethnic heritage to the motherly feature of nursing and nurturing. For Ren, moving to the cities entails a painful and involuntary abandonment of ethnic heritage, as cities refuse the "intrusion of the soil"—anyone with a rural or minority origin may face discrimination or marginalization in the cities. As a result, minority people like the Qiang choose to forget their ethnic identities and cut themselves off from their rural past. Yet such a separation only further marginalizes minority people in urban China, as Ren describes that these minority people are usually "caught in a dilemma and trapped in an impasse"—they can never be fully accepted into the cities, meanwhile they have lost their own ethno-rural roots and connections.

Indeed, the image of the mother is embraced by minority writers like Ren Dongsheng to signify the reunion with one's ethnic and cultural traditions, as "the redemptive maternal body constitutes the ahistorical other and the other of history against which modern identity is defined."[53] The sense of alienation resulting from the minority youth's departure from the ethnic homeland is only reconciled when the minority youth return to the mother's bosom to combat the painful self-delusions of renouncing one's ethnic past. The ethnic mother serves as a touchstone to the past, an almost "ahistorical other" that counterbalances the materialistic demands and industrializing ambitions in the nation's metropolises.

Like Wang Yong'an and Yang Zi that we studied in the first section, Ren also left his native village to become an elite intellectual in the cities. Yet after witnessing how young people in his native Qiang village have changed and become overtly materialistic upon his visit home, Ren starts to form a profound sense of intellectual and moral wandering: he left home to pursue a "better" life in the cities, but he believes that the very characteristics of urbanites have polluted minority youth like himself. It is only then that Ren realizes the moral and cultural value of his "muddy" homeland and yearns to return to his native village uncontaminated by urban culture:

> Every year at the end of the year, they [young Qiang people who migrate to cities to work] come home . . . They are fashionably dressed and stand straight, dandified in appearance. They have lost the mark of the soil given to them or

> forced on them by the earth . . . They bring with them the progressive thinking of the cities and show contempt for their parents for their foolish attachment to the land, including the cows and horses that accompanied them when they grew up. They detest the mud for making their leather shoes and pants dirty. They despise the order and rituals and laws handed down by the ancestors. They do not worship the white stone, nor do they worship the sacred mountains . . . *They start to measure everything anew through the lens of money, including the soil that gave birth to and nurtured them* (emphasis mine).[54]

This is a detailed passage of Ren's observations of the moral decline of a new generation of Qiang people, who have been poisoned by the materialistic and secular worldviews of the cities where they make a living. This passage bears striking resemblance to the critique of materialistic frenzy in Yu Yaoming's "The Fragrant Key," albeit in a more direct and didactic style. For Ren, the young Qiang people have changed into snobbish and pretentious human beings who are "dandified in appearance" and "measure everything anew through the lens of money." Ren laments that the moral and spiritual foundation of the Qiang has been lost in the younger generation: they would rather worship money and material success than worship the Qiang's traditional white quartz stone, a symbol of purity and life-giving energy. By denouncing the cows, horses, and the earth, the young generation of Qiang people have not only detached themselves from the physical space of their home villages, but they have also divorced themselves from the hardworking attitude, the spiritual beauty, and ancestral memories of their ethnic group. Eventually, Ren criticizes that young Qiang people lured by urban life renounce the soil that "gave birth to and nurtured them," detaching themselves from the motherly love of the land that nourished them and their communities.

It should come as no surprise that nostalgic autobiographies become the site of reclaiming the maternal ethnic heritage for minority writers. In autobiographical writings, minority writers seek to reconnect themselves to the land and call for a return to their ancestral memories. These writers engage in what Svetlana Boym calls "reflective nostalgia:" through narrating "longing and loss" and piecing together "the imperfect process of remembrance,"[55] minority writers use their nostalgic sentiments toward ethnic land and tradition to mediate between individual and collective memory. Ren Dongshen does so by sharply mocking young Qiang people's attachment to money and material gains at the cost of renouncing their ethnic roots. Minority writers like Ren Dongshen aim at awakening the moral and cultural consciousness of their fellow minority members, questioning the separation and divisions resulting from minority members' relentless pursuit of a modern lifestyle once they leave behind their villages.

Beyond the male minority writers we have studied so far, there has been a prolific group of female minority writers in contemporary China. Two minority female writers, the Qiang poet Lei Zi (雷子) and ethnic Va writer Burao Yilu (布饶依露), revitalize the image of the mother as the healer that prevents minority communities from detaching themselves from their traditions and collective memories. Like her male counterparts examined earlier in this chapter, Lei Zi is a productive Qiang poet: a member of the Chinese Writers Association, Lei Zi's poetry collection won the national Steed Award for Minority Literature (*Shaoshu minzu wenxue junma jiang* 少数民族文学骏马奖), and she has widely published her poetry and fiction in different regional and national newspapers and literary magazines.[56] In her 2016 essay collection, *Innocent Dreams and Songs in the Wilderness of the Qiang* (*Tianzhen de meng yu Qiangye de ge* 天真的梦与羌野的歌), Lei Zi engages in loving depictions of her mother as a symbol of hardworking seamstresses of "that era"—the bygone era of socialist China (1950s to 1980s) when people with handicraft skills like her mother were highly regarded.[57] Remembering her mother's younger days as a seamstress that connected the entire community, Lei Zi unveils the mother's superb skills of turning old clothes into new fashions. Being a humble female worker all her life, the mother knows the inevitable fate of the disappearance of the tradition of sewing clothes in the Qiang communities, but she still "resentfully and quietly complains how I [the daughter] failed to learn these skills from her."[58]

The mother's longing for the Qiang's traditions is inhered in the form of loss in her daughter: many members of the younger generation of Qiang people have lost interest and capability in the traditional sewing and weaving skills. The daughter, unable to pass down the Qiang sewing traditions, looks to her mother as a powerful feminine figure and as "emblematic of a nonalienated, nonfragmented identity" that symbolizes a deep connection to Qiang traditions.[59] Ironically, the "power" of the mother only resides in the memories of a bygone era in the form of a nostalgic essay: with the mechanization of cloth-making technologies, the mother's old skills are becoming less and less useful today. Yet still, the mother, especially the hardworking, honest, and loving mother, serves as an embodiment of the past that reverses the detachment from the native land and the dehumanizing processes of instrumental modernity that we saw in Qiang writers' critique of the minority's encounter with modernization.

The mother is portrayed not only as modernity's other, but also modernity's healer and challenger, in contemporary minority women's literature. Ethnic Va writer Burao Yilu of Yunnan province penned an essay titled "Four Generations of Va Women," which was included in a 2020 anthology of multiethnic Chinese women writers' work translated into English.[60] In this essay, Burao Yilu presents the life stories of four generations of Va women in her family by narrating the intergenerational connections fostered by the mother. Burao writes:

> The grass hut where my grandmother and mother used to live swayed on its stilts in the wind. My mother's laughter and my own laughter echoed in the village. My dreams and my daughter's dreams hovered over the mountain tops . . .[61]

The physical space and natural beauty of the Va valleys serve as vessels for the grandmother, the mother, the author herself, and her daughter to pass down and reinvent their identities as Va women. In this essay, Burao reveals the struggles of her grandmother and mother as daughters of Va chieftains who have witnessed the dramatic historical changes in China. The author's mother not only challenged the Va's traditional arranged marriages to find her own true love in life, but also questioned the anti-right-wing movements in the 1950s that implicated the family as she demanded the protection of the family's safety and property from her husband's factory.[62] Under Burao's pen, the ethnic mother is not only a hardworking woman true to her heart and her family, but also a rebellious challenger of social injustices.

Like the image of the mother we saw earlier in this chapter, such as the insular and caring mother that Yang Zi and Wang Yong'an depict, Burao's ethnic Va mother is far from cosmopolitan and never leaves her home region. Yet, the Va ethnic mother, like the Qiang mother, is resilient, brave, and all-encompassing: she allows the Va people to "harvest confidence and courage" amidst rapid changes and transformations in the Va communities.[63] In other words, the mother's embodiment of traditions should not be taken as a sign of backwardness, but should be celebrated as a source of ethnic pride, intergenerational connections, and strength to combat cultural assimilations for minority communities.

In this sense, the ethnic son's and daughter's return to the mother's bosom is a correction to the disruptions, divided selves, and cultural sacrifices experienced by ethnic communities in contemporary China. The mother, as a symbol of care and a master of traditional knowledge and cultural values, is the ultimate healer of the malaises of modernity. The mother also denotes a deep connection to the ethnic native land that many minority writers abandoned in their youth. Returning to the mother is returning to the ethnic homeland. The ethnic homeland serves as a cultural locus for minority writers to reconnect with their ancestral origins and to critique the cultural alienations modernity has created for minority groups. The painful realization that one should not abandon his or her native homeland in exchange for professional success and material gain only happens after the mature minority writer comes back to visit his or her home village, reconciling his or her relationship with ethnic traditions by acknowledging the importance of the ethnic mother as the centerpiece of minority traditions and roots.

Conclusion

In this chapter, we have investigated the question of gender in contemporary Chinese multiethnic literature. Particularly, we have seen how the ethnic mother and the Poisonous Cat embody the contradictory experience of modernity for China's ethnic minority groups: while the mother is often portrayed as a touchstone to a minority group's vanishing ethnic heritage and a healer to restore the minority group's cultural wholeness, the indigenous seductress bespeaks the bewitching but destructive power of commodifying minority cultures. Women and femininity bear the weight of minority groups' fraught encounter with modernization in China: while the ethnic mother is usually loathed by the immature ethnic son as a token of conservatism and slowness to change, the ethnic seductress is critiqued as a symbol of minority groups' self-Orientalization and sexualization, which contribute to the decline of minority virility in China's market economy.

In the eyes of minority writers, the market economy in China calls the nation's diverse minority people into the modernizing, homogenizing space of the nation-state and lures minority people to exchange their ethnic identities for the material wealth and professional success in the nation's urban centers. Yet minority writers have come to realize the moral deficiency and materialistic danger of that homogenizing space—they feel the urge to reclaim a moral power rooted in their ethnic heritage and rural origin. Often, minority writers resort to autobiography and family genealogies to make sense of their collective experience as they critically reflect on the evolution of one family and the coming-of-age story of one person. The various Qiang and Va authors examined in this chapter use autobiographies to situate minority identities vis-à-vis a fast-developing Chinese nation, narrating personal experiences into collective memories as they remember about the mother and her connections to minority traditions and moral foundations.

The irony of minority writers' return to their ethnic heritage lies in the fact that such a return is sometimes only imaginary and symbolic: minority intellectuals and elites can never truly go back to their ancestral past or native villages, as many of them continue to live and work in China's urban centers and towns, and more minority youth repeat the journey of leaving behind the ethnic homeland. The ethnic native land, therefore, serves as the site of a perpetual longing that can never be completely fulfilled: as many minority regions continue to be mired in developmental projects, modernizing transformations, and touristic commodification, minority writers' nostalgia is rooted in their desire for a pre-industrial past that can never truly return to the minority villages. How, then, should minority writers and the nation as a whole look into the future to re-construct minority cultural systems and values, particularly the spiritual values that are vital to ethnic communities in a secular China? What cultural, ideological, and political contestations lie in the process of protecting and re-constituting minority cultural and spiritual values in a nation racing into the future? The next and final chapter of this book will seek answers to these questions.

CHAPTER 6

Paradise Recrafted

The Problems of Secular Modernity in Chinese Multiethnic Literature and Village-Level Cultural Activism

Complementing the deep yearnings for the ethnic homeland and a critical reflection on the cost of abandoning ethnic heritage manifested in contemporary minority literature that we saw in Chapter 5, multiethnic literature in contemporary China is also characterized by its concern with secular modernity. Contrasting the inward-looking autobiographical writings studied in the previous chapter, which trace the emotional homecoming journeys of minority intellectuals, in this chapter, we will focus on the outward-looking multiethnic literature and village-level cultural activism in rural ethnic China, which challenge modern China's teleological worldviews and developmental agendas.

In this final chapter of this book, I analyze the cultural and social impetuses for minority writers and activists in southwest China to critique secular modernity. I will reveal how minority writers and activists detail the spiritual traditions of their ethnic groups, combining their efforts to document culture with their search for ethnic subjectivity in China, a nation with an alleged atheist state ideology. By translating a representative selection of minority literary works for the first time in English I will present how minority writers and activists claim ownership to their cultures and formulate powerful discourses to advocate for a spirituality-centered, alternative cultural system. In fictional and memoir accounts, ethnic Qiang and Yi writers in China voice discontent with the basic tenets of Chinese modernity as they reconstruct ethnic traditions through writing and cultural activism. Eventually, Qiang and Yi writers and activists re-enchant what they consider to be an overly secularized Chinese society by unveiling the social and aesthetic values of the mystic beliefs, spiritual quests, and cultural wonders of non-Han groups. Multiethnic authors and activists recraft the "paradise" of their spiritual worlds by critically re-evaluating minority traditions vis-à-vis the state's effort to delineate ethnic cultures. Against the backdrop of the Chinese state's ardent efforts to institutionalize and standardize cultural heritage (*wenhua yichan* 文化遗产), minority authors and village-level activists leverage state discourses and policies to increase the visibility of multiethnic communities. Meanwhile, minority writers and activists contest the state's definition of "culture" as they take ownership of interpreting their ethnic heritage and articulating a place of spirituality in secular China. This chapter takes readers into the enchanting spiritual landscape of minority shamanism and mysticism. The chapter introduces a host of fictional, autobiographical, and activist writing to reveal how China's multiethnic authors and grassroots activists question secular modernity and reconstruct the vitality of minority groups' indigenous worldviews to challenge the teleological, developmental agendas of modern China—minority groups present alternative ways of accounting for the tumultuous *longue durée* of twentieth-century Chinese history; meanwhile, they propose spirituality-inspired ways of construing China's future.

Recounting Socialist History and Defending Minority Spiritual Traditions in Contemporary Chinese Multiethnic Literature

Sichuan-based Qiang writer Ye Xingguang's (叶星光 b. 1954) short story "Sacred Mountain, Sacred Trees, Sacred Grove" (*Shenshan, shenshu, shenlin* 神山，神树，神林) is a historical fiction on how the Qiang spiritual traditions were severely attacked during the high socialist period. It enlivens the clashes between the industrializing socialist ideologies and the Qiang villagers, who hold their religious beliefs and spiritual traditions to be higher than anything else. The story takes place during the Great Leap Forward in the late 1950s. Under Mao Zedong's command, China made great efforts to industrialize itself and started a "backyard furnace" movement: all members of society were asked to collect various metals and instruments from their homes and smelt them to make steel and iron to contribute to the nation's industrial growth.[1]

A local Communist official, eager to impress his superiors, demands that the Qiang villagers in the story cut down their sacred grove to make room for a "steel and iron satellite." This causes great commotion and anxiety in the community. For the Qiang, a people defined by their pantheism, the sacred grove is made up of trees that are considered to have a special spiritual power. Like many indigenous and minority peoples of the world, the Qiang regard the natural environment with a religious reverence—for them, trees are like deities, which "possess agency and sociality" and can be "both nurturing and protective, and dangerous."[2] The Qiang people, therefore, never dare damage the trees in the sacred groves, for they believe that damaging the trees would offend the groves, causing calamities in the community.

Despite local people's protest, the official is determined to get rid of the sacred grove. As an atheist Party member, the official tells himself that the Qiang people are only deceiving themselves when they say that the groves have spiritual power. As an embodiment of the developmentalist, secular socialist nation, the official belittles the religious traditions of the minority people and dismisses their beliefs as superstitious. When Yu Bajin, the head of the village, also the son of a respected local shaman, tries to persuade the official to spare the sacred grove, he laughs it off and contests Yu's plea with the atheist state ideology:

> Ha-ha, sacred grove, what sacred grove? Total non-sense. Where are the gods? Ask them to come out and meet me . . . Comrade, we are all Communist Party members. We have to first be the vanguard fighters of the proletarian class. We have to be radical materialists. We should never believe in ghosts and gods whatsoever![3]

The Party official holds great contempt and suspicion for Qiang people's religious beliefs when he challenges Yu Bajin to ask the gods to "come out and meet [him]." He reminds Yu Bajin that as Communist Party members, they should be "radical materialists" and never believe in ghosts and gods. Such an atheist viewpoint apparently runs counter to Yu's religious beliefs as a Qiang person.

As Ralph Litzinger points out, during the high socialist period between the 1950s and late 1970s, the religious beliefs and rituals of minority peoples were glossed with the derogatory term "feudal superstition" (*fengjian mixin*); these beliefs and rituals were considered by the Party as a source of minority peoples' social and economic backwardness.[4] Political officials at the time took great pains to eradicate such beliefs from minority people's lives. The Party official depicted in the story epitomizes such efforts. Such secularization efforts were paired with industrializing projects, such as the backyard furnace movement, which worked together to diminish minority people's spiritual well-being and exacerbated their marginalizations.

When the official instigated a few members of the Qiang village to cut down the sacred grove, the old shaman of the village, Yu Tianbao (the father of Yu Bajin), becomes infuriated. He protests such violence with his death in the sacred grove on a stormy evening. His death helps save the sacred grove for the time being. In the story, Yu Tianbao's death is regarded by Qiang villagers as a journey to the spiritual world. Yu Tianbao becomes deified himself, and his death symbolizes the unification between humans and nature, a belief long upheld by the Qiang people. Author Ye Xingguang depicts the unique funeral Qiang villagers conduct for Yu with vivid ethnographic details:

> Niushan villagers do not want to see him [Yu Tianbao] separated from the old trees. According to the will of the gods, Niushan villagers conducted a solemn and unique ritual of tree funeral. They buried the remains of Mubi [the Qiang shaman Yu Tianbao] in the old trees. They buried him in the hinterland of the big mountains; they buried him at the bottom of Niushan villagers' hearts . . . [People] wished that he could also become a tree god, a tree god that had entered the sacred trees . . .
>
> Perhaps the soul of Abu [the old father Yu Tianbao] has already ascended to heaven . . . [he] yearns for the sacred grove to come back to life and yearns for the green origin of life.[5]

This passage shows us how the Qiang people, an ethnic minority in southwest China, hold a belief of life, death, and the natural world radically different from socialist China's secular state ideology. For the Qiang, the life and death of people are intricately entwined with the natural world. Trees, as an other-than-human form of life, have assumed divine functions in the Qiang community: trees enter into "close and lifelong relationships" with human beings and are an important source of protection and wisdom for the Qiang.[6] Yu Tianbao, the old shaman and patriarch of the village, has become one with the sacred trees through his sacrificial death to protect the sacred trees. People conduct a tree funeral to consummate the physical and spiritual communion between the old patriarch and the grove. Yu Tianbao is regarded by Qiang villagers as a deified ancestor who stands to guard them against the religious violence imposed on them. Most importantly, the merging of the man and the trees signifies the ecological worldview of the Qiang: by protecting the sacred grove, the Qiang defend the "green origin of life," carrying on a sustainable way of living in the sacred mountains that they revere as the giver of life (Figure 31).

Figure 31. Photograph of the Sacred Grove in Niuwei Qiang Village. Photograph by author.

In the story, Qiang villagers go through several other rounds of fighting and negotiation with the state after Yu Tianbao's death. As the Leap Forward continues, more officials come to the village and covet the sacred grove. Many Qiang villagers are imprisoned or physically hurt for fighting against the officials who want to take over the sacred grove. The sacred grove, as a site of the Qiang's spiritual reverence for nature, is eventually violently cut down. The story depicts a dramatic and tragic fight between a local official, Scar Liu, and villagers. Scar Liu wants to cut down the last remaining tree, the tree in which the old patriarch/shaman was buried. Aligning with Qiang people's beliefs, the author portrays the sacred tree as possessing human agency and capable of taking revenge: Scar Liu's ax is "eaten" by the tree, and a huge branch falls off from the tree, giving Scar Liu an inerasable scar on his face. Scar Liu's interventions and violent destructions of the symbols of the Qiang people's religious practice are characteristic of the Great Leap Forward Movement's relentless modernizing agendas that sought to control the ritual places of the people.[7]

"Sacred Mountain, Sacred Trees, Sacred Grove" is a poignant account of the Qiang people's struggle to guard their religious beliefs and spiritual traditions against the frenzy of socialist China's search for a secular and industrial nationhood. Yet the story ends abruptly in a pacifying tone—Scar Liu repents his violence to the villagers by writing them a letter and sending them money, and the Party provides great assistance to the Qiang when new officials come to help the villagers plant trees both for economic growth and recovering their religious practices. We can infer that, the ending is possibly motivated by the writer's desire to frame the story in an ideologically acceptable way. This ideological necessity is evident when the author Ye falls short of giving a credible explanation or detailing the psychological state of Scar Liu, who, after twenty years, suddenly admits his mistake. Yet despite this ideological compromise, the story reveals some of the most powerful episodes of minority people's endeavors to safeguard their spiritual traditions and their natural and cultural environments in socialist China, unveiling minority groups' struggle to maintain their religious beliefs in the backdrop of the state's secular and industrializing agendas.

If Ye's short story chooses a pacifying ending to neutralize its criticism of the historical violence to minority religious life, a younger Qiang writer by the pen name of Qiang Renliu (羌人六, b. 1987) insists on depicting the traumatizing effect of instilling a secular education on minority children in the post-Mao era. As a representative of a younger generation of minority writers, Qiang Renliu details his personal experience of growing up with a grandmother who is an exorcist in the local community in his memoir-style essay, "The Soul Pacifier" (*Ahun zhe* 安魂者).

Born in 1987 in Pingwu County, Sichuan, Qiang Renliu published an essay collection, *A Family That Survives on Mice* (*Shishu zhijia* 食鼠之家), under the China Multiethnic Literary Series (*Zhongguo duominzu wenxue congshu* 中国多民族文学丛书) in 2016. This Series is a national publication project that features the newest writing of younger writers from China's different ethnic groups. The naming of the series as *multiethnic literature* (*duo minzu wenxue* 多民族文学), as opposed to the long-upheld term, *minority literature* (*shaoshu minzu wenxue* 少数民族文学), is a subtle signal that ethnic literatures in China are increasingly recognized for their contribution to diversifying Chinese literature and culture, rather than their minoritarian status.

In "The Soul Pacifier," Qiang Renliu recounts his fragmented memories of and torn love for his maternal grandmother, or his Waipo, who plays the ambiguous role of an exorcist in his Qiang community. On the one hand, the

Waipo helps cure the diseases of people who have bizarre encounters with spirits and is deeply respected by those she helps. On the other hand, certain members of the community are suspicious of the Waipo's supernatural abilities and ridicule her for her "pretentious" superstitious practices: they believe that the Waipo is only deceiving people and making money under the pretense of spiritual healing.

When the author was an infant, his Waipo provided maternal love and boundless comfort for a little boy living away from his parents. The Waipo was the guardian of a shrine with the statues of different deities, including Han deities such as the Children-sending Guanyi (*songzi guanyin*) and the Earth God. Local people would come to her for treating strange diseases. The young author enjoyed the love of his Waipo, particularly when she gave the food others offered to the deities to him, telling him "you would not catch any disease after eating these [blessed] things."[8] For the young author, the statues of the deities that his Waipo and he revered were like family, serving as a source of comfort and joy.

Yet, as the author was growing up, he was gradually taught to be a skeptic of his Waipo's spiritual practices because his Waipo was ridiculed by certain members of the community. Most importantly, the atheist education he received at school contributed to shaking his faith and love for his Waipo. The most emotionally traumatizing and morally uneasy experience for the author was how in his Chinese class (*yuwen ke* 语文课), the teacher and his classmates alluded to the "pretentious" spiritual practice of his Waipo and made the author feel humiliated and publicly shamed.

Qiang Renliu details the episode in which he faced a moral judgment and emotional trial in his Chinese class. The class was reading a fourth-century Chinese short story titled "Songdingbo Catches the Ghost." This is a text about how a smart man called Songdingbo catches a ghost and watches it turn into a goat, selling it for money. It is a widely taught text in middle schools in China, with an ideological message of how human power can overcome and subdue spiritual forces. This simple text caused great shame and anxiety for the author. He feared the discussions about superstition that were to follow, for he knew that "My Waipo and I would have to face this trial on reality and nihility, superstition and morality."[9]

As expected, after reading the text, the Chinese teacher started the discussion by saying "Speaking about superstition, there are plenty of examples in our local region." This made the author sweat. Worse still, one of the author's classmates followed by satirically stating "A bowl of water can cure all diseases," alluding to the exorcist's practice of endowing ordinary objects, such as a bowl of water, with spiritual power to help treat the sick.[10] Even though the class never openly criticized the author's Waipo, the allusions and satires were enough to humiliate him. Qiang Renliu describes this experience in his Chinese class as unequivocally traumatizing: from this and other similar experiences surrounding the exorcist role of his Waipo, he learned to "hide the identity of Waipo as an exorcist and hold back my love for her" for many years.[11] The atheist, moralistic education at school served to alienate the minority author from his familial roots and the spiritual traditions entailed by such roots.

Even though the story happens in the post-Mao era, when the Chinese state is more relaxed in terms of its religious policies, minority children still have to grapple with the question of minority spiritual practice within a secular state ideology. In fact, in post-Mao China, local religious and spiritual practices remain a powerful signifier of backwardness, and some scholars believe that the state's desire to eliminate "superstitious" practices and bring potentially unruly, "unassailable" local cultures into "the universal, homogenizing . . . modernizing state" is still strong.[12] This marginalization of local spiritual practices is worsened when Qiang Renliu the minority boy had to face a moral trial in his Chinese class. Even though the author never specifies that his Qiang identity contributed to the social marginalization he had to endure, the role his Waipo took up in the local community—as a female exorcist and religious healer—is more common among the Qiang.[13]

The national educational system, which targets "feudal superstition" just like it did during the high socialist period, causes deep divides in the Qiang community by subjecting religious healers to social castigation.[14] Shamanism, manifested in its various forms from exorcism to ritual healing to divination, is important to the Qiang.[15] The exorcist, like other kinds of spiritual mediums, helps solve the problems in people's daily lives—such as treating bizarre diseases and sicknesses—by resorting to the soul and communicating with divine and spiritual powers.[16] The author's Waipo plays such a role. She serves as the "pacifier" of people's soul when she adroitly exorcises the bad spirits bothering local villagers. Qiang Renliu engages in detailed, ethnographic descriptions of the Waipo's healing process by assuming the voice of a detached observer:

> Waipo was not a doctor. She treated the patients without using medicine. With only a bowl of water, some incenses, and some rough paper towels, and

> some murmuring singing, she was able to identify the causes of the diseases and heal the people . . . There was never a shortage of locals coming to see Waipo for their diseases. When it was during festivals and holidays, there was an especially large number of people who came. After the healing was done, most patients would take out some money from their pockets, piously handing [their] money to Waipo. Waipo would not refuse the money; she directly put it on the shrine.[17]

This observation-based, seemingly objective passage reveals the relationship between the exorcist and the Qiang community. For local people, Waipo is a trustworthy healer. She also enjoys the respect of people when people "piously handed [their] money" to her. Therefore, contrary to the teacher's education and some people's misunderstanding of Waipo as a pretentious swindler who deceives people, the Waipo as an exorcist is deeply embedded in local social structure: as a religious healer, she changes undesirable situations, such as spiritually induced diseases, and restores "communal harmony" in the community.[18] The secular educational system thus inadvertently does violence to the spiritual well-being of the Qiang by educating minority children of the "evilness" of their traditional practices—such an education fails to recognize the social function of spiritual mediums like the exorcist in minority communities and imposes an atheist worldview on minority people.

For Qiang Renliu, the overly secular education he received at school not only deprived him of the opportunity to connect with his ethnic spiritual traditions, but has an emotionally traumatizing effect, as the Waipo that he loved as a child becomes the symbol of backward beliefs in the eyes of his classmates and teacher. In the essay, Qiang Renliu recounts how his denial of Waipo's identity and rejection of her love continued throughout his adolescent years. For many years, Waipo was reduced from a loving grandmother to a sign of superstition and stupidity for Qiang Renliu. The author is only able to reclaim his love and respect for Waipo after he has reached adulthood.

In the final two sections of the essay, the author unveils how his Waipo has taught him an important lesson about truth and reality and challenged the secular and rational worldview that has long permeated his thinking since he was in middle school. One time, when the adult Qiang Renliu went back to his home village for a visit, Waipo warned him of a potential tragedy between his parents in a fight. She used her spiritual power to see through the impending danger for the author's parent. She reminded Qiang Renliu, "Tell your parents to stop fighting. I saw that your [deceased] grandpa was waiting for your father on the ridges of a mountain. If [your parents] don't listen to me, a great calamity will follow."[19] Not believing Waipo's words, the author did not say anything to his parents. One month later, his father fell from a tree and died. It was only then did the author realize the power of Waipo's spiritual capacity: he realized that, contrary to what his school had taught him, there exists an alternative form of reality, the kind of mystical reality that only a pious spiritual medium like his Waipo could see through. "The world is much more mysterious than we imagine," Qiang Renliu concludes.[20] He realized that rather than being a pretentious swindler, his Waipo and the spiritual power she carries are "a measure of people's hearts and minds"—Waipo carries a transcendental spiritual and moral power that is direly needed in a secular society, restoring relationships and rebuilding communities.[21] She was trying to help people like the author's parents, who were in a grave fight and straying away from mutual respect and love. Through Waipo's supernatural power, she endows the community with emotional security and moral care.

This instance also taught the author that the atheist education and acculturation he has received since a teenager is often incapable of answering the deeper ethical questions of truth and reality. As Vincent Goossaert contends, the secularization of modern Chinese society is sometimes characterized by Chinese scholars as a disenchanting tendency, or the "collapse of idealism and adhesion to cosmological worldviews."[22] As a minority writer, Qiang Renliu finally recognizes the destructive effect of the disenchanting education he had received and chooses to renounce it in favor of the transcendental spiritual and healing power of his Waipo.

Qiang Renliu offers subtle but powerful critique of the secular and materialistic ideology in mainstream Chinese society by analyzing the dialectics between materialism and idealism, truth and hypocrisy:

> In my country, the running water is firmer than the bricks, and money is more reliable than feelings. Thus, truth will make people painful, will cause them muscle atrophy, and will make their faces look hideous. But hypocrisy will keep people intact and secure.[23]

Here, Qiang Renliu uses the metaphor of "running water" to indicate how the volatility of the water is like money, very unpredictable yet contradictorily "reliable" in a materialistic society. The author lays bare the operational logic of a disenchanting/disenchanted society, where truth will make people "painful" and "look hideous," whereas hypocrisy will "keep people intact." This can be read as a critique of the numerous scandals about faked identities and products in China, such as the fabrication of degrees and resumes, the highly profitable brand-name counterfeit industry, the manufacturing of harmful infant formula, and many other cases concerning "truth" and "fakeness." The author suggests that the secular education and materialistic acculturation he has received are powerless when it comes to solving moral problems and explaining the ultimate "reality" of the meaning of life and love. On the contrary, truth is to be found in the mystical, alternative spiritual practices that lead people to the core of a meaningful life.

At this moment, the Qiang author not only reconciles his relationship with his Waipo, but also reclaims his ethnic and spiritual roots that his Waipo embodies. This is indeed the author's moment of epiphany: he denounces the rational and atheist worldview that his education and socialization had bestowed on him for a more idealist understanding of the world. He finally comes to terms with his Waipo's identity as a *shenpo*, or female healer of the community. The author proclaims:

> [The idea that] my Waipo is a Shenpo [magical old lady] is a window through which the world and I confirm [our relationship] with each other. I mean, when I identify this strand of enchanting "power," my actions are being endowed with a brand-new meaning.[24]

The author uses the word "enchanting," or "charming" (*miren*), to describe the spiritual and emotional power generated by his Waipo. Enchanted is how he feels when he thinks about Waipo's capacities as both a loving grandmother and an adroit exorcist. For him, Waipo's double identity as a grandmother and a religious healer serves to re-enchant the secular and materialistic China: Waipo epitomizes both the feelings of genuine love mediated through a mystical relationship between humans and the cosmos and the moral desire for truth and authenticity that can never be satisfied by the materialistic manifestations of the world.

Lyrical Re-Enchantments of Modern Chinese History

The obsession over reconstituting ethnic identities through recounting spiritual traditions in indigenous communities is a common motif in contemporary Chinese multiethnic literature. In addition to the Qiang authors studied so far in this chapter, Yunnan-based ethnic Yi (彝族) writer Duan Haizhen (段海珍) exemplifies contemporary minority writers' efforts to write minority spiritual traditions and worldviews into modern Chinese history. Like Ye Xingguang and Qiang Renliu, the ethnic Yi fiction writer Duan Haizhen engages in vivid descriptions of the spirituality-inspired worldviews practiced by the Yi indigenous communities. In 2016, Duan published her novel *Heavenly Songs* (*Tian ge* 天歌), also under the China Multiethnic Literature Series, a national multiethnic literary publishing project spearheaded by the prestigious Zuojia Publishing House (作家出版社) in Beijing.

Duan Haizhen is a female ethnic Yi writer from Yunnan. Like the prominent Qiang writers discussed in this chapter, she is a prolific minority writer who has achieved national fame by winning several literary awards.[25] Her novel *Heavenly Songs* offers a first-person narrative of the life story of Gemei, the granddaughter of a (fictional) well-respected Yi shaman. The novel depicts how Gemei experiences the major historical and social changes in China from the Republican era (1930s) to the present day. Most importantly, it offers rich ethnographic accounts of the cosmological worldviews and practices of the Yi people, constructing a fascinating mystical temporality in parallel with historical temporality. Similar to Qiang Renliu's essay "The Soul Pacifier," *Heavenly Songs* challenges the rational modernity of China by presenting the truth and revelations only accessible through minority people's spiritually-inspired worldviews.

The novel can be read as an ethnographic novel, as the reader is guided by the narrator/protagonist to "witness" many rituals, ceremonies, and religious beliefs of the Yi with culturally intimate details. For example, when Gemei describes the funeral of the man whom she has loved for her entire life, she includes the ritual details of the funeral:

> The sound of the drum continued. The singing of the Saipo [religious singer] comes from the heavens. Fragrant campfire was burning in the yard. Thick and light liquid smoke pervaded the entire yard. That was because the villagers asked the Bimo [shaman] and the Saipo to come and do a divine dance and chant the scriptures for him [the dead]. The ritual was solemn and romantic . . . it enchanted me about death, like how I am enchanted by romance, elegance, and solemnity themselves.[26]

In this passage, the author first presents the Yi funeral in ethnographic "realist" details: people burn the campfire and liquid smoke and invite a Bimo and a Saipo to engage in religious singing and dancing for the dead. These ethnographic details endow the writing with what James Clifford calls an "ethnographic authority:" the narrator, through displaying carefully observed knowledge of the community, is in an authorial position of interpreting and educating the reader about Yi spiritual traditions.[27] Later, however, the passage turns to a more lyrical and poetic mode, as the narrator expresses her feelings, as well as the cultural feelings the ceremony conjures up for her community: the "solemn and romantic ritual enchanted [her] about death," just like how she is "enchanted by romance, elegance, and solemnity themselves." This "code switching" from an ethnographic realist style to a lyrical style appears frequently in the novel. It is a literary invention by minority writers like Duan Haizhen. Such an ethnographic-lyrical innovation not only endows the novel with an effective way of conveying knowledge about minority cultures, but also inserts the minority writer's interpretive subjectivity and ability to convey the overall cultural atmosphere and affective dimensions of her culture.

We can find many other examples of this innovative literary device throughout the novel. For example, when Duan describes how the narrator experiences the death of herself, the author combines the ethnographic mode with a lyrical mode:

> Bimo recites the *Scripture for Directions* for me over the distant mountains. Listen, it is the Yi's *Scripture for Directors*: Timbals sound now and then, friends and family come to pay homage to you. They bid farewell to you, sending you to the netherworld. Go happily and merrily, for it wouldn't do for you to stay. Leave joyfully, and walk cheerfully.
>
> Oh, so death turns out to be a necessity. Death is so joyful, so sad, so happy, so irrevocable. . . . I am a gust of wind; I am a consciousness. I am so joyful and so content. To be able to meet again the person one loves is to find paradise.[28]

Whereas the first passage is a detailed description of the Yi *Scripture for Directions*, a religious scripture sung to guide the souls of the dead, the second passage is the author's personal interpretation of and emotional response to the singing. The sentiments evoked by the singing, such as "joyful, sad," and "happy," are repeated in the second passage. Yet rather than a simple replication of the singing, the second passage interprets the values embedded in such singing in a lyrical way. "Oh, death turns out to be a necessity" is the narrator's interpretation of the positive and accepting attitude toward death manifested in the Yi ritual singing. Such interpretation becomes even more imaginative and achieves a stream-of-consciousness effect when the narrator feels that she is "a gust of wind" and "a consciousness," as she is running toward her loved one and believes that she has reached heaven by meeting her loved one in another world. The ethnographic details are thus more than "factual" and descriptive accounts of Yi people's culture, but have assumed affective and literary meanings when the narrator offers her poetic interpretations of and emotional responses to the religious customs.

Throughout the novel, the author presents Yi people's spiritual worldviews in tandem with the historical events and social changes taking place in twentieth century China, such as the Second Sino-Japanese War, which mobilized many soldiers in Yunnan, and the Cultural Revolution. More significantly, the narrator views historical events and social changes through the prism of Yi spiritual worldviews, shifting the center of Chinese modernity from the Han-led nation-state to the spiritually-informed minority experience. For instance, when the narrator Gemei's grandparents describe modern technological inventions, such as the airplane and the train, instead of lauding them as signs of progress, they lament these inventions as bad omens, for such inventions intrude upon the sacred spaces of the deities:

> [My] paternal grandma said that she heard from the masters in the temple that, when the iron birds [airplanes] are flying in the sky and iron horses [trains] are running on the earth, then the apocalyptical time will arrive . . . This prophecy also worried my maternal grandpa. My paternal grandpa said that he, too, felt that the world was going to change. The sky is the residence for gods. Now even the iron birds are flying up to the sky, competing for habitats with the gods. This profoundly unsettled my maternal grandpa.[29]

For the grandpa and grandma, modern technological innovations such as the airplane and the train will only cause chaos and disasters for human beings—these inventions proclaim human triumph over nature and the spiritual world by intruding on the divine spaces of the gods in the sky or occupying the earth. The grandpa and grandma's remarks are probably inspired by the Sino-Japanese War and the Chinese Civil War, which is the backdrop of this passage in the novel. Seeing the violence committed in the war with the help of technology, the grandpa and grandma voice their profound discontent with modern progress. The grandma is a Buddhist, whereas the grandpa is a Yi shaman. Despite their different religious backgrounds, they are both highly spiritual. The grandma uses the Buddhist terminology *saddharma-vipralopa* (the age of the decline of Buddhist dharma) to indicate the apocalypses she saw impending for humanity, if technological advancement was to compete for the divine spaces of the gods.

In the novel, such spiritually-driven worldviews are often invoked as the narrator offers critique of the historical events and social phenomena around her. Similar to the Qiang writers we have read, as a non-Han author, Duan Haizhen critically engages with the secular, teleological Chinese modernity by presenting the Yi (and in some cases, Buddhist) spiritual worldviews as an alternative but more illuminative worldview.

Indeed, religious communities often discover "alternative realities," or realities induced and inspired by a spirit, a god, or other forms of supernatural power.[30] Such realities are not based on experiences in the material world, but rather, experiences in religious rituals.[31] Yet such realities can be powerful enough to critique the regular, worldly reality, or the kind of reality derived from material everyday experience. For spiritually rich ethnic groups like the Yi and Qiang, religious beliefs and alternate realities lie at the very core of their existence: such beliefs and realities are handed down from generation to generation, assuming an ancestral authority that makes these groups "identifiable" from other non-religious groups.[32]

The author's intention of presenting Yi spiritual practices and religious worldviews against the historical background of modern China is complicated by her rhetorical move of assigning the role of cultural guardian to a Han student at the beginning and end of the novel. If the main body of the novel reads like an ethnographically detailed account of a Yi community and its religious and social life, then the beginning and end of the novel carry a cultural preservationist politics that reveals the minority writer's contradictory relationship with the nation. In Chapter 1 of the novel, the narrator Gemei introduces a character who appears again only in the last chapter. She is a Han Chinese college student newly returned from overseas. The student comes to visit Gemei and advocates for the protection of the "intangible cultural heritage" surrounding Gemei's living environment, such as the old vernacular house Gemei lived in, the folk artists, and funeral experts in the local Yi community. The student is depicted as an enthusiastic advocate for intangible cultural heritage in China. She tells Gemei: "When I was studying overseas, I read from an adventure magazine about the Yi creation epic by the name of Gemei [the same name as the narrator]. I was determined to engage in the kind of work to salvage folk culture (*minjian wenhua*)."[33] For the Han student, Gemei the Yi woman embodies the Yi ethnic culture that she has been dreaming about since her time overseas. Moreover, the student shows a keen awareness of the rapid disappearance of folk cultures, as she deliberates: "There should be no delay in the protection of intangible cultural heritage," as "a folk artist with a unique skill would be dying at the very moment she brushes her teeth."[34]

The inclusion of a Han Chinese student advocating for the protection of Yi and other folk cultures is an important move in the novel. It unveils the Yi author's anxiety for the preservation of her ethnic culture and extends the novel beyond the realm of "minority literature" to engage with the "cultural nationalism" informing much of China's nation-building strategies today. In the past decade or so, the valorization of "cultural heritage" (*wenhua yichan*) occupies a central place in China's national discourse and ideological space. In 2012, the then-president of China (Hu Jintao) enshrined the importance of "culture" in "strengthening the socialist nation" at the Eighteenth National Congress of the Communist Party.[35] He particularly emphasized the importance of allowing ethnic minority cultures to flourish.[36] In 2011, Hu signed an executive president's order (*zhuxi ling*) to pass the China Intangible Cultural Heritage Law. The term "intangible cultural heritage," (*fei wuzhi wenhua yichan* 非物质文化遗产), a UNESCO coinage, is deployed in the China Intangible Cultural Heritage Law to refer to a wide variety of non-material cultural properties, defined as "various kinds of expressions of traditional culture handed down from generation to generation by the different ethnic groups and considered by these groups as part of their heritage."[37] These "expressions of traditional culture" include oral literature, traditional art forms and performance, and, importantly for minority groups, "folklores such as traditional rituals and festivals."[38] The Law states that different levels of regional governments in China should take the responsibility to research, document, and preserve intangible cultural heritage.[39]

Despite the Law's encoding of the safeguarding of intangible cultural properties, for ethnic minority groups, the Law is a double-edged sword: while it promotes minority cultural expressions, it also propels minority groups to create cultures that fit into the state's ideological parameters.[40] Perhaps because of this, despite the novel's critical stance toward secular modernity in China and its desire to assert a distinctively Yi spiritual worldview, the author inserts passages about the Han student unrelated to the plot every now and then to display her understanding of and compliance with the national political discourse. By doing so, Duan as a minority author voices a common sentiment for minority cultures to be accepted by a broader national audience, a sentiment shared by many minority writers and cultural workers.

Indeed, the foregrounding of the novel as a Han student "discovering" minority cultural treasures complicates minority literary writing: the insertion of the Han student seems to diminish the ethnic and cultural integrity of the Yi that the novel otherwise asserts, reproducing the old cultural hierarchy of the Han as the superior ethnic group "civilizing" and helping the less advanced and less "mature" non-Han groups in China's cultural history.[41]

The self-contradictory process for minority writers like Duan Haizhen to both highlight and diminish their ethnic cultural traditions reveals the uneasy ideological liminal space of minority writing in contemporary China. On the one hand, minority writers feel a strong urge to claim their ethnic distinctiveness and engage in the critique of various aspects of Chinese modernity. On the other hand, the manufacturing and management of minority identities are closely tied to the state and state ideological and discursive apparatuses. The institutionalization of intangible cultural heritage in China is an Althusserian "cultural ideological state apparatus"—it "interpellates" minority members into the national ideological agendas of protecting cultures, encouraging minority communities to become the subjects of the nation by contributing to reinforcing its ideological and cultural institutions.[42] The ideological apparatus of institutionalizing intangible cultural heritage contradictorily both helps generate the confidence for minority writers like Duan to document and proclaim their ethnic distinctiveness *and* imposes on these writers a creative and ideological limitation that restrains them from engaging in full-fledged critique of modernity. The Han student in the novel personifies this ideological limitation when she becomes a spokesperson for an ethnic group that she has little knowledge about.

Village-level Cultural Activism and Grassroots Publication Projects in the Qiang Regions

In many ways, the same creative potential and ideological constraints we have seen in Duan Haizhen's work characterize the efforts made by Qiang villagers who write books about their ethnic traditions to challenge how "culture" is defined in mainstream and official domains in China. In this final section of the chapter, we will journey through village-level cultural activism initiated by members of A'er Qiang Village, exploring the grassroots cultural preservationist movements burgeoning in rural ethnic China in the twenty-first century.

A'er Qiang Village (*A'er qiangzhai* 阿尔羌寨) is tucked in the deep mountains of the Aba Tibetan and Qiang Autonomous Prefecture. At the time when I was doing my research (around 2017 and 2018), the village was only accessible through an extra hour or so of driving on a bumpy road after I left the main road paved for its neighbor, Longxi Qiang People's Valley, which is a well-designed tourist destination. Unlike many other minority tourism villages, at the time of my fieldwork, A'er had been underdeveloped and impoverished. Because of its distance from major tourist destinations, A'er had preserved more Qiang cultural traditions: many villagers were proficient or fluent in the Qiang language, and the village is also home to important Qiang intangible cultural heritage, such as the *shibi* shamanistic tradition.

During my fieldwork in the Qiang regions of Sichuan in 2017, I visited A'er Village and chanced into the household of the officially designated intangible cultural heritage inheritor (*feiwuzhi wenhua yichan chuanchengren* 非物质文化遗产传承人) of the village. The "inheritor" title, according to China's Intangible Cultural Heritage Law, designates representative figures of the specified skills listed in different regions.[43] Those given the title by various levels of government are expected to carry on the practice of their specified skills, showcase the skills occasionally, and train apprentices.[44] The household that I visited had an old shaman (*shibi* 释比) as an inheritor designated by Wenchuan County, where A'er Village is located.

The grandson of the old shaman, Mr. Yu, was in his mid-30s. He told me how he was inspired to initiate a cultural documentation project by the visit of several national cultural officials in A'er Village after the 2008 Wenchuan earthquake. According to Mr. Yu, existing accounts on A'er Village authored by Han writers were far from accurate, and Mr. Yu was determined to challenge what he considered to be the distortions of Qiang culture in mainstream media and scholarship.

As the grandson of the deceased and widely respected shaman/*shibi* in his region, Mr. Yu became well-versed in Qiang religious and cultural traditions at a young age. As discussed in Chapter 4, the *shibi* is an immensely important figure in Qiang culture. Despite the diversity of Qiang culture in different regions and villages, the *shibi* as an orator plays a key role in all Qiang communities. He is responsible for divination, sacrifices, exorcising evil spirits in the community, and managing other religious and social ceremonies and rituals, such as weddings and funerals.[45] Most importantly, the *shibi* is the main figure who transmits many oral cultural and literary traditions of the Qiang as a people: the *shibi* has to memorize Qiang creation epics, origin myths, and many religious scriptures to be used in religious ceremonies.[46] The *shibi*, in a word, embodies the moral and cultural order of the Qiang, as through religious ceremonies he often orates moral messages to the people and performs important cultural traditions.[47]

Mr. Yu shared the story about how, as he was growing up, he often listened to and watched his grandfather conducting religious ceremonies, forming a strong interest in these ceremonies. Mr. Yu also told me that his village was regulated by many customary laws, such as the law that everyone is expected to help those in need, and those who have received help have an obligation to repay their neighbors' kindness when it comes to their turn. Because A'er Village is nested deeply in the mountains of Wenchuan County, unlike other highly commercialized Qiang villages, many Qiang traditions are kept relatively intact there.

For someone like Mr. Yu, who grew up in a traditional Qiang community, religious ceremonies, customary laws, and other manifestations of Qiang "culture" were a part of his daily life. Yet in recent years, the discourse of cultural heritage has profoundly influenced his conceptualization of his Qiang roots: for him, the Qiang "culture" has become not only a way of life, but also an object to be documented and saved. During our conversations, Mr. Yu fluently deployed the lexicons popular in Chinese mass culture and official discourse to describe minority cultures, such as "*yuan shengtai*" ("pure and original," 原生态), a term coined by the CCTV (China Central Television) minority singing competitions to refer to the imaginarily uncontaminated minority artistic traditions.

Mr. Yu excitedly said that his wish was to document the "pure and original," or authentic, Qiang culture of his village. Frustrated by a certain Han scholar's account of A'er, which he deemed as "extremely inaccurate," Mr. Yu was determined to complete a book project with the help of his fellow villagers. Mr. Yu's desire to document his ethnic culture also stemmed from the visits paid to A'er by China's national officials and UNESCO officials after 2008, as the Wenchuan earthquake put Qiang culture under the spotlight of the global heritage community, and several Qiang cultural traditions, such as the Qiang New Year celebration, were inscribed on UNESCO's "List of Intangible Cultural Heritage in Need of Urgent Safeguarding."[48]

With the encouragement of a UNESCO official, Mr. Yu wrote a letter to the State Administration of Cultural Heritage in Beijing to request aid for his proposed project. The State Administration responded favorably and urged local governments in Sichuan to aid Mr. Yu in his project. With funding from the local governments in hand, Mr. Yu mobilized his fellow villagers in A'er and started a cultural documentation and preservation project: villagers from different age groups with different occupations began to research about and write down various aspects of the Qiang culture in A'er Village. This was a collective effort. Mr. Yu indicated that the young people of the village would usually interview the older members and ask questions about many different aspects of Qiang culture, from the local cuisine and marriage customs to legends, myths, and religious practices. The young members would record the interviews and then write up short articles based on these oral history projects. Mr. Yu and his fellow villagers also had to learn to be modern citizens in this process. Mr. Yu remembered with a laugh how he learned to use the computer for the first time. He had to type up interview scripts and struggled with mastering typing and saving his documents at first.

The research and publishing efforts of the book were also aided by Beijing Cultural Heritage Protection Center, a Beijing-based NGO organization aimed at "helping residents [citizens] to protect their own cultural heritage," particularly ethnic minority members.[49] Eventually, this collective effort culminated into a book called *A'er Archive*, published by the Cultural Heritage Publishing House in Beijing in 2011.

This book is an encyclopedic written documentation of various aspects of Qiang culture, particularly those unique to A'er Village (Figure 33). It is divided into eighteen chapters, and each chapter offers detailed accounts of the life and traditions in the village. Some of the chapters include "Customary Laws," "Clothing," "Architecture," "Folk Literature," as well as "Music and Dance." There are two sections devoted to the religious practice of the village, titled "Deities" and "*Shibi* Culture." Interestingly, within the "Folk Literature" chapter, there is a distinct section called "Mysterious Stories of A'er," which includes many short accounts of the bizarre encounters of A'er villagers, usually related to encounters with spirits.

Without being a part of any established institutions and lacking the elite status as a widely recognized "expert" of ethnic cultures, Mr. Yu is a grassroots activist who belongs to Sebastian Veg's definition of *minjian* intellectuals in China. According to Veg, *minjian* or unofficial intellectuals are mostly independent from state funding or state recognition; with a "low social marker," they usually highlight marginalized social groups and their rights.[50] Most importantly, *minjian* intellectuals operate outside of both state apparatuses

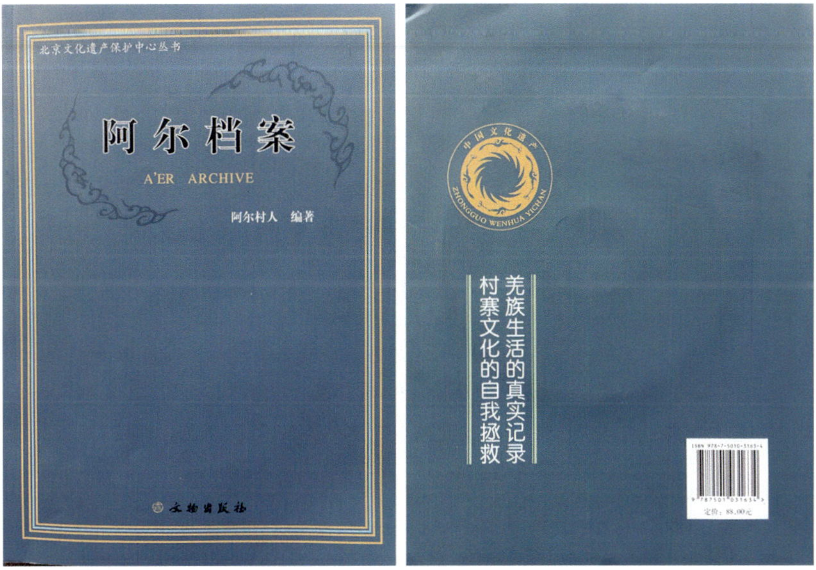

Figure 32. Front and back covers of *A'er Archive*.

and the market, endeavoring to "open space for a possible third sector" as they pluralize public discourses and diversify public spaces in China.[51] Even though Mr. Yu did obtain a certain amount of state funding, he is a self-advocate and village leader that does not belong to or conform to any institutions.

While a considerable amount of existing academic literature on ethnic minorities in China tends to be produced by ethnic Han scholars or other intuitionally-recognized figures, Mr. Yu's determination to create his own account of Qiang culture defies the stereotypes of minority communities as static, passive, and belonging to the past. Mr. Yu's endeavors testify to the creative energy and entrepreneurial spirit of China's multiethnic *minjian* intellectuals, who question the status quo of a cultural power that is usually controlled by academic elites and intuitionally-endorsed experts.

As an ethnic minority grassroots activist, Mr. Yu's efforts to spearhead the writing and publishing of *A'er Archive* further gives voice to the collective experience of his fellow Qiang villagers. Because the Qiang historically lacked a written script and a written tradition, writing lends contemporary Qiang people an effective instrument to articulate their identities and interpret their own culture. *A'er Archive* will impress its readers with its comprehensive, encyclopedic description of Qiang cultural traditions. This "near-mania to cast social life into categories and then to build up great edifices of written knowledge about [these categories]" is characteristic of the newly literate peoples of the world.[52] Anthropologist Susan Rodgers studied a similar phenomenon among the Batak people in Indonesia.[53] In a sense, writing and print technologies endow indigenous ethnic groups with a tool to imagine their communities and construct epistemological claims of their ethnic identities. The front cover of the book designates the authors as A'er Villagers, attributing collective authorship to the published material. The back cover of *A'er Arhieve* states that this book is an effort of the "self-salvation of village culture." Qiang villagers are taking authorship and credit of this collective cultural preservation project under Mr. Yu's leadership. They are reclaiming the power of self-representation and creating knowledge about ethnicity in China from their own lived experience, their memories, and their understandings. This book is a precious effort made by grassroots activists to produce knowledge about ethnic groups outside of academic institutions and to challenge established frameworks of ethnicity that are usually developed by ethnic Han and Western scholars.

Ironically, the empowering act of writing can also serve to secularize the villagers' spiritual identities and reduce their mystical, cosmological worldviews to folkloristic vignettes.[54] This is so because, by writing down and making publicly accessible the village's spiritual secrets and ritual procedures, the otherwise unspeakable, sacred power of ritual worlds lose their intrinsic supernatural forces to "bless or curse" and become signifiers of secular human knowledge.[55] In *A'er Archive*, for example, the details of certain religious rituals, including the number of people involved and the step-by-step breakdown of the ritual processes, are so meticulously depicted that they almost read like manuals. The ritual instruments of the *shibi* are also listed with corresponding pictures, generating a quasi-scientific feeling, as if these materials are presented for social scientific research purposes (Figure 33).

Indeed, like Duan Haizhen's novel *Heavenly Songs*, the conception and writing of *A'er Archive* exemplifies the precarious endeavors made by minority people to document and advocate for their own cultures in contemporary China. Such endeavors entail constant negotiations with the nation and the making of ethnic subjectivity within the framework of "culture" as a state apparatus. As Foucault argues, modern governments exercise their power in "pastoral" terms: they project themselves as the custodians and caregivers for people.[56] In the secular age, the pastoral power of governments means that governments legitimatize themselves as leaders who will help their peo-

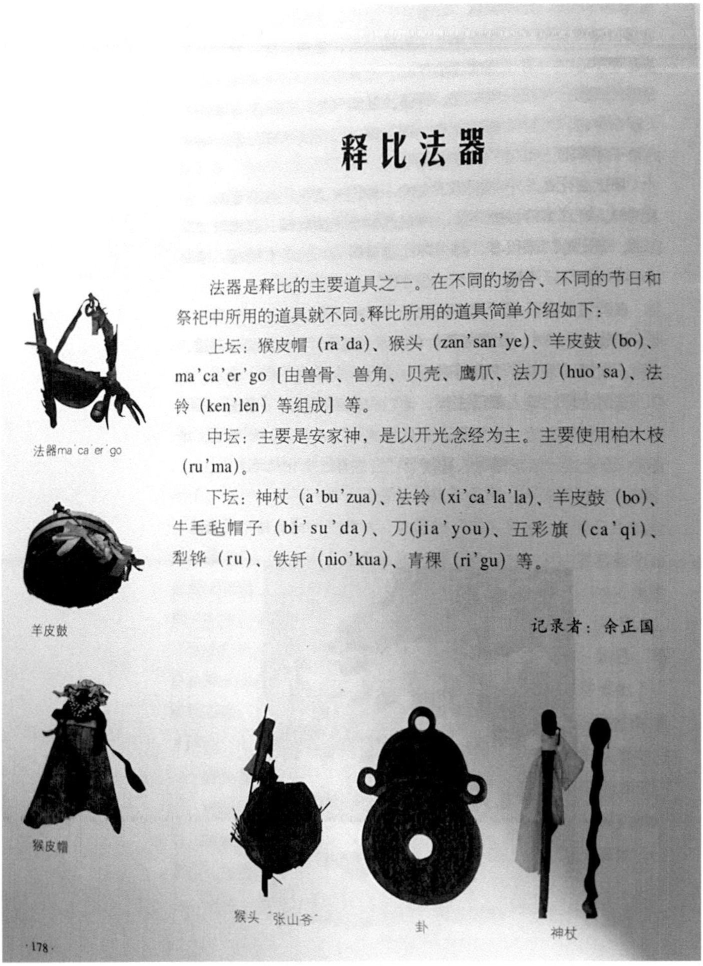
释比法器

法器是释比的主要道具之一。在不同的场合、不同的节日和祭祀中所用的道具就不同。释比所用的道具简单介绍如下：

上坛：猴皮帽（ra'da）、猴头（zan'san'ye）、羊皮鼓（bo）、ma'ca'er'go［由兽骨、兽角、贝壳、鹰爪、法刀（huo'sa）、法铃（ken'len）等组成］等。

中坛：主要是安家神，是以开光念经为主。主要使用柏木枝（ru'ma）。

下坛：神杖（a'bu'zua）、法铃（xi'ca'la'la）、羊皮鼓（bo）、牛毛毡帽子（bi'su'da）、刀(jia'you)、五彩旗（ca'qi）、犁铧（ru）、铁钎（nio'kua）、青稞（ri'gu）等。

记录者：余正国

法器ma'ca'er'go

羊皮鼓

猴皮帽

猴头"张山爷"

卦

神杖

·178·

Figure 33. Inner pages of *A'er Archive*.

ple achieve worldly satisfaction and "salvation" in terms of the people's well-being.[57] For the Chinese state, the discourse of cultural salvation, framed in the terminology of cultural heritage protection and preservation (*baohu*), is an important governmental technology. Since most ethnic minority groups in China have rich cultural traditions, framing governmentality in terms of cultural protection is effective at managing the nation's diverse peoples, such as the Qiang and the Yi. The discourse of culture and cultural preservation helps these peoples form ethnic subjectivity, as they learn to research the origins of their cultural traditions and see themselves as the creators and masters of their own cultures.[58]

Meanwhile, the discourse of cultural heritage and the institutionalization of traditional expressions of minority cultures as "heritage preservation" are not without their price. For the most part, such an institutionalization of culture sometimes serves to fragment and instrumentalize the collective memories embedded in cultural traditions, as well as induce a "folkorization," and therefore secularization, of otherwise sacred spiritual practices.[59] This folklorization of religious traditions reduces religious practices from social organizations informing the relationships among people and people's worldviews to classified secular knowledge subject to both scientific and political scrutiny. The institutionalization of "culture" also serves to objectify it, alienating "culture" from people's lived realities and reducing it to objects for guarding, processes for modeling, and sometimes even performances and entertainments.

As Danièle Hervieu-Léger suggests, the very idea of "tradition" is invented by modernity "to actualize the past in the present, to restore to human lives as they are lived in the living memory of an *essential core* which gives it existence in the present."[60] In other words, "tradition" or "traditional culture" itself is an imagined totality of the past that serves present political, social, and cultural needs in modern society. This does not mean that there exists no traditional or relatively stable forms of cultural expressions and values. But rather, the essentialization and institutionalization of "tradition" or "culture" as objects and specified processes of certain skills speak about modernity's anxiety to establish continuity with the past by using culture as a façade to cover up that which is lost in modern social life itself.

The instrumentalization and secularization of minority spiritual practices can be seen in the fact that, in many Qiang regions of Sichuan these days, the sacred *shibi* rituals have often "descended" to being performances for tourists and cultural galas, becoming a form of spectacle and entertainment. Because the *shibi* tradition is classified as a form of cultural heritage in China, it is contained in the ideological and political "box" designated by the state. A *shibi* would usually have to do the performance upon the request of tourists or cultural officials. In some villages, the *shibi* have even joined tourist performing teams to make money in their free time. The institutionalization of the *shibi* tradition as a form of cultural heritage to be displayed, performed, and protected, therefore, maintains only the appearance of this sacred tradition, whereas the spiritual function itself is sometimes lost and unsubstantiated.

As for the fragmentation of traditions, Mr. Yu revealed to me that some of the Qiang cultural practices defy institutionalization or standardization. For example, one time, Mr. Yu and a few other villagers were invited to perform a ritual dance for a TV show in Beijing. The director insisted on designing the choreography and lighting on stage in a way that would make the dance more attractive to the Han audience. Yet, Mr. Yu and his fellow villagers could never get it right. Mr. Yu remembered the awkwardness of trying to follow the Han director's mandate on stage: "After a whole day of rehearsal, we still could not perform it well. Our dances should not be designed that way. We usually improvise in our ritual dances according to our moods. If someone designs it for us, none of us can do it well." The Qiang *shibi* tradition is marked by its spontaneity, mysticism, and creativity. Distorting or standardizing any part of this tradition to cater to the director and the audience felt unnatural to the Qiang *shibi* invited to perform the ritual dance for a national audience. Eventually, the director gave in and let the performers follow their own rhythm, which allowed Mr. Yu and his friends to complete the performance. This instance is a telling example of how the standardization of ethnic cultural practices has the potential to essentialize "culture" and reducing it to sheer spectacles, taking the social meaning out of a cultural performance. Even though Mr. Yu and his friends were eager to present Qiang culture to a national audience, they were also conscious of the need to refute the fossilization and misrepresentation of their ethnic traditions, which motivates the writing and publication of *A'er Archive*.

From this chapter, we have seen that multiethnic activism and literary writing in contemporary China suggest the multiple sources of influence that converge to shape ethnic identities. On the other hand, whether it is minority writers/intellectuals or ordinary villagers, the efforts to preserve ancestral memories and document culture often entail a negotiation with the nation's existing political and cultural discourses. In order to make his book project possible, Mr. Yu made tremendous efforts to communicate with the national cultural heritage administrations and leveraged different kinds of influence that he could get, including the UNESCO official who had encouraged him and a supportive NGO in Beijing.

Furthermore, participating in both the discourse and practice of cultural heritage sometimes contributes to alienating spiritual and ethnic traditions from minority people's lived realities, reducing minority traditions to objects, entertainments, and performances divorced from minority cultural contexts. During my interview with a *shibi* in another Qiang village in Sichuan, the old *shibi* in his seventies told me that the ancestral tradition of handing down the *shibi* skills to the male members of the family is dying. Many young people find it meaningless and unprofitable to spend so much time learning a skill that would not help them with making a living. As a result, some *shibi* start to teach non-family male members of the community. In order to make this ancient skill "profitable," both the old *shibi* I interviewed and his apprentice routinely perform their ritual ceremonies and dances to tourists in the Qiang region. This is a poignant truth. While fewer and fewer Qiang people themselves are interested in their ancestral skills and spiritual traditions, such traditions have assumed a new life by becoming a form of touristic performance and entertainment. Inevitably, the *shibi* have to change parts of their traditions to cater to the taste of tourists and the imagination of "Qiang culture" produced in mainstream discourses of minority culture.

The institutionalization of *shibi* tradition as a "cultural heritage" is a double-edged sword. On the one hand, institutionalizing *shibi* (and other intangible minority) traditions ensures that there is always an audience and need, whether it is tourists or cultural officials or various cultural galas, for these traditions. Indeed, in many Qiang villages in Sichuan, *shibi* performances are part of the touristic package. Institutionalizing *shibi* rituals also makes it easier for older *shibi* to train young ones, providing old *shibi* with the financial support and social recognition they need to continue this spiritual and social tradition. Therefore, the institutionalization of *shibi* traditions may contribute to protecting the *forms* of the *shibi* tradition. Yet, on the other hand, training *shibi* in a standardized and ready-made format detaches the *shibi* traditions from their original sacred context. The *shibi* tradition has descended from a sacred and secretive tradition informing the worldview of the Qiang to a publicly accessible mass entertainment delighting Han Chinese tourists and cultural officials. In this sense, the documentation and performing of an awe-inspiring ethnic spiritual tradition, just like the Native American Powwow festivals in the U.S., contributes to its very secularization, if not commercialization.

A'er Archive ends with an afterword written by a Han professor from a university in Beijing. Lauding the courage and efforts of the Qiang to protect their own culture, the professor gives away her sense of superiority when she writes, "even though the villagers may not be very cultured (*wenhua shuiping bugao*), they are united in their love for Qiang culture and their desire to present Qiang culture to their descendants and outsiders."[61] The professor argues that even though the villagers participating in *A'er Archive* were not well-trained experts or scholars of culture, their efforts should be respected and taken seriously.[62] Whereas the rest of the book can be read more or less as A'er villagers' efforts of "writing against culture,"[63] as the villagers make concerted efforts to interpret the local manifestations and diversity of Qiang culture instead of mystifying it as a monolithic whole, this professor's afterword brings the entire book back to the institutionalized and hierarchized nature of knowledge production in China.

Just like how Duan Haizhen's novel *Heavenly Songs* is sandwiched between a beginning and an end with reference to a Han student's efforts of "salvaging" minority culture, the afterword authored by a Han professor in *A'er Archive* is not only a textual, but also a rhetorical and political move. Such a move, whether made by the minority writer and villagers themselves or by the book editors and funding agencies, is necessitated by a desire to comply with national political discourses. This political move delineates the limits of representing the "other" cultures in China.

As David Palumbo-Liu points out, in our increasingly globalized world, more and more distant peoples and spaces are "delivered" to a mainstream audience or readership.[64] Otherness can be understood both as a "thing," or a manifestation of cultural and ethnic difference in varying forms, and more importantly, as a relation.[65] Otherness can be understood as how ethnic and cultural differences are rendered in a hierarchal system and how various power relations come into play in mediating those differences. For minority-produced literary and cultural writings in China, the "otherness" of the non-Han people in terms of their cultural differences and spiritually-oriented ethnic subjectivities is oftentimes only acceptable when it is mediated through a hierarchized knowledge production system that privileges the viewpoint of the so-called Han "expert." The Han professor's afterword in *A'er Archive* and the fictional Han student's enthusiasm for saving minority cultures in *Heavenly Songs* are political necessities that put a limit on the otherwise excessively "other" non-Han cultures. By giving the Han expert the final word, the books seem to suggest that it is only through the legitimatization of the Han scholar that minority cultural claims are validated and valuable. Such a move, therefore, could potentially reinforce the entrenched social and cultural power hierarchy between the Han academic "center" and the minority "peripheries." Despite these books' alleged intentions to present minority worldviews and cultural traditions, they resonate with the "salvaging" discourse of the pastoral nation: minority communities cannot advocate for their cultures without the care of the Han intellectuals.

Yet there is more subtlety to this inclusion of the image of the Han scholar in these books. The minority people, working at the liminal space of national culture, deploy the images and discourses of the nation to introduce an "in-between" and ambiguous time and space for the nation.[66] These books' invocation of the Han is a strategic move to legitimatize minority groups' cultural claims. Minority writers and villagers mediate the power relations embedded in the production of difference, as they deliberately deploy the "state" and the Han other to expand the reach, legibility, and influence of their work. The mediating role of the Han state/intellectual in these books makes the books on minority cultural difference more legible to Han readers, who may otherwise feel at a loss when approaching minority cultures. In this sense, the inclusion of the Han does not have to mean the diminishing of minority voices, but can be an uncanny and strategic gesture that lends minority writing resilience as it explores the best ways to present minority groups' historical and contemporary experiences in the context of the ideological spaces and social realities in China.

It is precisely this ambiguity and uncanniness that generates a creative space for minority writers and villagers. The Qiang and Yi minority writers insist on highly localized, ethnically-specific, and spiritually-informed explanations of the modern nation. They resist the "empty, homogenous" national time that Anderson assigns to modern nation-states; minority writers and villagers thus become what Homi Bhabha calls the "performative subjects" that signify "temporalities of splitting, ambivalence and vacillation."[67] Minority writers such as Duan Haizhen and Qiang Renliu exemplify the "splitting" of national time when they present the spiritually-informed temporality of the non-Han and use such temporality to contest the secular, developmentalist temporality and educational system of the nation-state. Similarly, A'er villagers embody the "temporality of vacillation" when they vacillate between the bureaucratic nation and the local village to employ the nation's administrative forces to aid a decidedly local, village-level cultural preservationist project. It is exactly this liminal space of splitting and vacillation that enables creative energies—and tensions—for minority intellectuals and villagers to invent their identities and produce their narratives of difference vis-à-vis the nation. In other words, minority writers and villagers negotiate the spaces between the national and the ethnic and between a secular, developmentalist modern regime and its overlooked spiritual dimensions to critique the inadequacy of the teleological nation and suggest alternative truths that may leave the nation pondering its losses and pitfalls in its pursuit of secular modernization.

Conclusion

This chapter has presented how ethnic minority writers and grassroots activists are actively engaging with modernity in their literary and cultural productions. I have shown how minority writers from Qiang and Yi backgrounds voice skepticism of the secular visions of modern China. Most importantly, Qiang writers like Qiang Renliu and the Yi writer Duan Haizhen articulate how the mystical, cosmologically-informed worldviews of the non-Han can answer transcendental questions about truth and meaning that a secular, teleological worldview is not capable of answering. In particular, "The Soul Pacifier" and *Heavenly Songs* include many ethnographically-detailed descriptions of minority religious and spiritual practices, asserting the value of minority spiritual worldviews in a fast-developing China.

In line with minority writers' ethnographically-informed depictions of ethnic spiritual traditions, cultural preservation efforts made by the Qiang villagers in Sichuan speak about how the discourse of "cultural heritage" can be both liberating and limiting. The desire to categorize and make sense of ethnic traditions propels Qiang villagers to engage in the research and writing of their own culture. They produce epistemological claims that help them construct their ethnic identity. At the same time, the discourse and practice of "cultural heritage" entails the secularization and even commercialization of ancestral memories and spiritual traditions. The institutionalization of culture in contemporary China mobilizes minority peoples to safeguard their traditions and negotiate with the nation. Minority groups strategically navigate national and political discourses to assert their ethnic distinctiveness and cultural agencies, producing difference by deploying and mediating national discourses and policies. Therefore, many ethnic communities in China participate in national discourses and policies in their effort to invent and re-create their "culture."

The ethnic heteroglossia of Chinese literature and cultural activism is generated when writing entails a constant act of self-examination and negotiation with the "other," be it the Han other (for minority groups) or the minority others (for the Han readers coming into contact with minority cultures). Minority writers and villagers are thus stepping outside of their immediate concerns of protecting their own ethnic traditions and actively engaging with a modernizing nation, sculpting an "in-between" place where the national and the ethnic interact to give rise to more creative voices and potentialities.

CONCLUSION

The "Qiang" as Concept, History, and People

A few years ago, when I traveled in the Qiang regions of Sichuan, I encountered a funeral that was taking place on the farmland near a small village. As I was watching the funeral, the Qiang villagers invited me, a stranger and passer-by, to join the group dance. The villagers were dancing around an earthen tomb where the dead had been buried. A cup of orange juice was being passed along, and I was instructed by the Qiang villagers to take a sip of the juice, as it was a token of blessing bestowed by the dead. The celebratory and inviting atmosphere of the funeral deeply struck me. In Han culture, funerals are always occasions for mourning accompanied by solemnity. As I danced with the villagers, I asked myself: Who are the Qiang? How did a group of people with cultural customs so different from the Han come to be defined as Chinese? Who decides the "Chinese-ness" of ethnic minority groups? And what constitutes the boundaries between the Han and the non-Han, who together make up the diverse populations of China?

This book has traced the invention of the Qiang identity in Chinese cultural history and contemporary Chinese society. I have argued that the Qiang identity has been intertwined with the national identity of China since antiquity. The concept of "Qiang" has been an important signifier of the changing ethno-national relations between the non-Han peoples and China from the earliest recorded history to the present day. In pre-modern China, the idea of "Qiang" mainly signified the barbarian racial others west of China proper, who came to be assimilated into Confucian cultural and social systems in the Ming and Qing dynasties. In modern China, "Qiang" has become an ethnonym signifying great cultural and musical traditions, such as the *Qiangdi* (Qiang flute), and the Qiang as an ethnic group has been portrayed in Communist national narratives as guardians of important aspects of Chinese civilization.

Even though the signified content is always shifting and evolving, the signifier (the concept of "Qiang") has always been recognized by different Chinese regimes and has been extant during different periods of Chinese history. "Qiang" takes on different symbolic, ethno-national and cultural meanings at different moments of history. Whether it is used as a marker for the barbarian western groups or a symbol for the guardians of national musical heritage, the idea of "Qiang" has been mythologized and tokenized in Chinese national discourses, and it references the Chinese political and cultural center's changing relationships with its ethnic and geographical "peripheries" represented by non-Han groups. In modern China, "Qiang" has become solidified as an ethnic group and a tangible community of people, and those classified as Qiangzu have inherited the rich symbolic and historical meanings associated with the sign "Qiang" to re-create their identities. This is particularly the case in the reform era (1980–present). The growing market economy and the political economy of multiculturalism in contemporary China have led to the blossom of ethnic tourism and China's official policies for enshrining multiethnic cultural heritage. These recent developments have allowed Qiang elites and villagers alike to reimagine their identities and reconfigure a minority group's relationship with national discourses and cultural memories.

In this sense, the story of the "Qiang" is more than the story of one ethnic group, but encapsulates how ethnic relations can be conceived, how ethnic identities can be imagined, and how ethnic minorities' status in the nation can be construed across the "pre-modern" and "modern" divide. Too often, we regard the past simply as a source of historical imagination or a somehow static treasure trove of culture and civilization. Yet, as we have seen in this book, the past is never past: both China's state historians during the socialist period and contemporary Qiangzu writers and cultural workers have animated the rich and long textual traditions of the "Qiang" to invent new realities for ethno-national purposes. As China's national discourses and national imagination are almost always formed through the relationship between the ethnic majority (known as the "Han" today) to minority peoples, the symbolic meaning of Qiang has been appropriated by the nation and is now reinterpreted and re-created by those categorized as Qiangzu themselves in the creative realms of scholarly and creative literature, cinema and the built environment, as well as local history-making and cultural preservation projects.

Through the six chapters of this book, I have presented an interdisciplinary picture of how the Qiang identity has been invented through three major means. These three means are: first, the contemporary re-interpretation of historical and textual sources revered in Sinitic Chinese tradition, such as Tang-dynasty poetry and the myths of Da Yu (Chapters 1 and 2). This first means aims at constructing the historical longevity and legitimacy of the Qiang in China's national memory and civilizational imagination. The second means is the visual construction of the image of the "Qiang" through cinema and other visual technologies, such as contemporary blockbusters shot in Taoping Qiang Village and indigenous Qiang cinema (Chapters 3 and 4). This second means aims at visualizing the Qiang as a tangible, creative group of people and renders Qiang architecture and living environments legible and sensational to the global media imagination. Finally, the third means of constructing the Qiang is through the self-articulation of the future of the "Qiang" through the vehicle of literature and cultural activism. Such writing efforts aim to construct minority identities and to challenge the widely accepted premises of modernity, such as secularism and consumerism (Chapters 5 and 6). If the first means of reinventing historical narratives in the hands of ethnic Qiang and Han historians is oriented toward the past of the Qiang, then the second means of visualizing the Qiang as a creative people in the works of filmmakers is oriented toward the present of the Qiang. Eventually, the third means of Qiang literary writing is oriented toward the future of the Qiang. Through such critical lenses spanning vast historical periods and spatial configurations, I hope I have presented a multifaceted, rich, and complex portrait of the Qiang.

The six chapters in this book have demonstrated that both the national political center's imagination of the minorities (such as the state history-making projects examined in Chapter 1) and minority groups' response to national imagination is not static or one-sided. On the contrary, such ethnonational imagination is dynamic and mutually constitutive: just as national discourses appropriate the *shaoshu minzu* in the textual and visual constructions of a multiethnic China, minority groups deploy national discourses, historical materials, and Sinitic cultural myths to assert minority identities and pasts within the broader spectrum of Chinese history. Minority writers, entrepreneurs, scholars, and village activists are becoming increasingly savvy at leveraging multiple resources at the local, national, and global levels to carve out spaces of "creative belonging" as they assert both their ethnic distinctiveness and their worldliness.

My study of the "Qiang" thus takes on a triple meaning: I have treated the "Qiang" as a historical concept open to immense interpretations, an ethnic signifier denoting changing ethno-national relations, and a real group of people concerned with their ancestral memories and contemporary livelihoods. Through such cross-disciplinary and transhistorical examinations of

Figure 34. The author interviewing an old Qiang *shibi* and his apprentice. Photograph by author.

the "Qiang," this book can hopefully provide a fresh conceptual and methodological framework conducive to the study of the making and re-making of ethnic identities for other minority groups in the world.

Indeed, the invention of the Qiang identity is representative of how the creation of ethnic identities in the modern world can mobilize a myriad of symbols and resources. The study of the Qiang will contribute to the growing scholarship on global indigenous and minority cultures and movements: the experience of the Qiang (and many similar minority groups in China) shows us that indigenous claims on local roots, ancestral memories, and spiritual traditions do not always have to run counter to state discourses or challenge state hegemony. Rather, minorities and indigenous groups like the Qiang can creatively re-make state discourses and locate their claims to their originary status in the nation by placing their claims within the state's larger political-cultural frameworks.[1] As the case of the Qiang has shown, by creatively engaging with Chinese and even global cultural-historical sources, ethnic Qiang scholars, writers, artists, and villagers unsettle the dichotomy between the Chinese cultural "center" and its "peripheries," and they contest certain hierarchies, such as that between China and the West, in minority-related visual and literary productions.

The fluidity and capaciousness of the signifier "Qiang" throughout Chinese history have created the rich discursive spaces for contemporary Qiangzu elites and villagers alike to reimagine the "Qiang" identity in the climate of China's pursuit of a multicultural national identity. Ethnic minorities are not—and have never been—passive receivers of external forces; rather, minority groups have always exhibited creativity and inventiveness as they deploy local, national, and global sources to situate themselves in our ever-changing world. The invention of the Qiang identity—and the identities of many other ethnic minority groups in China and the world—will keep evolving and adapting to new situations. Minority identities will incorporate new inspirations and become open to new imaginings in order to create the many futures of ethnicity.

GLOSSARY OF CHINESE TERMS

Note: This glossary is a reference to important concepts and terms discussed in this book. It contains both traditional and simplified Chinese characters. The author respects the origin of the Chinese sources. For Chinese terms that appeared in traditional Chinese in their original contexts, the author maintains the traditional characters; likewise, for Chinese characters that appeared in simplified characters in their original contexts, the author maintains the simplified characters. If the original term is in traditional Chinese, the simplified Chinese version is supplemented in parenthesis, and vice versa. For terms that are already included in a previous chapter or section, when they appear again in another chapter or section, they will not be included again, unless the same term is discussed in significant length in the next appearance. Italics indicates book or film titles. Pinyin romanizations follow Chinese characters, accompanied by English translations or explanations of the words.

Introduction

羌	Qiang	Qiang
羌族	Qiangzu	Qiang ethnic group
少数民族	shaoshu minzu	Ethnic minorities in China
阿来 (阿來)	Alai	An ethnic Tibetan author's name
阿库乌雾 (阿庫烏霧)	Aku Wuwu	An ethnic Yi poet's name
蕃	Fan	The Fan "barbarians" in classical Chinese literature and historiography

蛮	Man	The Man "barbarians" in classical Chinese literature and historiography
後漢書 (后汉书)	*Hou Hanshu*	*The Book of Later Han*
范曄 (范晔)	Fan Ye	The author of *The Book of Later Han*
西羌傳 (西羌传)	*Xiqiang zhuan*	"Biography of the West Qiang" (a section in *The Book of Later Han*)
蔡文姬	Cai Wenji	Poet from Eastern Han dynasty
曹操	Cao Cao	Military general of the Eastern Han dynasty and an important figure in the Three Kingdoms Period
中華民族 (中华民族)	The Chinese people/nation/race	*Zhonghua minzu*
民族走廊	Minzu zoulang	Ethnic corridor
藏彝走廊	Zangyi zoulang	Tibetan-Yi corridor
古堡之吻	*Gubao zhiwen*	*Forbidden Kiss* (Title of a film)
非物质文化遗产 (非物質文化遺產)	Feiwuzhi wenhua yichan	Intangible cultural heritage
杀生 (殺生)	*Shasheng*	*Design of Death* (Title of a film)
田芬	Tian Fen	Name of a Chinese American film director

Chapter 1

国殇 (國殤)	Guo shang	National trauma
中华民族文化 (中華民族文化)	Zhonghua minzu wenhua	Chinese culture (culture of the Chinese people)
民族生命	Minzu shengming	National life
金氣 (金气)	Jinqi	The golden energy

戎, 戎狄	Rong, Rongdi	The Rong "barbarians" in classical Chinese literature and historiography
諸戎 (诸戎)	Zhurong	The "various Rong barbarians"
詩經 (诗经)	*Shijing*	*The Classic of Poetry*
殷武	Yinwu	A king portrayed in *The Classic of Poetry*
南匈奴	Nan Xiongnu	Southern Xiongnu
南蛮西南夷	Nanman Xinanyi	Southern Barbarians and Southwestern Savages
民族	Minzu	Ethnic groups, ethnic minorities
莊學本 (庄学本)	Zhuang Xueben	Photographer and ethnographer of Republican-era China
羌戎考察記 (羌戎考察记)	*Qiangrong kaochaji*	*Expeditions into the Land of the Qiang and Rong*
同胞	Tong bao	Compatriots
民族學 (民族学)	Minzuxue	Ethnology
蔡元培	Cai Yuanpei	Scholar in Republican-era China
赫哲族	Hezhezu	Hezhe, an ethnic group in northeast China
苗族	Miaozu	The Miao ethnic group
羅羅 (罗罗)	Lolo	A Republican-era term to refer to an indigenous ethnic group in southwest China, often known as the Yi ethnic group in post-1949 China
回民	Huimin	The Hui people (a group of Chinese-speaking Muslim people in China)

中國民族史 (中国民族史)		*History of the Races in China* (Title of a book) *Zhongguo minzushi*
林惠祥	Lin Huixiang	Scholar of ethnicity and history in Republican-era China
王桐齡 (王桐龄)	Wang Tongling	Scholar of ethnicity and history in Republican-era China
宋文炳	Song Wenbing	Scholar of ethnicity and history in Republican-era China
夷 Yi, 狄 Di, 東胡 (东胡) Donghu, 氐羌 (Diqiang), 百越 (Baiyue)		Terms used in classical Chinese literature to refer to the various "barbarians" residing in China's borderlands
藏系	Zangxi	The "Tibetan lineage" (an ethno-racial term used in Republican-era scholarship to refer to the collective identity of various Tibetan groups)
氐羌系	Diqiangxi	The "Diqiang lineage" (an ethno-racial term used in Republican-era scholarship to refer to the historical Diqiang people, which was believed to be the ancestors of the modern Tibetan groups by Chinese ethnologists and historians at the time)

嘉绒藏族 (嘉絨藏族)	Jiarong zangzu	Gyalrong Tibetans (This refers to certain Tibetan groups residing in the Aba Tibetan and Qiang Autonomous Prefecture and the Garze Tibetan Prefecture in Sichuan Province, though "Gyalrong Tibetan" is not an officially recognized ethnic group in China and is considered as a branch of the greater Tibetan group.)
费孝通 (費孝通)	Fei Xiaotong	An important and influential ethnologist and sociologist in twentieth-century China
民族融合	Minzu ronghe	Ethnic conglomeration/ assimilation/ acculturation
中国少数民族简史丛书	*Zhongguo shaoshu minzu jianshi congshu*	*Series of Concise Histories of Chinese Ethnic Minorities*
国家民族事务委员会 (國家民族事務委員會)	Guojia minzu shiwu weiyuanhui	National Ethnic Affairs Committee
羌族简史(羌族簡史)	*Qiangzu jianshi*	*Concise History of Qiangzu*
人民	Renmin	The people
羌笛	Qiangdi	The Qiang flute (reed pipe)
塞上聞笛 (塞上闻笛)	"Saishang wendi"	"Listening to the Flute on the Frontiers" (title of a Tang-dynasty poem)
金城北樓 (金城北楼)	"Jincheng beilou"	"The North Tower of Golden Fort" (title of a Tang-dynasty poem)

吐蕃	Tubo	A classical Chinese term referring to the historical Tibetan Kingdom
涼州詞(凉州词)	"Liangzhou ci"	"The Lyrics of Liangzhou" (Title of a Tang-dynasty poem)
民族识别(民族識別)	Minzu shibie	Ethnic Classification Project (spearheaded by the Chinese Communist Party in post-1949 China)
民族传统 (民族傳統)	Minzu chuantong	Ethnic traditions

Chapter 2

理县 (理縣)	Lixian	Li County (a county in Sichuan with a relatively large concentration of Qiang population)
西羌文化	*Xiqiang wenhua*	*The Culture of West Qiang* (title of a journal)
尧	Yao	A legendary ancient king in China
舜	Shun	A legendary ancient king in China
禹, 大禹	Yu, Da Yu	King Yu the Great, a legendary ancient king in China
耿少将 (耿少將)	Geng Shaojiang	An ethnic Qiang historian
羌族通史	*Qiangzu tongshi*	*A Complete History of the Qiangzu*
史记 (史記)	*Shiji*	*The Records of the Grand Historian*
揚雄 (扬雄)	Yang Xiong	A historian in the Western Han dynasty in China

岷江流域 (岷江流域)	Minjiang liuyu	The Min River Valley in Sichuan
华阳国志 (華陽國志)	*Huayang guozhi*	*Chronicles of Huayang* (gazetteer from the Jin dynasty in China)
李冰	Li Bing	Hydro-engineer and official of the Shu region during the Warring State period
天府之国 (天府之國)	"Tianfu zhiguo"	"Country of Heaven" (nickname for Sichuan)
桃坪史话 (桃坪史話)	*Taoping shihua*	*Historical Accounts on Taoping*
杨光成 (楊光成)	Yang Guangcheng	An ethnic Qiang scholar
谷运龙(谷運龍)	Gu Yunlong	An ethnic Qiang writer and scholar

Chapter 3

桃坪羌寨	Taoping Qiangzhai	Taoping Qiang Village
碉楼	Diaolou	Fortified, tower-form Qiang and Tibetan architecture with both spiritual and historically military functions
神秘的东方古堡 神秘的東方古堡	"Shenmi de dongfang gubao"	"Mysterious Oriental Castle" (a popular culture reference to Taoping Qiang Village)
记住乡愁 (記住鄉愁)	*Jizhu xiangchou*	*Remembering Home* (title of a national TV program in China featuring Taoping Qiang Village)
管虎	Guan Hu	Name of a Chinese Six-Generation director

杀生 (殺生)	*Shasheng*	*Design of Death* (title of a Chinese film by Guan Hu)
方言	Fangyan	Local dialects
四川话 (四川話)	Sichuan hua	Sichuanese dialect
古堡之吻	*Gubao zhiwen*	*Forbidden Kiss* (title of a film by Tian Fen)
寨花	"Zhaihua"	"Beauty of the Village" (a term referring to Ms. Long, widely considered the most beautiful and most capable woman in Taoping Qiang Village)

Chapter 4

十年寻羌 (十年尋羌)	*Shinian xunqiang*	*Ten Years in Search for the Qiang* (title of a documentary film by Gao Tunzi)
高屯子	Gao Tunzi	Name of a documentary filmmaker in the Qiang regions
木姐珠	Mujiezhu	Name of a celestial goddess in Qiang mythology
斗安珠	Dou'anzhu	A monkey-headed man considered as ancestor to human beings in Qiang mythology
图经 (圖景)	Tujing	Shamanistic pictographic writings in Qiang, Naxi, and other indigenous traditions in southwest China

东巴 (東巴)	Dongba	An indigenous shamanistic, animalist religious practice of the Naxi people of Yunnan; "dongba" can refer to both the priest of the Naxi's indigenous religious practice and the practice itself
纳西 (納西)	Naxi	An ethnic minority group in Yunnan province
尔玛的婚礼 (爾瑪的婚禮)	*Erma de hunli*	*Erma's Wedding* (title of a film produced in the Qiang regions of Sichuan)
韩万峰 (韓萬峰)	Han Wanfeng	Name of the director who directed *Erma's Wedding*
黎族	Lizu	An ethnic minority group mainly distributed in Hainan, Guangxi, and other southern provinces in China
红双喜 (紅雙喜)	Hong shuangxi	The double-happiness symbol

Chapter 5

毒药猫 (毒藥貓)	"Duyao mao"	"Poisonous Cat," a Qiang term that refers to women who are believed to have bewitching and dangerous powers over their fellow villagers
个人随笔 (個人隨筆)	Geren suibi	A genre of autobiographical and personal

回忆性随笔 (回憶性隨筆)	Huiyixing suibi	Memoir-style writing popular among ethnic Qiang writers in contemporary China
乡土 (鄉土)	Xiangtu	The native soil, a literary motif in modern Chinese literature
羊子	Yang Zi	An ethnic Qiang writer
王永安	Wang Yong'an	An ethnic Qiang writer
任冬生	Ren Dongsheng	An ethnic Qiang writer
羌族文学 (羌族文學)	*Qiangzu wenxue*	*Qiangzu Literature* (title of a Qiang literary journal)
汶川县文联 (汶川縣文聯)	Wenchuanxian wenlian	Wenchuan County Liteature and Art Association
山中的母亲 (山中的母親)	"Shanzhong de muqin"	"Mother in the Mountains" (title of an essay by Yang Zi)
老家	"Laojia"	"Homeland" (title of an essay by Wang Yong'an
余耀明	Yu Yaoming	A Qiang ethnic writer
芬芳朵哟喂	"Fenfang duoyowei"	"The Fragrant Key" (title of a short story by Yu Yaoming)
中国作家协会 (中國作家協會)	Zhongguo zuojia xiehui	Chinese Writers Association
羌风遍野 (羌風遍野)	*Qiangfeng bianye*	*Qiang Wind All Over the Wilderness* (title of a book by Ren Dongsheng
雷子	Lei Zi	A Qiang ethnic writer
少数民族文学骏马奖 (少數民族文學駿馬獎)	Shaoshu minzu wenxue junma jiang	Steed Award for Minority Literature
天真的梦与羌野的歌	*Tianzhen de meng yu Qiangye de ge*	*Innocent Dreams and Songs in the Wilderness of the Qiang* (title of a book by Lei Zi)

Chapter 6

文化遗产 (文化遺產)	Wenhua yichan	Cultural heritage
叶星光 (葉星光)	Ye Xingguang	A Qiang ethnic writer
神山，神树，神林 (神山，神樹，神林)	"Shenshan, shenshu, shenlin"	"Sacred Mountain, Sacred Trees, Sacred Grove" (title of a short story by Ye Xingguang)
羌人六	Qiang Renliu	A Qiang ethnic writer
安魂者	"An'hun zhe"	"The Soul Pacifier" (title of an essay by Qiang Renliu)
食鼠之家	*Shishu zhijia*	*A Family That Survives on Mice* (title of an essay collection by Qiang Renliu)
中国多民族文学丛书	*Zhongguo duominzu wenxue congshu*	*China Multiethnic Literary series* (a series of multiethnic literary works published in China)
多民族文学 (多民族文學)	Duominzu wenxue	Multiethnic literature
少数民族文学	Shaoshu minzu wenxue	Ethnic minority literature
彝, 彝族	Yi, Yizu	The Yi ethnic group
段海珍	Duan Haizhen	An ethnic Yi writer
天歌	*Tiange*	*Heavenly Songs* (title of a novel by Duan Haizhen)
作家出版社	Zuojia chubanshe	A publishing house in China that publishes various ethnic minority literatures discussed in this chapter
非物质文化遗产 (非物質文化遺產)	Feiwuzhi wenhua yichan	Intangible Cultural Heritage
非物质文化遗产传承人 (非物質文化遺產傳承人)	Feiwuzhi wenhua yichan chuanchengren	Designated inheritors for Intangible Cultural Heritage

释比	Shibi	The Qiang shamanistic ritual master
原生态 (原生態)	Yuan shengtai	“pure and original” (a term used to describe traditional art and cultural forms for minority groups)
阿尔档案 (阿爾檔案)	*A'er Dang'an*	*A'er Archive* (title of a book authored by A'er Villagers)

NOTES

Introduction

1. Qtd. in Andre Dudemaine, Gabrielle Marcoux, Isabelle St-Amand, 42, emphasis original.

2. Salah El Moncef, "Minor Literature," *The Oxford Research Encyclopedia, Literature*, 1.

3. *Global Indigenous Media: Cultures, Poetics, and Politics* (Durham: Duke University Press, 2008), p. 40.

4. Pamela Wilson and Michelle Stewart, *Global Indigenous Media*, 2.

5. Mark Bender, "Cry of the Silver Pheasant: Contemporary Ethnic Poetry in Sichuan and Yunnan," in *Chinese Literature Today* 2, no. 2 (2012): 70.

6. Bender, "Cry of the Silver Pheasant," 69–74 and my fieldwork.

7. Yang Yumei 杨玉梅, *Minzu wenxue de jianshou yu chyaoyue* 民族文学的坚守与超越 [The persistence and transcendence of ethnic literature] (Beijing: Zuojia chubanshe, 2013), 12–19.

8. Alai 阿来 and Lu Yiping 卢一萍, Alai: Wo yizhi douzai zhuiwen, weishenme 阿来：我一直都在追问,为什么？ [Alai: I have been questioning: Why?], Zhongguo zuojia wang 中国作家网 [China Writers' Site], last modified June 30, 2017, http://www.chinawriter.com.cn/n1/2017/0630/c405057-29373267.html (accessed May 16, 2018).

9. D. Dayton, "Growing New Forms of Literature: A Conversation with Tibetan Author Alai." https://www.worldliteraturetoday.org/2019/spring/growing-new-forms-literature-conversation-tibetan-writer-alai-d-dayton.

10. *Aku Wuwu's Coyote Traces: East Asian Audio Books, Voices from Past and President.* Translated by Wen Peihong and Mark Bender. The Ohio State University. https://u.osu.edu/eaab/aku-wuwus-coyote-traces/coyote-traces-page-1/.

11. Wen Peihong and Mark Bender, trans., *Aku Wuwu's Coyote Traces.*

12. Recent monographs on Chinese minority literatures include Yuqing Yang's *Mystifying China's Southwest Ethnic Borderlands: Harmonious Heterotopia* (Lexington Books, 2018), in which the author studies three particular sites in southwest China and their representations in literary works by both Han and non-Han writers and Mark Bender's *Butterfly Mother: Miao (Hmong) Creation Epics from Guizhou, China* (Hackett Publishing Company, 2006), in which the author translates and studies Miao creation epics and folklore. In 2019, Mark Bender and Qingchun Luo also translated Yi creation epic in their book The *Nuosu Book of Origins: A Creation Epic from Southwest China* (University of Washington Press, 2019).

13. Louisa Schein, *Minority Rules: The Miao and The Feminine in China's Cultural Politics* (Durham: Duke University Press, 2000).

14. Other recent publications in the anthropological understandings of China's ethnic minorities include Yu Luo's writings about the indigenous experience of the Buyi people of Guizhou (2017, 2018) and Andrew Grant's 2022 book on the urbanization of Tibetan communities, *The Concrete Plateau: Urban Tibetans and Chinese Civilizing Machine.*

15. Robin Visser, *Questioning Borders: Ecoliteratures of China and Taiwan* (Columbia University Press, 2023), 2.

16. Shu-mei Shih, "Introduction: What is Sinophone Studies," in Shu-mei Shih, ed., *Sinophone Studies: A Critical Reader* (Columbia University Press, 2013), 7.

17. Andre Dudemaine, Garbrielle Marcoux and Isabelle St-Amand, "Introduction: Indigenous Cinema and Media in the Americas: Storytelling, Communities, and Sovereignties," in *Canadian Journal of Film Studies*, Vol. 29, Iss. 1, 24.

18. *Learning from Experience: Minority Identities, Multicultural Struggles* (University of California Press, 2002), 13.

19. Homi K. Bhabha, "DissemiNation," in *The Location of Culture* (London: Routledge 1994), 212; Homi Bhabha, "The Third Space: Interview with Homi Bhabha," in *Identity: Community, Culture, Difference*, ed. Jonathan Rutherfold (London: Lawrence and Wishart, 1990), 221; Homi Bhabha, "Culture's In-Between," in *Multicultural States: Rethinking Difference and Identity*, ed. David Bennett (London: Routledge, 1998), 34.

20. Pamela Kyle Crossley, "Thinking about Ethnicity in Early Modern China," 10.

21. Shu-mei Shih, "Introduction: What is Sinophone Literature?" in *Sinophone Studies: A Critical Reader*, ed. Shu-mei Shih (Columbia University Press, 2013).

22. Not all ethnic groups in China experience the same relationship with national policies and official national narratives. Some other, larger groups in the borderlands of China may experience religious expressions and cultural identities very differently from the smaller, indigenous groups, such as the Qiang.

23. El Moncef, "Minor Literature," 5.

24. Pamela Kyle Crossley, "Thinking about Ethnicity in Early Modern China," 24.

25. Stuart Hall, "Introduction: Who Needs 'Identity'?," in *Questions of Cultural Identity*, ed. Stuart Hall and Paul du Gay (London: Sage Publications, 1996), 2.

26. Hall, "Introduction," 2–3 and Lawrence Grossberg and Stuart Hall, "On Postmodernism and Articulation," in *Journal of Communication Inquiry*, 10, no. 2 (1986), 53.

27. Hall, "Introduction," 4–5.

28. Fan Ye 范曄, *Hou Hanshu* 後漢書 西羌傳 [The book of later Han: biographies of the Xiqiang]. Zhongyang yanjiu yuan hanji dianzi wenxian ziliaoku 中央研究院漢籍電子文獻資料庫 [Academia Sinica hanji electronic database], volume 87.

29. For example, in the *Book of Tang* 唐書 and the *History of Ming* 明史, there were similar passages that depict the cultural otherness of the non-Sinitic groups.

30. *The Red Brush: Writing Women of Imperial China*, Wilt Idema and Beata Grant, eds. (Cambridge: Harvard University Asia Center, 2004), 117. Emphasis mine. The authorship of Cai Wenji's poems is up for debate, as some scholars argue that male poets assumed her voice and personified her in these poems. Even so, the sentiments of Cai's poems uncontestably convey a sense of personal and cultural loss and humiliation when Chinese women

and Chinese culture fell prey to the militant power of non-Chinese groups residing in China's borderlands.

31. Idema and Grant, ed., *The Red Brush*, 118.

32. *Race: The New Critical Idiom*, Martin Orkin and Alexa Alice Joubin (New York: Routledge), 9.

33. *Race: The New Critical Idiom*, 12.

34. This book respects the origin of the primary sources. When traditional Chinese characters are used in the primary sources, I maintain the traditional characters. Likewise, when simplified characters are used, I maintain the simplified characters.

35. "Deconstructing the Chinese Nation: How Recent is It?" In *The Global and Regional in China's Nation-Formation* (London: Routledge, 2009), 103.

36. The Qiangic language, itself highly diverse with many regional variations, belongs to the Sino-Tibetan language family and falls under the Tibetan-Burmese language group (藏缅语支). These groups were likely glossed as West Qiang in pre-modern historical cannons, such as *The Book of Later Han* discussed earlier.

37. Fei Xiaotong 费孝通 "Guanyu woguo minzu de shibie wenti" 关于我国民族的识别问题 [Questions about the identification of our nation's ethnic groups], *Zhongguo shehui kexue* 中国社会科学 [Social sciences of China], no. 1, 1980.

38. Fei Xiaotong 费孝通 "Tan shenru kaizhan minzu diaocha wenti 谈深入开展民族调查问题 [On the deepening of the questions of ethnic investigations], *Zhongnan Minzu Xueyuan xuebao* 中南民族学院学报 [Journal of Zhongnan Nationalities College], no.3, 1982, 4.

39. Fei Xiaotong, "Tan shenru," 4.

40. "Thinking about Ethnicity in Early Modern China," 23.

41. Paula M.L. Moya, *The Social Imperative: Race, Close Reading, and Contemporary Literary Criticism* (Stanford: Stanford University Press, 2016), 112.

42. Moya, *The Social Imperative*, 112.

43. James Leibold, *Reconfiguring Chinese Nationalism: How the Qing Frontier and its Indigenes Became Chinese* (New York: Palgrave Macmillan, 2007), 8.

44. Benedict Anderson, *Imagined Communities: Reflections on the Origin and Spread of Nationalism* (London: Verso, 1991), 7.

45. Benedict Anderson, *Imagined Communities*, 7.

46. Leibold, *Reconfiguring Chinese Nationalism*, 11 and Xiuyu Wang, *China's Last Imperial Frontier: Late Qing Expansion in Sichuan's Tibetan Borderlands* (Lanham: Lexington Books, 2011), 13.

47. Liang Qichao 梁启超, "Zhongguoshi xulun" 中国史叙论 [Introduction to the history of China], in Liang Qichao quanji 梁启超全集 [The Complete Works of Liang Qichao] (Beijing: Beijing chubanshe, 1999), Vol. 1, 499.

48. Leibold, *Reconfiguring Chinese Nationalism*, 10.

49. Liang, "Zhongguoshi xulun," 499 and Leibold, *Reconfiguring Chinese Nationalism.*

50. Leibold, *Reconfiguring Chinese Nationalism*, 2.

51. Leibold, *Reconfiguring Chinese Nationalism*, 115.

52. Thomas Mullaney, *Coming to Terms with the Nation: Ethnic Classification in Modern China* (Berkeley: University of California Press, 2011), 4.

53. Mullaney, *Coming to Terms*, 15.

54. Mullaney, *Coming to Terms*, 15.

55. Mullaney, *Coming to Terms*, 19.

56. Minglang Zhou, "Nation-state building and multiculturalism in China" in *Handbook on Ethnic Minorities in China*, ed. Xiaowei Zang (Cheltenham: Edward Elgar Publishing, 2016), 121.

57. Chinese ethnic studies scholar Ma Rong distinguishes between two types of policies for managing ethnic relations, politicization and culturalization. For him, politicization entails making policies that emphasize the "integrity, political power, and 'territorial' conservation of ethnic groups," whereas culturalization entails "emphasizing the cultural characteristics of ethnic groups" and "treating ethnic relations as cultural relations." Ma Rong, "A New Perspective in Guiding Ethnic Relations in the 21st Century: 'De-politicization of Ethnicity in China," in *De-politicization of Ethnic Questions in China*, ed. Lizhong Xie (Singapore: World Scientific 2014), 6.

58. Ma, "A New Perspective," 6.

59. Leibold, *Reconfiguring Chinese Nationalism*, 8.

60. Leibold, *Reconfiguring Chinese Nationalism*, 8.

61. Thomas Mullaney, "Critical Han Studies: Introduction and Prolegomenon," in Thomas Mullaney, James Leibold, Stephane Gros, and Eric Vanden Bussche, ed., *Critical Han Studies: The History, Representation, and Identity of China's Majority*, 4–8.

62. Mullaney, "Critical Han Studies," 13.

63. Ralph Litzinger, "Memory Work: Reconstituting the Ethnic in Post-Mao China," in *Cultural Anthropology* 13, no. 2 (1998): 225.

64. Hu Jintao 胡锦涛, "Hu Jintao tichu, zhashi tuijin shehui zhuyi wenhua qiangguo jianshe" 胡锦涛提出,扎实推进社会主义文化强国建设 [Hu Jintao proposes: firmly push forward the construction of a culturally strong socialist state], last modified November 8, 2012, http://cpc.people.com.cn/18/n/2012/1108/c350821-19526764.html (accessed May 20, 2018).

65. Hu Jintao, "Hu Jintao tichu."

66. Shen Guiping 沈桂萍 and Ou Guangming 欧光明, *Zhongguo minzu lilun zhengce gailun* 中国民族理论政策概论 [Introduction to China's ethnic theories and policies] (Beijing: Minzu chubanshe, 2007), 192–201.

67. Susan K. McCarthy, *Communist Multiculturalism: Ethnic Revival in Southwest China* (Seattle: University of Washington Press, 2009), 32.

68. For discussions on ethnic tourism in Yunnan, see Bai Zhihong, "Ethnic Identities under the Tourist Gaze," in *Asian Ethnicity* 8, no. 3 (2007): 245–259; for similar topics on Guizhou and Guangxi, see Tim Oakes, *Tourism and Modernity in China* and Jenny Chio, *A Landscape of Travel: The Work of Tourism in Rural Ethnic China* (Seattle: University of Washington Press, 2014); for similar topics on Sichuan, see Chapter 2 of this dissertation.

69. For example, Tim Oakes argues that the development of ethnic tourism in many southwestern provinces has led an influx of Han in-migration to minority regions, and Han developers and entrepreneurs have exacerbated a "trend of accumulation by dispossession," exploiting the resources and labor in minority regions. See Tim Oakes, "Ethnic tourism in China" in *Handbook on Ethnic Minorities in China*, ed. Xiaowei Zang (Cheltenham: Edward Elgar Publishing, 2016), 291–315.

70. Dru C. Gladney, "Representing Nationality in China: Reconfiguring Majority/Minority Identities," in *The Journal of Asian Studies* 53, no. 1 (1994): 92–123.

71. China has been publishing many national journals to study minority groups since the early 1980s. For example, a journal devoted to the study of ethnic minority literatures, *National (Minzu) Literature* (*minzu wenxue* 民族文学), was created in 1981 and is under the administration of the Chinese Writers' Association. This journal has been featuring many minority writers and their literary works. Another national journal, *Ethno-national Studies* (*Minzu yanjiu* 民族研究), under the administration of the Chinese Academy of Social Sciences, is devoted to the study of minority societies, education, law, and history.

72. Bhikhu Parekh, "What is Multiculturalism?" in *The Ethnicity Reader: Nationalism, Multiculturalism and Migration*, ed. Montserrat Guibernau and John Rex (Cambridge: Polity, 2010), 238–242.

73. Stuart Hall, "The Multicultural Question," in *Stuart Hall: Essential Essay, Volume 2: Identity and Diaspora*, ed. David Morley (Durham: Duke University Press, 2019), 95–96.

74. Hall, "The Multicultural Question," 96–97.

75. Jin Wen, *Pluralist Universalism: An Asian Americanist Critique of U.S. and Chinese Multiculturalisms* (Columbus: The Ohio State University, 2012), 5, 43.

76. Tim Oakes, "Ethnic tourism in China" in *Handbook on Ethnic Minorities in China*, ed. Xiaowei Zang (Cheltenham: Edward Elgar Publishing, 2016), 291–315.

77. McCarthy, *Communist Multiculturalism*, 33.

78. McCarthy, *Communist Multiculturalism*, 33.

79. McCarthy, *Communist Multiculturalism*, 33.

80. Eric Hobsbawm, "Introduction: Inventing Traditions," in *The Invention of Tradition*, ed. Eric Hobsbawm and Terence Ranger (Cambridge: Cambridge University Press, 1983), 1.

81. Similar experiences can be found among other ethnic minority groups in China, such as the Yi, who who, like the Qiang, engage in revisionist writing of Chinese cultural history to construct alternative histories as they "question the centrality of . . . Han culture in the development of the Chinese nation" (Stevan Harrell and Li Yongxiang. 2003. "The History of the History of the Yi, Part II." *Modern China* 29, no. 3: 364).

82. Certain larger ethnic groups, such as the Tibetans and the Uighurs, experience a different relationship with the state and face more severe surveillance for their identity claims.

83. Charles R. Hale, "Neoliberal Multiculturalism: The Making of Cultural Rights and Racial Dominance in Central America," in *Political and Legal Anthropology Review*, 28, no. 1 (2005): 12, 13. Emphasis original.

84. Erik Mueggler, "Dancing Fools: Politics of Culture and Place in a 'Traditional Nationality Festival,'" 7.

85. Mueggler, "Dancing Fools," 27.

86. In this book, when I use quotation marks around the word Qiang, I am using the word in the context of the Qiang as a historical construction and ethno-national imaginary. When I omit the quotation marks around the word Qiang, I use the word in the context of the Qiang as a modern *shaoshu minzu*. As the reader will see, sometimes the boundary between two meanings is blurred, and sometimes they are interchangeable. It is precisely this fluid nature of "Qiang" that gives the modern Qiang ethnic group its power of imagining its place in Chinese culture and history.

Chapter 1

1. Xu Chao 徐超, "Wen Jiabao zongli guanyu baohu Qiangzu wenhua yichan de liangci pishi 温家宝总理关于保护羌族文化遗产的两次批示——记民进中央副主席、中国民间文艺家协会主席冯骥才与羌族文化的不解情缘" [Two comments by Premier Wen Jiabao on the safeguarding of Qiangzu cultural heritage: on the close bonds between Feng Jicai, Vice President of China Democracy Promotion Association and President of Chinese Folk Literature and Art Association, and Qiang culture], last modified August 1, 2013, http://www.mj.org.cn/zsjg/mz/200811/200812/t20081230_86659.htm (accessed May 20, 2016).

2. Xu Chao, "Wen Jiabao zongli." Emphasis mine.

3. Xu Chao, "Wen Jiabao zongli."

4. Qiangzu wenhua zao dizhen yanzhong pohuai 羌族文化遭地震严重破坏 [Qiang ethnic culture was severely damaged by the earthquake], last modified June 2, 2008. http://www.china.com.cn/aboutchina/zhuanti/qiangwenhua/2008-06/02/content_15596515.htm (accessed May 21, 2016).

5. "Qiangzu" 羌族 [Qiang ethnic minority group]. http://www.china.com.cn/ch-shaoshu/index39.htm (accessed May 21, 2016).

6. Mark Edward Lewis, *Writing and Authority in Early China*, 1.

7. Lewis, *Writing and Authority*, 2.

8. Lewis, *Writing and Authority*, 4.

9. Edward Said: *Orientalism*, 55.

10. Fan Ye 范曄, *Hou Hanshu* 後漢書 西羌傳 [The book of later Han: biographies of the Xiqiang]. Zhongyang yanjiu yuan hanji dianzi wenxian ziliaoku中央研究院漢籍電子文獻資料庫 [Academia Sinica hanji electronic database], volume 87.

11. Fan Ye, *Hou Hanshu*.

12. For detailed depictions of these conflicts between China and the Xiqiang tribes, see Hou Han Shu, Xiqiangzhuan.

13. http://m.haoshiwen.org/view.php?id=301. The Chinese original of the these lines are the follows: 昔有成湯，自彼氐羌，莫敢不來享，莫敢不來王。日商是常.

14. *The Red Brush: Writing Women of Imperial China*, Wilt Idema and Beata Grant, eds. (Cambridge: Harvard University Asia Center, 2004), 117. Emphasis mine. The Chinese original of these verses are: 嗟薄祜兮遭世患。宗族殄兮門戶單。身執略兮入西關。歷險阻兮之羌蠻.

15. Idema and Grants, ed., *The Red Brush*, 118.

16. https://www.jianshu.com/p/d4c7e07618ed. The Chinese original of these lines are: 平土人脆弱，來兵皆胡羌.

17. Frank Dikotter, *The Discourse of Race in Modern China*, 2.

18. Dikotter, *The Discourse of Race*, 11–12.

19. Dikotter, *The Discourse of Race*, 2.

20. Fan Ye, *Hou Hanshu*, Nanman xinanyi liezhuan, no. 76.

21. Fan Ye, *Hou Hanshu*, Nanman xinanyi liezhuan, no. 76.

22. Fan Ye, *Hou Hanshu*, Xiqiangzhuan.

23. Fan Ye, *Hou Hanshu*, Nanman xinan yi liezhuan.

24. Fan Ye, *Hou Hanshu*, Nanman xinan yi liezhuan.

25. Fan Ye, *Hou Hanshu*, Nanman xinan yi liezhuan.

26. James Leibold: *Reconfiguring Chinese Nationalism: How the Qing and Its Indigenes Became Chinese*, "Introduction." Other relevant scholarship includes John Fitzgerald's "The Nationless State: The Search for a Nation in Modern Chinese Nationalism" and Stevan Harrell's "Civilizing Projects and the Reaction to Them." Xiuyu Wang's *China's Last Imperial Frontier: Late Qing Expansion in Sichuan's Tibetan Borderlands* details how the frontier lands in Sichuan under the rule of local chieftains became integrated into the Qing empire as the Qing government sent officials to replace the chieftains and attempted to impose Confucian education and "Sinicize" the Tibetans on the borderland of the Qing empire.

27. James Leibold, *Reconfiguring Chinese Nationalism: How the Qing and Its Indigenes Became Chinese*. "Introduction" and Chapter 1.

28. James Leibold, 7.

29. Ma Naihui, Wang Zhaohu, Zhuang Wenjun, ed. *Chenfen de lishi shunjian: shengying dashi Zhuang Xueben ershi shiji sanshi niandai de xibu renwen tanfang* [Sealed historical moments: photographic master Zhuang Xueben's humanist explorations and visits to the west, 1934–1939), 12. 尘封的历史瞬间：摄影大师庄学本20世纪30年代的西部人文探访：1934年—1939年.

30. Whereas Xiqiang is used in *Hou Hanshu* to denote the ethnic others in Sichuan's ethnic frontiers, Xifan is used in late imperial historical writing, such as *Mingshi* (History of Ming), to refer to the peoples residing in the ethnic frontiers of Sichuan, who would later be categorized as the Tibetans, Qiang, and Yi. See 明史 四川土司，漢籍電子文獻資料庫, No. 199.

31. Zhuang Xueben, *Qiangrong kaochaji*, 2.

32. Zhuang Xueben, *Qiangrong kaochaji*, 2.

33. Cai Yuanpei, *Shuo minzuxue*, 1

34. Yanshuo Zhang, "Transforming the 'Barbarian' Margins into Multiethnic National Centers: Photographic Reportage and Ethnic Imagination in Republican-era China," 9.

35. For example, Ling Chunsheng 凌純聲 published *The Hezhe Ethnic Group in the Lower Tributaries of the Songhua River* (Songhua jiang xiayou de Hezhezu 松花江下游的赫哲族) in 1934; Ling Chunsheng and Rui Yifu 芮逸夫 published *Investigative Reports of the Miao Ethnic Group in Western Hunan* (Xiangxi Miaozu diaocha baogao 湘西苗族調查報告) in 1947. Zhuang Xueben himself also published lots of photography about the Lolo in *Liangyou* magazine 良友畫報.

36. Zhuang Xueben, *Qiangrong kaochaji*, 134–135.

37. Zhuang Xueben, *Qiangrong kaochaji*, 134–135.

38. Zhuang Xueben, *Qiangrong kaochaji*, 138–139.

39. Zhuang Xueben, *Qiangrong kaochaji*, 138–139.

40. Mullaney, *Coming to Terms with the Nation*. Chapter 2.

41. Mullaney, *Coming to Terms with the Nation*, 56.

42. Wang Tonglin; *Zhongguo minzushi*, Song Wenbing, *Zhongguo minzu shi*,; Zhongguo Minzu Shi, Lin Huixiang.

43. Lin Huixiang, *Zhongguo minzushi*, 6.

44. Lin Huixiang, *Zhongguo minzushi*, 5. I respect the way words like "Mongolo-Tarar" and "Thibetan" were spelled in the original sources cited and are reproducing them here for historical discussions, despite the fact that these words are spelled differently now.

45. Lin Huixiang, *Zhongguo minzushi*, 10.

46. Mullaney, "Critical Han Studies," 8–9.

47. Mullaney, "Critical Han Studies," 16.

48. Mullaney, "Critical Han Studies," 16.

49. Mullaney, "Critical Han Studies," 37.

50. Lin Huixiang, *Zhongguo minzushi*, 1

51. Lin Huixiang, *Zhongguo minsushi*; Ren Qiu and Wang Tongling, *Zhongguo Minzu Shi*.

52. Lin Huixiang, *Zhongguo minsushi*, Vol. 2, 111.

53. Pamela Kyle Crossley, "Thinking About Ethnicity in Early Modern China," *Late Imperial China* 11, no. 1 (1990): 20.

54. Crossley, "Thinking about Ethnicity," 20.

55. James Leibold, "Searching for the Han: Early Twentieth-Century Narratives of Chinese Origins and Development," in *Critical Han Studies: The History, Representation, and Identity of China's Majority*, ed. Thomas S. Mullaney, James Patrick Leibold, Stéphane Gros and Eric Armand Vanden Bussche (Berkeley: University of California Press, 2012), 217.

56. Michel Foucault, *The Order of Things: An Archaeology of the Human Sciences*, 139.

57. Foucault, *The Order of Things*, 139.

58. Foucault, *The Order of Things*, 140.

59. Alai 阿来. "Zai yiben shu zhong youli guxiang 在一本书中游历故乡 [Journeying into the homeland within a book]." In Zhuang Xueben 庄学本, *Qiangrong kaocha ji: Sheying dashi Zhuang Xueben ershi shiji sanshi niandai de xibu renwen tanfang* 羌戎考察记：摄影大师庄学本20世纪30年代的西部人文探访 [Expeditions into the land of the Qiang and Rong: photographic master Zhuang Xueben's humanist explorations and visits to the west in the 1930s], ed. Ma Naihui 马鼐辉, Wang Zhaohu 王昭武, Zhuang Wenjun 庄文骏, 1–3. Chengdu: Sichuan chubanjituan, Sichuan minzu chubanshe, 2007.

60. Alai, "Zai yiben shuzhong," 3.

61. William Schaefer discusses how images of the "primitive" and "savage" others were used in fragmented ways to project an image of China in a global space in photographic productions in journals published in Republican-era Shanghai in his article "Shanghai Savage."

62. Ralph Litzinger, "Memory Work: Reconstituting the Ethnic in Post-Mao China," *Cultural Anthropology* 13, no. 2 (1998): 226.

63. Harrell and Li, 362.

64. Ralph Litzinger, *Other Chinas: the Yao and the Politics of National Belonging* (Durham: Duke University Press 2000), 2.

65. Litzinger, *Other Chinas*, 2–3. For a more thorough discussion of the cultural institutionalization of ethnic traditions, please see Chapter 6 of this book.

66. Arif Dirlik, *Culture and History in Postrevolutionary China: The Perspective of Global Modernity* (Hong Kong: The Chinese University Press 2012), 17–18.

67. Dirlik, *Culture and History*, 17–18.

68. Jason McGrath, *Postsocialist Modernity: Chinese Cinema, Literature, and Criticism in the Market Age* (Stanford: Stanford University Press 2008), 7.

69. McGrath, *Postsocialist Modernity*, 9.

70. Fei Xiaotong, "Zhonghua minzu de duoyuan yiti geju," 中华民族的多元一体格局 1988.

71. See, for example, an edited volume, *Zhongguo minzu guanxi shilun wenji* 中国民

族关系史论文集 [Collection of papers on China's ethnic relations] edited by the Guojia minzu shewu weiyuanhui (国家民族事务委员会 State Ethnic Affairs Commission of the People's Republic of China) published by Minzu chubanshe in 1982.

72. Qiangzu Jianshi Bianxiezu 羌族简史编写组 [Editorial board of *A Concise History of Qiangzu*], *Qiangzu jianshi* 羌族简史 [A concise history of Qiangzu] (Beijing: Minzu chubanshe 2008), 2.

73. Qiangzu Jianshi Bianxiezu, *Qiangzu jianshi*, 1.

74. Qiangzu Jianshi Bianxiezu, *Qiangzu jianshi*, 1.

75. Qiangzu Jianshi Bianxiezu, *Qiangzu jianshi*, 1.

76. Qiangzu Jianshi Bianxiezu, *Qiangzu jianshi*, 105.

77. Douglas Howland, "The Dialectics of Chauvinism: Minority Nationalities and Territorial Sovereignty in Mao Zedong's New Democracy," *Modern China* 37, no. 2 (2011): 177.

78. Howland, "The Dialectics," 174.

79. Qiangzu Jianshi Bianxiezu, *Qiangzu jianshi*, 2.

80. Qiangzu Jianshi Bianxiezu, *Qiangzu jianshi*, 2.

81. Qiangzu Jianshi Bianxiezu, *Qiangzu jianshi*, 180–219.

82. Qiangzu Jianshi Bianxiezu, *Qiangzu jianshi*, 216.

83. Qiangzu Jianshi Bianxiezu, *Qiangzu jianshi*, 216.

84. In this poem and other poetic accounts, I translate *Qiang di* as the Qiang flute to make the translation more economical, even though in other places, the *Qiang di* can be more appropriately rendered as the Qiang reed pipe to denote its material and musicality. I thank Gibb Schreffler of Pomona College for pointing out that *Qiang di* can be translated as the Qiang reed pipe.

85. Qiangzu Jianshi Bianxiezu, *Qiangzu jianshi*, 216. Translation mine. All translations in this chapter are mine unless otherwise noted. For any Chinese materials that first appeared in classical Chinese contexts or the pre-1949/Republican era and those published in Taiwan, I am using traditional Chinese characters to be faithful of the original context. Any Chinese materials published in simplified Chinese will be reproduced here in their simplified forms.

86. Ming-ke Wang 王明珂, *Qiang zai Han Zang zhijian: yige Huaxia bianyuan de lishi renleixue yanjiu* 羌在漢藏之間：一個華夏邊緣的歷史人類學研究 [Qiang between the Han and the Tibetans: a historical-anthropological study of a people on the periphery of China]. (Taipei: Lianjing chuban sheye gufen youxian gongsi, 2003), 174.

87. Ming-Ke Wang, *Qiang zai Han Zang zhijian*, 174.

88. Ming-ke Wang, "Searching for Qiang Culture in the First Half of the Twentieth Century," *Inner Asia* 4, no.1 (2002): 136.

89. Ming-ke Wang, "Searching for Qiang Culture," 133.

90. Ming-ke Wang, "Searching for Qiang Culture," 135.

91. Ming-ke Wang, "Searching for Qiang Culture," 135. Geng Shaojiang 耿少将, *Qiangzu tongshi* 羌族通史 [A comprehensive history of Qiangzu] (Shanghai: Shanghai renmin chubanshe, 2010), 223–225.

92. Stephen Owen, *The Great Age of Chinese Poetry: The High T'ang* (New Haven: Yale University Press, 1981), 149.

93. Owen, *The Great Ages*, 151. Translation by Owen.

94. Owen, *The Great Ages*, 151. Translation by Owen.

95. Owen, *The Great Ages*, 155–156. Translation by Owen.

96. Owen, *The Great Ages*, 92. Translation by Owen. In the first line, the Yellow Sand can be replaced by Yellow River（黃河）. For this alternative version, see *Quan Tang shi* [Complete poems of Tang], 439.

97. Harumi Befu, quoted by Arthur Waldron in "Representing China: The Great Wall and Cultural Nationalism in the Twentieth Century," in *Cultural Nationalism in East Asia: Representation and Identity*, ed. Harumi Befu (Berkeley: University of California Press 1993).

98. Harumi Befu, quoted by Arthur Waldron in "Representing China," 37–38.

99. Thomas S. Mullaney, *Coming to Terms with the Nation: Ethnic Classification in Modern China* (Berkeley: University of California Press, 2011).

100. Harumi Befu, quoted by Arthur Waldron in "Representing China," 20–21.

101. Eric Hobsbawm, "Introduction: Inventing Traditions," in *The Invention of Tradition*, ed. Eric Hobsbawm and Terence Ranger (Cambridge: Cambridge University Press, 1983), 9.

102. Ran Guangrong 冉光荣, Li Shaoming 李绍明, Zhou Xiyin 周锡银, *Qiangzu shi* 羌族史 [The History of Qiangzu] (Chengdu: Sichuan minzu chubanshe, 1985), 358–359.

103. Ran, Li, and Zhou, *Qiangzu shi*, 5.

104. http://m.xinhuanet.com/2018-05/10/c_1122814554.htm.

105. http://m.xinhuanet.com/2018-05/10/c_1122814554.htm.

Chapter 2

1. In this book, I use the term "Qiangzu" (羌族 Qiang ethnic group) to refer to the modern Qiang ethnic group, which is classified as a distinct ethnic group as a result of the Ethnic Classification Project in post-1949 China. By contrast, I use the word "Qiang" to refer to all the symbolic, cultural, and historical construction and invention of an identity that is at times mystified, at times nationalist, and at times ethnic. Sometimes these two are used interchangeably, as the modern Qiangzu is inherently mythologized in both national narratives and local scholarly inventions, as Chapters 1 and 2 reveal.

2. Zhang Shanyun, "Qianyan," 1.

3. Yanshuo Zhang, "Entrepreneurs of the National Past," 425.

4. Yanshuo Zhang, "Entrepreneurs of the National Past," 425.

5. Robin McNeal, "Constructing Myth in Modern China," 438.

6. McNeal, "Constructing Myth in Modern China," 438.

7. McNeal, "Constructing Myth in Modern China," 455.

8. Rosemary J. Coombe, "Managing Cultural Heritage as Neoliberal Governmentality," 380.

9. Coombe, "Managing Cultural Heritage," 380.

10. Geng Shaojiang, *Qiangzu Tongshi*, 26–27.

11. Geng, *Qiangzu Tongshi*, 26–27.

12. Geng, *Qiangzu Tongshi*, 26–27.

13. Geng, *Qiangzu Tongshi*, 28.

14. "Da Yu Zhi Shui" (Da Yu managing floods) 大禹治水 http://www.ebaomonthly.com/window/discovery/history/china/ch100/100_1.htm.

15. “Da Yu Zhi Shui.”

16. “Da Yu Zhi Shui” (Da Yu managing floods) http://www.nongli.com/Doc/0409/2410021.htm.

17. Coombe, “Managing Cultural Heritage,” 380.

18. Tan Jiehe and Wang Chunwu, “Xia yu wenhua de xin tansuo—Sichuan xuezhe xia yu wenhua yanjiu xinzuo zonglun [New explorations of the culture of Xia Dyansty and Da Yu—a synthesis of the new works of Sichuan scholars' research on Xia Dynasty and Da Yu], 1.

19. Tan and Wang, “Xiayu wenhua de xin tansuo,” 3.

20. Tan and Wang, “Xiayu wenhua de xin tansuo,” 3.

21. Long Xianzhao, “Yuxing shudi, huize fangxia Yu Rose from the Land of Shu [the ancient name of Sichuan], Nurturing All of China.” 禹兴蜀地，惠泽方夏,” 9.

22. Robin McNeal, “Constructing Myth in Modern China,” 689.

23. McNeal, “Constructing Myth in Modern China,” 689.

24. Robin McNeal, “Moral Transformation and Local Identity: Reviving the Culture of Shun at Temples and Monuments across China,” 443, 444.

25. Mark Edward Lewis, *Flood Myths of Early China*, 28.

26. Lewis, *Flood Myths of Early China*, 17.

27. Lewis, *Flood Myths of Early China*, 30.

28. Lewis, *Flood Myths of Early China*, 17.

29. Lewis, *Flood Myths of Early China*, 46.

30. Lewis, *Flood Myths of Early China*, 46.

31. Long Xianzhao, “Yuxing shudi, huize fangxia [Yu Rose from the Land of Shu [the ancient name of Sichuan], Nurturing All of China.” 禹兴蜀地，惠泽方夏,” 10.

32. Lewis, *Flood Myths in Early China*, 31.

33. 世界文化遺產：青城山，都江堰 [World Cultural Heritage: Mt. Qingcheng, Dujiangyan] http://big5.xinhuanet.com/gate/big5/news.xinhuanet.com/ziliao/2003-09/24/content_1097516.htm.

34. Long, “Yuxing shudi,” 10.

35. Lewis, *Flood Myths in Early China*, 46.

36. Lewis, *Flood Myths in Early China*, 46.

37. Long, “Yusheng shudi,” 11.

38. Harrell and Li, “History of *The History of Yi*,” 385.

39. Ralph Litzinger, *Other Chinas*, 53.

40. Harrell and Li, “The History of the History of Yi,” 364.

41. Ming-ke Wang, “Genji lishi: Qiangzu de xiongdi gushi,” 16.

42. Wang, “Genji lishi: Qiangzu de xiongdi gushi,” 16.

43. Wang, “Genji lishi: Qiangzu de xiongdi gushi,” 16.

44. “Yu xing Shudi, huize Fangxia.” [Yu Flourished from the Land of Shu [the ancient name of Sichuan], Nurturing All of China.] *Xiqiang Wenhua*, 2007, 6.

45. James Leibold, “Searching for Han: Early Twentieth-century Narratives of Chinese Origins and Development,” 226.

46. Harrell and Li, 384.

47. Charles Hall, “Neoliberal Multiculturalism: The Making of Cultural Rights and Racial Dominance in Central America,” 12, 13. Emphasis original.

48. Stuart Hall, "New Ethnicities," 446.

49. Long Xianzhao, 9. This narrative of the multiethnic origin of the *Zhonghua minzu*, as I have argued in another article titled "Entrepreneurs of the Past: Contemporary China's Indigenous Cultural Writing and the Ethnicization of *Zhonghua minzu* (Chinese race)," has its roots in the Communist version of China's ethnic history in *Zhongguo tongshi jianbian* (*A Concise General History of China*) written by Communist historian Fan Wenlan in the 1940s.

50. Yang Guangcheng, "Yandi—Zhongguo qiangyan wenhua shizu" [The Yan Emperor—the ancestor of China's Qiang-Yan culture]. 炎帝：中国羌炎文化始祖 http://www.china001.com/show_hdr.php?xname=PPDDMV0&dname=EEB6H51&xpos=3.

51. James Clifford, *Returns: Becoming Indigenous in the Twenty-first Century*, 14.

52. Clifford, *Returns*, 27.

53. Clifford, *Returns*, 60.

54. Stevan Harrell, "Civilizing Missions and Reactions to Them," 5–6.

55. Geng Shaojiang, *Qiangzu tongshi*, 357–358.

56. Geng, *Qiangzu tongshi*, 362–363.

57. Scholars such as Pamela Crossley have pointed out that the concept of "Sinicization" is somewhat flawed, since it assumes that Chinese culture was a static entity that remained unchanged throughout history and attracted ethnic "others" to integrate into the Chinese cultural system automatically. Crossley argues that in reality, such factors as economic necessity and political coercion played a crucial role in bringing these "others" into the Chinese system (see "Thinking About Ethnicity in Early Modern China"). However, it is undeniable that the Chinese political and cultural center did try to assimilate and pacify its frontier peoples throughout history, as evidenced by the various imperial records cited in this chapter and elsewhere. Therefore, I find the concept of "Sinicization" useful in explaining cultural assimilations such as the ones that happened to the Qiang.

58. Liu Biyun, "From Kinship to State and Back Again: Lineage and History in a Qiang Village," 36.

59. *Zhongguo shaoshu minzu guji zongtiyao*, 15.

60. Kai-wing Chow, "Imagining Boundaries of Blood: Zhang Binglin and the Invention of the Han 'Race' in Modern China."

61. Paul Cohen, *History in Three Keys: The Boxers as Event, Experience, and Myth*. Introduction.

62. Cohen, *History in Three Keys*, 212.

63. The concept of "tourism imaginary" was broached by Nelson Graburn and Maria Gravari-Barbas in their "Introduction: Tourism Imaginaries at the Disciplinary Crossroads" to their book *Tourism Imaginaries at the Disciplinary Crossroads*.

64. Bai Zhihong, "Ethnic Identities under the Tourist Gaze," 246.

65. Bai, "Ethnic Identities," 255.

66. Bai, "Ethnic Identities," 245.

67. Graburn and Gavari-Barbas, "Introduction," 1.

68. Graburn and Gavari-Barbas, "Introduction," 21, 22.

69. Graburn and Gavari-Barbas, "Introduction," 21.

70. Yang Guangcheng, *Taoping shihua*, 6.

71. Yang Guangcheng, *Taoping shihua*, 17.
72. Yang Guangcheng, *Taoping shihua*, 21.
73. Yang Guangcheng, *Taoping shihua*, 17.
74. Judith N. Shklar, "Subversive Genealogies," 130.
75. Paul Cohen, *History in Three Keys*, 212.
76. Stuart Hall, "Ethnicity and Difference in Global Times," 106.
77. Hall, "Ethnicity and Difference," 106.
78. Yi-fu Tuan, *Topophilia: A Study of Environmental Perception, Attitudes, and Values*, 93.
79. Tuan, *Topophilia*, 99.
80. Gu Yunlong "Minjiang fu," [Ode to Min River]," 1.
81. Gu Yunlong, "Minjiang fu," 1.
82. Gu Yunlong, "Minjiang fu," 1.
83. Gu Yunlong, "Minjiang fu," 1.
84. Gu Yunlong, "Minjiang fu," 1.
85. Hombi Bhabha, "DisseminNation: Time, Narrative and the Margins of the Modern Nation," 147, 148.
86. Bhabha, "DissemiNation," 149.
87. Bhabha, "DisseminNation," 202.
88. Henri Lefebvre, *The Production of Space*, 39.
89. Lefebvre, *The Production of Space*, 39.

Chapter 3

1. https://whc.unesco.org/en/tentativelists/5815/.
2. http://www.mzfxw.com/e/action/ShowInfo.php?classid=15&id=30358.
3. Douban Dianying. https://movie.douban.com/subject/4176542/reviews.
4. Shasheng paishe huaxu, http://movie.mtime.com/135313/behind_the_scene.html.
5. "Shasheng huojiang qingkuang." https://movie.douban.com/subject/4176542/awards/.
6. https://movie.douban.com/subject/4176542/.
7. Zeynep Çelik and Leila Kinney, "Ethnography and Exhibitionism at the Expositions Universelles," 55.
8. Prasenjit Duara, "Local Worlds: The Poetics and Politics of the Native Place in Modern China," 13.
9. Duara, "Local Worlds," 14.
10. Gina Anne Tam, doctoral dissertation, "Sounding the Nation: Dialect and the Making of Modern China," Introduction.
11. Jason McGrath, *Postsocialist Modernity: Chinese Cinema, Literature and Criticism in the Market Age*, 7
12. McGrath, *Postsocialist Modernity*, 12.
13. Gina Anne Tam, doctoral dissertation, "Sounding the Nation: Dialect and the Making of Modern China," Introduction.
14. Tani Barlow, *The Question of Women in Chinese Feminism*, 42, 45.
15. http://you.ctrip.com/travels/lixian1445566/3339060.html. For example, Mafeng

Wo features many netizens' posts and photographs of the "Mysterious Oriental Castle." http://www.mafengwo.cn/poi/8662.html.

16. For studies on this period, see Chen Jie's dissertation.

17. McGrath, Chapter 1; David Harvey, *A Brief History of Neoliberalism.*

18. I discuss in detail how non-Han peoples were portrayed in imperial Chinese historiography and poetry in Chapter 1.

19. Douban Dianying. https://movie.douban.com/celebrity/1274919/.

20. Jeff Kyong-Mc.Clain, "Missionary Archaeology on Republican China's Southwestern Frontier," 4.

21. Kyong-Mc.Clain, "Missionary Archeology," 4.

22. Western La Barre, "Book Review."

23. Examples of Japanese scholars include Matsuoka Masako of Aichi University, who has studied about Qiang villages and cultural preservations in the post-2008/post-earthquake era. http://edu.aichi-u.ac.jp/tsearch/AUT_detail.aspx?pid=11250. American scholarship on Taoping Qiang Village includes a research project conducted by University of Washington in collaboration with Sichuan University, titled "Community-based Earthquake Recovery in Taoping, Sichuan, China," conducted in 2009. http://courses.washington.edu/belab09/work/508studio/final_studio_report/01_Introduction_A3.pdf. The earliest American and British missionary studies of the Qiang dates back to the nineteenth and early twentieth centuries, when Thomas Torrance (1871–1959) from Britain and David Crockett Graham (1884–1961) from the U.S. studied Qiang religious customs and folk traditions.

24. For example, Qiaoyun Zhang, an American-trained anthropologist, has studied about the Qiang's reconstruction of their homeland and published extensively on this topic.

25. UNESCO, "Diaolou Buildings and Villages for Tibetan and Qiang Ethnic Groups."

26. Michel Foucault, "Of Other Spaces: Utopias and Heterotopias," 353.

27. Foucault, "Of Other Spaces," 353.

28. Yuqing Yang, *Mystifying Chinas' Southwest Ethnic Borderlands: Harmonious Heterotopia*, 16.

29. Louisa Schein, "Gender and Internal Orientalism in China," 269. Emphasis original.

30. See Laura Hostetler, *The Art of Ethnography: The Miao Album of Guizhou Province* and Hu Xiaozhen (in Chinese), *The Southwest in Ming-Qing Literary Imagination* (明清文學中的西南敘事).

31. Schein "Gender and Internal Orientalism," 269.

32. Jiawen Ai, "'Selecting the refined and discarding the dross': the post-1990 Chinese leadership's attitude towards cultural tradition," 131.

33. See Thomas Campanella, *The Concrete Dragon: China's Urbanization and What It Means for the World*; Robin Visser: *Cities Surround the Countryside: Urban Aesthetics in Postsocialist China.*

34. Tim Oakes, *Tourism and Modernity in China*, 24.

35. For discussions on this issue, see Haiyan Lee, *The Stranger and the Chinese Moral Imagination*; James Leibold, *Reconfiguring Chinese Nationalism: How the Qing and Its Indigenes Became Chinese*; Chris Berry and Mary Farquhar, *China on Screen: Cinema and Nation.*

36. Haiyan Lee, *The Stranger and the Chinese Moral Imagination*, 251.

37. Schein, "Gender and Internal Orientalism," 73.

38. Kyong-McClain, "Missionary Archaeology," 4.

39. See Dru Gladney, "Representing Nationality in China: Refiguring Majority/Minority Identities" and Louisa Schein, "Gender and Internal Orientalism in China," 75.

40. Jenny Chio, *A Landscape of Travel: The Work of Tourism in Rural Ethnic China*, xxv.

41. Chio, A Landscape of Travel, "Introduction."

42. Choi, *A Landscape of Travel*, 17.

43. Quoted in Chio, *A Landscape of Travel*, xxvi.

44. Admittedly, the idea of the native village was first used and became infamously popular in the context of colonial encounters, such as the French Empire's display of Egyptian native villages in the *Expositions Universelles* in Paris. However, contemporary ethnic minority groups in China, and perhaps many other countries of the world, have started to reclaim the concept of "native village" in the context of indigenous cultural empowerment. I choose to adhere to the term "native village" to show that the perspective of appreciating indigenous aesthetics is a product of cultural encounters between the Qiang ethnic group and translocal, transnational influences.

45. Susan Sontag, "Melancholy Objects," from *On Photography*, 75.

46. Tim Oakes, *Tourism and Modernity in China*, 32.

47. Guy Debord, *Society of the Spectacle*, 12.

48. John A. Smith, "Three Images of the Visual: Empirical, formal and normative," 258.

49. Walter Benjamin: "The Work of Art in the Age of Mechanical Reproduction," in *Illuminations: Essays and Reflections.*

50. Bai Zhihong, "Ethnic Identities under the Tourist Gaze," 246.

51. Bai, "Ethnic Identities," 255.

52. Bai, "Ethnic Identities," 245.

53. Graburn and Gavari-Barbas, "Introduction," 1.

54. I interviewed Mr. Zhou in 2017 and followed him on his trips to his native village. He shared with me his plans to develop his native village into a culturally important site for tourism and his recent endeavors of hiring a film crew to make a documentary about his native Zengtou village.

55. Tim Oakes and Louisa Schein, "Translocal China: An Introduction," 19.

56. Oakes and Schein, "Translocal China," 19.

57. "Indigenous Media: Faustian Contract or Global Village?" 96.

Chapter 4

1. P. Kerim Friedman, "Defining Ethnographic Film," 17.

2. Friedman, "Defining Ethnographic Film," 21.

3. Buffalohead, Eric L., Marubbio, M. Elise, "Native Americans on Film," 7.

4. Buffalohead, Eric L., Marubbio, M. Elise, "Native Americans on Film," 9.

5. Dudemaine, Marcoux, and St-Amand, "Indigenous Cinema and Media," 5.

6. This film has an alternative title, *Qiang's Journey* (Xunqiang 寻羌). In some public showings, the alternative title is used.

7. "Gao Tunzi jianjie," https://www.wenweipo.com/a/202306/21/AP6491f3f6e4b043f3863611a5.html.

8. Friedman, "Defining Ethnographic Film," 21.

9. For example, in his article, "The Question of Minority and Indigeneity in Post-Colonial China," anthropologist Dru Gladney argues that "The rubric [of *shaoshu minzu*] does [the native people] a disservice, obscuring not only their own indigenous identities but also the nature of multiculturalism and multiethnicity in China" (50). Similarly, in her chapter "Tibetan Indigeneity: Translations, Resemblances, and Uptake" in the book *Indigenous Experience Today*, geographer Emily Yeh contends that the Chinese state generally considers "indigeneity" as irrelevant to the minorities of China, as the government of China has long claimed that "all of the nation's citizens are equally indigenous" (81), making no distinction between the indigeneity of the Han and the minority groups of China.

10. Yanshuo Zhang, "Entrepreneurs of the National Past," 426.

11. Michael Hathaway, "The Emergence of Indigeneity," 303, 304.

12. Christine Mathieu, "The Dongba Religion," 59.

13. Yu Yaoming, "Qiangzu shibi tujing," 69.

14. Li Xianglin. "Binwei de Qiangzu koutou yichan he tuxiang jingdian," http://www.artanthropology.com/show.aspx?id=1889&cid=16.

15. Li Xianglin. "Binwei de Qiangzu koutou yichan."

16. Yu Yaoming, "Qiangzu shibi tujing," 69.

17. Christine Matthieu, "The Dongba Religion," 81.

18. Matthieu, *Ancestral Realms*, 54–87.

19. Matthieu, *Ancestral Realms*, 72.

20. Mark Bender, *The Borderlands of Asia*, 13.

21. Bender, *The Borderlands*, 13–14.

22. Faye Ginsburg, "Decolonizing Documentary On-screen and Off," 39.

23. Personal communication.

24. Gao Tunzi, *Shinian xunqiang: renyushen de beihuanlihe*, 19.

25. Gao Tunzi, *Shinian xunqiang*, 15.

26. Dudemain, Marcoux, and St-Amand, "Indigenous Cinema and Media," 7.

27. "Docufiction" is Hisu-Chuang Deppman's coinage in her article "Reading docufiction: Jia Zhangke's *24 City*."

28. Zou Huafen and Liu Jing, "Jilu quanqiuhua beijingxia shaoshu minzu de shengcun zhuangtai," 21.

29. Zou Huafen and Liu Jing, "Jilu quanqiuhua beijingxia," 21.

30. Maotao Wen, "The Creation of the Qiang Ethnicity," 6.

31. Maotao Wen, "The Creation of the Qiang Ethnicity," 73.

32. In the context of a powerful political figure speaking of "recommending" someone to an organization in China, "recommendation" is usually used as a euphuism for such a political figure to get someone to be accepted for employment or academic opportunities at said organization under the influence of the speaker.

33. Zou Huafen and Liu Jing, "Jilu quanqiuhua," 21.

34. Zou Huafen and Liu Jing, "Jilu quanqiuhua," 21.

35. Walter Benjamin, "The Work of Art in the Age of Mechanical Reproduction," 6.

36. Walter Benjamin, "The Work of Art," 6.

37. Clifford Geertz, "Religion as Cultural System," 89.

38. For example, in chapter 3, I discussed how some Chinese-language blockbusters,

such as *Design for Death*, alienate certain Qiang cultural symbols, such as the Qiang fortressed villages, to create spectacles.

39. Oxford Refence, https://www.oxfordreference.com/display/10.1093/oi/authority.20110803103943993.

Chapter 5

1. Michael M.J. Fischer, "Ethnicity and the Post-modern," 199.
2. Michael M.J. Fischer, "Ethnicity and the Post-modern," 197, 198.
3. Eileen Cheng, *Literary Remains*, 141.
4. Cheng, *Literary Remains*, 149.
5. Rita Felski, "Introduction: Myths of the Modern," 1.
6. Felski, "Introduction: Myths of the Modern," 2.
7. Qiangzu wenxue and https://books.google.com/books/about/%E8%A1%80%E7%A5%AD.html?id=2bt5nQEACAAJ.
8. Yin Lianteng, "Dashan shenchu," 70.
9. Yin Lianteng, "Dashan shenchu," 70.
10. Yin Lianteng, "Dashan shenchu," 70, 71.
11. Wang Yong'an, *Yong'an sanwen ji*, book jacket.
12. Wang Yong'an, *Yong'an sanwen ji*, book jacket.
13. Ren Dongsheng, *Qiangfeng bianye*, biographic page.
14. Yang Zi, "Shanzhong de muqin," 198.
15. Yang Zi, "Shanzhong de muqin," 198.
16. Yang Zi, "Shanzhong de muqin," 198.
17. Yang Zi, "Shanzhong de muqin," 199.
18. Yang Zi, "Shanzhong de muqin," 200.
19. Rita, Felski, *The Gender of Modernity*, 2.
20. Rita, Felski, *The Gender of Modernity*, 2.
21. "Shenzhen: tequ chuchuang, tizhi youshi."
22. "Shenzhen: tequ chuchuang, tizhi youshi" and "Zhuzhong rende ganshou."
23. Yang Zi, "Shanzhong de muqin," 200.
24. Yang Zi, "Shanzhong de muqin," 200.
25. Svetlana Boym, *The Future of Nostalgia*, 52.
26. Michael M.J. Fischer. "Ethnicity and the Post-Modern," 197.
27. Michael M.J. Fischer. "Ethnicity and the Post-Modern," 197.
28. Wang Yong'an, "Laojia," 130.
29. Wang Yong'an, "Laojia," 130.
30. Wang Yong'an, "Qiangnian xujiu," 29.
31. *Shiren de Qiangzu jilu* 十人的羌族纪录 [The documentary about Qiang created by ten people]. https://wh.cnki.net/article/detail/LVZZ200905018.
32. Tenzen and Bai Gengsheng, "Zhanshi yu qidian," 4.
33. Yu Yaoming, "Fenfang duoyowei," 78.
34. Yu Yaoming, "Fenfang duoyowei," 78.
35. Yu Yaoming, "Fenfang duoyowei," 79.
36. Rita Felski, *The Gender of Modernity*, 4.

37. Ming-ke Wang, "Nüren, bujie," 725.
38. Rita Felski, *The Gender of Modernity*, 62.
39. Yu Yaoming, "Fenfang duoyowei," 82.
40. Rita Felski, *The Gender of Modernity*, 62
41. Ming-ke Wang, "Nüren, bujie," 718–719.
42. Ming-ke Wang, "Nüren, bujie," 722, 723.
43. Ming-ke Wang, "Nüren, bujie," 722, 723.
44. Yu Yaoming, "Fenfang duoyowei," 79.
45. Yu Yaoming, "Fenfang duoyowei," 79.
46. Dru Gladney, "Representing Nationalities in China," 94.
47. Yuqing Yang, *Mystifying China's Southwest Ethnic Borderlands*, 143–161.
48. Ben Hillman and Lee-Anne Henfry, "Macho Minority," 254.
49. Ben Hillman and Lee-Anne Henfry, "Macho Minority," 254.
50. Ben Hillman and Lee-Anne Henfry, "Macho Minority," 254.
51. Rita Felksi, *The Gender of Modernity*, 58.
52. Ren Dongsheng, "Minshan zhidian," 163.
53. Rita Felski, *The Gender of Modernity*, 38.
54. Ren Dongsheng, "Minshan zhidian," 163.
55. Svetlana Boym, *The Future of Nostalgia*, 41, 54.
56. Lei Zi, *Tianzhen de meng*.
57. Lei Zi, "Muqin de Shuguang fengrenshe," 5.
58. Lei Zi, "Muqin de Shuguang fengrenshe," 7.
59. Rita Felksi, *The Gender of Modernity*, 37.
60. The collection is titled *Chinese Women Writers on the Environment: A Multi-ethnic Anthology of Fiction and Nonfiction*, edited by Dong Isbister, Xiumei Pu and Stephen D. Rachman, published by McFarland & Company Inc., North Carolina.
61. Burao Yilu, "Four Generations of Va Women," in *Chinese Women Writers on the Environment: A Multi-ethnic Anthology of Fiction and Nonfiction*, edited by Dong Isbister, Xiumei Pu and Stephen D. Rachman (McFarland & Company Inc., North Carolina), 13.
62. Burao Yilu, "Four Generations of Va Women," 18.
63. Burao Yilu, "Four Generations of Va Women," 21.

Chapter 6

1. David Kenley, *Modern Chinese History*, 62.
2. Tim Ingold, "Ancestry, generation," 145.
3. Ye Xingguang, "Shenshan," 42.
4. Ralph Litzinger, *Other Chinas*, 12, 185.
5. Ye Xingguang, "Shenshan," 50.
6. Tim Ingold, "Ancestry, generation," 141.
7. Ann Anagnost, 222, "The Politics of Ritual Displacement," 222.
8. Qiang Renliu, "Anhun zhe," 17.
9. Qiang Renliu, "Anhun zhe," 23.
10. Qiang Renliu, "Anhun zhe," 23.
11. Qiang Renliu, "Anhun zhe," 24.

12. Ann Anagnost, "The Politics of Ritual Displacement," 222.

13. During my field trips in the Qiang regions in Sichuan, I interviewed people who told similar stories about female exorcists healing local people with spiritual powers. One Qiang woman told me about how her mother-in-law helped cure many diseases for local people without resorting to modern medicine. Therefore, exorcism is popular in the Qiang regions, especially in the more distant villages, or villages deep in the mountains.

14. Ann Anagonost, 224.

15. Piers Vitebsky, "Shamanism," 59; Yu Ronggen, "Qiangzu xiguan fa," 329.

16. Piers Vitebsky, "Shamanism," 57, 58, 61.

17. Qiang Renliu, "Anhun zhe," 16, 17.

18. Piers Vitebsky, "Shamanism," 61.

19. Qiang Renliu, "Anhun zhe," 25.

20. Qiang Renliu, "Anhun zhe," 25.

21. Qiang Renliu, "Anhun zhe," 25.

22. Vincent Gossaert, "State and Religion in Modern China: Religious Policy and Scholarly Paradigms," 10.

23. Vincent Gossaert, "State and Religion," 14.

24. Qiang Renliu, "Anhun zhe," 26.

25. Duan Haizhen, *Tiange*, author's biographic page.

26. Duan Haizhen, *Tiange*, 9.

27. James Clifford, "On Ethnographic Authority," 31.

28. Duan Haizhen, *Tiange*, 3.

29. Duan Haizhen, *Tiange*, 80–81.

30. James Cox, *From Primitive*, 78.

31. James Cox, *From Primitive*, 78.

32. James Cox, *From Primitive*, 85, 86.

33. Duan Haizhen, *Tiange*, 80–81.

34. Duan Haizhen, *Tiange*, 5.

35. Hu Jintao, "Hu Jintao tichu."

36. Hu Jintao, "Hu Jintao tichu."

37. Zhonghua Renmin Gongheguo Zhongyang Renmin Zhengfu.

38. Zhonghua Renmin Gongheguo Zhongyang Renmin Zhengfu.

39. Zhonghua Renmin Gongheguo Zhongyang Renmin Zhengfu.

40. McCarthy, quoted in Silverman and Blumenfield "Introduction," 8.

41. Stevan Harrell has argued that there are usually three metaphors used by the Han to refer to the minorities: the educational metaphor, the sex metaphor, and the historical metaphor (1995). While the educational metaphor sees minority people as more child-like compared to the Han; the sex metaphor relegates minorities to the status of women, who are exotic, erotic, but lack agency; the historical metaphor sees minority people as occupying the less advanced ladders of history and need the Han's help for historical progress.

42. Louis Althusser, "Ideology and Ideological State Apparatuses."

43. Zhonghua Renmin Gongheguo Zhongyang Renmin Zhengfu.

44. Zhonghua Renmin Gongheguo Zhongyang Renmin Zhengfu.

45. Yu Ronggen, *Qiangzu xiguan fa*, 301, 302.

46. Yu, *Qiangzu xiguan fa*, 303.

47. Yu, *Qiangzu xiguan fa*, 303.

48. UNESCO, "Intangible Cultural Heritage." https://ich.unesco.org/en/USL/qiang-new-year-festival-00305.

49. "Beijing wenhua."

50. Sebastian Veg, *Minjian: The Rise of China's Grassroots Intellectuals*, 8.

51. Sebastian Veg, *Minjian: The Rise of China's Grassroots Intellectuals*, 13.

52. Rodgers, "A Batak Antiquarian," 104.

53. See Susan Rodgers' essay, "A Batak Antiquarian Writes His Culture: Print Literacy and Social Thought in an Indonesian Society."

54. Sebastian Veg, *Minjian: The Rise of China's Grassroots Intellectuals*, 8.91, 92.

55. Sebastian Veg, *Minjian: The Rise of China's Grassroots Intellectuals*, 100.

56. Foucault, "The Subject," 782.

57. Sebastian Veg, *Minjian: The Rise of China's Grassroots Intellectuals*, 8.

58. Not every single ethnic group in China applies such cultural preservation strategies equally or benefits equally from national cultural policies. Certain groups may have ideas about preserving their cultural symbols and histories somewhat differently from the state's construction of these groups' identities. This needs to be studied on a case-by-case basis. Many smaller minority groups in southwest China tend to benefit from the discourse and practice of "intangible cultural heritage."

59. Hervieu-Léger, *Religion*, 90.

60. Hervieu-Léger, *Religion*, 88; emphasis mine.

61. Wang, *Houji*, 244.

62. Wang, *Houji*, 244.

63. "Writing Against Culture" is the title of a 1991 essay written by anthropologist Lila Abu-Lughod. In this essay, she challenges the coherence and timelessness that anthropologists usually attribute to cultures and the ways "others" and differences are written about in anthropological scholarship. She suggests that anthropologists should avoid the tendency to essentialize cultures and try to write "ethnographies of the particular" to reveal the diversity and individual experiences of cultures and communities.

64. Palumbo-Liu, *The Deliverance*, 3.

65. Palumbo-Liu, *The Deliverance*, 3.

66. Bhabha, "DissemiNation," 212.

67. Anderson, *Imagined Communities*, 24; Bhabha, "DissemiNation," 208, 211.

Conclusion

1. Existing scholarship on indigenous movements in other parts of the world points out that many indigenous groups make claims about the territorial integrity of their ancestral lands and demand political rights from the state (for examples, see Anna Tsing "Indigenous Voice." In *Indigenous Experience Today*, edited by Marisol de la Cadena and Orin Starn, 33–68. Oxford: Berg and Marisol De la Cadena and Orin Starn. 2007. "Introduction." In *Indigenous Experience Today*, edited by Marisol de la Cadena and Orin Starn, 1–32. Oxford: Berg).

BIBLIOGRAPHY

Aba Sheke 阿坝社科 [Aba social sciences]. "Geng Shaojiang 耿少将 gen." Last modified December 8, 2016. http://www.abzsk.cn/detail.action?id=14235.

Abu-Lughod, Lila. "Writing Against Culture." In *Recapturing Anthropology: Working in the Present*, edited by Richard G. Fox, 137–162. Santa Fe: School of American Research Press, 1991.

A'er Cunren 阿尔村人 [A'er villagers]. *A'er Dang'an* 阿尔档案 [A'er archive]. Beijing: Wenwu chubanshe, 2011.

Ai, Jianwei. "'Selecting the Refined and Discarding the Dross': The Post-1990 Chinese Leadership's Attitude towards Cultural Tradition." In *Routledge Handbook of Heritage in Asia*, edited by Patrick Daly and Tim Winter, 129–138. Oxon: Routledge, 2012.

Aku Wuwu. *Aku Wuwu's Coyote Traces: East Asian Audio Books, Voices from Past and President*. Translated by Wen Peihong and Mark Bender. The Ohio State University. https://u.osu.edu/eaab/aku-wuwus-coyote-traces/coyote-traces-page-1/.

Aku Wuwu. *Coyete Traces: Aku Wuwu's Poetic Sojourn in America* 凯欧蒂神迹：阿库乌雾旅美诗歌选.Translated by Peihong Wen and Mark Bender. Beijing: The Ethnic Publishing House and the Ohio State University National East Asian Languages Resource Center, 2015.

Aku Wuwu, and Peihong Wen. "Erdu kua wenming xiezuo: Aku Wuwu lvmei shige ch uangzuo beijing fangtanlu." 二度跨文明写作：阿库乌雾旅美诗歌创作背景访谈录 ["Twice-cross-cultural writing: An interview on Aku Wuwu's poems concerning his sojourn in the USA"]. In *Coyete Traces: Aku Wuwu's Poetic Sojourn in America* 凯欧蒂神迹：阿库乌雾旅美诗歌选. Translated by Peihong Wen and Mark Bender, 312–347. Beijing: The Ethnic Publishing House and the Ohio State University National East Asian Languages Resource Center, 2015.

Aku Wuwu, and Peihong Wen. "Muyu: Xiaoshizhong de jianshou" 母语：消逝中的坚守 ["Mother tongue: Persistence in vanishing"]. In *Coyete Traces: Aku Wuwu's Poetic Sojourn in America* 凯欧蒂神迹：阿库乌雾旅美诗歌选. Translated by Peihong Wen and Mark Bender, 270–311. Beijing: The Ethnic Publishing House and the Ohio State University National East Asian Languages Resource Center, 2015.

Alai 阿来. "Zai yiben shu zhong youli guxiang 在一本书中游历故乡 [Journeying into the homeland within a book]." In Zhuang Xueben 庄学本, *Qiangrong kaocha ji: Sheying dashi Zhuang Xueben ershi shiji sanshi niandai de xibu renwen tanfang* 羌戎考察记：摄影大师庄学本20世纪30年代的西部人文探访 [Expeditions into the land of the Qiang and Rong: Photographic master Zhuang Xueben's humanist explorations and visits to the west in the 1930s]. Edited by Ma Naihui 马鼐辉, Wang Zhaohu 王昭武, Zhuang Wenjun 庄文骏, 1–3. Chengdu: Sichuan chubanjituan, Sichuan minzu chubanshe, 2007.

Alai 阿来, and Lu Yiping 卢一萍. "Alai: Wo yizhi douzai zhuiwen, weishenme 阿来：我一直都在追问，为什么?" [Alai: I have been questioning: Why?] "Zhongguo zuojia wang 中国作家网" [China writers' site]. Last modified June 30, 2017. http://www.chinawriter.com.cn/n1/2017/0630/c405057-29373267.html.

Althusser, Louis. "Ideology and Ideological State Apparatuses: Notes Toward an Investigation." In *Lenin and Philosophy and Other Essay.* Translated by Ben Brewster, 121–176. London: NLB, 1971.

Anagnost, Ann. "The Politics of Ritual Displacement." In *Asian Visions of Authority: Religion and the Modern States of East and Southeast Asia.* Edited by Charles F. Keyes, Laurel Kendall and Helen Hardacre, 221–254. Honolulu: University of Hawai'i Press, 1994.

Anderson, Benedict. *Imagined Communities: Reflections on the Origin and Spread of Nationalism.* London: Verso, 1991.

Appadurai, Arjun. *Modernity at Large: Cultural Dimensions of Globalization.* Minneapolis: University of Minnesota Press, 1996.

Bachner, Andrea, and Pedro Erber. "Remapping the Transpacific: Critical Approaches between Asia and Latin America." *Verge: Studies in Global Asias* 3, no. 2 (2017): vi–xiii.

Bai, Zhihong, "Ethnic Identities under the Tourist Gaze." *Asian Ethnicity* 8, no. 3 (2007): 245–259.

Barlow, Tani. *The Question of Women in Chinese Feminism.* Durham: Duke University Press, 2004.

Barthes, Roland. "Mythologies Today." In *Mythologies.* Translated by Richard Howard and Annette Lavers, 213–274. New York: Hill and Wang, 2012.

Befu, Harumi. Introduction to *Cultural Nationalism in East Asia: Representation and Identity,* 1–5. Edited by Harumi Befu. Berkeley: Institute of East Asian Studies, University of California, Berkeley, 1993.

Beijing Wenhua Yichan Baohu Zhongxin 北京文化遗产保护中心 [Beijing Cultural Heritage Protection Center]. Accessed May 20, 2018. http://www.bjchp.org/.

Bender, Mark. "Cry of the Silver Pheasant: Contemporary Ethnic Poetry in Sichuan and Yunnan." *Chinese Literature Today* 2, no. 2 (2012): 68–74.

Bender, Mark. "Introduction: Poems from Borderlands in Asia." *The Borderlands of Asia: Culture, Place, Poetry.* Amherst: Cambria, 2017.

Bender, Mark. "Poet of the Late Summer Corn: Aku Wuwu and Contemporary Yi Poetry." In *The Oxford Handbook of Modern Chinese Literatures.* Edited by Carlos Rojas and Andrea Bachner, 498–520. New York: Oxford University Press, 2016.

Benjamin, Walter. "The Work of Art in the Age of Mechanical Reproduction." In *Illuminations: Essays and Reflections.* Translated by Harry Zohn, edited by Hannah Arendt, 217–253. New York: Schocken Books, 1968.

Berry, Christopher, and Mary Farquhar. *China on Screen: Cinema and the Nation.* New York: Columbia University Press, 2006.

Bhabha, Homi K. "Culture's In-Between." In *Multicultural States: Rethinking Difference and Identity.* Edited by David Bennett, 29–36. London: Routledge, 1998.

Bhabha, Homi K. "DissemiNation." In *The Location of Culture*, 199–244. London: Routledge. 1994.
Bhabha, Homi K. "The Third Space: Interview with Homi Bhabha." In *Identity: Community, Culture, Difference*. Edited by Jonathan Rutherfold, 207–221. London: Lawrence and Wishart, 1998.
Blaeser, Kimberley M. "Native Literature: Seeking a Critical Center." In *Learn, Teach, Challenge: Approaching Indigenous Literatures*. Edited by Deanna Reder, and Linda M. Morra. Waterloo: Wilfrid Laurier University Press, 2016.
Blumenfield, Tami, and Helaine Silverman. *Cultural Heritage Politics in China*. New York: Springer New York, 2013.
Boym, Svetlana. *The Future of Nostalgia*. New York: Basic Books, 2001.
Brubaker, Rogers. "Ethnicity without Groups." In *The Ethnicity Reader: Nationalism, Multiculturalism and Migration*. Edited by Montserrat Guibernau and John Rex, 33–45. Cambridge: Polity, 2010.
Buffalohead, Eric L., and Elise M. Marubbio. "Introduction: Talking Back, Moving Forward." In *Native Americans on Film: Conversations, Teaching, and Theory*. Edited by Eric L. Buffalohead and Elise M. Marubbio. Lexington: University of Kentucky Press, 2018.
Burao, Yilu. "Four Generations of Va Women." In *Chinese Women Writers on the Environment: A Multi-ethnic Anthology of Fiction and Nonfiction*. Edited by Dong Isbister, Xiumei Pu and Stephen D. Rachman, 13–25. McFarland & Company, North Carolin, 2000.
Cai, Yuanpei 蔡元培. Shuo minzuxue 說民族學 [On ethnology]. In *Cai Yuanpei minzuxue lunzhu* 蔡元培民族學論著 [Cai Yuanpei's works on ethnology]. Edited by Zhongguo minzu xuehui [China association of ethnology], 1–11. Taipei: Taiwan zhonghua shuju, 1962.
Casanova, Pascale. *The World Republic of Letters*. Translated by M. B. DeBevoise. Cambridge: Harvard University Press, 2004.
Çelik, Zeynep, and Leila Kinney. "Ethnography and Exhibitionism at the Expositions Universelles." *Assemblage* no. 13 (1990): 35–59.
Chao, Emily. "Hegemony, Agency, and Re-presenting the Past: The Invention of Dongba Culture among the Naxi of Southwest China." In *Negotiating Ethnicities in China and Taiwan*. Edited by Melissa J. Brown, 208–239. Berkeley: Institute of East Asian Studies, University of California, Berkeley, 1996.
Chen, Jie. "Nationality, Ethnicity, and Cultural Strategies: Three Waves of Ethnic Representation in post-1949 China." PhD diss. The State University of New Jersey, 2008.
Cheng, Eileen J. *Literary Remains: Death, Trauma, and Lu Xun's Refusal to Mourn*. Honolulu: University of Hawaii Press, 2013.
China-UNESCO World Heritage Centre. 2016. http://whc.unesco.org/en/statesparties/cn.
United Nations. 2007. "United Nations Declaration on the Rights of Indigenous Peoples." http://www.un.org/esa/socdev/unpfii/documents/DRIPS_en.pdf.
Chio, Jenny. *A Landscape of Travel: The Work of Tourism in Rural Ethnic China*. Seattle: University of Washington Press, 2014.
Chow, Kai-wing. "Imagining Boundaries of Blood: Zhang Binglin and the Invention of the Han 'Race' in Modern China." In *The Construction of Racial Identities in China and Japan*. Edited by Frank Dikotter, 34–52. London: C. Hurst & Co., 1997.

Clark, Paul. "Ethnic Minorities in Chinese Films: Cinema and the Exotic." *East-West Film Journal* 1, no. 2 (1987): 15–31.

Clifford, James. "On Ethnographic Authority." *The Predicament of Culture: Twentieth-century Ethnography, Literature, and Art.* Cambridge: Harvard University Press, 1988. 21–54.

Clifford, James. *Returns: Becoming Indigenous in the Twenty-first Century.* Cambridge: Harvard University Press, 2013.

Coggins, Chris, and Gesang Zeren. "Animated Landscapes: Nature Conservation and the Production of Agropastoral Sacred Space in Shangrila." In *Mapping Shangrila: Contested Landscapes in the Sino-Tibetan Borderlands*, edited by Chris Coggins and Emily T. Yeh, 149–164. Seattle: University of Washington Press. 2014.

Cohen, Paul A. *History in Three Keys: The Boxers as Event, Experience, and Myth.* New York: Columbia University Press, 1997.

Comaroff, John L., and Jean Comaroff. *Ethnicity, Inc.* Chicago: University of Chicago Press, 2009.

Coombe, Rosemary J. "Managing Cultural Heritage as Neoliberal Governmentality." In *Heritage Regimes and the State.* Edited by Regina F. Bendix, Aditya Eggert, and Arnika Peselmann, 375–387. Gottingen: Gottingen University Press, 2016.

Cox, James L. *From Primitive to Indigenous: The Academic Study of Indigenous Religions.* Hampshire: Ashgate Publishing Limited, 2007.

Crossley, Pamela Kyle. "Thinking About Ethnicity in Early Modern China." *Late Imperial China* 11, no. 1 (1990): 1–35.

Danzeng 丹增 and Bai Gengsheng 白庚胜. "Zhanshi yu qidian" 展示与起点 [Demonstrations and beginnings]. In Dazeng and Bai Gengqing ed. and General Editorial Committee, *Xinshiqi Zhongguo shaoshu minzu wenxue zuopin xuanji: Qiangzu juan* 新时期新时期少数民族文学作品选集：羌族卷 [Selected works of Chinese ethnic minority literatures in the new era, Volume on the Qiang]. Beijing: Zuojia chubanshe, 2014, 1–4.

Dayton, D. "Growing New Forms of Literature: A Conversation with Tibetan Author Alai." https://www.worldliteraturetoday.org/2019/spring/growing-new-forms-literature-conversation-tibetan-writer-alai-d-dayton.

Da Yu Zhi Shui 大禹治水 [Da Yu controls floods]. Accessed May 20, 2016. http://www.ebaomonthly.com/window/discovery/history/china/ch100/100_1.htm.

Debord, Guy. *The Society of the Spectacle.* New York: Zone Book, 1995.

De la Cadena, Marisol, and Orin Starn. "Introduction." In *Indigenous Experience Today.* Edited by Marisol de la Cadena and Orin Starn, 1–32. Oxford: Berg. 2007.

Deleuze, Gilles, and Félix Guattari. "What Is a Minor Literature?" In *Kafka: Toward a Minor Literature.* Translated by Dana Polan, 16–27. Minneapolis: University of Minnesota Press, 1986.

Dikotter, Frank. *The Discourse of Race in Modern China.* London: C. Hurst 1992.

Dirlik, Arif. *Culture and History in Postrevolutionary China: The Perspective of Global Modernity.* Hong Kong: The Chinese University Press 2012.

Douban Dianying 豆瓣电影. "Guan Hu 管虎." Accessed April 30, 2018. https://movie.douban.com/celebrity/1274919/.

Douban Dianying 豆瓣电影. "Shasheng de yingping"《杀生》的影评 [Commentaries for *Design of Death*]. Accessed April 13, 2016. https://movie.douban.com/subject/4176542/reviews.

Duan, Haizhen 段海珍. *Tiange* 天歌 [Heavenly songs]. Beijing: Zuojia chubanshe, 2016.

Duara, Prasenjit. "Deconstructing the Chinese Nation: How Recent Is It?" In *The Global and Regional in China's Nation-Formation*, 97–116. London: Routledge. 2009.

Duara, Prasenjit. "Local Worlds: The Poetics and Politics of the Native Place in Modern China." *The South Atlantic Quarterly* 99, no. 1 (2000): 13–45.

Duara, Prasenjit. "Superscribing Symbols: The Myth of Guandi, Chinese God of War." In *The Global and Regional in China's Nation-Formation*. 76–96. London: Routledge, 2009.

Dudemaine, Andre, Garbrielle Marcoux, and Isabelle St-Amand, "Introduction: Indigenous Cinema and Media in the Americas: Storytelling, Communities, and Sovereignties." *Canadian Journal of Film Studies* 29, no. 1, 2020: 1–39.

Editorial Committee. *Zoubian wenchuan—Dayu wenhua lüyouqu xilie congshu* 走遍汶川—大禹文化旅游区系列丛书 [Walking all over Wenchuan: Da yu scenic cultural tourism book series]. Vol. 2. *Wenchuan xinlv* 汶川新旅 [Wenchuan new tourism]. Beijing: Dazhong wenyi shubanshe, 2011.

Fan, Ye 范曄. *Hou Hanshu* 後漢書 西羌傳,南蠻西南夷列傳 [The book of later Han: Biographies of the Xiqiang and biographies of the southern *man* and southwestern *yi*]. *Zhongyang yanjiu yuan hanji dianzi wenxian ziliaoku* 中央研究院漢籍電子文獻資料庫 [Scripta Sinica electronic database of traditional Chinese classics]. Taipei: Academia Sinica. http://hanchi.ihp.sinica.edu.tw/ihp/hanji.htm.

Fan, Yihong 樊义红. *Wenxue de minzu rentong texing jiqi wenxuexing shengcheng: yi zhongguo dangdai shaoshu minzu xiaoshuo wei zhongxin* 文学的民族认同特性及其文学性生成：以中国当代少数民族小说为中心 [The ethnic identification features of literature and the emergence of its literary qualities: Centering on contemporary China's ethnic minority fiction]. Beijing: Zhongguo shehui kexue chubanshe, 2016.

Fariello, M. Anna. "Making and Naming: The Lexicon of Studio Craft." In *Extra/ordinary: Craft and Contemporary Art*, edited by Maria Elena Buszek, 23–42. Durham: Duke University Press, 2011.

Fei, Xiaotong 费孝通. "Guanyu woguo minzu de shibie wenti" 关于我国民族的识别问题 [Questions about the identification of our nation's ethnic groups], *Zhongguo shehui kexue* 中国社会科学 [Social sciences of China], no.1 (1980): 147–162.

Fei, Xiaotong. "Tan shenru kaizhan minzu diaocha wenti 谈深入开展民族调查问题 [On the deepening of the questions of ethnic investigations], *Zhongnan minzu xueyuan xuebao* 中南民族学院学报 [Journal of Zhongnan Nationalities College] no. 3 (1982): 2–6.

Fei, Xiaotong. "Zhonghua minzu de duoyuan yiti geju," 中华民族的多元一体格局 [The diversity in unity frame of *Zhonghua minzu*]. In *Zhonghua minzu duoyuan yiti geju* 中华民族多元一体格局 [The diversity in unity frame of *Zhonghua minzu*].Edited by Chen Kejin 陈克进, 1–36. Beijing: Zhongyang minzu xueyuan chubanshe, 1988.

Felski, Rita. *The Gender of Modernity*. Cambridge: Harvard University Press, 1995.

Fischer, Michael M.J. "Ethnicity and the Post-Modern Arts of Memory." In *Writing Cul-*

ture: The Poetics and Politics of Ethnography. Edited by James Clifford and George E. Markus, 194–233. Berkeley: University of California Press, 1986.

Foucault, Michel. "Of Other Spaces: Utopias and Heterotopias." In *Rethinking Architecture: A Reader in Cultural Theory*. Edited by Neil Leach, 350–356. London: Routledge, 1997.

Foucault, Michel. *The Order of Things: An Archaeology of the Human Sciences*. New York: Vintage Books, 1973.

Foucault, Michel. "The Subject and Power." *Critical Inquiry* 8, no. 4 (1982): 777–795.

Foucault, Michel. "Subjectivity and Truth." In *Michel Foucault: Ethics, Subjectivity, and Truth: The Essential Works of Foucault, 1954–1984, Volume 1*. Edited by Paul Rabinow. Translated by Robert Hurley and others, 87–92. New York: The New Press, 1994.

Friedman, P. Kerim. "Defining Ethnographic Film." The Routledge International Handbook of Ethnographic Film and Video. Edited by Phillip Vannini. London: Routledge, 2020.

Gao Tunzi jianjie 高屯子简介 [brief bio of Gao Tunzi] https://www.wenweipo.com/a/202306/21/AP6491f3f6e4b043f3863611a5.html.

Gao, Tunzi, dir. Shinian xunqiang [十年寻羌 Ten years in search for the Qiang], 2019. Emei dianying jituan, Chengdu shengshi wenjing gongsi.

Gao, Tunzi. *Shinian qunxiang: renyushen de beihuanlihe* 十年寻羌：人与神的悲欢离合 [Ten years in search of the Qiang: The unions and separations between humans and gods]. Shanghai: Shanghai sanlian shudian, 2022.

Garcia, Edgar. "Introduction, Unnatural Signs." In *Signs of the Americas: A Poetics of Pictography, Hieroglyphs, and Khipu*. Edited by Edward Garcia, 1–36. Chicago: University of Chicago Press, 2020.

Geertz, Cliford. "Religion as a Cultural System." In *The Interpretation of Cultures: Selected Essays*, 87–125. New York: Basic Books, 2000.

Geng, Shaojiang 耿少将. Qiangzu tongshi 羌族通史[A comprehensive history of Qiangzu]. Shanghai: Shanghai renmin chubanshe, 2010.

Ginsburg, Faye. "Decolonizing Documentary On-screen and Off." *Film Quarterly* 72, no. 1 (2018).

Ginsburg, Faye. "Indigenous Media: Faustian Contract or Global Village?" *Cultural Anthropology* 6, no. 1 (1991): 92–112.

Gladney, Dru C. *Dislocating China: Muslims, Minorities, and Other Subalterns*. Chicago: University of Chicago Press, 2003.

Gladney, Dru C. "The Question of Minority and Indigeneity in Post-colonial China." *Cultural Survival Quarterly* 21, no. 3 (1997): 50–54.

Gladney, Dru C. "Representing Nationality in China: Reconfiguring Majority/Minority Identities." *The Journal of Asian Studies* 53, no. 1 (1994): 92–123.

Gossaert, Vincent. "State and Religion in Modern China: Religious Policy and Scholarly Paradigms." *communication au colloque du cinquantenaire de l'Institut d'Histoire Moderne de l'Academia Sinica* (2006): 1–29. https://halshs.archives-ouvertes.fr/halshs-00106187/document.

Graburn, Nelson, and Maria Gravari-Barbas. "Introduction: Tourism Imaginaries at the Disciplinary Crossroads." In *Tourism Imaginaries at the Disciplinary Crossroads: Place, Practice, Media*. Edited by Nelson Graburn and Maria Gravari-Barbas, 1–33. Oxon: Routledge, 2016.

Gramsci, Antonio. "Prison Notebooks: The Intellectuals." In *An Anthology of Western Marxism: From Lukacs and Gramsci to Socialist-Feminism*. Edited by Roger S. Gottlieb, 113–119. New York: Oxford University Press, 1989.

Guan, Hu 管虎, dir. *Shasheng* 杀生 [Design of Death]. Beijing: Xingmei yingye youxian gongsi, 2012. Accessed June 2, 2018. https://www.youtube.com/watch?v=KvRq-oD8pbw&t=1611s.

Guojia Minwei Minzu Wenti Wuzhong Congshu Bianji Weiyuanhui 国家民委民族问题五种丛书编辑委员会 [Editorial Committee on the Five Ethnic Questions of the State Ethnic Affairs Commission] and Zhongguo Shaoshu Minzu Jiashi Congshu Bianjizu 《中国少数民族简史》丛书编辑组 [Editorial Board of *Concise Histories of Chinese Ethnic Minorities Series*]. "*Zhongguo shaoshu minzu jianshi congshu* chuban shuoming"《中国少数民族简史丛书》出版说明 [Note on the publication of *Concise Histories of Chinese Ethnic Minorities Series*]. In *Qiangzu jianshi* 羌族简史 [A concise history of Qiangzu]. Edited by Qiangzu Jianshi Bianxiezu. Beijing: Minzu chubanshe, 2008.

Guojia Minzu Shiwu Weiyuanhui Zhengce Yanjiushi. 国家民族事务委员会政策研究室 [Research Unit of Policies of the State Ethnic Affairs Commission of the People's Republic of China]. *Zhongguo minzu guanxishi lunwenji* 中国民族关系史论文集 [Collection of papers on China's ethnic relations]. Beijing: Minzu chubanshe, 1982.

Guojia Minzu Shiwu Weiyuanhui Zhongguo Shaoshu Minzu Guji Zhengli Yanjiushi 国家民族事务委员会全国少数民族古籍整理研究室 [Unit of the Research and Compilation of National Ethnic Minority Groups' Ancient Relics and Documents, State Ethnic Affairs Commission of the People's Republic of China], *Zhongguo shaoshu minzu guji zongmu tiyao: Qiangzu juan* 中国少数民族古籍总目提要:羌族卷 [General catalogue of grand summaries of Chinese ethnic minorities' ancient relics and documents: volume of Qiangzu]. Beijing: Zhongguo da baike quanshu chubanshe, 2009.

Hale, Charles. "Does Multiculturalism Menace? Governance, Cultural Rights, and the Politics of Identity in Guatemala." *Journal of Latin American Studies* 34, no. 3 (2002): 485–524.

Hall, Stuart. "Ethnicity and Difference in Global Times." In *The Fateful Triangle: Race, Ethnicity, Nation*. Edited by Kobena Mercer, 80–124. Cambridge: Harvard University Press, 2017.

Hall, Stuart. "Introduction: Who Needs 'Identity'?" In *Questions of Cultural Identity*. Edited by Stuart Hall and Paul du Gay, 1–17. London: Sage Publications, 1996.

Hall, Stuart. "New Ethnicities." In *Stuart Hall: Critical Dialogues in Cultural Studies*. Edited by David Morley and Kuan-Hsing Chen, 441–449. New York: Routledge, 1996.

Hall, Stuart, and Lawrence Grossberg. "On Postmodernism and Articulation: An Interview with Stuart Hall." *Journal of Communication Inquiry* 10, no. 2 (1986): 45–60.

Harrell, Stevan. "Introduction: Civilizing Projects and the Reactions to Them." In *Cultural Encounters on China's Ethnic Frontiers*. Edited by Stevan Harrell, 3–36. Seattle: University of Washington Press, 1995.

Han, Wanfeng 韩万峰, dir. *Erma de hunli* 尔玛的婚礼 [Erma's wedding]. Xiaoxiang dianying jituan, 2008.

Harrell, Stevan, and Li Yongxiang. "The History of the History of Yi." *Modern China* 29, no. 3 (2003): 362–396.

Harvey, David. *A Brief History of Neoliberalism*. New York: Oxford University Press, 2005.
Harvey, David. *The Condition of Postmodernity: An Enquiry into the Origins of Cultural Change*. Oxford: Basil Blackwell, 1989.
Hathaway, Michael. "The Emergence of Indigeneity: Public Intellectuals and an Indigenous Space in Southwest China." *Cultural Anthropology* 25, no. 2 (2010): 301–333.
Hathaway, Michael. *Environmental Winds: Making the Global in Southwest China*. Berkeley: University of California Press. 2013.
Hervieu-Léger, Danièle. *Religion as a Chain of Memory*. Translated by Simon Lee. New Brunswick: Rutgers University Press, 2000.
Hillier, Bill, and Julienne Hanson. *The Social Logic of Space*. Cambridge: Cambridge University Press, 1984.
Hilman, Ben, and Lee-Anne Henfry. "Macho Minority: Masculinity and Ethnicity on the Edge of Tibet." *Modern China* 32, no. 2 (Apr. 2006): 251–272.
Hobsbawm, Eric. "Introduction: Inventing Traditions." In *The Invention of Tradition*. Edited by Eric Hobsbawm and Terence Ranger, 1–14. Cambridge: Cambridge University Press, 1983.
Hostetler, Laura. "Introduction to *The Art of Ethnography: The Miao Album of Guizhou Province*." Translated by David M. Deal and Laura Hostetler, xvii–lxvii. Seattle: University of Washington Press, 2006.
Howland, Douglas. "The Dialectics of Chauvinism: Minority Nationalities and Territorial Sovereignty in Mao Zedong's New Democracy." *Modern China* 37, no. 2 (2011): 170–201.
Hu, Jintao 胡锦涛. "Hu Jintao tichu, zhashi tuijin shehui zhuyi wenhua qiangguo jianshe" 胡锦涛提出,扎实推进社会主义文化强国建设 [Hu Jintao proposes: firmly push forward the construction of a culturally strong socialist state]. Last modified November 8, 2012. http://cpc.people.com.cn/18/n/2012/1108/c350821-19526764.html.
Hu, Siao-chen 胡曉真. *Mingqing wenxue zhongde xinan xushi* 明清文學中的西南敘事 [The southwest in Ming-Qing literary imagination]. Taipei: Taida chuban zhongxin, 2017.
Idema, Wilt, and Beata Grant, ed. *The Red Brush: Writing Women of Imperial China*. Cambridge: Harvard University Asia Center, 2004.
Ingold, Tim. "Ancestry, Generation, Substance, Memory, Land." In *The Perception of the Environment, Essays on Livelihood, Dwelling and Skill*. 132–151. London: Routledge, 2000.
Jidi Majia. *Identity*. Translated by Qian Kunqiang. Nottingham: Aurora Publishing, 2016.
"Jidi Majia jianjie" 吉狄马加简介 [A brief introduction to Jidi Majia]. Zhongguo zuojiawang. http://www.chinawriter.com.cn/n1/2018/0521/c419344-30003294.html.
Kenley, David. *Modern Chinese History*. Ann Arbor: Association for Asian Studies, 2012.
Kyong-McClain, Jeff. "Missionary Archaeology on Republican China's Southwestern Frontier." *The Newsletter* no. 65, Autumn 2013. https://www.iias.asia/the-newsletter/article/missionary-archaeology-republican-chinas-southwestern-frontier.
Lefebvre, Henri. *The Production of Space*. Translated by Donald Nicholson-Smith. Oxford: Blackwell, 1991.
Lei, Zi 雷子. "Muqin de Shuguang fengrenshe" 母亲的曙光缝纫社 [Mother's Shuguang sewing Unit]. In *Tianzhen de meng yu Qiangye de ge*. 3–8. Beijing: Zhongguo wenlian chubanshe, 2016.

Lei, Zi 雷子. *Tianzhen de meng yu Qiangye de ge* 天真的梦与羌野的歌 [*Innocent dreams and songs in the wilderness of the Qiang*]. Beijing: Zhongguo wenlian chubanshe, 2016.

Leibold, James. *Reconfiguring Chinese Nationalism: How the Qing Frontier and its Indigenes Became Chinese*. New York: Palgrave Macmillan, 2007.

Leibold, James. "Searching for the Han: Early Twentieth-Century Narratives of Chinese Origins and Development." In *Critical Han Studies: The History, Representation, and Identity of China's Majority*. Edited by Thomas S. Mullaney, James Patrick Leibold, Stéphane Gros and Eric Armand Vanden Bussche, 210–233. Berkeley: University of California Press, 2012.

Le Montec, Katiana, and Qiangyun Zhang. "Heritagization of Disaster Ruins and Ethnic Culture in China: Recovery Plans after the 2008 Wenchuan Earthquake." *China Information* 31, no. 3 (2017): 349–370.

Lewis, Mark Edward. *Flood Myths of Early China*. Albany: State University of New York, 2006.

Lewis, Mark Edward. *Writing and Authority in Early China*. SUNY, 1999.

Li, Xianglin 李祥林. "Binwei de Qiangzu koutou yichan he tuxiang jingdian" 濒危的羌族口头遗产和图像经典 [Endangered Qiang oral cultural heritage and pictographic classics]. http://www.artanthropology.com/show.aspx?id=1889&cid=16.

Liang, Qichao 梁启超 "Zhongguoshi xulun" 中国史叙论 [Introduction to the history of China]. In *Liang Qichao quanji* 梁启超全集 [The complete works of Liang Qichao]. Edited by Zhang Pinxing 张品兴, 448–454. Vol. 1 of *The Complete Works of Liang Qichao*. Beijing: Beijing chubanshe, 1999.

Lin, Huixiang 林惠祥. *Zhongguo minzushi* 中國民族史 [History of the ethnicities of China]. 2 vols. Beijing: Shangwu yinshuguan, 1939; reprint: Beijing: Shangwu yinshuguan, 1993.

Litzinger, Ralph. "Memory Work: Reconstituting the Ethnic in Post-Mao China." *Cultural Anthropology* 13, no. 2 (1998): 224–255.

Litzinger, Ralph. *Other Chinas: The Yao and the Politics of National Belonging*. Durham: Duke University Press, 2000.

Liu, Biyun. "From Kinship to State and Back Again: Lineage and History in a Qiang Village." In *Modalities of Change: The Interface of Modernity and Tradition in East Asia*. Edited by James Wilkerson and Robert Parkin. New York: Berghahn Books, 2013.

Liu, Yingying 刘颖颖. "Jidi Majia huo Guayajier 2020 guoji shigejiang." 吉狄马加获2020 瓜亚基尔国际诗歌奖 ["Jidi Majia won the 2020 Guayaquil International Poetry Award"]. http://www.yizuren.com/literature/wyzx/41046.html.

Long, Colin, and Sophia Labadi. Introduction to *Heritage and Globalization*. Edited by Sophia Labadi and Colin Long, 1–16. London: Routledge, 2010.

Luo, Qingchun 罗庆春. "Cong 'wenhua hunxue' dao 'wenxue hunxue:' lun Yizu hanyu shige de wenhua goucheng yu jingshen zhixiang." 从 "文化混血" 到 "文学混血" ：论彝族汉语诗歌的文化构成与精神指向 ["From cultural hybridity to literary hybridity: on the cultural components and spiritual directions of Yi poetry in Chinese-language."] In *Ling yu ling de duihua: Zhongguo shaoshu minzu hanyu shilun* 灵与灵的对话：中国少数民族汉语诗论 [Soul to soul: on the Chinese-language poetry of China's ethnic minorities], 51–58. Hong Kong: Tianma tushu, 2001.

Luo, Qingchun 罗庆春. "Houji." 后记 [Afterword]. In *Ling yu ling de duihua: Zhongguo shaoshu minzu hanyu shilun* 灵与灵的对话：中国少数民族汉语诗论 [Soul to soul:

on the Chinese-language poetry of China's ethnic minorities], 238–239. Hong Kong: Tianma tushu, 2001.

Luo, Yu. "Alternative Indigeneity in China? The Paradox of the Buyi in the Age of Ethnic Branding." *Verge: Studies in Global Asias* vol. 4, no. 2 (2018): 107–134. http://m.xinhuanet.com/2018-05/10/c_1122814554.htm.

Luo, Yu. "An Alternative to the 'Indigenous' in Early Twenty-First-Century China: Guizhou's Branding of Yuanshengtai." *Modern China* 2017: 1–35.

Ma, Rong, "A New Perspective in Guiding Ethnic Relations in the 21st Century: 'De-politicization' of Ethnicity in China." In *De-politicization of Ethnic Questions in China*. Edited by Lizhong Xie, 1–27. Singapore: World Scientific, 2014.

Mathieu, Christine. "The Dongba Religion." In *Quetin Roosevelt's China: Ancestral Realms of the Naxi*. Edited by Christine Matthieu, 54–91. New York: Rubin Museum of Art, 2011.

McCarthy, Susan K. *Communist Multiculturalism: Ethnic Revival in Southwest China*. Seattle: University of Washington Press, 2009.

McGrath, Jason. *Postsocialist Modernity: Chinese Cinema, Literature, and Criticism in the Market Age*. Stanford: Stanford University Press, 2008.

McNeal, Robin. "Constructing Myths in Modern China." *Journal of Asian Studies* 71, no. 3 (2012): 679–704.

McNeal, Robin. "Moral Transformation and Local Identity: Reviving the Culture of Shun at Temples and Monuments across China." *Modern China* 41, no. 4 (2015): 436–464.

Merlan, Francesca. "Indigeneity Global and Local." *Current Anthropology* 50, no. 3 (2009): 303–333.

Moncef, Salah El. "Minor Literature." In *Oxford Research Encyclopedia, Literature*, 1–24. Oxford University Press USA, 2020.

Moretti, Franco. *Distant Reading*. London: Verso, 2013.

Moya, Paula M.L. *Learning from Experience: Minority Identities, Multicultural Struggles*. Berkeley: University of California Press, 2002.

Moretti, Franco. *The Social Imperative: Race, Close Reading, and Contemporary Literary Criticism*. Stanford: Stanford University Press, 2016.

Mullaney, Thomas. *Coming to Terms with the Nation: Ethnic Classification in Modern China*. Berkeley: University of California Press, 2011.

Mullaney, Thomas. "Critical Han Studies: Introduction and Prolegomenon." In *Critical Han Studies: The History, Representation, and Identity of China's Majority*. Edited by Thomas Mullaney, James Leibold, Stephane Gros, and Eric Vanden Bussche, 1–22. University of California Press, 2012.

Nonini, Donald. "Is China Becoming Neoliberal?" *Critique of Anthropology* 28 no. 2 (2008): 145–176.

Oakes, Tim. "Cultural Strategies of Development: Implications for Vnillage Governance in China." *The Pacific Review* 19, no. 1 (2006): 13–37.

Oakes, Tim. "Ethnic Tourism in China." In *Handbook on Ethnic Minorities in China*. Edited by Xiaowei Zang, 291–315. Cheltenham: Edward Elgar Publishing, 2016.

Oakes, Tim. *Tourism and Modernity in China*. London: Routledge, 1998.

Oakes, Tim, and Louisa Schein. "Translocal China: an introduction." In *Translocal China:*

Linkages, Identities, and the Reimagining of Space. Edited by Tim Oakes and Louisa Schein, 1–35. London: Routledge, 2006.

Okin, Martin, and Alexa Alice Joubin. *Race: The New Critical Idiom*. New York: Routledge, 2019.

Owen, Stephen. *The Great Age of Chinese Poetry: The High T'ang*. New Haven: Yale University Press, 1981.

Oxford Refence. https://www.oxfordreference.com/display/10.1093/oi/authority.20110803103943993.

Palumbo-Liu, David. *The Deliverance of Others: Reading Literature in a Global Age*. Durham: Duke University Press 2012.

Parekh, Bhikhu. "What is Multiculturalism?" In *The Ethnicity Reader: Nationalism, Multiculturalism and Migration*. Edity by Montserrat Guibernau and John Rex, 238–243. Cambridge: Polity, 2010.

Peck, Jamie. *Constructions of Neoliberal Reason*. New York: Oxford University Press, 2010.

Qian, Weipin 钱伟品. "Liuzhu qingshan lüshui, bixu jizhu xiangchou: Xi zongshuji quanshi chengzhenhua" 习近平：留住青山绿水，必须记住乡愁：习总书记诠释城镇化 [Xi Jinpin: To preserve green mountains and rivers, we must protect our feelings of homesickness: General Secretary Xi explains urbanization]. Accessed April 10, 2018. http://www.mzfxw.com/e/action/ShowInfo.php?classid=15&id=30358.

Qiang, Renliu 羌人六. "Anhun zhe" 安魂者 [The soul pacifier]. In *Shishu zhijia* 食鼠之家 [The household that survives on eating mice]. Beijing: Zuojia chubanshe, 2016, 14–27.

Qiangzu Jianshi Bianxiezu 羌族简史编写组 [Editorial board of *The Concise History of Qiangzu*] and Qiangzu Jianshi Xiudingben Bianxiezu 羌族简史修订本编写组 [Editorial board of the revised version of *Qiangzu Jianshi*]. *Qiangzu jianshi* 羌族简史 [The concise history of Qiangzu]. Revised edition. Beijing: Minzu chubanshe 2008.

Qiangzu wenhua zao dizhen yanzhong pohuai 羌族文化遭地震严重破坏 [Qiang ethnic culture was severely damaged by the earthquake]. Last modified June 2, 2008. http://www.china.com/cn/aboutchina/zhuanti/qiangwenhua/2008-06/-2/content_15596515.htm.

Qing, Lidong 青理东. "Huashuo Wenchuan" 话说汶川 [Discussing about Wenchuan]. In *Zoubian wenchuan—Dayu wenhua lüyouqu xilie congshu* 走遍汶川—大禹文化旅游区系列丛书 [Walking all over Wenchuan: Wenchuan Da Yu scenic cultural tourism book series, Volume 2], 1–2. Beijing: Dazhong wenyi shubanshe, 2011.

Ran, Guangrong 冉光荣, Li Shaoming 李绍明, and Zhou Xiyin 周锡银. *Qiangzu shi* 羌族史 [The history of Qiangzu]. Chengdu: Sichuan minzu chubanshe, 1985.

Rao, Shuguang. *A Film History of Chinese Minorities*. Translated by Wu Biyu and Wang Jianguo. Reading: Paths International Ltd, 2017.

Ren, Dongsheng 任冬生. "Minshan zhidian de mimi" 岷山之巅的秘密 [Secrets on the top of the Min Mountain]. In *Qiangfeng bianye* 羌风遍野 [Qiang wind all over the wilderness]. Chengdu: Dianzi keji daxue chubanshe, 2014, 153–164.

Ren, Dongsheng 任冬生. *Qiangfeng bianye* 羌风遍野 [Qiang wind all over the wilderness]. Chengdu: Dianzi keji daxue chubanshe, 2014.

Robbins, Joel. "Beyond the Suffering Subject: Toward an Anthropology of the Good." *Journal of the Royal Anthropological Institute* 19, no. 3 (2003): 447–462.

Rodgers, Susan. “A Batak Antiquarian Writes His Culture: Print Literacy and Social Thought in an Indonesian Society.” In *Anthropology and Literature*, edited by Paul Benson, 89–106. Urbana: University of Illinois Press, 1993.

Said, Edward. *Orientalism*. New York: Vintage Books, 1979.

Schaefer, William. “Shanghai Savage.” *positions: east asia cultures critique* 11, no. 1 (2003): 91–133.

Schein, Louisa. “Gender and Internal Orientalism in China.” *Modern China* 23, no. 1 (1997): 69–98.

Schein, Louisa. *Minority Rules: The Miao and The Feminine in China's Cultural Politics*. Durham: Duke University Press, 2000.

Schein, Louisa with Luo Yu. “Representations of Chinese Minorities.” In *Handbook on Ethnic Minorities in China*. Edited by Xiaowei Zang, 263–290. Cheltenham: Edward Elgar Publishing, 2016.

Schoppa, R. Keith. *Revolution and Its Past: Identities and Change in Modern Chinese History*. third edition. Boston, Prentice Hall, 2011.

Scott, James C. *Seeing Like the State: How Certain Schemes to Improve the Human Condition Have Failed*. New Haven: Yale University Press, 2005.

Shang, Guangqin 尚光琴. “Wei minzu shuxie, wei shidai ou'ge: Yang Zi changshi Wenchuan Qiang zai Zhongguo Xiandai Wenxueguan zhaokai” 为民族抒写，为时代讴歌：羊子长诗《汶川羌》在中国现代文学馆召开 [Writing for an ethnic group, singing for an era: Yang Zi's long poem *Wenchuan Qiang* debuted at National Museum of Modern Chinese Literature]. *Caodi* 草地. no. 1 (2012): 73–80.

“Shasheng paishe huaxu《杀生》拍摄花絮” [Sidelights of the shooting of *Design of Death*]. Accessed April 9, 2018. http://movie.mtime.com/135313/behind_the_scene.html.

“Shasheng 2012《杀生》2012” [*Design of Death* 2012]. Accessed April 9, 2018. https://movie.douban.com/subject/4176542/.

Shen Guiping 沈桂萍, and Ou Guangming 欧光明. *Zhongguo minzu lilun zhengce gailun* 中国民族理论政策概论 [Introduction to China's ethnic theories and policies]. Beijing: Minzu chubanshe, 2007.

“Shenzhen: tequ chuchuang, tizhi youshi 深圳：特区橱窗，体制优势” [Shenzhen: window of the special economic zone, advantage of the system]. Last modified August 25, 2005. http://finance.people.com.cn/GB/8215/52335/52348/52355/3642456.html.

Shih, Shu-mei. “Introduction: What is Sinophone Literature?” In *Sinophone Studies: A Critical Reader*. Edited by Shu-mei Shih, 1–16. New York City: Columbia University Press, 2013.

“Shijie wenhua yichan: Dujiangyan, Qingchengshan 世界文化遗产：都江堰、青城山” [World Cultural Heritage: Dujiangyan, Mt. Qingcheng]. Accessed May 23, 2016. http://big5.xinhuanet.com/gate/big5/news.xinhuanet.com/ziliao/2003-09/24/content_1097516.htm.

Shiren de Qiangzu jilu 十人的羌族纪录 [The documentary about Qiang created by ten people]. https://wh.cnki.net/article/detail/LVZZ200905018.

Shklar, Judith K. “Subversive Genealogies.” *Daedalus: Myth, Symbol, and Culture* 101, no. 1 (Winter 1972): 129–154.

Sichuan Lüyou Qingbao 四川旅游情报 [Information on Tourism in Sichuan]. Wenchuan dayu lüyou wenhuajie ji kangyang minsu zhuanchang tuijiehui kaimu 汶川大禹旅游

文化节暨康养民宿专场推介会开幕 [Wenchuan Da Yu cultural tourism festival and wellness resort guesthouses promotional conference opens]. Sohu.com. https://m.sohu.com/a/163649668_406858.

Smith, John A. "Three Images of the Visual: Empirical, Formal and Normative." In *Visual Culture*. Edited by Chris Jenks, 238–259. London: Routledge, 1995.

Sontag, Susan. "Melancholy Objects." In *On Photography*, 51–84. New York: Picador, 1977.

Sorace, Christian. *Shaken Authority: China's Communist Party and the 2008 Sichuan Earthquake*. Ithaca: Cornell University Press, 2017.

Tam, Gina Anne. "Sounding the Nation: Dialect and the Making of Modern China." PhD diss., Stanford University, 2016.

Tan, Jihe 谭继和, and Wang Chunwu 王纯五. "Xiayu wenhua de xin tansuo—Sichuan xuezhe Xiayu wenhua yanjiu xinzuo zonglun" 夏禹文化的新探索—四川学者夏禹文化研究新作综论 [New explorations of the culture of Xia Dynasty and Da Yu—a synthesis of the new works of Sichuan scholars' research on Xia Dynasty and Da Yu]. *Xinqiang Wenhua* 西羌文化 2007: 1–4.

"Taoping Qiangzhai 桃坪羌寨" [Taoping Qiang Village]. Accessed April 28, 2018. http://www.mafengwo.cn/poi/8662.html.

Tian, Fen 田芬, dir. *Gubao zhiwen* 古堡之吻 [Forbidden kiss]. 2014; Chengdu: Sichuan Ao'tu wenhua chuanbo youxian gongsi. Accessed April 30, 2018. https://www.youtube.com/watch?v=wh4sL05bvfs&t=1565s.

Trouillot, Michel-Rolph. "Anthropology and the Savage Slot: The Poetics and Politics of Otherness." In *Global Transformations: Anthropology and the Modern World*, 7–28. New York: Palgrave Macmillan, 2003.

Tsing, Anna. "Indigenous Voice." In *Indigenous Experience Today*. Edited by Marisol de la Cadena and Orin Starn, 33–68. Oxford: Berg, 2007.

Tuan, Yi-fu. *Topophilia: A Study of Environmental Perception, Attitudes, and Values*. New York: Columbia University Press, 1974.

UNESCO (Intangible Cultural Heritage). "Qiang New Year Festival." Accessed May 18, 2018. https://ich.unesco.org/en/USL/qiang-new-year-festival-00305.

Veg, Sebestian. *Minjian: The Rise of China's Grassroots Intellectuals*. New York: Columbia University Press, 2019.

Visser, Robin. *Questioning Borders: Ecoliteratures of China and Taiwan*. Columbia University Press, 2023.

Vitebsky, Piers. "Shamanism." In *Indigenous Religions: A Companion*. Edited by Graham Harvey, 55–67. London: Cassell, 2000.

Waldron, Arthur. "Representing China: The Great Wall and Cultural Nationalism in the Twentieth Century." In *Cultural Nationalism in East Asia: Representation and Identity*. Edited by Harumi Befu, 36–60. Berkeley: Institute of East Asian Studies, University of California, Berkeley, 1993.

Wang, Ming-ke 王明珂. "Genji lishi: Qiangzu de dixiong gushi" 根基歷史：羌族的弟兄故事 [Histories of the roots: the Qiangzu's stories about brotherhood]. In *Shijian, lishi yu jiyi* 時間、歷史與記憶 [Temporality, history, and memory]. Edited by Huang Ying-gui 黃應貴. Institute of Ethnology, Academia Sinica, 1999.

Wang, Ming-ke 王明珂. "Nüren, bujie, yu cunzhai rentong: Minjiang shangyou de duyaomao gushi 女人、不潔與村寨認同：岷江上游的毒藥貓故事 [Women, pollution, and village identities: the stories of the Poisonous Cat in the upper reaches of the Min River"]. *Journal of the Institute of History and Philology, Academia Sinica* 70, no. 3 (1999): 699–738.

Wang, Ming-ke 王明珂. *Qiang zai Han Zang zhijian: yige Huaxia bianyuan de lishi renleixue yanjiu*羌在漢藏之間：一個華夏邊緣的歷史人類學研究 [Qiang between the Han and the Tibetans: a historical-anthropological study of a people on the periphery of China]. Taipei: Lianjing chuban shiye gufen youxian gongsi, 2003.

Wang, Ming-ke 王明珂. "Searching for Qiang Culture in the First Half of the Twentieth Century." *Inner Asia* 4, no.1 (2002): 131–148.

Wang, Tongling 王桐齡. *Zhongguo minzushi* 中國民族史 [History of the ethnicities of China]. Wenhua Xueshe, 1934; reprint. Shanghai: Shanghai shudian, 1989.

Wang, Xiuyu. *China's Last Imperial Frontier: Late Qing Expansion in Sichuan's Tibetan Borderlands.* Lanham: Lexington Books, 2011.

Wang, Yong'an 王永安. "Laojia" 老家 [Homeland]. In *Yong'an sanwenji* 永安散文集 [Collection of essays of Yong'an], 129–132. Chengdu: Sichuan renmin chubanshe, 2013.

Wang, Yong'an 王永安. "Qiangnian xujiu" 羌年叙旧 [Talking about the old days during the Qiang New Year]. In *Yong'an sanwenji* 永安散文集 [Collection of essays of Yong'an]. Chengdu: Sichuan renmin chubanshe, 2013, 27–29.

Wang, Yunxia 王云霞. "Houji" 后记 [Afterword]. In A'er Villagers, *A'er Dang'an* 阿尔档案 [A'er archive]. Beijing: Wenwu chubanshe, 2011.

Weber, Marx. "What Is an Ethnic Group?" In *The Ethnicity Reader: Nationalism, Multiculturalism and Migration.* Edited by Montserrat Guibernau and John Rex, 17–26. Cambridge: Polity, 2010.

Wen, Jin. *Pluralist Universalism: An Asian Americanist Critique of U.S. and Chinese Multiculturalisms.* Columbus: The Ohio State University, 2012.

Wen, Maotao. "The Creation of the Qiang Ethnicity, Its Relation to the Rme People and the Preservation of Rme Language." Master thesis, Duke University.

Wenchuanxian Renmin Zhengfu 汶川县人民政府 [Wenchuan County People's Government]. www.wenchuan.gov.cn.

Wilcox, Emily. "Beyond Internal Orientalism: Dance and Nationality Discourse in the Early People's Republic of China, 1949–1954." *Journal of Asian Studies* 75, no. 2 (2016): 363–386.

Wilson, Pamela, and Michelle Stewart. "Introduction: Indigeneity and Indigenous Media on the Global Stage." In *Global Indigenous Media: Cultures, Poetics, and Politics.* Edited by Pamela Wilson and Michelle Stewart, 1–36. Durham: Duke University Press, 2008.

Xie, Hong 谢洪, dir. Zhongguo zui juyou shibiedu de gu cunluo: yunshang Zeng Tou 中国最具有识别度的古村落：云上增头 [China's most distinctive ancient village: Zengtou Village above the clouds]. https://v.youku.com/v_show/id_XMzI3OTQ1NzQ3Ng==.html?refer=seo_operation.liuxiao.liux_00003303_3000_Qzu6ve_19042900. 2017.

Xu, Chao 徐超. "Wen Jiabao zongli guanyu baohu Qiangzu wenhua yichan de liangci pishi 温家宝总理关于保护羌族文化遗产的两次批示—记民进中央副主席、中国民间文艺家协会主席冯骥才与羌族文化的不解情缘" [Two comments by Premier Wen Jiabao on the safeguarding of Qiangzu cultural heritage: on the close bonds between

Feng Jicai, Vice President of China Democracy Promotion Association and President of Chinese Folk Literature and Art Association, and Qiang culture]. Last modified August 1, 2013. http://www.mj.org.cn/zsjg/mz/200811/200812/t20081230_86659.htm.

Xu, Xueshu 徐学书. "Qiangzu" 羌族 [Qiang ethnic group]. Last modified July 23, 2009. http://www.hprc.org.cn/gsgl/zggk/rmin/shaoshumz/200907/t20090713_15896.html.

Yang, Guangcheng 杨光成. *Taoping shihua* 桃坪史话 [Historical accounts of Taoping]. Wenchuan: Xiqiang wenhua bianjibu, 2007.

Yang, Yumei 杨玉梅. *Minzu wenxue de jianshou yu chyaoyue* 民族文学的坚守与超越 [The persistence and transcendence of ethnic literature]. Beijing: Zuojia chubanshe, 2013.

Yang, Yuqing. *Mystifying China's Southwest Ethnic Borderlands: Harmonious Heterotopia*. Lanham: Lexington Books, 2018.

Yang, Zi 羊子. "Shanzhong de muqin" 山中的母亲 [Mother in the mountains]. In *Xinshiqi Zhongguo shaoshu minzu wenxue zuopin xuanji: Qiangzu juan* 新时期新时期少数民族文学作品选集：羌族卷 [Selected works of Chinese ethnic minority literatures in the new era, volume on the Qiang]. Edited by Danzeng 丹增, Bai Gengsheng 白庚胜, and General Editorial Committee, 198–200. Beijing: Zuojia chubanshe, 2014.

Yang, Zi 羊 子. *Wenchuan Qiang* 汶川羌. Chengdu: Sichuan chuban jituan, Sichuan wenyi chubanshe, 2010.

Ye, Xingguang 叶星光. "Shenshan, shenshu, shenlin" 神山 神树 神林 [Sacred mountain, sacred trees, sacred grove]. In *Xinshiqi Zhongguo shaoshu minzu wenxue zuopin xuanji: Qiangzu juan* 新时期新时期少数民族文学作品选集：羌族卷 [Selected works of Chinese ethnic minority literatures in the new era, volume on the Qiang]. Edited by Danzeng 丹增, and Bai Gengsheng 白庚胜, and General Editorial Committee, 31–61. Beijing: Zuojia chubanshe, 2014.

Yeh, Emily T. "The Rise and Fall of the Green Tibetan: Contingent Collaborations and the Vicissitudes of Harmony." In *Mapping Shangrila: Contested Landscapes in the Sino-Tibetan Borderlands*. Edited by Chris Coggins and Emily T. Yeh, 255–278. University of Washington Press, 2014.

Yeh, Emily T. "Tibetan Indigeneity: Translations, Resemblances, and Uptake." In *Indigenous Experience Today*. Edited by Marisol de la Cadena and Orin Starn, 69–98. Oxford: Berg, 1997.

Yin, Tenglian 尹腾连. "Dashan shenchu de baihe: 1988 nian zhi 2009 nian *Qiangzu wenxue zazhi* yanjiu" 大山深处的百合—1988年至2009年《羌族文学》杂志研究 [A White lily deep in the great mountains: a study on *Qiangzu Wenxue* from 1988 to 2009]. *Qiangzu wenxue* 羌族文学 [Qiangzu literature] (March 2016): 64–78.

Yu, Ronggen 俞荣根. *Qiangzu xiguan fa* 羌族习惯法 [The customary laws of Qiangzu]. Chongqing: Chongqing chubanshe, 2000.

Yu, Yaoming 余耀明. "Fenfang duoyowei" "芬芳朵哟喂 [The fragrant key]. In *Xinshiqi Zhongguo shaoshu minzu wenxue zuopin xuanji: Qiangzu juan* 新时期新时期少数民族文学作品选集：羌族卷 [Selected works of Chinese ethnic minority literatures in the new era, volume on the Qiang]. Edited by Danzeng 丹增, Bai Gengsheng 白庚胜, and General Editorial Committee, 72–82. Beijing: Zuojia chubanshe, 2014.

Yu, Yaoming 余耀明. "Qiangzu shibi tujing shualeri de shoucang yu yunyong" 羌族释比图经图经《刷勒日》的收藏与运用 [The collection and use of shualeri Qiang shamanistic pictographs]. *Sichuan tushuguan xuebao* 四川图书馆学报 [Journal of libraries in Sichuan] 4 (2007): 68–70.

Zhang, Qiaoyun. "Heritage Making After the Earthquake: Safeguarding the Intangible Heritage of the Qiang People in China." *The Newsletter of International Association of Asian Studies* no. 80 (Summer 2018): 37–38.

Zhang, Shanyun 张善云. "Qianyan" 前言 [Preface]. In *Fengzhou qiangge sanbaishou* 凤州羌歌三百首 [Three hundred Qiang songs from Feng County], 1–6. Chengdu: Sichuan minzu chubanshe, 2011.

Zhang, Tingyu 張廷玉. *Mishi*: Sichuan tusi 明史 四川土司 [History of Ming: Sichuan chieftains]. Edited by Yang Jialuo 楊家駱. *Zhongyang yanjiu yuan hanji dianzi wenxian ziliaoku* 中央研究院漢籍電子文獻資料庫 [Scripta Sinica electronic database of traditional Chinese classics]. Taipei: Aacademia Sinica. http://hanchi.ihp.sinica.edu.tw/ihp/hanji.htm.

Zhang, Yanshuo. "Entrepreneurs of the National Past: The Discourse of Ethnic Indigeneity and Indigenous Cultural Writing in China." *positions: asis critique* 29, no. 2 (2021), 423–450.

Zhang, Yanshuo. "Transforming the 'Barbarian' Margins into Multiethnic National Centers: Photographic Reportage and Ethnic Imagination in Republican-era China." In *Reportage in the Chinese-speaking World*. Edited by Charles A. Laughlin and Li Guo. University of Michigan Press, forthcoming 2026.

Zhang, Yingjin. "From 'Minority Film' to 'Minority Discourse:' Questions of Nationhood and Ethnicity in Chinese Cinema." In *Transnational Chinese Cinemas: Identity, Nationhood, Gender*. Edited by Sheldon Hsiao-peng Lu, 81–104. Honolulu: University of Hawai'i Press, 1997.

Zhongguo shaoshu minzu guji zongtiyao: Qiangzujuan, 中国少数民族古籍总目提要：羌族卷 [Abstracts and indexes to general catalogues of ancient documents about China's ethnic minorities: the volume on Qiangzu]. Edited by Guojia Minzushiwu Weiyuanhui 国家民族事务委员会[National Committee on Ethnic Minority Affairs]. Beijing: Zhongguo dabaikequanshu chubanshe, 2009.

Zhonghua Renmin Gongheguo Minzu Quyu Zizhifa 中华人民共和国民族区域自治法 [The People's Republic of China Law on Regional Autonomy of Minority Nationalities].1984.

Zhonghua Renmin Gongheguo Zhongyang Renmin Zhengfu 中华人民共和国中央人民政府 [The Central People's Government of the People's Republic of China]. "Zhonghua renmin gongheguo feiwuzhi wenhua yichan fa 中华人民共和国非物质文化遗产法" [The People's Republic of China Intangible Cultural Heritage Law]. Last modified February 25, 2011. http://www.gov.cn/flfg/2011-02/25/content_1857449.htm.

Zhou, Ba 周巴. Qiangzu wenhua qiangjiu shinian huiwang (羌族文化抢救十年回望) [A retrospective look at the rescuing of Qiang culture after ten years]. *Xiqiang wenhua* 西羌文化 2018–2019. vol. 24: 105–111.

Zhou, Mingliang. "Nation-state Building and Multiculturalism in China." In *Handbook on Ethnic Minorities in China*. Edited by Xiaowei Zang, 111–137. Cheltenham: Edward Elgar Publishing, 2016.

Zhuang Xueben 庄学本. *Chenfeng de lishi shunjian: sheying dashi Zhuang Xueben ershi shiji sanshi niandai de xibu renwen tanfang* 尘封的历史瞬间：摄影大师庄学本20世

纪30年代的西部人文探访 [Sealed historical moments: photographic master Zhuang Xueben's humanist explorations and visits to the west]. Edited by Ma Naihui 马鼐辉, Wang Zhaohu 王昭武, and Zhuang Wenjun 庄文骏. Chengdu: Sichuan chuban jituan, Sichuan minzu chubanshe, 2005.

Zhuang Xueben 莊學本. *Qiangrong kaochaji* 羌戎考察記 [*Expeditions into the land of the Qiang and Rong*]. Shanghai: Liangyou tushu yinshua gongsi, 1937.

Zhuang Xueben 庄学本. *Qiangrong kaochaji: Sheying dashi Zhuang Xueben ershi shiji sanshi niandai de xibu renwen tanfang* 羌戎考察记：摄影大师庄学本20世纪30年代的西部人文探访 [Expeditions into the land of the Qiang and Rong: photographic master Zhuang Xueben's humanist explorations and visits to the west in the 1930s]. Edited by Ma Naihui 马鼐辉, Wang Zhaohu 王昭武, and Zhuang Wenjun 庄文骏. Chengdu: Sichuan chubanjituan, Sichuan minzu chubanshe, 2007.

"Zhuzhong rende ganshou: Shenzhen chongxin dingwei xiandaihua 注重人的感受：深圳重新定位现代化" [Emphasizing the feelings of people: Shenzhen redefines modernization]. Last modified August 25, 2005. http://finance.people.com.cn/GB/8215/52335/52348/52355/3642281.html.

Zou, Huafen 邹华芬, and Liu Jing 刘敬. "Jilu quanqiuhua beijingxia shaoshu minzu de shengcun zhuangtai—*Erma de hunli* daoyan fangtan" 纪录全球化背景下少数民族的生存状态—尔玛的婚礼导演访谈 [Documenting the living realities of ethnic minorities in the backdrop of globalization—an interview with the director of *Erma's Wedding*]. *Dianying pinglun* 电影评论 [Film review] 2 (2009): 20–24.

INDEX

Note: The format of the Chinese characters for each entry is based on the original source referred to. If the original source uses traditional Chinese, traditional characters are included for the entry; if the original source uses simplified Chinese, simplified Chinese is included for the entry.

Aba Tibetan and Qiang Autonomous Prefecture (阿坝藏族羌族自治州), 20, 44, 82, 114, 125, 161, 230
activism, 10, 87; village-level, 39, 213, 229, 237, 241, 244
A'er Archive, 232–35, 237–39
A'er Qiang Village (*A'er qiangzhai* 阿尔羌寨), 12, 229–34, 240
aesthetics of accountability (concept from Faye Ginsburg), 168–69
Aku Wuwu (阿库乌雾), 7
Alai (阿来) (b. 1959), 6, 64–65
alternative modernities (concept from Arif Dirlik), 68
ancestral memory, 79, 82, 102, 108, 167, 181, 192, 196, 208, 237, 241, 244–45
Anderson, Benedict, 25–26, 240
Asian-ness, 8. *See also* Chinese-ness
assimilation, cultural, 16, 59, 69, 71, 108–10, 141, 195–96, 210
atheism, Chinese state ideology of, 39, 213, 215, 218–23. *See also* secularism, indigenous critiques of
aura (concept from Walter Benjamin), 177
authenticity, cultural, 58, 137, 142, 151–52, 169, 176–77, 206, 231
autobiographical essays, 37, 188–98, 205, 208, 212–14
Backyard Furnace Movement, 214–15
Bai Zhihong, 110, 152
barbarian (as epithet for non-Sinitic peoples), 18–19, 26, 35, 44–55, 62, 102, 243
Bender, Mark, 9, 167
Benjamin, Walter, 151, 177
Bhabha, Homi, 14, 119, 178, 240
bilingualism, 10, 14, 92, 147, 153, 189–90. *See also* minority elites
Biographies of the Southern Barbarians and Southwestern Savages (work by Fan Ye), 51
The Biography of the West Qiang (*Xiqiang zhuan* 西羌傳), 47
The Book of Later Han (*Houhanshu* 後漢書) (work by Fan Ye), 18, 46–51
Boym, Svetlana, 195, 208
Buddhism, 165, 226–27
Buffalohead, Eric L., 159
Burao Yilu, 209–10

Cai Wenji (蔡文姬) (c. 132–192), 18–19, 48–49, 250n30
Cai Yuanpei (蔡元培), 55–56
Cao Cao (曹操) (155–220), 19, 49
center-periphery relationship, 4, 16, 18, 35, 45–46, 50–52, 66, 88–89, 92, 108, 116, 121, 137, 141, 239, 243, 245

Chang Qu (常璩), 99
Chengtang (king), 48
China Multiethnic Literary Series (*Zhongguo duominzu wenxue congshu* 中国多民族文学丛书), 218
Chinese and Sinophone studies, 11–12, 15, 161
Chinese-ness, 4, 15–17, 28, 32–33, 40, 60, 67, 89, 121, 179, 242. *See also* Asian-ness
Chinese state history, 9, 16, 27, 71, 78–79, 83, 121, 243–44. See also *The Concise Histories of China's Ethnic Minorities* (*Zhongguo shaoshu minzu jianshi congshu* 中国少数民族简史丛书); *Concise History of Qiangzu* (*Qiangzu jianshi* 羌族简史)
Chio, Jenny, 8, 148
cinema of sovereignty (concept from Eric Buffalohead and M. Elise Marubbio), 159–60
Classics of Poetry (*Shijin* 詩經), 48
Clifford, James, 107–8, 225
Cohen, Paul, 109
collaborative (Qiang and Han) filmmaking, 159–61, 169–70, 172, 183. *See also* indigenous cinema
commercialization of culture, 1, 30, 33, 125, 152–54, 201–5, 236–38, 241. *See also* cultural entrepreneurialism; tourism, ethnic
commodification of culture, 30, 188, 200–201, 212
Communist China, conceptions of ethnic minorities in, 27, 30, 45, 71, 79
compatriots (*tongbao* 同胞), 54–55
A Complete History of the Qiangzu (*Qiangzu tongshi* 羌族通史) (book by Geng Shaojiang), 96
The Concise Histories of China's Ethnic Minorities (*Zhongguo shaoshu minzu jianshi congshu* 中国少数民族简史丛书), 27, 70–71, 80
Concise History of Qiangzu (*Qiangzu jianshi* 羌族简史), 70–74, 78–80
Confucian moral values, 50–52, 97, 131, 134–36
Confucian Sinitic self, 17–18, 46–47, 108–9. *See also* Sinitic Chinese identity
consumerism and consumption, 111, 181–82, 200, 202, 204–5, 244
Coombe, Rosemary, 95
creative agency, 10, 11, 32, 88, 90
creative belonging, 4, 11–13, 29–34, 87, 244
creative space, 178, 182, 240
Crossley, Pamela Kyle, 16, 23, 62, 260n57
cultural activism, 39, 213–14, 229–40
cultural assimilation, 16, 59, 69, 71, 108–10, 141, 195–96, 210
cultural entrepreneurialism, 13, 92, 110–11, 153, 155, 162, 199–203. *See also* commercialization of culture; tourism, ethnic
cultural exhibitionism, 176, 202
cultural hybridity, 7, 14, 22, 103, 106, 157–58, 163, 165–66, 170, 173, 178
culturalization (concept from Ma Rong), 27
cultural nationalism, 79, 228
cultural preservation, Qiang efforts of, 23, 86
Cultural Revolution (1966–1976), conceptions of ethnic minorities in, 29, 67–68

Davies, H.R., 57
Da Yu/King Yu the Great (大禹), 29, 36, 88, 93–104, 106, 109, 118–19
Debord, Guy, 151
Design of Death (*Shasheng* 杀生) (film by Guan Hu), 36, 126–27, 129–38
dialects, role of in identity formation, 132–33. *See also* Mandarin Chinese; Sichuanese dialect; Tibetan language; Qiang language (*xiangtan* 鄉談)
diaolou (The towering, fortressed architecture that belongs to the Qiang and Tibetan groups of Sichuan province碉楼), 125, 139, 200–201
Dikotter, Frank, 49
Di people (狄), 48, 58–59

Diqiang (氐羌), 58, 62
Diqiangxi (氐羌系, the Diqiang lineage), 62
Dirlik, Arif, 68
discursive self-fashioning, 3, 87–88, 90, 121
disseminated identities (concept from Michael M.J. Fischer), 189
Dongba (东巴) religion, 165
Dong people (侗), 172
Douanzhu (斗安珠) (Qiang deity), 163
Duan Haizhen (段海珍), 224–25, 228–29
Duara, Prasenjit, 20, 131–32
Dudemaine, Andre, 11
Dujiangyan Irrigation System, 100, 118–19

earthquake (Sichuan, 2008), 1, 22, 43, 81, 90, 130, 139–40, 160, 168–69, 230–31
embroidery, Qiang culture of, 22–23, 81, 168
entrepreneurial identity, 13
Erma's Wedding (*Erma de hunli* 尔玛的婚礼) (film by Han Wanfeng), 170–81
eroticization of ethnic minorities, 141, 146, 168, 198–201, 203–5, 267n41. *See also* seductress as symbol for modernization
Ethnic Classification Project (*minzu shibie* 民族识别), 20, 27–28, 79–80
Ethnic Corridor (*minzu zoulang* 民族走廊), 22
ethnicity, 16, 25, 33, 44–45, 83, 127; Chinese constructions of, 3, 52, 57–58, 62–63, 105, 155. *See also* indigeneity, Chinese constructions of; race
ethnic minorities. See *shaoshu minzu* (China's ethnic minority people or groups)
ethnic minority literature. *See* minority literature
ethnographic authority (concept from James Clifford), 225
ethnographic poetics, 5, 37, 157–59, 163, 169–70, 182–83
ethnography and ethnology in China, 44, 55–56, 58, 61, 63
ethno-national identities, 24
ethno-national imagination, 25, 36, 244
ethno-national traditions, 23
exorcists, 218–23. *See also* Qiang religious traditions and spirituality
exoticization of ethnic minorities, 64–65, 88, 127–28, 136–38, 146, 153, 203–5. *See also* commercialization of culture; tourism, ethnic
Expeditions into the Land of the Qiang and Rong (*Qiangrong kaochaji* 羌戎考察記) (work by Zhuang Xueben), 53–56, 61, 64–66

Fan (蕃), 16
Fangyan (方言 dialects), 132–33
Fan Ye (范曄) (398–445), 18–19, 46–48, 50–51
Fei Xiaotong (费孝通) (1910–2005), 22, 69
Felski, Rita, 190, 206
feminization of ethnic minorities, 141–42
Feng Jicai, 43–44
fetishization of Qiang culture, 200–201. *See also* exoticization of ethnic minorities
fire, importance of in Qiang culture, 112, 114
Fischer, Michael M.J., 189, 195
fluid indigeneity, 37, 161, 163, 166, 170, 183
folk culture, 43, 72–73, 81, 92, 175, 227–28; symbols of, 179
folklore, 90, 228, 234
folklorization of minority cultures, 236
Forbidden Kiss (*Gubao zhiwen* 古堡之吻) (film by Tian Fen), 22, 24, 36, 138–47
Foucault, Michel, 63, 140, 234
"Four Generations of Va Women" (memoir by Burao Yilu), 210
"The Fragrant Key" (*Fenfang duoyowei* 芬芳朵哟喂) (story by Yu Yaoming), 198–205, 208
funerals, 134, 165, 177, 201, 224, 227, 230, 242; tree, 216

Gao Shi (高適) (ca. 704–765), 73, 75–77
Gao Tunzi (高屯子), 160–61, 168–70

Geertz, Clifford, 177
gender symbolism in modernization discourse, 8, 145–46; 188, 190–91, 194, 199–205, 211–12. *See also* mother as symbol for traditional life; Poisonous Cats
Geng Shaojiang (耿少将), 95–96
Ginsburg, Faye, 154, 168
Gladney, Dru, 146, 204
goats and goat skin, 163, 192–93, 219
Goossaert, Vincent, 222
Graburn, Nelson, 111, 114
Graham, David Crockett (1884–1961), 139, 145
Gravari-Barbas, Maria, 111, 114
Great Leap Forward Movement, 214, 217
Guan Hu (管虎), 36, 126–27, 129, 136–37
Gu Yunlong (谷运龙) (b. 1957), 117–19

Hale, Charles, 33, 105
Hall, Stuart, 16–17, 30
Han (as an ethnic group and ethnic concept in China), 28–29, 60–61, 104; interethnic origins of, 20, 59, 69; shared ancestry of with the Qiang, 2, 20, 32, 43–44, 92, 94, 106. *See also* multiethnic Chinese identity; Qiang culture and identity, relationship of to the Han
Han centralism, 7–8, 59–60, 69, 108–9, 229, 237–40; resistance against, 11, 87–88, 92 101–3, 105, 115–16, 119, 121, 136–37, 240. *See also* Confucian Sinitic self; Sinitic Chinese identity
Han Wanfeng (韩万峰), 172–73, 176
Harrell, Stevan, 101–2, 105, 108
Hathaway, Michael, 162–63
healer, religious (*shenpo*), 220–21, 223. *See also* Qiang religious traditions and spirituality
Heavenly Songs (*Tian ge* 天歌) (novel by Duan Haizhen), 224–26, 239
Henfry, Lee Ann, 204
Hervieu-Léger, Danièle, 236
heterotopia (Foucauldian concept), 140–41
Hezhe people (赫哲族), 56
Hillman, Ben, 204
historical mentality (*lishi xinxing*) (concept from Ming-ke Wang), 102
historiography, imperial Chinese, 35, 44–52, 54, 58, 62, 66, 98
The History of Qiangzu (*Qiangzu shi* 羌族史), 81
The History of the Races in China (*Zhongguo minzushi* 中國民族史), 20, 58, 62
Hobsbawm, Eric, 80
"Homeland" (*laojia* 老家) (essay by Wang Yong'an), 196
Huaxia, 59–60, 88, 121
Huayang guozhi (*Chronicles of Huayang* 华阳国志) (work by Chang Qu), 99–100
Hui people (回民), 56
Hu Jintao, 29, 228
hybridity. *See* cultural hybridity.

image-mediated mobility, 155
image solidarity, 128
indigeneity, Chinese constructions of, 161–63, 166, 170. *See also* ethnicity; race
indigenous articulation (concept from James Clifford), 107–8
indigenous cinema, 14, 37, 157–60, 170, 182. *See also* collaborative (Qiang and Han) filmmaking
indigenous docufiction, 170–71
Innocent Dreams and Songs in the Wilderness of the Qiang (*Tianzhen de meng yu Qiangye de ge* 天真的梦与羌野的歌) (book by Lei Zi), 209
institutionalization of minority cultures, 236–38, 241. *See also* commercialization of culture
intangible cultural heritage, 22, 33, 68, 95, 227–31
Intangible Cultural Heritage Law, 228, 230
interethnic romance, 170, 172

Jade Gate Barrier, 77–78
Japanese (language), 15, 28, 62, 139
Jiang River, 106

Jidi Majia, 15
Ji River, 106

Keane, A.H., 59
key (traditional Qiang object), 200–201, 205
Khitan (or Huren 胡人), 76

Latin America and Latin Americans, 4–5, 33
Lefebvre, Henri, 120
Leibold, James, 8, 25, 52
Lei Zi (雷子), 209
Lewis, Mark Edward, 45, 98–100
Liang Qichao (1873–1929), 26, 28, 63
Li Bai (701–762), 73
Li Bing (李冰), 100–101, 118–19
Li County (理县), 85, 172
Lin Huixiang (林惠祥), 58–60, 62
Li people (黎族), 172
"Listening to the Flute on the Frontiers" (塞上聞笛) (poem by Gao Shi), 73–74
Litzinger, Ralph, 68, 102, 215
Li Yongxiang, 101–2, 105
Lolo people (羅羅), 56
Long Xianzhao, 97, 99–101, 103–4, 106
Luobo Qiang Village, 1–2
lyrical mode, 15, 158, 163, 169, 182, 223, 225
"Lyrics of Liangzhou" (涼州詞) (poem by Wang Zhihuan), 77

Man (蛮), 16, 58–59
Manchu people, 26, 60
Mandarin Chinese, 14, 132–33, 173–74
masculinity, 197, 202, 204–5
Maotao Wen, 173
Mao Zedong, 2, 71, 214. *See also* post-Mao China
Marcoux, Gabrielle, 11
Ma Rong, 27
Marubbio, M. Elise, 159
Marxism, 70–71, 97, 102, 142
Mathieu, Christine, 165
May Fourth Movement, 56, 190
McCarthy, Susan K., 31
McGrath, Jason, 69
McNeal, Robin, 94–95, 98
memory work (concept from Ralph Litzinger), 68
Miao people (苗族), 8, 20, 26, 56, 141
minjian (民间), 232–33
minority elites, 112, 147–49, 153–55, 190. *See also* bilingualism
minority literature, 6, 8, 10, 30, 37, 39, 187–88, 198, 218, 228–29, 240–41
minor thought, 4
Min River Valley, 73, 98, 101, 103, 117–20
minzu (民族) minority nationality, 10, 25–28, 43, 62–63, 71, 79
minzu chuantong 民族传统 (ethnic traditions or ethnic heritage), 80
minzu ronghe 民族融合 (ethnic assimilation and acculturation), 69
modernization: conflicts of with traditional life, 188–211; conflicts of with traditional spirituality, 213–27, 234, 237–38. *See also* Qiang religious traditions and spirituality
Mongols, 8, 26, 165, 204
monkey-skin hats, 85, 163, 176. *See also* *shibi* (释比) (shaman)
Mosuo people, 204
mother as symbol for traditional life, 37, 188, 190–98, 206–11. *See also* gender symbolism in modernization discourse
"Mother in the Mountains" (*Shanzhong de muqin* 山中的母亲) (essay by Yang Zi), 192–95
mouth harp (*kouxian*) (traditional Qiang instrument), 65–66, 82
Moya, Paula M.L., 14
Mubita (Qiang deity), 167
Mueggler, Erik, 34
Mujiezhu (木姐珠) (Qiang deity), 163
Mullaney, Thomas, 8, 28, 57, 79
multiculturalism, 3, 5, 13, 29–33, 33, 60, 67–68, 72, 87, 121, 243

multiethnic Chinese identity, 30–32, 62–63, 105, 108, 161, 228–29, 235; historical development of, 27–29, 54–56, 58–60, 69–70, 79–81; Liang Qichao's conception of, 26, 28, 63; origin myths of, 45, 52, 62, 69. See also *Zhonghua minzu* 中華民族/中华民族 (the Chinese people)
multiethnic literature, 6, 39, 188, 211, 213–14, 218, 223–24
Mysterious Oriental Castle (*Shenmi de dongfang gubao* 神秘的东方古堡), 125, 136, 139

National Ethnic Affairs Committee (*Guojia minzu shiwu weiyuanhui* 国家民族事务委员会), 70
national identity, 22–23, 25, 36, 39, 45, 52, 58–59, 87, 137, 143, 146, 242, 246
national narratives, 3, 13, 15–16, 35, 44–45, 67, 69, 81, 83, 87, 101, 242
national trauma (*guoshang* 国殇), 43
nation-states, 4, 25, 58, 107, 119, 211, 240
Native Americans, 4, 6–7, 13, 15, 238; cinema of, 159–60 (*see also* indigenous cinema)
neoliberalism, 5, 33, 69, 88, 95, 101, 104–5, 107, 120–22, 137, 140
"The North Tower of Golden Fort" (金城北樓) (poem by Gao Shi), 76–77
Naxi people (纳西), 10, 165–66

"On Ethnology" (*Shuo minzuxue* 說民族學) (work by Cai Yuanpei), 55
orality and oral traditions, 10, 57, 61, 90, 92, 150, 165, 228. *See also* writing
Orientalization, 178, 182, 205, 211
other (sociological and cultural concept), 14, 17, 129, 131, 137, 141–42, 241; foreign, 143–44, 201; internal, 143–45, 201; non-Han/non-Sinitic peoples as, 13, 17–20, 26, 46, 48, 74–75, 87, 155, 205, 239
Owen, Stephen, 77

Palumbo-Liu, David, 239
patriarchy, 134–35, 201, 203–4
performative subjects (concept from Homi Bhabha), 240
place, role of in constructing ethnic identity, 116–20. *See also* Min River Valley, Sichuan
poetry: classical Chinese, 18, 44–52, 141; Tang dynasty, 9, 74–75, 77–80
Poisonous Cats, 37, 187–88, 198–205
post-Mao China, 29, 43, 67-68, 101, 105, 218, 220
post-socialist China, 68–69, 127, 129, 133, 136, 141–43, 146, 155

Qiang culture and identity: contemporary construction of, 3, 14–15, 20–24, 28, 32–33, 70–71, 87–90, 101–3, 109–12; construction of through film and photography, 36, 128, 147–53, 157–59; evolution of the concept of, 10, 17–20, 35, 45–75, 242–46; origins of, 2–3, 20, 32, 36, 117, 163, 242; recognition of as distinct, 52–54, 57, 61–63, 173; relationship to the Han, 2–3, 20, 43–44, 106, 108–9, 113, 242 (*see also* Han, shared ancestry of with the Qiang); relationship to Tibetans, 2–3, 20–21; reviving/reinvention of, 13, 16, 81–82, 89–92, 101, 110, 196 (*see also* discursive self-fashioning); suppression of, 108–9
Qiang language 20, 57, 61, 172–74
Qiang marriage traditions, 18, 47, 50, 57, 140, 144, 170, 174–81
Qiang reed pipe (*Qiangdi* 羌笛), 45, 72–74, 76–82, 242
Qiang religious traditions and spirituality, 2, 39, 57, 163–70, 213–23, 227. *See also* spirituality and spiritual worldviews
Qiang Renliu (羌人六) (b. 1987), 218–22
Qiangrong kaochaji 羌戎考察記 (*Expeditions into the Land of the Qiang and Rong*) (work by Zhuang Xueben), 53–56, 61, 64–66
Qiangzu Literature (*Qiangzu wenxue* 羌族文学) (journal), 191

Qing dynasty, conceptions of the Qiang in, 52

race, 19, 25, 45, 59, 83; Chinese constructions of, 26–28, 49–50, 59, 62–63. *See also* ethnicity; indigeneity, Chinese constructions of
The Records of the Grand Historian (*Shiji* 史记) (work by Sima Qian), 96, 98, 115
reflective nostalgia (concept from Svetlana Boym), 208
Reform and Opening-up era China, conceptions of ethnic minorities in, 29, 67–71, 80, 105
regime of reference (concept from Erik Mueggler), 34
relational practices, 3, 159, 161
Remembering Home (*Jizhu xiangchou* 记住乡愁) (documentary series), 126
Ren Dongsheng (任冬生) (b. 1978), 190–92, 206–9
renmin 人民 (the people), 71
Ren Qiu, 58
representational space (concept from Henri Lefebvre), 120
Republican era China (1911/1912–1949), conceptions of ethnic minorities in 20, 45, 53, 55, 57, 60–63, 72
rhetorical legitimacy, 11
Rme language, 173
rrmea ("locals" or "indigenes"), 173
Rodgers, Susan, 234
Rongdi (戎狄), 48
Rong people (戎), 26, 48, 54–57, 59, 61–66
rural villages, role of in Qiang identity, 126–27, 131–32, 166–69, 189, 192–93, 196–98, 207–8

sacred grove, 214–17. *See also* Qiang religious traditions and spirituality
"Sacred Mountain, Sacred Trees, Sacred Grove" (*Shenshan, shenshu, shenlin* 神山，神树,神林) (short story by Ye Xinguang), 214–18
Said, Edward, 47
Scar Literature, 43
Schein, Louisa, 8, 141, 144, 146
secondary language (Foucauldian concept), 63–64
Second Sino-Japanese War, 173, 226
"Secrets on the Top of the Min Mountain" (*Minshan zhidian de mimi* 岷山之巅的秘密) (essay by Ren Dongsheng), 206–9
secularism, indigenous critiques of, 4, 39, 213, 215–23, 227–28, 240–41
secularization of indigenous culture, 234–36, 241
seductress as symbol for modernization, 37, 188, 198–204. *See also* gender symbolism in modernization discourse
self, sense of, 14, 17, 20; Chinese national, 17–18, 20, 27, 46, 48, 51–52, 75, 102, 131, 144; ethnic minority, 3, 121, 189, 196, 205–6, 234; Qiang, 15, 64, 149
shamanism, 57, 181, 214, 220. See also *shibi* 释比 (shaman)
Shangshu, 99
shaoshu minzu (China's ethnic minority people or groups), 3, 9–10, 28, 70, 88, 161, 244, 253n86, 264n9
shenpo (female healer), 223
shibi (释比) (shaman), 43, 163, 165, 169, 176–79, 205, 216, 230–31, 236–38. *See also* Qiang religious traditions and spirituality
Shih, Shu-mei, 11
Shklar, Judith, 116
Shun (舜) (king), 94, 98
Shuwang benji (work by Yang Xiong), 99
Sichuan, 117–20; earthquake in (2008), 1, 22, 43, 81, 90, 130, 139–40, 160, 168–69, 230–31; origin of Da Yu in, 32, 88, 94, 97–106, 117; Sinicization of, 108–9; Zhuang Xueben's travels to, 54–56, 61
Sichuanese dialect, 57, 61, 132–33, 173–74
Sichuan Provincial Qiang Studies Association (*Sichuansheng Qiangxue xuehui* 四川省羌学学会), 88–89, 172

Sinitic Chinese identity, 18, 46–52, 60, 75, 88, 102. *See also* Confucian Sinitic self
Sinophone Studies, 11, 15
Sino-Tibetan language family, 20, 173, 251n36
socialist China, 29, 70–71, 142, 209, 214–16, 218, 220, 228, 243. *See also* post-socialist China; post-Mao China
"Songdingbo Catches the Ghost" (short story), 219
"Song of Yen" (燕歌行) (poem by Gao Shi), 75–76
Song Wenbing (宋文炳), 58
"The Soul Pacifier" (*Ahun zhe* 安魂者) (essay by Qiang Renliu), 218–23
spirituality and spiritual worldviews, 4, 7, 13, 39, 165, 169, 182, 196, 201, 208, 212–14, 223–28, 234, 236–41. *See also* Qiang religious traditions and spirituality
St-Amand, Isabelle, 11
stereotypes, 5, 19, 51–52, 138, 141, 146, 159–60, 233
Stewart, Michelle, 5
superstition, 215, 219–20; feudal, 67, 215, 220
symbols for Qiang culture. *See* gender symbolism in modernization discourse; goats and goat skin; monkey-skin hats; mother as symbol for traditional life

Tam, Gina Anne, 132
Tang dynasty: conceptions of the Qiang in, 75; poetry of, 74–75, 77–80
Tangut Qiang people (*Dangxiang Qiang* 党项羌), 90
Tangut script, 90–92
Tan Jihe 谭继和, 97
Taoping Qiang Ethnic Culture Museum, 85–87
Taoping Qiang Village, 36, 38, 82–83, 85–86, 112–14, 146–49, 151–54; appearance of in films 125–46
Taoping shihua 桃坪史话 (*Historical Accounts on Taoping*) (book by Yang Guangcheng), 112–14
Ten Years in Search of the Qiang (*Shinian xunqiang* 十年寻羌) (documentary by Gao Tunzi), 160–70
third space (concept from Homi Bhabha), 14, 178
Three Hundred Qiang Songs from Feng County (*Fengzhou Qiangge Sanbaishou*) (book by Zhang Shanyun), 92–93
Three Sovereigns and Five Emperors, 115–16, 120
Tian Fen (田芬), 36, 138–40
Tibetan language, 61
Tibetan religion, 165
Tibetans, 2–3, 6, 22, 26, 55, 62, 66, 117, 173, 204; Gyalrong Tibetan (嘉绒), 64–65
Tibetan-Yi Corridor, 22
Torrance, Thomas (1871–1959), 138, 145
tourism, ethnic, 1, 22, 30, 86–87, 92, 94, 110, 114, 127, 129, 148–55, 199–204, 238. *See also* commercialization of culture; Taoping Qiang Village
tourism imaginary, 110–11, 114–15, 152
tourism literature, 29, 88, 110–11, 114–15, 121
tradition, invention of, 236
transnational tribal solidarity, 15–16
trauma (cultural and religious), 43, 190, 193–94, 197, 206, 218–21
Tubo (吐蕃), 75
tusi (chieftain system), 108

UNESCO, 114, 125, 139, 147, 228, 231, 237

Veg, Sebastian, 232
Visser, Robin, 8–9
visual sovereignty (concept from Eric Buffalohead and Elise Marubbio), 159–60

Wang, Ming-ke, 74–75, 102, 202
Wang Chunwu, 97
Wang Tongling (王桐龄), 58
Wang Yong'an (王永安) (b. 1954), 190–92, 196–97

Wang Zhihuan (688–742), 73, 75–77
Wenchuan County (*Wenchuan xian* 汶川县), 187, 198, 230–31
Wenchuan Qiang 汶川羌 (poem by Yang Zi), 191
Wen Jiabao, 43–44, 81
Western epistemologies and values, 31, 45, 59; decentering of, 7, 23, 52, 59, 69, 129, 144–46
West Qiang. *See* Xiqiang
Wilson, Pamela, 5
women as guardians of tradition. *See* gender symbolism in modernization discourse
writing, 10, 46, 57, 165, 233–34. *See also* orality and oral traditions; Tangut script

Xia dynasty, 32, 96–97
xiangtu 乡土 (native soil), 168, 190
Xifan, 54, 255n30
Xige Qing Village, 160
Xi Jinping, 126
Xiongnu, Southern (南匈奴), 19, 48–49
Xiqiang (West Qiang), 47–48, 50–51, 54, 89–90, 96, 98, 115, 255n30
Xiqiang wenhua 西羌文化 (*The Culture of West Qiang*) (journal), 88–93, 96–97
Xiqiang zhuan 西羌傳 (*Biography of the West Qiang*), 47
Xixia (West Xia) empire, 90–92

Yandi/Emperor Yan/the Fire Emperor (炎帝), 36, 88, 106–8, 112, 115
Yang, Yuqing, 141, 204
Yang Guangcheng (杨光成) (1938–2011), 106–7, 112–15
Yangtze River Valley, 32, 103–4, 119
Yang Xiong (扬雄), 99–100
Yang Zi (羊子) (b. 1969), 15, 190–96
Yao (尧) (king), 94
Yao people, 102
Yellow Emperor, 94, 104, 106–7, 109, 115
Yellow River Valley, 103–4, 119–20
Ye Xingguang (叶星光) (b. 1954), 214, 216, 218, 224
Yi (彝), 6–7, 101–2, 224, 227–28; religious traditions of, 224–27
Yi (夷), 58–59
Yi-fu Tan, 118
Yinwu (殷武) (poem), 48
Yu Yaoming (余耀明) (b. 1963), 198–201, 205, 208

Zhang Binglin (章炳麟) (1869–1936), 60, 109
Zhang Shanyun (张善云), 92, 172
Zhitai Qiang Village, 160
Zhongguo minzushi (*The History of the Races in China*; book by Lin Huixiang), 59
Zhonghua minzu 中華民族/中华民族 (the Chinese people), 2, 32, 44–45, 85, 88; interethnic ancestry of, 20, 26–29, 45, 60, 63, 69, 71, 79, 82, 106–7, 161; invention and development of the concept of, 9, 26–29, 59–60, 63, 69, 71, 109; *Qiangdi* as symbol of, 73, 82
Zhuang Xueben (莊學本) (1909–1984), 26, 53–57, 61, 63, 64–65